Is Jesus of Nazareth the Predicted Messiah?

Is Jesus of Nazareth the Predicted Messiah?

A Historical-Evidential Approach to Specific Old Testament Messianic Prophecies and Their New Testament Fulfillments

Douglas D. Scott

FOREWORD BY
Leo Percer

WIPF & STOCK · Eugene, Oregon

IS JESUS OF NAZARETH THE PREDICTED MESSIAH?
A Historical-Evidential Approach to Specific Old Testament
Messianic Prophecies and Their New Testament Fulfillments

Copyright © 2018 Douglas D. Scott. All rights reserved. Except for brief quotations in critical publications or reviews, no part of this book may be reproduced in any manner without prior written permission from the publisher. Write: Permissions, Wipf and Stock Publishers, 199 W. 8th Ave., Suite 3, Eugene, OR 97401.

Wipf & Stock
An Imprint of Wipf and Stock Publishers
199 W. 8th Ave., Suite 3
Eugene, OR 97401

www.wipfandstock.com

PAPERBACK ISBN: 978-1-5326-5851-8
HARDCOVER ISBN: 978-1-5326-5852-5
EBOOK ISBN: 978-1-5326-5853-2

Manufactured in the U.S.A.

Foremost among those who have contributed to this work is my wife Suzan. You have, by faith, waited patiently through the years for me to complete my doctoral degree. Without your encouragement during moments of despair or fatigue, I certainly would have chosen an easier way. The dedication of this dissertation to you as a testimony to your patience, love, and endurance seems a woefully inadequate way to express my love and gratitude. Better days are coming soon. I love spending life with you!

Doug

Abstract

THE PRIMARY PURPOSE OF this dissertation is to establish if critically acceptable historical-evidential reasons exist for believing that Jesus Christ is the direct fulfillment of the specific OT messianic texts included in the study. The study presupposes many of the conclusions of historical-critical scholarship and employs historical-evidential criteria to evaluate the evidence and attempt to establish the historical warrant for affirming such belief. Secondarily, this study seeks to find *minimal facts* related to these specific OT prophetic texts. To qualify as a *minimal fact*, two conditions must be met: (1) there must be more than adequate scholarly evidences usually consisting of several critically ascertained lines of argumentation; and (2) there must be agreement among the majority of contemporary scholars about the historicity of the event or the specific claim the *minimal fact* affirms.

This investigation envisions the existence of three possible outcomes for each prophecy examined: (1) Jesus directly fulfilled the prophecy and sufficient historical evidence establishes the claim as probable, (2) Jesus directly fulfilled the prophecy, but the available historical evidence is insufficient to establish the claim as probable, and (3) sufficient historical evidence exists to refute the claim that Jesus directly fulfilled the prophecy.

The historical-evidential approach employed by this study yields the probability of two direct fulfillments and the emergence of fifteen *minimal facts*. The author thus concludes that the historical evidence supports the probability that the two specific OT passages affirmed in this study (2 Samuel 7:13, 16; Micah 5:2) directly prophesy regarding some aspect of Jesus' life and ministry. On three other occasions (Psalm 2:7; Psalm 16:10; Malachi 3:1), a distinct possibility exists that these texts directly prophesy regarding some aspect of Jesus' life and ministry.

Contents

Foreword by Leo Percer | xiii
Acknowledgements | xv

Part I: Introduction and Literature Review

Chapter 1: Introduction to the Study | 3

Background and Preliminary Considerations | 3
Statement of the Problem | 6
Significance of the Problem | 6
The Study's Contribution to Professional Knowledge and Practice | 8
An Overview of the Components of the Dissertation | 10
    Key Elements | 10
    Reasons for Including Each Element | 12
Overview of Methodology, Key Terms, and Presuppositions | 13
    Basic Rationale | 13
    Evaluative Framework for Biblical Data | 15
    Evaluative Framework for Historical Data | 16
    Definitions of Key Terminology | 16
    Authorial Presuppositions | 18
    Summary of Important Literature | 18
    Conclusion | 21

Chapter 2: Literature Review | 23

Overview of the Literature Review | 23

Elements in and Rationale for Section 1 of the Literature Review | 24

Section 1. A Progressive Review of the Traditional Argument from Messianic Prophecy | 25

Alexander Keith: Evidence of the Truth of the Christian Religion | 25

Eduard Riehm: Messianic Prophecy: Its Origin, Historical Character, and Relation to New Testament Fulfillment | 26

Franz Delitzsch: Messianic Prophecies in Historical Succession | 28

Ed Hindson: "Messianic Prophecy" | 29

Bernard Ramm: Protestant Christian Evidences | 29

Kenny Barfield: The Prophet Motive | 30

Robert C. Newman: Jesus: The Testimony of Prophecy and History | 33

Robert C. Newman: "Fulfilled Prophecy as Miracle" | 34

Robert C. Newman: Prophecies About the Coming Messiah | 36

J. Barton Payne: Encyclopedia of Biblical Prophecy | 37

Herbert W. Bateman, Darrell L. Bock and Gordon H. Johnston: Jesus the Messiah: Tracing the Promises, Expectations, and Coming of Israel's King | 40

Section 2. Key Authors and Arguments that Alter or Eliminate the Traditional Approach to Predictive Prophecy | 41

Elements in and Rationale for Section 2 of the Literature Review | 42

John J. Collins: The Bible after Babel: Historical Criticism in a Postmodern Age | 41

Ernest A. Edghill and Herbert E. Ryle: An Inquiry into the Evidential Value of Prophecy | 43

Gurdon C. Oxtoby: Prediction and Fulfillment in the Bible | 46

Dewey Beegle: Prophecy and Prediction | 48

Joseph Fitzmyer: The One Who Is to Come | 49

Section 3. The Possibility of Miracles | 51

    Elements in and Rationale for Section 3 of the Literature Review | 51

    Hume's Arguments against Miracles | 52

    Hume's Argument and Predictive Prophecy | 55

    Conclusion | 57

Part II: Exegesis Analysis and Synthesis

Introduction to Part II | 59

Chapter 3: The First Group of Biblical Texts | 61

    Introduction to the First Group of Biblical Texts | 61

    Genesis 49:10 | 61

        Literary and Textual Analysis | 61

        The Interpretation of Genesis 49:10 in Exilic and Post-exilic Judaism | 68

        Summary | 71

    Psalm 118 | 72

        Literary and Textual Analysis | 72

        Summary | 80

    Haggai 2:1–9 | 82

        Literary and Textual Analysis | 82

        Summary | 90

    Malachi 3:1 | 91

        Literary and Textual Analysis | 91

        Summary | 103

Chapter 4: The Second Group of Biblical Texts | 106

    Introduction to the Second Group of Biblical Texts | 105

    2 Samuel 7:13 | 105

        Literary and Textual Analysis | 105

        Summary | 123

Chapter 5: The Third Group of Biblical Texts | 125

Introduction to the Third Group Biblical of Texts | 125
Micah 5:2 | 126
    Literary and Textual Analysis | 126
    Summary | 142

Chapter 6: The Fourth Group of Biblical Texts | 145

Introduction to the Fourth Group of Biblical Texts | 145
Jesus the Miracle-Worker: A Synopsis | 145
Did the Jews Expect a Miracle-Working Messiah? | 148
    Old Testament Evidence Supporting a Jewish Expectation of a Miracle-Working Messiah | 148
Extra-Biblical Data | 157
    New Testament Evidence | 160
    Summary | 163

Chapter 7: The Fifth Group of Biblical Texts | 166

Introduction to the Fifth Group of Biblical Texts | 166
Psalm 2:1–12, Emphasizing Verse 7 | 166
    Literary and Textual Analysis | 166
    Summary | 184
Psalm 16, Emphasizing Verses 9–10 | 187
    Literary and Textual Analysis | 187
    Summary | 201
Psalm 22:1–31, Emphasizing Verse 16 | 203
    Literary and Textual Analysis | 203
    Summary | 209
Summary of Chapters 3–7 | 211

Part III: Conclusions

Chapter 8: The Results of the Study and Recommendations for Future Research | 215

   Introduction | 215

   Results of the Study | 215

      The First Group of Biblical Texts | 215

      The Second Group of Biblical Texts | 218

      The Third Group of Biblical Texts | 220

      The Fourth Group of Biblical Texts | 221

      The Fifth Group of Biblical Texts | 223

      Minimal-Fact Statements as Related to the Statement of the Problem | 225

      Applying the Criteria for Justifying Historical Descriptions | 227

      Recommendations for Future Research | 229

Bibliography | 231

Subject Index | 249

Ancient Document Index | 275

Foreword

ORIGINALLY CHAMPIONED BY DR. Gary Habermas, a method of historical apologetics based on an idea of "minimal facts" creates a lot of discussion (especially in the area of the historicity of narratives in the Christian Scripture). This approach acknowledges that a minimal fact is something that passes two basic tests: 1) Are there sufficient, multiple attestations or multiple evidence to consider the historical issue a minimal fact? 2) Is there sufficient consensus among contemporary scholars to label the event/issue a minimal fact? Christian apologists utilize some version of this historical approach to defend specific events depicted in the Christian Scripture as historical facts (especially the issue of the resurrection of Jesus). The focus typically has been on showing some of the contents of Christian Scripture to fit criteria as historical fact. What has been lacking in this approach is an application of the minimal facts method to the claims of Hebrew Scripture (and especially prophecy). While debates on prophecy in the Hebrew Scripture find their way into some apologetic discourse, very little (if any) of the literature raises the issue of minimal facts as a means to defend these materials.

I have known Doug Scott for several years, primarily as one of my students in the PhD in Theology and Apologetics program at Liberty University. As both the director and an instructor in that program, I had the privilege of becoming familiar with Doug and his work. When Doug Scott first came to me with an idea for his dissertation that involved the application of a minimal facts approach to specific biblical prophecies in the Hebrew Bible, I admit that my first response was a bit skeptical. I was familiar with Dr. Habermas and his teaching on the minimal facts approach, but as a biblical studies instructor, I admit I was unable to see how the method could help in regards to understanding particular portions of prophecy. Doug pressed his case (supported by the insistence of Dr. Habermas), and a committee formed to walk with him through this research.

As a member of that committee, I remember reading some of the first materials researched and written for the dissertation, and I saw an idea developing that had merit. The book you hold in your hand is the result of a great deal of research and wrestling. In the end, Doug won his committee over, and I have the honor to introduce his work to you. In this volume, Dr. Scott offers you his argument. He states his intention clearly; he defines his approach well; he offers exegesis of the passages considered; and he supports his conclusions with solid research and passionate conviction. I am honored to recommend this work to you, and I hope as you read it you will find that the claims of Christianity (even on the issue of prophecies hundreds of years old) are indeed based on historical realities and supported by some minimal facts.

Leo Percer, PhD

Director, PhD in Theology and Apologetics
Associate Professor in Biblical Studies
Rawlings School of Divinity
Liberty University
Lynchburg, VA

Acknowledgements

I WOULD BE REMISS in my duties as an author if I did not acknowledge the scholarly and professional contributions of several people who have influenced this work. First, I want to thank Drs. Ed Hindson, Gary Yates, and Leo Percer of Liberty University for guiding me during the process that produced this dissertation. Their collective theological expertise and critical evaluations helped generate a work that is important to messianic studies and of interest to the reader with an investigative mindset.

Second, I would like to publicly appreciate the editing and scholarly suggestions provided by Dr. Marvin Gilbert and Heather Van Allen. Laboring through more than 300 pages of text without growing despondent is a testimony to your commitment to professionalism and to me.

Last, I would like to thank Wipf and Stock for accepting this dissertation for publication. Their willingness to work closely with a publishing novice has made the experience pleasant.

Part I

Introduction and Literature Review

Chapter 1

Introduction to the Study

Background and Preliminary Considerations

Is JESUS OF NAZARETH the ultimate anointed messianic king (משיח/ Χριστός)[1] who was to rule Israel from the throne of David as predicted by the Old Testament (OT) prophets?[2] Since circa AD 30, a number of people proudly—some even defiantly—claimed that Jesus is this Messiah. In some cases, his followers made these claims despite persecution, threats, and even martyrdom by antagonists who were vehement in their opposition to the growing sect. According to biblical data, John the Baptist (JTB) was the first to provide public witness affirming that Jesus was the fulfillment of OT prophetic messianic predictions. He identified Jesus as the anointed one (Mark 1:10; John 1:32; Q 3:21–22).[3]

Jesus himself affirmed his status as Χριστός during interviews with the High Priest Caiaphas and the Sanhedrin by overtly stating, "I am, and you will see the Son of Man seated at the right hand of Power, and coming with the clouds of heaven" (Mark 14:62b, English Standard Version).[4] The

---

1. All lexical work in the Masoretic text, unless otherwise designated, will utilize Koehler et al., *Hebrew and Aramaic Lexicon of the Old Testament*, 250.

All lexical work in the Septuagint, unless otherwise designated, will utilize Lust et al., *Greek-English Lexicon of the Septuagint*.

All lexical work in the NT, unless otherwise designated, will utilize Arndt et al., *Greek-English Lexicon of the New Testament and other Early Christian Literature*.

2. Koehler et al., *Hebrew and Aramaic Lexicon*, 694.

3. Robinson et al., *Critical Edition of Q*, 20. Throughout this dissertation, NT references will be weighed in accordance with accepted standards for textual and historical evaluation. Although not an exhaustive list, these standards include: independent or multiple attestation, criterion of dissimilarity, contextual credibility, and the criterion of embarrassment. Also considered are factors such as eyewitness testimony, whether the documents are primary or secondary in nature, archeological evidence, and current critical scholarship.

4. Unless otherwise indicated, Bible passages rendered in English use the English

implication is that by evoking the image of the transcendent "son of man," appearing in Daniel 7:13–14, Jesus was claiming status as both the predicted Messiah and the judge of those present during this trial.[5] Pontius Pilate also inquired about Jesus' status when he asking, "'Are you the King of the Jews?' And Jesus answered him, 'You have said so'" (Mark 15:2b). On the Day of Pentecost, Peter proclaimed Jesus as the fulfillment of OT promises (Acts 3:18–25), especially those related to messianic suffering.[6] Later, at the house of Cornelius, Peter again referred to the prophets while describing Jesus as judge and redeemer (Acts 10:42–43). In 1 Peter 1:10–12, providing salvation as a distinctly messianic function is also attributed to Jesus; Peter contends this was foretold by the prophets. Stephen ties prophetic prediction to Jesus: Stephen specifically is reported as mentioning the coming of the Righteous One (Acts 7:52) which, in context, can only be referring to the crucifixion Jesus.

The work of the apostle Paul is of major importance for this study because of his repeated references to the OT prophets. Saul of Tarsus was one of the primary persecutors of believing Jews. His persecutions began shortly after the formation of the new Jewish sect (Christians) and its initial expansion into the regions surrounding Judea. His conversion experience profoundly changed both the direction of his life and his religious belief system (Gal 1:11–17; 1 Cor 15:8). The cornerstone of Paul's arguments advocating Jesus as the Messiah are the words of the OT prophets; these figure prominently in several of his recorded speeches (Acts 13:27; 26:22ff; 28:23; Rom 1:2–3; 3:21; 1 Cor 15:3–4). When Paul became the persecuted rather than the persecutor, his interlocutors pressed him for answers as to the basis for his affirmation of Jesus as the predicted Messiah. Paul's responses routinely included reasons based on fulfilled OT prophecy. The normative Jewish interpretations of the early first century would not unambiguously have delineated Jesus as the Messiah. Even so, Paul almost certainly expected any Jew with the requisite knowledge of the *Tanakh* to follow his arguments and reach the same conclusion.[7]

Standard Version.

5. Mark 14:62 appears in one of the most well attested passages in the NT. Jesus apparently identifies himself as the transcendent figure and judge who receives the kingdom described in Daniel 7:13–14. This figure receives a kingdom and dominion over all peoples.

6. Paul also affirms the suffering of the Messiah in a creedal hymn (1 Cor 15:3) that seems to predate his own writing and probably stems from the earliest Palestinian Christian thoughts about the Messiah. Witherington, *Jesus, Paul, and the End of the World*, 191.

7. This seems to be the implication of Acts 26:27. Paul speaks as though belief in the prophets equals belief that Jesus is the fulfillment of those prophecies. Similarly,

Several of the early Christian fathers add their voices to those of Peter and Paul by supplementing the biblical data concerning the vital role OT prophecy plays as an apologetic tool. They did this when demonstrating the truth of the Christian religion and its assertions about the messianic status of Jesus. Two examples will suffice to support this observation. The first extant apologetic documents of the church are those of Justin Martyr (Justin), in which prophecy is frequently appealed to as evidence for the truth of Christianity.[8] Another influential writer, Origen, in his well-known work *Against Celsus*, employs OT prophecy to defend the Messiah being born of a virgin within the house of David. Interestingly, in this case, OT prophecy is used to argue in a way reminiscent of Paul's letters because the Jew Celsus believes in predictive prophecy, but rejects Christianity:

> And these arguments I employ as against a Jew who believes in prophecy. Let Celsus now tell me, or any of those who think with him, with what meaning the prophet utters either these statements about the future, or the others which are contained in the prophecies? Is it with any foresight of the future or not? If with a foresight of the future, then the prophets were divinely inspired; if with no foresight of the future, let him explain the meaning of one who speaks thus boldly regarding the future, and who is an object of admiration among the Jews because of his prophetic powers.[9]

The goal at this juncture of the dissertation is not to provide an exhaustive list of apologetic data but to bring attention to the early and wide-ranging use of fulfilled prophecy as a legitimate apologetic tool. It is ironic that many within Christendom—as well as agnostics and atheists—now dismiss a once valuable and often deployed apologetic evidence for Christianity. The proposed remedy for this condition is a revitalization of the study of messianic prophecy for apologetic purposes by applying contemporary historical-critical methods to these ancient oracles and drawing conclusions based on strict verification criteria. Criteria-verifying conditions include: (1) primary fulfillments, (2) critical dating, (3) the impossibility of staging fulfillments, (4) *minimal facts*,[10] and (5) justifiable historical descriptions based on probabilities as indicated by adequate historical data.

Paul confirms this assertion by citing OT prophecy stating that those who reject his argument are both unable to perceive and dull (Acts 28:26–27).

8. Martyr, "First Apology of Justin," 411.

9. Origen, "Origen against Celsus," 1.35.

10. Habermas asserts that minimal facts are "well-evidenced, usually for multiple reasons, and they are generally admitted by critical scholars who research this

Statement of the Problem

This study will seek to establish if critically acceptable historical-evidential reasons exist for believing that Jesus is the direct fulfillment of the specific OT messianic texts included in the study. This investigation envisions the existence of three possible outcomes for each prophecy examined: (1) Jesus directly fulfilled the prophecy and sufficient historical evidence establishes the claim as probable, (2) Jesus directly fulfilled the prophecy, but the available historical evidence is insufficient to establish the claim as probable, and (3) sufficient historical evidence exists to refute the claim that Jesus directly fulfilled the prophecy.

Significance of the Problem

The problem under investigation seeks to identify and to examine critically acceptable historical-evidential reasons for believing that Jesus is the direct fulfillment of the OT messianic texts. Questions about the status, nature, and person of Jesus have been the subject of many scholarly investigations. A significant lacuna exists in critical scholarly data, however. The lacuna lies in the treatment of the relationship of Jesus to his purported fulfillment of major OT prophetic predictions. This scholarly void is at least partly attributable to the *a priori* anti-supernatural, rationalist arguments of the Enlightenment. In his now infamous "ugly broad ditch" statement, G. E. Lessing presses the issue of how "accidental truths of history could never become necessary truths of reason."[11] Although not denying the possibility of supernatural events outright, Lessing apparently considers assertions of the supernatural historically indemonstrable because of their dissimilarity to natural events.[12] The difficulty involved in justifiably "jumping the ditch" between the historical and the metaphysical, or the contingent and the necessary, remains key to understanding the reasons for this lacuna.

---

particular area" (Habermas, "Evidentialist Apologetics," 100). In addition, he gives priority to the "well-attested grounds" since the opinions of scholars can be mistaken for "intellectual climate changes." For a more complete definition see "Definition of a Minimal Fact" below. Throughout this work, the term *minimal facts* will be italicized because of their methodological significance in the study.

11. Chadwick, *Lessing's Theological Writings*, 53.

12. Chadwick, *Lessing's Theological Writings*, 53. Lessing, borrowing Aristotle's phrase, describes history and assertions of the supernatural as "μεταβασις εις αλλο γενος."

It also reveals the reticence of scholars to exegete and interpret data that is inherently ambiguous and subject to hermeneutical manipulation.[13]

Lessing was not the first to point out the ambiguity of historical descriptions as indicators of supernatural activity, or even the difficulty of an unqualified identification of primary fulfillments of prophecy. Celsus reproached the idea of Christians employing prophecy as an apologetic defense based on his contention that "prophecies agree with ten thousand other things more credibly than with Jesus."[14] What is the evidential and factual basis of these claims? In the spirit of true scholarship, it is incumbent on skeptics, including Celsus, historically-evidentially, "to have demonstrated with regard to each particular prophecy that it can apply to other events with equal or greater probability than to Jesus."[15] Bare assertions of absolute certainty made about alleged historical events are misplaced. Rational, historical, and empirical data must support such claims, regardless of the advocated position.

Recent scholarship and popular media are no less critical of the possibility of genuine predictive prophecy. Most recent discussions have centered specifically on the related issue of biblical inerrancy, the impossibility of miracles, or speculative eschatological issues.[16] Few outside of the Internet press have actually dealt directly with specific messianic prophecies.

With these difficulties in mind, what may one conclude? If demonstrated historically-evidentially probable that Jesus' life and claims are the fulfillment of certain OT messianic prophecies, such fulfillment would lend credibility to his claim as King of the Jews. It would also support claims made of his resurrection, a future second coming, and the realization of the kingdom of God on earth. If the positive claims of Jesus regarding his messiahship are probabilistically true and, therefore, warranting belief, so

---

13. Other scholars engaged in evidential approaches to OT messianic prophecy include Gauch Jr., "Best Practices for Prophecy Arguments," 255–82, and Gauch Jr. et al., "Public Theology and Scientific Method," 45–88. Cf. the four-part dialogue between Christian physicist Robert C. Newman and atheist philosopher Evan Fales: Newman, "Fulfilled Prophecy as Miracle"; Fales, "Successful Defense?"; Newman, "On Fulfilled Prophecy as Miracle," 63–67; and Newman's final response, included in the Gauch Jr. et al. article above, 77–78.

14 Origen, "Origen against Celsus," 2.28.

15. Origen, "Origen Against Celsus," 2.28.

16. Ulrich states, "By way of evaluation, Klein, Eichrodt, Barr, and Carroll have either made God subject to the vicissitudes of history or made him so transcendent that he cannot recognizably enter his own universe" (Ulrich, "Dissonant Prophecy," 131). Cf. Carroll, *When Prophecy Failed*, 11–40. Carroll negatively assesses the possibility that God knows the future and reveals it to prophets. Such ideas are, "archaic metaphors" . . . requiring "hermeneutical gymnastics" and among the theological ideas that are better discarded (Carroll, *When Prophecy Failed*, 34–35).

must his equally potent assertions of eternal punishment for those who fail to heed his call to repent and follow him. If certain events of Jesus' life and ministry ("accidental truths of history") are demonstrated as probabilistically true, those events imply supernatural agency and, consequently, a rationally necessary being actualizing those historical truths.

The Study's Contribution to Professional Knowledge and Practice

The initial survey of the literature pertaining to this dissertation has revealed few modern full-length scholarly works that treat OT prophecies and their purported NT fulfillment from a critical, exegetical, and historical-evidential perspective. Further, none has attempted to reduce the data to *minimal facts*. The available works treating prophecy date from the early church fathers, followed by centuries during which few additional insights were offered. Scholarly interest in OT messianic prophecy resumes in the nineteenth century, followed by important corpora of twentieth-century works. In proportion to other theological interests, however, few full scholarly treatments exist.

In contrast, several recent studies on the life and resurrection of Jesus employ historical-evidential and *minimal-facts* criteria or other forms of critical scholarship to advocate that he was a real historical person,[17] a miracle worker,[18] an itinerant preacher, an apocalyptic prophet,[19] and resurrected from the dead.[20] The lacuna in current literature is a treatment of OT prophecies that link aspects of Jesus' life and ministry to purported fulfillments from the perspective of historical-evidential criteria and critical scholarship by attempting to sift the data for the historical bedrock.[21]

Critical scholarship disallows presuppositions such as the authority and inerrancy of the Bible or evangelical presuppositions on the dating and authorship of texts. With few exceptions, contemporary treatments of OT prophecy tend to be overly broad or written for popular audiences.[22] These deficiencies do not necessarily make these treatments incorrect, but an in-depth analysis of the facts, supported by concomitant intellectual restraint,

17. Ehrman, *Did Jesus Exist*.
18. Habermas, *Risen Jesus and Future Hope*, 90.
19. Ehrman, *Jesus: Apocalyptic Prophet*.
20. Licona, *Resurrection of Jesus*.
21. Licona, *Resurrection of Jesus*. The term "bedrock" is one employed by Licona in his expansive study on the historical Jesus.
22. One recent exception to this statement is Bateman et al., *Jesus the Messiah*.

should produce a composition that will begin to fill the lacuna associated with this subject. The study will open up new research possibilities for messianic prophecy, and thus will contribute to the theological and scholarly advancement in the field.

In addition to the theological and scholarly contribution of the study, the apologetic contribution is noteworthy for three reasons. First, with few exceptions, skeptical scholars have avoided predictive prophecy as subject matter in scholarly works because of naturalistic assumptions based on *a priori* rejection of miracles as a possible explanation for otherwise unexplained phenomena.[23] Second, other writers have eschewed anything labeled prophecy because of the gullibility of the public, manipulative approaches adopted by some televangelists, or authors overstating their conclusions.[24] Third, conclusions drawn from historical descriptions are neither certain, exhaustive, nor unassailable; as a result, they leave the researcher open to criticism. Nevertheless, this lack of certainty does not eliminate the possibility that disciplined research into many historical events yields valid and substantial knowledge of those events. Apologetically, during the course of this study, the author will seek to overcome all three of these problems with appropriate methodological neutrality.

---

23 Three of Hume's quotes are important in relation to the rejection of miracles (See Hume, *Enquiry Concerning Human Understanding*, 120–22):

First: "A miracle is a violation of the laws of nature; and as a firm and unalterable experience has established these laws, the proof against a miracle, from the very nature of the fact, is as entire as any argument from experience can possibly be imagined."

Second: "The plain consequence is (and it is a general maxim worthy of our attention), 'That no testimony is sufficient to establish a miracle, unless the testimony be of such a kind, that its falsehood would be more miraculous, than the fact, which it endeavours to establish; and even in that case there is a mutual destruction of arguments, and the superior only gives us an assurance suitable to that degree of force, which remains, after deducting the inferior.'"

Third: "For *first*, there is not to be found, in all history, any miracle attested by a sufficient number of men, of such unquestioned good-sense, education, and learning, as to secure us against all delusion in themselves; of such undoubted integrity, as to place them beyond all suspicion of any design to deceive others; of such credit and reputation in the eyes of mankind, as to have a great deal to lose in case of their being detected in any falsehood; and at the same time, attesting facts performed in such a public manner and in so celebrated a part of the world, as to render the detection unavoidable: All which circumstances are requisite to give us a full assurance in the testimony of men."

24. Callahan, *Bible Prophecy*, 179–251.

An Overview of the Components of the Dissertation

Key Elements

This dissertation proposes to conduct an analysis of particular OT texts and their NT counterparts that Christians claim are both messianic and primarily fulfilled in the life and ministry of Jesus of Nazareth. The available literary, historical, and archeological methods will be utilized to verify or disprove these claims. The process will begin with a literature review in chapter 2, which includes works from a broad spectrum of scholarship addressing the specific issues of messianic prophecy. The works will be discussed in light of their methodology and especially as they relate to evidential approaches to the question of fulfillment. This portion of the work will also include critical analysis of the relationship between historiography and prophecy as miracle, since predictive prophecy, if it exists, is a sub-species of miracle.

The heart of the dissertation, chapters 3–7: "Exegesis, Analysis, and Synthesis," will approach the texts in three phases. First, the work will be narrowly focused on specific allegedly-predictive OT messianic texts and their alleged NT fulfillment texts. Second, exegetical analysis of relevant biblical and historical data will isolate relevant evidence. Some of this evidence may rise to a level of certainty that qualifies as *minimal facts*. In the final chapter, evidence rising to this level will be separated and highlighted in relation to data not as clearly attested. Specific OT prophecies and any relationship they may have to alleged NT fulfillments will be of primary significance at this final stage of the study.

Third, the conclusions gleaned from the historical evidence, including evidence rising to the level of *minimal facts*, will be applied to and weighed against plausible competing hypotheses proposed by other scholars. This component of the study will focus on evaluating theories (and their critiques) of the primary and best-known scholars who have addressed *the specific prophecy*.[25] Elements of the texts that will be considered include: rejecting the predictive component, denying the messianic character of the text, or disconnecting the prophecy from Jesus of Nazareth.

---

25. The more general treatment of whether predictive prophecy is possible is appropriate as an element of the second component.

INTRODUCTION TO THE STUDY 11

Chapter 3 the First Group of Biblical Texts

In reference to the five groups of biblical texts selected for this study. The first group of texts investigates the claim that the *terminus ad quem* for the coming of the Messiah must occur before Israel loses its status as self-governing (Gen 49:10) and before the destruction of the temple in AD 70 (Ps 118; Hag 2:7, 9; Mal 3:1).

Chapter 4 the Second Group of Biblical Texts

The second group of texts probe the claim that the Messiah would spring from the linage of King David and, correspondingly, that Jesus is a descendant of King David (2 Sam 7:13; Isa 11:1–2; Jer 23:5–6; Ezek 34:23–24; Hos 3:4–5). The NT genealogical data (Matt 1:1–17; Luke 2:4; 3:23–38) and Paul's comments on the issue (Rom 1:3) are important during this phase of study.

Chapter 5 the Third Group of Biblical Texts

The third group of texts relates to the geographical location associated with the birth and early life of the Messiah. Micah 5:2 will be examined to substantiate the claim that the Messiah would be born in Bethlehem of Judea, and the parallel claim that Jesus was born in this small village (Matt 2:1–12; Luke 2: 1–7).

Chapter 6 the Fourth Group of Biblical Texts

In the fourth set of passages, Jesus' miracles in relation to the expectations of the messianic age, the Messiah himself, and the predictions of the OT prophets are analyzed. Jesus' self-described *titular nomens* such as "prophet" (Luke 4:17–19), "son of man," "son of the Blessed" (Mark 14:61–62), and "son of David" (Matt 9:27; 12:23; 15:22; 21:9; Mark 10:47) all bear implications for his assertion of a future "seated at the right hand of God" (Mark 14:62). The best (and perhaps the only currently available) verification of whether these titles attributed to Jesus are justifiable is an examination of whether Jesus performed the miracles that the OT prophets allegedly predicted would accompany the messianic age (Deut 18:15–18; Isa 29:18; 35:5–6; 61:1–2; Matt 9:35; 11:4–6; Luke 7:22–23).[26]

26. That Messiah would have a ministry that includes miracles is the opinion of

Chapter 7 the Fifth Group of Biblical Texts

The fifth group of biblical texts includes Psalm 2:1–12, emphasizing verse 7; Psalm 16, emphasizing verses 9–10; and Psalm 22:1–31, emphasizing verse 16. Psalm 2 is often interpreted as a description of the unique relationship Jesus claimed to have with the God the Father. Psalm 22 is allegedly messianic and some interpreters claim it reports circumstances related to the crucifixion of Jesus. Finally, no investigation of allegedly fulfilled messianic prophecy in Psalms would be complete without a treatment of the resurrection claims made by Christians about Jesus. Psalm 16 contains language that may be indicative of the resurrection of Jesus. This portion of the work will not deal in depth with the actual NT data concerning the reported resurrection of Jesus because the resurrection proper has been extensively treated by other scholars.[27] The connection between the alleged OT predictions and the reported resurrection of Jesus will be treated without an *a priori* rejection of its historicity.

Reasons for Including Each Element

Five criteria were used to select the texts for this dissertation. First, in combination, the biblical texts must potentially span the entire life of Jesus from his birth to purported resurrection. Second, a straightforward contextual reading of an OT text must envision the sort of event alleged to be its NT fulfillment.[28] Third, a prophecy must have been made decades (or even centuries) prior to its alleged fulfillment. Fourth, all of the prophecies under investigation must be incapable of staged fulfillments, either individually or collectively. Given all the relevant evidence, if the historicity of the event is probable, the most likely explanation must be either the revealed foreknowledge of God or another type of miracle—not mere chance or collusion. Fifth, the prophecies selected must contain enough data to argue for or against Jesus as the probable fulfillment based on evidence or, if necessary, inference to the best explanation. If adequate sources and data are not available for a specific text, it will be eliminated from consideration.

Norman Geisler among others (Geisler, *Christian Apologetics*, 340).

27. See Habermas, *Historical Jesus*. Cf. Licona, *Resurrection of Jesus*, or Craig et al., *Jesus' Resurrection*.

28. Newman, "Fulfilled Prophecy as Miracle," 215. No person or group of persons could possibly arrange for any one individual to fulfill the diverse group of prophecies selected for this investigation.

INTRODUCTION TO THE STUDY 13

Overview of Methodology, Key Terms, and Presuppositions

Basic Rationale

This study will seek to establish if critically acceptable, historical-evidential, or factual reasons exist for believing that Jesus is the direct fulfillment of the OT messianic texts included in the study. The study proposes to answer this primary question by critically examining specific OT prophecies and their NT counterparts to determine what historical-evidential facts about these prophecies and their purported fulfillment can be established. The study will use criteria and methods that many contemporary scholars would accept as yielding methodologically valid evidence. If this objective is successful, the credibility of some of the facts will be distinguished by posing evidence or lines of argumentation that even skeptics and critical scholars will accept (*minimal facts*).[29] The author will make every attempt to assume a neutral stance on each of the issues and interpret the evidence according to the criteria outlined below. The results of the study will provide the reader with prudential verification, epistemic warrant for belief, and moral reasons for believing or rejecting Jesus as the fulfillment of these prophecies.

This author will employ several of the general methodological guidelines used by Michael Licona in *The Resurrection of Jesus: A New Historiographical Approach*. In doing so, however, the author acknowledges his "horizons" (i.e., preunderstanding), which are impossible to eliminate from the process.[30] No historical investigation proceeds from a value-neutral position. Each historian comes to the text with bias and dispositions that incline his or her work one way or another. The most prudent approach is to develop a historiographical method that reduces opportunity for subjectivity, discloses the presuppositions and *Weltanschauung* of the historian, and submits the conclusions to the scrutiny of other scholars. The results of any investigation of this sort will not be exhaustive; however, if properly conceived and executed, the study should yield adequate historical-evidential justification for its conclusions.

In each of the cases analyzed in this study, probabilities will be determined by the methodology explicated by C. Behan McCullagh: "inference

---

29. See the definition of a scholar under "Definitions of Key Terminology" below.

30. Licona, *Resurrection of Jesus*, 29–132. Licona lists six points that must be addressed for a fully developed historiographical approach: (1) method; (2) peer pressure; (3) submitting ideas to unsympathetic experts; (4) disclosing authorial horizons; (5) detachment from bias; and (6) accounting for historical bedrock (Licona, *Resurrection of Jesus*, 94).

to the best explanation" for justifying historical descriptions.[31] Although all seven criteria used by McCullagh will not apply in every case, all that do will be applied to the subject prophecies and their purported fulfillment.[32] These seven criteria are:

> 1. The statement, together with other statements already held to be true, must imply yet other statements describing present, observable data. (We will henceforth call the first statement "the hypothesis," and statements describing observable data, "observation and statements").
>
> 2. The hypothesis must be *of greater explanatory scope* than any other incompatible hypothesis about the same subject; that is, it must imply a greater variety of observation statements.
>
> 3. The hypothesis must be *of greater explanatory power* than any other incompatible hypothesis about the same subject; that is, it must make the observation statements it implies more probable than any other.
>
> 4. The hypothesis must be *more plausible* than any other incompatible hypothesis about the same subject; that is, it must be implied to some degree by a greater variety of accepted truths than any other and implied more strongly than any other; and its probable negation must be implied by fewer beliefs and implied less strongly than any other.
>
> 5. The hypothesis must be *less ad hoc* than any other incompatible hypothesis about the same subject; that is, it must include fewer new suppositions about the past which are not already implied to some extent by existing beliefs.
>
> 6. It must be *disconfirmed by fewer accepted beliefs* than any other incompatible hypothesis about the same subject; that is, when conjoined with accepted truths, it must imply fewer observation statements and other statements.
>
> 7. It must exceed other incompatible hypotheses about the same subject by so much that there is little chance of an incompatible hypothesis (characteristics 2–6) and, after further investigation, soon exceeding it in these respects.[33]

---

31. McCullagh, *Justifying Historical Descriptions*, 15–33.
32. McCullagh, *Justifying Historical Descriptions*, 19.
33. McCullagh, *Justifying Historical Descriptions*, 19.

When applied, these criteria disallow speculative or novel conclusions that might require the setting aside of relevant evidence. They also demand that the probability that the advocated historical description will be displaced by another more plausible description be remote.

Evaluative Framework for Biblical Data

Biblical data will be analyzed using the grammatical-historical method.[34] The grammatical-historical method consists of interpreting the biblical text in its literal sense while allowing for theological implications, figurative language, the literary forms and genres, and specific, historical *sitz im leben*. From the biblical authors' perspective, this means the prophecies predict literal events—though the descriptions do not necessarily portray the events literally.[35] Milton S. Terry expresses the appropriate sentiments and practices regarding this method:

> Its fundamental principle is to gather from the Scriptures themselves the precise meaning that the writers intended to convey. It applies to the sacred books the same principles, the same grammatical process and exercise of common sense and reason, which we apply to other books. The grammatico-historical exegete, furnished with suitable qualifications, intellectual, educational, and moral, will accept the claims of the Bible without prejudice or adverse prepossession, and, with no ambition to prove them true or false, will investigate the language and import of each book with fearless independence.[36]

After the lexical, grammatical, and historical data are collected from biblical texts, the second step of interpretation involves asking interpretative questions of those data and formulating a hypothesis capable of answering those questions. This need arises because prophetic language is often ambiguous.[37] A case in point is the attribution of prophetic speech to Caiaphas, when he states: "You know nothing at all. Nor do you understand

---

34. See Kaiser and Silva, *Introduction to Biblical Hermeneutics*. Specifically addressing the issue of prophecy, Gregory V. Trull identifies seven hermeneutical approaches of modern scholarship: (1) Hermeneutical Error, (2) Jewish Hermeneutics, (3) *Sensus Plenior*, (4) Canonical Approach, (5) Typology, (6) Single Message, and (7) Direct Prophecy. See Trull, "Views on Peter's Use of Psalm 16:8–11 in Acts 2:25–32," 198.

35. Klein et al., *Introduction to Biblical Interpretation*, 443.

36. Terry, *Biblical Hermeneutics*, 70.

37. The actual content of the original author's conception cannot be fully known. Therefore, the use of the grammatical-historical method in this dissertation will not prohibit either typology or *sensus plenior* understandings of texts.

that it is better for you that one man should die for the people, not that the whole nation should perish" (John 11:49c–50). John (ironically) extends the meaning intended by Caiaphas beyond the concern for Roman retribution for messianic aspirations in Israel to include propitiation of the wrath of God. These secondary meanings presented by biblical data from both the Old and New Testaments must be given due consideration, even though they often transcend the understanding of the original oracle, author, and recipients. The data and hypothesis (this author's interpretation) will then be coordinated with any historical data from extra-biblical sources, with priority given to the most-well-attested, earliest scholarly sources. No data will be given a privileged position arbitrarily.[38]

Evaluative Framework for Historical Data

This study requires the analysis of texts and other historical evidence that are not a part of the books traditionally included in the Protestant canon. These include, but are not limited to, the Apocrypha/Pseudepigrapha, Josephus, Roman historians, the Talmudic writings, and early non-canonical Christian works. The strategy for analyzing ancient texts and archeological evidence consists of pairing descriptions drawn from the biblical account with verifiable historical events. Historical and archeological data will receive the same treatment and status as the biblical documents in an effort to support and historically justify the conclusions generated by the study.

Definitions of Key Terminology

Evidence: Evidence is information drawn from personal testimony, a document, or a material object that in some way establishes facts or other indications capable of confirming or disconfirming an event or claim.

History: History is the genre, content, and description of past events expressed through many mediums of communication.[39]

Fulfillment: When applied in this historical-evidential study, fulfillment of an OT prophecy means literal direct fulfillment. Every component of the prediction must have historical-evidential grounds that indicate the

---

38. The present author makes no affirmations of authorship for any canonical or other works unless explicitly stated. The use of traditional attributions and authorship are employed only for convenience.

39. History may include events of social, political, or other significant aspects of human existence and should consist primarily of factual data extracted from primary or original source documents.

event or action has transpired in a manner consistent with the original prediction. Specifically eliminated from consideration are fulfillment concepts such as progressive revelation and deeper meaning, typological fulfillment, double fulfillment, manifold fulfillment, theological fulfillment, and analogous fulfillment.[40]

Minimal fact: A *minimal fact* will conceptually align with the definitions previously provided by Gary R. Habermas and Licona.[41] Habermas contends that there are "at least two major prerequisites for an occurrence to be designated as a *Minimal Fact*."[42] First, more than adequate scholarly evidences usually containing several critically ascertained lines of argumentation must be available. Second, agreement must exist among the majority of contemporary scholars about the historicity of the event. In this study, the second criteria has been modified as follows: there must be agreement among the majority of contemporary scholars about the historicity of the event or the specific claim the *minimal fact* affirms.

When referring to a spoken prophecy, a *minimal fact* could consist of—but need not be limited to—agreement that: (1) a prophecy was spoken before the alleged fulfillment, (2) non-canonical texts interpret the prophecy as messianic, (3) the prophecy is considered messianic by certain individuals or sects within Judaism, (4) the complete implication of the prophecy

---

40. See Sailer et al., *Religious and Theological Abstracts*. These theories of how OT prophecy may be understood as fulfilled are listed in reference to Weir, "Analogous Fulfillment."

41. Licona, *Resurrection of Jesus*, 279.

42. Habermas, "Minimal Facts Approach to the Resurrection of Jesus," 16. Habermas notes that of the two prerequisite criteria for acceptance, the first is by far the most important because it establishes historicity. The second criteria is subject to human error and the changing views of scholars.

For example, Habermas suggests the following twelve facts about Jesus that meet the criteria: "(1) Jesus died by crucifixion and (2) was buried. (3) Jesus' death caused the disciples to despair and lose hope, believing that his life was ended. (4) Although not as widely accepted, many scholars hold that the tomb in which Jesus was buried was discovered to be empty just a few days later. Critical scholars further agree that (5) the disciples had experiences which they believed were literal appearances of the risen Jesus. Because of these experiences, (6) the disciples were transformed from doubters who were afraid to identify themselves with Jesus to bold proclaimers of his death and resurrection. (7) This message was the center of preaching in the early church and (8) was especially proclaimed in Jerusalem, where Jesus died and was buried shortly before. As a result of this preaching, (9) the church was born and grew, (10) with Sunday as the primary day of worship. (11) James, who had been a skeptic, was converted to the faith when he also believed that he saw the resurrected Jesus. (12) A few years later, Paul was converted by an experience which he, likewise, believed to be an appearance of the risen Jesus" (Habermas, *Historical Jesus*, 158). Habermas believes that only numbers one, five, six, and twelve are necessary to prove the likely historicity of Jesus' resurrection.

has not been fulfilled, (5) specific NT writers believed the prophecy was fulfilled, (6) specific post-apostolic sources believed the prophecy was fulfilled, and (7) other historical sources claim the prophecy was fulfilled by Jesus.

Scholar: A scholar possesses a terminal academic degree in a field of study relevant to this dissertation and is actively engaged in academic research and writing.

Authorial Presuppositions

The author maintains a realist view of history, one that allows for the possibility that properly conducted historical investigation into actual events may yield some or even adequate knowledge to determine the historicity of those events.

The author maintains that the correspondence theory of truth is the primary test of true descriptions of the world. Further, the correspondence theory must interact closely with the coherence theory and pragmatic livability, since truth actualized in time and space will display each of these elements.[43]

The author will apply the basic laws of logic throughout the research.[44] The author maintains that any *a priori* rejection of a theistic worldview or supernatural activity invalidates the conclusions of a given study. Therefore, this study will initially accept the possibility of miracles, but will require evidential support before concluding *a posteriori* that supernatural activity is a probable conclusion.

The author is a Christian. For purposes of this study, however, claims of privileged status for biblical documents such as divine inspiration, inerrancy, authorship, or date of writing, are suspended. To the extent possible, each text will be examined objectively.

Summary of Important Literature

This summary of the literature related to messianic prophecy and claims of its fulfillment in the person and work of Jesus of Nazareth is limited in both scope and analysis. The purpose at this juncture is to demonstrate the author's familiarity with the primary sources—not to provide a full literature review with critical evaluations.

---

43. Geisler and Feinberg, *Introduction to Philosophy*, 235–51.

44. Three key laws of logic include, (1) the law of identity: A is A; (2) the law of noncontradiction: A is not non-A; (3) the law of the excluded middle: either A or non-A, but not both.

In addition, this summary highlights the scarcity of modern scholarly works that even briefly address the topic; full-length treatments not written for the popular audience are scarcer still. No treatment of OT prophecy employing a historical-evidential approach or *minimal-facts* methodology has been uncovered by the preliminary search. A full literature review that includes critical evaluation of primary sources and other material integral to the dissertation will form the content of chapter 2. Some of the works that are important to the study are commented on below.

Jesus the Messiah: Tracing the Promises, Expectations, and Coming of Israel's King is important to this study because of its detailed expositon of the progressively revealed and multi-layered nature of OT prophecy.[45] Simplistic fulfillment claims are few; OT messianic prophecies rarely limit their perspective to a single indisputable referent. Most prophecies have temporally near and far referents, but only one ultimate fulfillment is possible. This information sheds light on texts such as Genesis 49:10, where, despite a textual difficulty, traditional interpreters have often identified both David and Jesus as fulfillments of this oracle.

In addition, this work provides perspective on the general development of Jewish messianic thought with its differing strands as recorded in the literature of various sects within Judaism. Messianism was far from ubiquitous or of a monolithic nature in the minds of most Israelites prior to the growing discontent with the Hasmonean royal priesthood about 152 BC. After this date, messianism gained increasing significance and its influence felt during the life of Jesus. According to Herbert W. Bateman, Darrell L. Bock, and Gordon H. Johnston, 152 BC delineates the approximate dating of earliest non-biblical sources at our disposal for studying messianic thought in the second temple period, while AD 70 and the period immediately after are the latest.

Another issue that this dissertation must address is how the NT writers used, appropriated, and applied the OT when attributing prophetic fulfillments to Jesus. There are difficulties encountered regardless of the method employed. Help addressing these difficulties is available in *Three Views on the New Testament Use of the Old Testament*.[46] Before the contributing authors of this work explain their approaches to this issue, the introductory material poses five key questions that each scholar must answer during the course of his exposition:

1. Is *sensus plenior* an appropriate way of explaining the New Testament use of the Old Testament?

---

45. Bateman et al., *Jesus the Messiah*.
46. Kaiser Jr. et al., *Three Views*.

2. How is typology best understood?

3. Do the New Testament writers take into account the context of the passages they cite?

4. Does the New Testament writers' use of Jewish exegetical methods explain the New Testament use of the Old Testament?

5. Are we able to replicate the exegetical and hermeneutical approaches to the Old Testament that we find in the writings of the New Testament?[47]

These are important questions for the proposed study because each of the NT texts examined are in some way interpretations of the OT. Further, the research conclusions, such as those generated in this study, add yet another layer of interpretation. Nevertheless, in order to meet the *minimal-facts* criteria, the evidence must indicate a single direct referent.

Two works by Robert C. Newman are worthy of mention because of their direct relevance to the topic of OT prophecy. *Fulfilled Prophecy as Miracle* is a brief but well-written defense of prophecy as a subspecies of miracle: something that can only be consistently produced by supernatural agency. Without an *a priori* rejection of miracles, the possibility of predictive prophecy must be given a fair hearing. In Newman's second work, *Prophecies about the Coming Messiah*, he highlights OT prophecies that he believes could not have been invented or staged by the NT church. Significant among these for this study is Psalm 22. Newman contends that this Psalm depicts a suffering person who has pierced hands and feet and is crying out in anguish as a result of his abandonment by God. Although some recent scholarship dissents from this view, an examination is still warranted to see if facts can be ascertained.

Part of this dissertation will involve interactions with non-biblical sources predating the historical Jesus. These include the Apocrypha/Pseudepigrapha and the Dead Sea Scrolls. It is also possible that Egyptian or other Near Eastern sources may contain information bearing on the issues of messianic understanding in relation to establishing facts about purported NT fulfillment. In each of these cases, modern and critical editions will be employed where applicable.

---

47. Lunde, "Introduction to Central Questions," 12.

Sources studying the historical Jesus have received substantial attention by scholars such as Gary Habermas[48] and Darrell Bock.[49] Bock in particular deals with much of the non-biblical literary evidence of the life of Jesus while providing a brief outline of the political and social history of the period.

This dissertation is not an extension of the *Third Quest for the Historical Jesus*. Nevertheless, it presupposes some of the conclusions of other scholars about the historical Jesus and will interact as needed with the texts produced by the Jesus Seminar. The text of *The Five Gosples*, in particular, will be utilized to help rank biblical sources and begin discussion about the historicity of the NT texts. The fellows of the Jesus Seminar are considered by many to be hypercritical in approaching the historical Jesus.[50] Thus, it is certain that any conclusions drawn from NT data in the current work that agree with those of the Jesus Seminar will be critically acceptable.

In summary, the literature that will be included in the study includes works that cover a broad spectrum of past and present messianic thought. Sources from evangelical, critical, and skeptical sources will be given consideration in chapter 2 (the Literature Review) and subsequent research.

Conclusion

The proposed methodology for this dissertation involves the study of OT messianic prophecy and the purported NT fulfillments from a historical-evidential and facts-centered perspective as described earlier in this chapter. It must be emphasized that this method has not been fully developed for this type of application and is not the traditional approach to the topic of messianic prophecy. Rather than embracing an uncritical acceptance of the texts, relevant prophecies will be analyzed to discover if the events they depict can be established by meeting historical-evidential requirements and both the criteria defining *minimal facts*. Those events or assertions that can satisfy the criteria constitute the historical bedrock. They are not merely matters that must be accepted on the basis of faith or tradition.

---

48. Habermas, *Historical Jesus*, 250. Habermas contends that there are at least 45 ancient sources for the study of the historical Jesus. Notably, he focuses much attention on the early creedal statements within the four gospels and the undisputed Pauline letters. These creedal statements are the earliest expressions of how the church understood Jesus.

49. Bock, *Studying the Historical Jesus*.

50. Funk and Hoover, *Five Gospels*.

It is this author's opinion that the historical bedrock will provide solid apologetic evidence that Jesus is the direct fulfillment of specific OT messianic texts. Consequently, the intellectual rationale for believing otherwise will be narrowed, and honest fact-focused doubters, especially among scholars, will be compelled to reckon with the data.

Chapter 2

Literature Review

Overview of the Literature Review

THE LITERATURE DEALING WITH the overarching phenomena of Hebrew prophecy as recorded in the OT is immense. The scope of this body of literature requires some narrowing in order to better suit the current purpose. First, the works must specifically treat messianic prophecy. Second, the scope of the literature is further constricted by including only works that have a definite apologetic interest or that do not approach the topic with uncritical presuppositions. These qualifications reduce the relevant literature to a manageable quantity. The copious number of volumes devoted to the study of biblical prophecy is justified by the vital role it plays in Christian thought and practice. John Ankerberg and John Weldon, commenting on the importance of prophecy and prophets in the Bible, note that Scripture contains more than 600 direct references to prophecy and prophets; approximately 27 percent of the Bible contains prophetic material.[1]

In contrast to the immense amount of literature dedicated to prophecy in general, and the vital role of messianic prophecy in the Bible, an extreme paucity of sources exist that approach the topic from an evidential, apologetic, and critical perspective. None combines all of these elements into a single, thorough treatment. This noticeable deficiency is what the present study hopes to alleviate.

The first section of the Literature Review highlights the progression of modern thought regarding OT messianic prophecy. The first section begins with works that forward reasons for the beliefs of Christianity in what might be termed the *classic* or *traditional* argument from prophecy and progresses toward its end with more critical and apologetic works. The second section of the Literature Review highlights authors and arguments that alter or

---

1. Ankerberg and Weldon, *Handbook of Biblical Evidences*, 216.

eliminate the traditional approach to predictive prophecy. The third section of the Literature Review critiques and analyzes David Hume's *An Enquiry Concerning Human Understanding*. His work contributed significantly to the establishment of the Enlightenment paradigm for skepticism about miracles; including prophecy as a species of miracle. To this point, the current work has made no attempt to demonstrate the possibility of miracles. However, the third section of this chapter seeks to disclose the rationale for not rejecting miracles *a priori*.

Elements in and Rationale for Section 1 of the Literature Review

The basis for the traditional argument from prophecy is fairly straightforward. An OT prediction is tied textually to a NT fulfillment based on the reader's presupposition of supernatural inspiration of the prophet, Christian traditional teachings, and perhaps some historical support.[2] Other presuppositions include such concepts as the analogy of faith, reading the texts canonically (or possibly anachronistically), and belief that the autographs were inerrant. The result of this approach is unquestionably a circular course of reasoning. This course usually proceeds retrogressively from a perceived NT connection to an image drawn in OT prophecy, and results in a subsequent leap of faith to the conclusion that the same hand that drew the prophetic image also molded the portrait or NT connection in historical realization.[3] These connections—and their associated leaps of faith—all seem reasonable to the uncritical reader. This allows the fulfillment data to be cited in support of the contention that the Bible is the inspired Word of God. Further, this course of reasoning makes three key assumptions: (1) the God of the Bible is the only One capable of genuine predictive prophecy; (2) the God of the Bible is both all-knowing and all-powerful; and (3) Jesus perfectly fulfilled OT predictions and therefore is the Messiah, the Savior of the world, the Son of the living God.[4] The circularity is obvious.

A second frequently observed element in the traditional approach to OT prophecy and alleged NT fulfillments is the mistaken notion that interpretive perfection is within the reader's grasp. In fact, no scholarly consensus exists on hermeneutical principles that must be applied to biblical literature, or on how each prophecy is rightly understood. The quintessential example of this error is, perhaps, the profusion of explanations

---

2. See the definition of fulfillment in chapter 1, "Definition of Key Terminology."
3. Meldau, *Prophets Still Speak*, 4.
4. Meldau, *Prophets Still Speak*, 4.

purporting to solve the conundrum of Daniel 9:24–27. Several possible solutions to the problem of when the seventy weeks begin and when they end have been proffered. There are also several conflicting ideas as to when, if at all, breaks in the time sequence should be inserted. Some interpreters do not even accept the idea that literal time periods are actually intended. In addition, there is no consensus on a solution to the textual issue of whether the prophecy is actually messianic in the ultimate sense, at all. Nevertheless, many authors employing the traditional argument from prophecy dogmatically affirm something similar to Earle Rowell's statement: "Daniel gives the exact year of Christ's appearance as the Messiah, and of His crucifixion."[5] Perhaps Daniel's prophecy does this, but as of yet no scholarly consensus, *a leviori* agreed-upon facts, have emerged to support such a claim.

Section 1. A Progressive Review of the Traditional Argument from Messianic Prophecy

Alexander Keith: Evidence of the Truth of the Christian Religion

Alexander Keith authored a classic work on OT prophecy entitled, *Evidence of the Truth of the Christian Religion*. Keith presupposes an inspired biblical text and the concept of canon. The term "*canon*" here implies that prophetic texts are best understood when read from a perspective where later texts interpret or illuminate earlier texts. This method facilitates the reading of OT texts as preparatory and the reading of NT texts anachronistically, back into the OT documents. Stated another way, a canonical reading allows for the discovery of meaning that may not have been apparent to the original audience. For example, Keith maintains that the time of Jesus' first advent was predicted in several different ways.[6] First, for our current purpose, is his reference to Genesis 49:10 and the assertion that the Savior must come during the time that Judah remained as a united people with a reigning king.[7] However, he neither offers an explanation of his proposed solution to the well-documented textual difficulty regarding the term שילה nor does he explain his conclusion that this text refers to the person of the Savior. His conclusion remains an unsupported assertion. Much the same is evident when Malachi 3:1 is championed as a demand that the Messiah come into his (the second) temple before its destruction. Again, Keith avows that the

---

5. Rowell, *Prophecy Speaks*, 55.
6. Keith, *Evidence of the Truth of the Christian Religion*, 23–52.
7. Keith, *Evidence of the Truth of the Christian Religion*, 26.

prophecy regarding the glory of the second temple exceeding that of the first (Hag 2:9) is a messianic prophecy: it demands that the Messiah come before the demolition of the temple in AD 70. In addition, Keith adds to the flood of interpretations of Daniel 9:24–27, but his interpretation of this passage is methodologically unclear and does nothing to clarify the already complicated morass of interpretations proffered in the literature.[8]

In general, the allegedly messianic nature of the prophecies Keith treats are the common stock of Christian belief. Negatively, however, he supplies little early Jewish interpretive data to support a historical-contextual messianic interpretation for his claims. To his credit, he does cite the lack of any credible contradicting testimony when alluding to the genealogies of Jesus, including some early church support.

The zenith of Keith's research, ironically, is a footnote, quoting four historical persons (Tacitus, Suetonius, Josephus, and Philo) who he believes affirm the approximate time of the Messiah's appearance as predicted by the texts cited above.[9] Each of these historians make direct mention of prophecies and they do interpret the prophecies as dealing with the first-century period. The problem with these sources, however, is they all remain vague in what they are claiming to reference in regard to specific Jewish prophetic texts. Much the same conclusion is drawn from Keith's exposition of Christ's birth, life, and death and the character of the Christian religion. Everything presented is plausible and reasonable. However, facts that can be derived from his work on messianic texts are few. In the end, the critical reader comes away from Keith's work with more questions than answers.

Eduard Riehm: Messianic Prophecy: Its Origin, Historical Character, and Relation to New Testament Fulfillment

Eduard Riehm produced a work on messianic prophecy in 1876 that takes a distinct approach to the subject. For Riehm, the key to understanding prophecy was the historical sense; that is, how the prophet wished to be understood by his contemporaries. Riehm contends that "what we do not learn until the period of fulfillment cannot be in the prophecy itself."[10] He adamantly rejected any attempt to read the OT anachronistically from the NT perspective and he refused to affirm those who did. In his mind, the goal of the study of messianic prophecy was to work toward understanding

---

8. Keith, *Evidence of the Truth of the Christian Religion*, 27–30.
9. Keith, *Evidence of the Truth of the Christian Religion*, 30.
10. Riehm, *Messianic Prophecy*, xxii.

the "germ" and then progress to understanding the "full flower."[11] The sense in which the prophets and their contemporaries understood the contents of the prophecies was to be kept separate from the reference ultimately intended in the counsels of God and later revealed through Christ.[12]

Riehm also argues that prophecy was not so much a mosaic to be constructed as it was a multi-strand work of preparation; a living organism whose leaves grow, mature, and then fall away, with the final form being hidden until fully manifest in Christ. Thus, unfulfilled or partially fulfilled messianic prophecies were of little concern because they were controlled by history and historical context and elucidated by history. They did not mandate exhaustive concrete fulfillment. Riehm contends that the OT forms that contained prophetic meaning were "mere drapery" (opaque drapery) the higher forms and development of messianic prophecy had taken away. Among the drapery were Jewish ceremony, the temple, and even the city of Jerusalem.[13] In other words, the OT features were temporary forms, separate from the fully matured type. Consistently applied, this approach allows for prophetic fulfillment in Christ without a demand for the historicity of every aspect of the prophecy or prophecies being subject to evidential verification, except in their ideal sense.

Historically verifiable fulfillments are possible to see in some prophecies, but in order to properly understand fulfillment, the typological sense is paramount. Conversely, Riehm is critical of incorrect or allegorized interpretation that allowed Christ to be inserted in unlikely places and in ways that misconstrue the true historical sense of the prophetic text. In short, the historical sense, on the one hand, and the type on the other are both important aspects of prophecy.

The strength of Reihm's work lies in his commitment to a proper historical sense for the texts, including making place for the individual psychology of the prophet. In addition, he affirmed that messianic prophecy developed along a continuum—from germ to the full flower.

The weakness of Reihm's work is the indistinct line of separation between what can be demonstrated as historically concrete in relation to messianic prophecy and what is merely the spiritualization of prophetic fulfillment through the "drapery" of the OT forms. Such forms include (1) Israelite nationalism; (2) the offices of prophet, priest, and king; and (3) the functions of temple cult. Reihm's point about the ideal contained in the historical features of a given prophecy seems plausible as the essential demanding fulfillment.

---

11. Riehm, *Messianic Prophecy*, 151. Kaiser Jr., *Messiah in the Old Testament*, 23–28.
12. Riehm, *Messianic Prophecy*, 151.
13. Riehm, *Messianic Prophecy*, 164–67.

One question remains, however, with reference to Reihm's work: what, if anything, can verify a claim if it is not concrete and historical? Verification of a type or ideal is so tenuous that virtually nothing of apologetic value can be salvaged. There is much value in what Riehm proposes, and the present study takes his approach with due deference. If, however, Jesus as an historical person existed and is the ultimate antitype and ideal of OT messianic prophecy, then some concrete verification must be available. Otherwise, the honest skeptic is left without hope or direction.

Franz Delitzsch: Messianic Prophecies in Historical Succession

A prominent scholar of the nineteenth century, Franz Delitzsch approaches the topic of messianic prophecy from both a mildly critical and chronological perspective, treating them in historical succession. Delitzsch recognizes the difficulties involved in presupposing supernatural intervention as an explanation for prophecy and fulfillment. He devotes a short section to help the reader understand his position. Essentially, Delitzsch grants that affirmations of past supernatural activity are highly suspicious if present supernatural activity does not support its existence. Supernatural activity ("interchange" in his terminology) is a necessary inference if there is to be any communion between God and his creation. The presuppositions, therefore, that God exists and that redemptive communion is the goal of revelation carry the weight of the rest of his work.[14]

Delitzsch details the treatment of specific messianic prophecies, often using exegetical conclusions based on Hebrew texts, but with noticeable restraint in speculative extensions that go beyond what is reasonably supported. This exegetical restraint is an example of a gradually ascending paradigm that has contributed much to the scholarly treatment of biblical texts when compared to other less critical approaches.

A primary weakness of Delitzch's work, as is the case with many others, is that he makes little attempt to support his conclusions or affirmations with historical (or other) sources external to the biblical texts. He provides limited interaction with opposing views or critical scholarship, which limits the use of this work as an apologetic tool. The approach chosen by Delitzsch is a testament to his faith, but does little to commend the Bible to the skeptic as authoritative and accurate.[15]

---

14. Delitzsch, *Messianic Prophecies*, 13–14.

15. E. W. Hengstenberg authored another significant work treating OT messianic prophecy. It is not included in this review because he generally approaches the biblical texts with many of the traditional presuppositions. In some cases, he does reference

Ed Hindson: "Messianic Prophecy"

The Popular Encyclopedia of Bible Prophecy contains an article addressing messianic prophecy. Ed Hindson encapsulates the traditional argument as have few other works. As the title of the book suggests, the article is intended for a popular audience, not scholars. However, it is representative of how presuppositions play a paramount role in the traditional argument from OT messianic prophecy to the conclusion that Jesus is the Messiah.

The presuppositions surfacing in this article include the notion that Jesus' life, ministry, death, and resurrection are all predicted in the OT. The NT events related to these aspects of Jesus' life are presumed to be the best indicators of fulfillment and are factually related by inspired authors.[16] This approach works as intended when read uncritically. When the intended reader is well-versed in critical methodology, however, questions that require longer and detailed treatments of the topic emerge. This truncation is perhaps the only shortcoming of the article. Given greater space, issues such as evidence external to the Christian Bible and whether a given claim of prophetic fulfillment is legitimately messianic might have received treatment.[17]

One of the primary strengths of Hindson's article is its recognition of the early apologetic use of OT prophecy as "proof" for believing the claims of Jesus and, subsequently, the preaching of the apostles. The NT records several occasions in which the OT prophets are appealed to as evidence for Jesus as the fulfillment of their prophecies; any treatment of the topic must take these sources seriously.

Bernard Ramm: Protestant Christian Evidences

Bernard Ramm decisively moved the discussion of messianic prophecy in a scholarly direction. Ramm acknowledges the multifaceted role of the prophet in the Hebrew economy. Unlike some critical scholars, past and present, he does not relegate the teaching and proclamations of the OT prophet to that of an ethical and spiritual symbol. A prophecy, for Ramm, included genuinely predictive elements that neither violated the human personality nor constituted an "amoral thrust of knowledge upon the

---

historical sources to support his conclusions, but includes little critical interaction with these sources. See Hengstenberg, *Christology of the Old Testament*.

16. Hindson, "Messianic Prophecy," 217.

17. Such treatment is forthcoming in the proposed *Moody Dictionary of Messianic Prophecy*, edited by Michael Rydelnik, in which Hindson contributes numerous detailed chapters.

prophet."[18] The foretelling was intended to influence the present conduct of the people; in that regard, it constituted a behaviorally focused insight coming from an omniscient God.[19]

Ramm also notes the importance of prophecy as an apologetic device for the Christian religion. The idea that prophecy functions as an apologetic device, he contends, is based on two primary OT passages: Deuteronomy 18 and Isaiah 41. Deuteronomy 18:15–22 specifically promises that *Yahweh* will raise up a prophet like Moses. The key to distinguishing true prophets and prophecy from false prophets and prophecy, according to this passage, is whether the prophecies are actualized in human experience. If they are not, those prophecies are false. Similarly, Isaiah 41:22–23 appeals to predictive prophecy as a test for distinguishing between the work of false gods and the authentic work of *Yahweh*.

One of the strengths of Ramm's work is his interaction with the objections of critical scholars. Noting a few of the most virulent among them, he affirms their claim that issues such as the vague nature of some prophecies, the possibility of artificial or staged fulfillments, and interpretive disagreement make certainty about fulfillments difficult. He also addresses the need for "concrete data"[20] if fulfillments are to be verified. Ramm, however, does not go to the full measure that critical scholarship demands. That additional measure would require approaching the biblical material as one would any other set of historical documents. For Ramm, the inspired quality of the biblical texts and the existence of the supernatural are still presuppositions rather than conclusions based on his research.

Kenny Barfield: The Prophet Motive

Kenny Barfield represents another step toward a scholarly, critical, and objective approach to OT prophecy and its alleged fulfillments.[21] Barfield devotes a short chapter to predictive prophecy as a key element in prophetic literature. The character of the prophet also receives treatment. Barfield observes that some of the OT prophets become unintelligible if predictive elements as verification of their status are *a priori* dismissed as impossibilities. Examples include Jeremiah 28:9 and Ezekiel 33:33. The same idea is generally applicable to the NT documents and personalities as well. For example, in his first public address, Jesus specifically claims to be fulfilling

---

18. Ramm, *Protestant Christian Evidences*, 81–82.
19. Ramm, *Protestant Christian Evidences*, 81.
20 Ramm, *Protestant Christian Evidences*, 91–96.
21. Barfield, *Prophet Motive*.

the predictions of Isaiah 61:1–2 (Luke 4:21). If this statement is somehow not true or if the life of Jesus is not an actualization of the prophecy, Jesus himself becomes unintelligible.

Herein lies the difficulty with the study of OT prophecy as an apologetic for Christianity. Predictions and alleged fulfillments that are partial, generalized, or intangible are, in most cases, less than convincing and rarely possess the weight of evidence necessary to be affirmed as fact. Barfield attempts to address these issues by making space for a discussion of the apologetic value of prophecy and introducing his principles for verification. Barfield lists six standards he claims are "reasonable criteria for assessing the claims of predictive prophecy."[22] These criteria, quoted below, closely align with those employed for the current work—with the exception of a commitment to interact with critical scholars:

> 1. The prediction should occur well in advance of the fulfillment. There should be no valid reason to suspect that the event occurred after-the-fact.
>
> 2. The prediction should be accurate. It must conform to historical fact.
>
> 3. Fulfillment should occur in an impartial manner. There should be no evidence of collusion or manipulation of the events.
>
> 4. The fulfillment should be obvious to a reasonable person. Absent bias toward either position, an individual should be able to weigh evidence on both sides of the argument and conclude that the predictions was made prior to an event and was later confirmed to have occurred through valid testimony. This does not suggest that the prediction has to be totally free from ambiguity, but that the fulfillment should be obvious.
>
> 5. Predictive prophecy should be dynamic. It must be ongoing, repetitive, and consistent. Anyone can be lucky, so to eliminate the chance of an accidental fulfillment, the number of accurate predictions should be significant.
>
> 6. The prediction should suggest supernatural guidance. Prediction capable of being based on human reasoning or genius is not sufficient to establish one's claim as a prophet.[23]

In his chapter focusing on messianic prophecy, Barfield highlights several cultural-historical characteristics that affect the way prophecy and

---

22. Barfield, *Prophet Motive*, 31–32.
23. Barfield, *Prophet Motive*, 31–32.

the hope for a utopian golden age are envisioned. Barfield's analysis gives the reader reason to believe that messianism is a universal phenomenon. First, he notes, the modern tendency to place hope for a resolution to mankind's problems in the realms of education and science. Second, Barfield observes that, despite this tendency, the idyllic superhuman figure often remains as part of the vision. Mankind is constantly seeking a messiah in some form. Third, Barfield describes the general disposition of the Jewish people toward some form of messianic expectation. The factuality of this assertion can be traced in the earliest historical records of Israel. Fourth, he cites Roman historians Suetonius and Tacitus to verify that the same general type of expectation was present in cultures far removed from Judea. Suetonius verifies this assertion when he writes:

> A firm persuasion had long prevailed through all the East that it was fated for the empire of the world, at that time, to devolve on someone who should go forth from Judaea. This prediction referred to a Roman emperor, as the event shewed; but the Jews, applying it to themselves, broke out into rebellion, and having defeated and slain their governor, routed the lieutenant of Syria, a man of consular rank, who was advancing to his assistance, and took an eagle, the standard of one of his legions. As the suppression of this revolt appeared to require a stronger force and an active general, who might be safely trusted in an affair of so much importance, Vespasian was chosen in preference to all others.[24]

Another well-developed aspect of Barfield's book is the section dealing with Genesis 49:10, addressing whether adequate evidence exists to support a messianic interpretation of the text. Barfield marshals substantial evidence to support his position; the present work will draw upon this text in an attempt to establish what, if any, *minimal facts* exist.

Barfield, however, is not immune to some of the same weaknesses as those who use the traditional argument in its less critical form. He attempts, unsuccessfully, to establish the time of the Messiah's coming by appealing to Daniel 2 and 9. The reason for skepticism about proofs from Daniel 9 have been documented above,[25] and the same type problem exists with his appeal to Daniel 2. First, the date of the composition of the book of Daniel is disputed. Most critical scholars reject Daniel's purported authorship with its

24. Tranquillus, *Suetonius*. Barfield also cites the well-known passage from Tacitus, *Historiae*, in which general messianic prophecy and expectation is attributed by the general Jewish population to mean rulers from Judea. However, Tacitus believes it referred to Vespasian. Cornelius Tacitus, *Historiae (Latin)*, 5.13.

25. See section above, "Elements and Rationale for Section 1."

concomitant 5th-6th century BC date. Second, in the context of Nebuchadnezzar's dream and the empires represented by the statue, not only is the exact correspondence of the strata of the statue with world empires disputed but also the apocalyptic nature of the image and the interpretation of dreams as a legitimate way to establish historical facts is tenuous. Third, the meaning of a "kingdom that shall never be destroyed . . . [and] shall stand forever" (Dan 2:44) is ambiguous. These statements are problematic since they appear to be foretelling of a kingdom that, as of this writing, has no current physical manifestation and is therefore completely speculative.

In the final analysis, both Ramm and Barfield represent significant steps in the right direction. Neither, however, incorporates all of the necessary elements for a full-length critical treatment of OT prophecy and NT fulfillment.

Robert C. Newman: Jesus: The Testimony of Prophecy and History

Robert Newman has published three important works bearing on the issue at hand. The first is *Jesus: The Testimony of Prophecy and History*.[26] The focus of this short book is exclusively on messianic prophecy and the historical evidence for Jesus as the fulfillment of certain OT messianic texts. The book treats the OT texts pertaining to "Messiah as a light to the Gentiles" (Isa 42:6–7; 49:5–6) together with several other significant OT prophetic texts. These texts include those listed in the table below:[27]

Biblical Text	Heading
Micah 5:2	Born yet Pre-existent
Daniel 7:13–14 and Zechariah 9:9	Humble yet Exalted
Psalm 22, Zechariah 12:10, and Isaiah 52:13–53:12	Suffering yet Reigning
Psalm 110 and Genesis 14:18–20	King yet Priest
Genesis 49:10	The Messiah was to come while Judah had its own rulers
Haggai 2:3–9	The Messiah was to come while the second Temple stood

26. Newman, *Jesus*, 39.
27. Newman, *Jesus*, 10.

Biblical Text	Heading
Daniel 9:24–27	The Messiah was to come after the sixty-ninth sabbath cycle

A primary strength of this book is its focused treatment of messianic prophecy. Newman does not digress into areas unrelated to messianic prophecy while marshaling a handful of historical evidences for his conclusions. The individual treatments of various passages include some exegetical and lexical work, but an extended treatment of these issues is needed if the conclusions are to be accepted by critical scholars.

Another strength of Newman's work is his implicit recognition that mere assertion will not persuade the unconvinced; documentation bearing upon the issue must be readily available and cited. Despite its brevity, Newman's book contains an abundance of citations from several Jewish and other historical sources.

The primary weakness of Newman's approach is its failure to provide adequate interaction with the assertions of critical scholarship on the various issues of both a textual and contextual nature. Ambiguities in the Hebrew text must be addressed in greater detail and the rationale for conclusions supported by a more robust engagement. Scholarly interaction is lacking between (1) how each of the cited biblical texts would likely have been interpreted by the first audience and (2) how the Jewish interpretation of these texts may have developed through the intertestamental, NT, and Christian era. It does not appear plausible to argue that every text currently held to be fully messianic by Christians was understood as such by the original readers. If claims of fulfillment are to find widespread acceptance, the work of skeptical scholars must not be omitted. Solid argumentation, to whatever extent possible, is crucial to making Newman's case a plausible alternative to skepticism.

Robert C. Newman: "Fulfilled Prophecy as Miracle"

The second important contribution from Newman is a chapter in a larger edited volume. In "Fulfilled Prophecy as Miracle," Newman makes the case for predictive prophecy as a species of miracle.[28] The primary thrust of this chapter is the contention that if genuine predictive prophecy occurred in the form presented in the OT, it is miraculous in nature. As previously stated, many critical scholars reject this possibility *a priori*. The

---

28. Newman, "Fulfilled Prophecy as Miracle."

early part of Newman's work seeks to address this prejudicial rejection by critiquing various techniques skeptics employ to explain the phenomenon of predictive prophecy by naturalistic means. On some occasions, Newman notes, texts are simply subjected to reinterpretation or the literature is declared *ex eventu* by postdating. On other occasions, the application of a reductionist hermeneutical methodology disallows any long-term perspective by the prophet. In this latter case, the immediate horizon is the only allowable context. If there is no identifiable fulfillment, skeptical scholars argue, either the prophet was mistaken in his prediction or perhaps a later prophet invented a fulfillment.

In an attempt to address these difficulties, Newman sets down five criteria to evaluate if a miraculous prophecy is present in a biblical text.[29] These criteria are much like those other authors have suggested; they supply some of the needed foundation for the study of OT prophecy that moves from a naïve examination of the biblical text to informed interaction with critical scholarship.

This particular work by Newman addresses three types of OT prophecy: (1) those referring to Israel as a nation, (2) those addressing city-states such as Tyre and Sidon, and (3) those describing the coming Messiah. The portion of Newman's work dedicated to messianic prophecy is painfully brief. It treats nothing beyond the concept of the Servant from Isaiah 40–56 and the seventy weeks from Daniel 9:24–27.[30] First, Newman's evidence for Jesus being the fulfillment of the Servant texts of Isaiah is essentially a restatement of his previous work. He notes the fact that Jesus is the founder of a religion currently having 1.4 billion adherents and that no other messianic claimant has ever established a religion among Gentile nations. Second, Newman observes that the vast majority of the Jewish people historically and currently reject Jesus, whereas many Gentiles have embraced him as the Messiah. Of what other Jewish person could Isaiah have spoken? Newman's answer to this important question is that no other person could fit the criteria.

The single most important contribution Newman brings to the discussion is the mention of criteria or techniques that skeptics often employ to disallow the existence of genuine predictive prophecy. Newman desires to begin interacting with these skeptical ideas. The present study will include, and in some instances embrace, these criticisms to engage the issue of predictive prophecy from a fresh perspective.

29. Newman, "Fulfilled Prophecy as Miracle," 215.

30. To avoid redundancy, Daniel 9:24–27 will not be treated extensively, even though it remains one of the most popular (and frequently cited) texts. Some interpreters reference it as specifically identifying the time of Messiah's appearance.

Robert C. Newman: Prophecies About the Coming Messiah

Newman's third contribution is contained in *Prophecies About the Coming Messiah*. The focus in this short work is those OT prophecies he believes could not have been invented or staged by the NT church. These include the following: (1) the light-to-the-Gentiles prophecy of Isaiah 42 and 49, (2) the seventy-weeks prophecy of Daniel 9, (3) the suffering-servant prophecy of Isaiah 53, and (4) the pierced-one prophecy of Psalm 22.

The most important additon to the biblical texts mentioned in his other works is the short treatment of the pierced one as described in Psalm 22. A straightforward reading of this Psalm gives the impression that it is depicting a suffering person who has pierced hands and feet and is crying out in anguish as an expression of his feelings of abandonment by God. Newman points out that two of the NT writers appropriate this text in reference to utterances made by the suffering Jesus during his crucifixion (Matt 27:46; Mark 15:34). Besides this obvious connection, the following statements approximate Newman's reasons for viewing the Psalm as a depiction of the suffering of Jesus:

1. The sufferer depicted feels abandoned by God.
2. The sufferer trusts God completely.
3. The sufferer is despised and mocked by the people around him.
4. The hands and feet of the sufferer are pierced.
5. Lots are cast for the sufferer's clothing.
6. The sufferer is weak, thirsty, and his bones are out of joint.
7. Though the sufferer expects or is experiencing death, God somehow rescues him.
8. The effects of these events will be recognized in future generations and to the ends of the earth.
9. The families of the nations will turn to the Lord.[31]

The point of the enumerations above is to demonstrate the improbability of a single human death containing all of the elements described in the Psalm. Whether the Psalm in its original context is actually describing a crucifixion is another matter—one this dissertation will address. One thing is certain about Psalm 22, however: the NT writers apply the image to the death of Jesus.

---

31. Newman, *Prophecies about the Coming Messiah*, 234.

J. Barton Payne: Encyclopedia of Biblical Prophecy

The next important text for our consideration is *Encyclopedia of Biblical Prophecy* by J. Barton Payne. This book is possibly the most comprehensive work on biblical prophecy in existence. Like most works on biblical prophecy, it presupposes the biblical *autographa* as inspired by God and inerrant in content. Beyond these presuppositions, however, Payne takes a serious scholarly approach when addressing the topic of prophecy. Issues speaking directly to the possibility of predictive prophecy and the functions of the Hebrew prophet are detailed, along with hermeneutical guidelines that undergird his study methodologically. The value of prophecy for the Jewish people, according to Payne, was its verification that alleged prophets were indeed messengers of *Yahweh* or, alternatively, were inspired oracles of assurance. Most important was the prophet's role as a motivator calling Israel to holiness.[32] While noting that the value of prophecy for the first audiences was important, Payne believes the significance of prophecy actually grows over time because the overall body of fulfillment grows. This growth is the means whereby the apologetic value of prophecy becomes a noticeable, viable tool for defense of the Christian faith in the modern and postmodern intellectual climate.

At this important juncture in his work, Payne introduces the opinions of critical scholars who dismiss the possibility of genuine predictive prophecy.[33] The modern reader must function as an interpreter of the texts; he or she cannot witness historic fulfillments first-hand. As such, a naturalistic or anti-supernaturalistic view of the Hebrew prophets has become fashionable. These views demand either *ex eventu* prophets or over-spiritualized interpretations. When describing the current state of the prophetic/apologetic question, Payne intimates that higher critics have reduced the apologetic value of prophecy as "proof" for unbelievers to embarrassingly low level. He proposes to alleviate this embarrassment with his work.

To establish a framework for his approach to prophecy and to restore its apologetic value, Payne introduces several criteria for determining legitimate predictive elements and their corresponding fulfillment. These limiting criteria (and those similar criteria developed by other writers) constitute a corrective to the traditional approach often taken in works dealing with prophecy. However, the nature of the criteria offered by Payne differ from those used in the present study. He is treating prophecy in multiple forms—rather than only the messianic—and his approach does not require direct

---

32. Payne, *Encyclopedia of Biblical Prophecy*, 14.
33. Payne, *Encyclopedia of Biblical Prophecy*, 15.

fulfillment. More importantly, acceptance of Payne's method and conclusions by critical scholars is not required. Nevertheless, Payne's criteria are worth considering for their applicability to the study of biblical prophecy and their interaction with the criteria used in the present study.

Payne's first criterion is the proper limitation placed on various oracles contained within the biblical corpus. He applies limitations to predictive figures, symbols, and types by closely analyzing the texts to ensure that they are predictive rather than textual misrepresentations, incorrect translations, or simply not intended to be predictive in the first place. Extending this criterion, Payne argues that if the predictive element is identified from inference rather than by explicit statements, the analogy of faith principle is applied. When the analogy of faith principle applies, in a given passage, support for the presence of a predictive element must be confirmed from biblical cross references.

Similar criteria are applied to biblical figures. Both predictive and non-predictive figures confront the exegete in the study of prophecy. Eliminating the non-predictive figures from consideration is crucial to working accurately with the material. Much the same is true of the symbols and symbolic behavior portrayed in many biblical texts. Those with an actual bearing on the future must be distinguished from those that do not.

Perhaps the most difficult aspect of predictive prophecy, requiring detailed explanation, is that of typology.[34] Payne's treatment of this controversial topic is thoughtful and worth referencing when the need arises. For example, certain persons who were part of the Davidic dynasty (such as Zerubbabel) are sometimes understood in a typological relationship to the Messiah.

No consensus exists on the issues pertaining to Payne's treatment of typology and limitations on what should be considered as typological. Even so, his work is an excellent primer on prophecy. The two-step approach adopted by Payne first makes the most drastic reduction in what is an allowable type; he then describes the expansions that will be considered. This initial drastic reduction is achieved by limiting types to those elements that have both direct divine origin and redemptive character, with the additional

---

34. G. K. Beale provides a good primer on the subject, describing typological interpretation as "one of the thorniest issues to face in OT-in-the-NT studies in the twentieth and early twenty-first centuries" (Beale, *Handbook on the New Testament*, 13). The descriptions of typological prophecies usually have similar elements, although there are differences among dispensationalist, non-dispensationalist, and progressive dispensationalist thinkers. See also Blaising and Bock, *Progressive Dispensationalism*, 102–4; Corley et al., *Biblical Hermeneutics*, 84–87; and Bateman, *Three Central Issues*.

requirement that these elements be demonstrated as such by the declarations of Christ or the apostles.[35]

Payne's subsequent expansion of what constitutes a type then proceeds by noting the objection of Patrick Fairbairn that interpreters do not demand that each prophecy contained in the biblical corpus be demonstrated or explicitly stated in order to be considered inspired. Such a requirement on types is too restrictive, therefore, Fairbairn (and Payne) also allow types that present themselves as matters of deduction in addition to those explicitly stated.[36] Further expansion is provided by understanding certain symbols that were conceptually redemptive to those first exposed to them, but also possess a prophetic, futuristic element or antitype. Without belaboring the point, the criteria for identifying prophecy in its various forms moves significantly forward with Payne's work. As will be seen below, so does the list of criteria for determining fulfillment.

Determining fulfillment of particular prophecies is often difficult, especially when little or no evidence is available. Under such circumstances, the interpretive process may become a matter of presupposition rather than a consistently applied hermeneutical or historical method. Many of these difficulties are resolved by Payne in his rigorous approach to both the texts and their contexts and by advocating a thorough knowledge of history. Payne argues that recognizing the appropriate limitation on texts, symbols, and types does not reduce prophetic fulfillment to mere history. Some degree of literal fulfillment is usually intended, whether through the use of analogous symbols and types or by a straightforward, point-by-point correspondence. Concisely stated, it appears that a given OT prediction is best understood as fulfilled (1) when other OT texts confirm the predictive element; (2) when fulfillment is confirmed canonically, whether literally or by analogy; and (3) if possible, by secular history.

The great strength of Payne's work is his detailed and consistently applied methodology. He adequately treats the textual difficulties, his conclusions are well supported, and the criteria (22 of them) tightly control the process of exegesis. The primary weakness lies in his sparse interaction with critical scholarship.

---

35. Payne, *Encyclopedia of Biblical Prophecy*, 51.
36. Fairbairn, *Typology of Scripture*, 377.

Herbert W. Bateman, Darrell L. Bock and Gordon H. Johnston: Jesus the Messiah: Tracing the Promises, Expectations, and Coming of Israel's King

The last text this section discusses is *Jesus the Messiah: Tracing the Promises, Expectations, and Coming of Israel's King*.[37] Bateman, Bock, and Johnston examine messianic prophecy from both a historical and canonical point of view. The term *canon*, however, is used in the limited sense of the OT canon and how the prophecies it contained would have been understood in light of the whole (OT). The authors also take pains to note the progressive nature of messianic prophecy within the OT. Their approach allows for meaning in the original context and also for a development as understood by later, second-temple Judaism. Last, as is appropriate, they consider the prophecy from the NT christological perspective.

By admitting the possibility of a canonical reading of the OT, the authors presuppose some form of inspiration in which the messianic ideas contained in the prophecies become more visible and understandable. This emergent process is similar to the various pieces of a puzzle (their analogy) gradually revealing the whole picture.[38]

According to Bateman, Bock, and Johnston, the problem with many treatments of OT prophecy is that individual prophecies (especially the earlier ones) are interpreted as explicit and direct prophecies concerning the Messiah. They argue that OT texts are capable of containing implicit, ambiguous messianic concepts that are not necessarily exclusively attributable to the ultimate Messiah. In other words, when the dynamic nature of "*pattern* and *prophecy*"[39] is properly valued, OT prophecies may indirectly refer to Messiah or prefigure Messiah or point directly to other persons. Concisely stated, the strategy employed by Bateman, Bock, and Johnston requires the use of a three-fold hermeneutic: first, contextual-canonical; second, messianic; and third, christological.

The strengths of this approach are manifold. The reader gains much insight into the wording and original historical context, including its attending ambiguities. The additional information supplied by later literature often illuminates those ambiguities, uncovering the latent eschatological potential of the prophecy. The historical research and attendant sources are well-cited by Bateman, Bock, and Johnston. Further, the insights of critical

---

37. Bateman et al., *Jesus the Messiah*.
38. Bateman et al., *Jesus the Messiah*, 22.
39. Bateman et al., *Jesus the Messiah*, 26.

scholarship are, at least, partially taken into account by the explication of a method that begins with the original historical context.

Only two weaknesses limit the value of this important work. First, the sparse interaction with specific arguments of critical scholars on particular texts limits the value of the book for apologetic purposes. Ignoring skeptical opinions reduces the credibility and, consequently, the viability of OT prophecy as a legitimate tool for the twenty-first century Christian. The second weakness is the presupposition of an inspired text and canonical readings. This weakness is far more difficult to remedy because empirical proofs of divine inspiration are as impossible to establish with certainty as the existence of God. The best that can be obtained is the logical necessity of a divine being[40] and the probability that miracles (prophecy included) attest divine participation in the events described by the documents.[41]

Section 2. Key Authors and Arguments that Alter or Eliminate the Traditional Approach to Predictive Prophecy

Elements in and Rationale for Section 2 of the Literature Review

The second section of this literature review features some key authors and arguments that in one way or another discount the significance of, or legitimacy of, predictive prophecy. This discounting is often the result of conclusions reached by applying criteria associated with the historical-critical method to the biblical texts. The presuppositions of authors who wholly embrace the historical-critical methodology, as will be demonstrated below, differ significantly from those who take an uncritical or even moderately critical approach to the topic. Consequently, their conclusions also differ significantly.

John J. Collins: The Bible after Babel: Historical Criticism in a Postmodern Age

John Collins has commented that the last quarter of the twentieth century witnessed a crisis in the historiographical study of ancient Israel. Specifically,

---

40. Moreland and Craig, *Philosophical Foundations*, 502–4.

41. Cf. Kligerman, *Messianic Prophecy*; Hays, *Message of the Prophets*; and Smith, *Prophets as Preachers*. In addition, dozens of works specifically dealing with OT messianic texts will also be consulted.

a progressive loss in confidence of the accuracy of the biblical narratives has occurred. This loss has taken concrete form in the writings of some scholars who deny the historicity of certain persons and events. In some extreme cases, biblical chronologies and large portions of the patriarchal period (the stories of Abraham, Isaac, and Jacob in the book of Genesis) have been deemed unhistorical.[42] Collins notes that virtually all "mainline" scholars date the finalization of the Torah, prophets, and historical books no earlier than the Persian period.[43]

According to Collins, the crisis in ancient Israelite historiography is not based on philosophical predispositions; rather, it arises from the limitations of the available evidence.[44] This assertion becomes self-evident when one scrutinizes the general methodology developed for historical-critical investigations. Although the wording and explanations are not identical in every case, the three generally accepted criteria are: (1) the principle of autonomy of the historian, (2) the principle of analogy, and (3) the principle of criticism.[45] With employment of these strict criteria, the problematic aspects of ancient historiography in general and how prophetic oracles were historically understood—and should presently be understood—becomes apparent.

From within the framework of the historical-critical method, other criteria are applied specifically to prophetic texts; this process further diminishes the likelihood of evidential verification. This attenuating effect is achieved by utilizing any of the following devices: (1) reducing the prophecy to an ideal rather than concrete historical prediction, (2) asserting later redaction or interpolation, (3) claiming *vaticinium ex eventu* prophecy (late dating), (4) reducing the scope to a strictly localized context, and (5) outright denying the possibility of historical fulfillment. Collins's book establishes parameters such as those listed above and prepares the reader to follow the rationale reflected in the books examined in this section of the work.[46]

---

42. See, for example, Thomson, *Historicity of the Patriarchal Narratives*, 315.
43. Collins, *Bible after Babel*, 33.
44. Collins, *Bible after Babel*, 34.
45. Collins, *Bible after Babel*, 5–6. Cf. Krentz, *Historical-Critical Method*, 55–72.
46. Other works by John J. Collins and Adela Yarbro Collins consulted during this study include Collins and Collins, *King and Messiah* and Collins, *Scepter and the Star*.

Ernest A. Edghill and Herbert E. Ryle: An Inquiry into the Evidential Value of Prophecy

Ernest A. Edghill and Herbert E. Ryle authored a book with a very provocative title, *An Inquiry into the Evidential Value of Prophecy*. At first glance, the title suggests an approach to prophecy similar to that employed in the current study. This first suggestion is not supported by the content of their work, however. Edghill and Ryle approached the subject of the evidence of prophecy from an idealistic perspective, seeing the "fundamental conceptions of prophecy . . . in 'preparing the way of the Lord.'"[47] This preparation is treated under three thoughts central to the OT: "The Kingdom, the Covenant, and the Church and Priest."[48] The authors follow each of these dominant themes as they relate to the growth of the fundamental concept.

Edghill and Ryle are very specific in that they intend to treat prophecy as a whole—as a religious and historical phenomenon—and not as a collection of individual passages or even individual prophets. They avoid discussing key issues such as the geniuses of the oracle, authorship, dating, or the possibility of redaction. Their contention is that the prophetic phenomenon prepares the way of the Lord and thereby constitutes evidence of the truth of the Christian religion.

The evidence, Edghill and Ryle believe, surfaces through four streams of biblical thought. First, prophecy progressively prepared the world for the "*teaching* of Christ,"[49] who brought perfected standards of ethics, morality, and knowledge about the metaphysical attributes of God. Second, prophecy prepared the way for the "*office* of Christ and his Church."[50] Prophecy depicts Christ as prophet, priest, and king: as king from David's line, with David's character, and endued with the Spirit to fulfill the ideal image; as prophet from the ideal image of the prophet as a teacher knowing God, revealing God to all of mankind; and as priest as mediator, offering sacrifice and minister of grace.

The third stream of biblical thought, according to Edghill and Ryle, emphasize that prophecy prepared the way for the "*the true apprehension of his person.*"[51] The Christ as conceived by the OT prophets progressively became more than merely human; he was described as having abundant gifts of grace, functioning as the perfect mediator, and even becoming the

---

47. Edghill and Ryle, *Inquiry into the Evidential Value of Prophecy*, 43.
48. Edghill and Ryle, *Inquiry into the Evidential Value of Prophecy*, 43.
49. Edghill and Ryle, *Inquiry into the Evidential Value of Prophecy*, 35.
50. Edghill and Ryle, *Inquiry into the Evidential Value of Prophecy*, 36.
51. Edghill and Ryle, *Inquiry into the Evidential Value of Prophecy*, 39.

son of God and Mighty God. All of these prophetic images coalesce leading to the incarnation.

Finally, prophecy prepared the way for the "historical life of Christ."[52] This element is the most interesting aspect of the book. Edghill and Ryle discuss the life of Christ from the perspective of his titles: *Son of man*, *Son of God*, and *Son of David*. The title *Son of man*, they assert, has very early origins and is centered in the frailty of man as demonstrated in the Fall. This frailty later finds hopeful expression in Psalm 8. The designation of Ezekiel as *son of man* seems to indicate his dependence on God in light of his mortality and human weakness. Yet in Daniel, the phrase *son of man* and its meaning take a dramatic shift by becoming a messianic designation in the mind of the author and his subsequent readers. Edghill and Ryle imply that in Daniel, the dominion over creation lost in the Fall is regained by man—by a man who encapsulates all the ideals of Israel, even superseding the ideal, and becoming truly messianic. The authors of the Synoptic Gospels clearly believed that Jesus applied the phrase to himself both as an identification with the frailty associated with the early use of the phrase and as a clear self-identification with the cosmic figure portrayed in the book of Daniel.

Edghill and Ryle discuss the title *son of God* as used in Israelite settings, differentiating it from how the phrase was employed by other nations. They contend that the phrase was used as a moral designation based on protective love and election. This designation involved the duties of filial love, but did not imply physical decent in any sense. It was a title of official sonship. Such is the case in Psalm 82:6–7, where no hint of essential deity is indicated; rather, a place of privilege is described. Contrasting with this clearly human designation for the phrase is the description of what may be angelic beings as *sons of God* in Genesis 6:2 (cf. Job 1:6). The use of this phrase, according to Edghill and Ryle, designates beings of a higher metaphysical order, as it most clearly does in Daniel 3:25. Combining all of these ideas, one may argue that Judaism was never understood as a limited monotheism; it was, rather, a system that looked for the real union between God and man. This leads to the conclusion that the phrase *son of God* is, from the beginning, a preparation for a Son of God who encapsulates the theocratic, theanthropic, and metaphysical ideal of the phrase: one who is both God and man.

In their discussion about the title *Son of David* in relation to how OT prophecy prepared the way for Christ, Edghill and Ryle begin to distance themselves from what traditionally would be described as verifiable evidence. In their minds, historical events and details are not excluded in

---

52. Edghill and Ryle, *Inquiry into the Evidential Value of Prophecy*, 41.

fulfillment criteria. The evidential significance of the historical life of Christ lies in his fulfillment of the messianic ideal, the spiritual ideal. They argue that the ideal supersedes the historical as evidence. A key example of what the authors mean is found in their discussion of the Davidic Covenant. The promise of a seed of David as the Messiah is affirmed; even the eternal significance of the promise is acknowledged. In a dubious exegetical move, however, Edghill and Ryle abandon literal Davidic descent in light of Jeremiah 22:30 and Isaiah 11:1. They ask if it is not possible to assert a religious conception? The authors offer several rationales for this move, including the denial that Isaiah 7:14, regarding a future birth in that clan, is directed to the house of David. They also assert that the prophecy of Micah regarding the birthplace of the Messiah may indicate a reincarnation of David himself. Edghill and Ryle suggest that if the prophecy concerned the birth of a king, Jerusalem would be the setting.

The primary argument against a literal descendant of David is the correspondence between גדועים (hewn down) in relation to the Assyrians in Isaiah 10:33 and גדועים (stump) in Isaiah 11:1. Edghill and Ryle contend that the connotation of being hewn down is present in both verses. The hewn down tree, in combination with the mention of Jesse instead of David, indicates that Isaiah expected neither a literal descendant of David nor a revival of the monarchy. Isaiah, they argue, only expected a second David from some undesignated place; a second David with the character of the first. The name *David*, they contend, connotes certain ideas and theocratic reflections but cannot be pressed to demand literal physical decent. The Messiah will have the character of David, perhaps even being a second David. However, the Messiah's relationship to David must not be taken in a strict literal sense. The emphasis of the prophets, Edghill and Ryle contend, is on the Davidic character of the Messiah, not lineal decent.

Taking these messianic ideals and transferring them to the NT context, Edghill and Ryle proceed to strip virtually all hope from the historian in search of verifiable evidence regarding the evangelists' claim that Jesus was a descendant of David. Their examination of the question Jesus posed to the Pharisees in Mark 12:35 is interpreted as a denial that Jesus could be both the son of David and David's Lord. These authors claim that Jesus simply wanted to convey the idea that he was the spiritual son of David: "He is son of David only insofar as he is son in the Spirit."[53] If he was the

---

53. Edghill and Ryle, *Inquiry into the Evidential Value of Prophecy*, 423. Later in their book, the authors admit that the early Christians believed in the physical decent of Jesus from the stock of David (Edghill and Ryle, *Inquiry into the Evidential Value of Prophecy*, 579).

son of David genetically, Jesus valued it only as an outward pledge of his spiritual kingship.

In the final analysis, Edghill and Ryle believe that the true evidence of prophecy is not found in literal fulfillment of predictions; rather, it lies in the "spiritual correspondence of the fact with the essential ideas of the prophecy which it fulfills."[54] Thus, what began as an evidential inquiry by Edghill and Ryle ends as little more than an allegorized philosophizing of the biblical data on the *son of David* concept. Their book includes lucid evaluation of phrases like *son of man* and *son of God*—and how those concepts progressed into an understanding of the person of Jesus—and yet, with something actually containing the potential to place real evidence in front of the skeptic, Edghill and Ryle offer nothing. Their retreat to an ideal *son of David* cannot be classified as evidence; it can in no way withstand the scrutiny of a verification principle. It is even possible that such a notion is exegetically falsifiable.

Gurdon C. Oxtoby: Prediction and Fulfillment in the Bible

Another work that takes a mildly critical view of predictive prophecy is entitled *Prediction and Fulfillment in the Bible*.[55] Oxtoby's primary goal appears to be the explanation of the concept of fulfillment in ways that clarify how the NT writers appropriated OT texts. He does not completely idealize the concept of fulfillment, but he diminishes the expectation that specific OT prophets could foresee NT historical realizations of their oracles. His argument proceeds by treating the semantic range of the expression *fulfillment*. The resulting terms are familiar: complete, consummate, finish, realization, and actuality. His purpose, however, is to move the reader to

---

54. Edghill and Ryle, *Inquiry into the Evidential Value of Prophecy*, 581. The authors also assert that if Jesus' Davidic linage was only through Joseph, then he could not actually be a son of David. This observation seems plausible.

Another author who reduces the historical significance of the NT fulfillments to merely spiritual status is Abraham Kuenen. He grounds the OT predictive elements of prophecy solidly in their original contexts and then completely dismisses any thought of the NT interpretation as exegetical ground. He describes the method of the NT writers when utilizing the OT in prediction and fulfillment claims as sometimes contradictory and in opposition. Kuenen contends that one must abandon scientific exegesis or cease to acknowledge the authority of the NT in exegesis. His reason is clearly stated: the NT writers often read into the prophecies things they did not contain. See Kuenen, *Prophets and Prophecy in Israel*.

55. Oxtoby, *Prediction and Fulfillment*.

think of fulfillment as "correspondence."[56] This correspondence may be as slight as phraseology and illustrative correspondence or as prominent as that of a genuine anticipation of what the NT writer is presenting. Jesus as a historical person corresponds to the ideal of the *Son of Man*, *Son of God*, and *Messiah*. These assertions are valid, as far as they go.

Conversely, Oxtoby appears to be ambivalent about the assertions of biblical prophecy when specifics are investigated. He asserts that, on several occasions, the OT prophets predicted events that did not and, "in the very nature of the case, never can come to pass."[57] Throughout the book, however, Oxtoby affirms fulfillment of other oracles; particularly those historically proximate to the prophet. These distinctions uncover the first methodological difficulty in Oxtoby's work. How can someone trust a prophet whose predictions fail?[58] Oxtoby rightly corrects those who believe that the magical or superstitious forms of divination often associated with pagan prophets are somehow appropriate to Christian understanding. In so doing, however, he blunts any thought of supernatural aid at work in the mind of the prophet. This is why he is able to reject the entire concept of specific, long-range predictions by the biblical prophets. In fact, long-range prediction is the target of Oxtoby's most disparaging comments; he describes the concept of long-range predictions as historically presupposing, predestining, and fatalistic.[59]

Ironically, Oxtoby affirms the methods of historical critical studies and then, in his summary, appropriates the story of the transfiguration of Jesus without any demonstration of its historicity. To his credit, Oxtoby notes the conditional nature of some predictions and accepts some short-range predictive prophecies. He then turns and rejects most, if not all, long-range predictions. He speaks of the fulfillment of prophecy in terms of conceptual cooperation and verification, yet rejects the idea that the biblical prophets possessed "extraordinary powers of second sight."[60] He accepts the resurrection of Jesus, yet rejects the notion that the career of Jesus was predicted.

---

56. Oxtoby, *Prediction and Fulfillment*, 67.

57. Oxtoby, *Prediction and Fulfillment*, 79.

58. The best responses to date on the issue of what are perceived to be failed prophecies are: Chisholm Jr., "When Prophecy Appears to Fail," 561–77 and Chisholm Jr., "Does God 'Change His Mind'?," 387–99. If prophecy (as biblically construed) actually fails, with no mitigating conditionality, all but the most learned historians struggle to separate what is true from what is false. This introduces a plethora of problematic elements into the historic understanding of the biblical text in relation to the intended and extended audience and the perspicuity of the documents.

59. Oxtoby, *Prediction and Fulfillment*, 77.

60. Oxtoby, *Prediction and Fulfillment*, 77.

When considered in light of the whole biblical corpus, the problem lurking beneath Oxtoby's method is inconsistency. The Bible's prophetic corpus does not betray any notion that it is limited to oracles directed to past events. If current scholarship is at all correct, future events have also been predicted. At least part of the reason for anticipating their fulfillment is the concrete actuality of past predictions, not vagaries about conceptual realization. How are inquirers to react if some prophecies fail and others are realized? What is to be believed and what is to be rejected? Adequate, non-speculative answers to these questions require a historical-evidential approach rather than the inconsistent method of Oxtoby.

Dewey Beegle: Prophecy and Prediction

Prophecy and Prediction by Dewey Beegle marks an approximate half-way point between the classical view of predictive OT prophecy and the outright rejection of its actuality. Beegle affirms the existence of predictive prophecy and even certain fulfillments. One of the problems with OT prophecies, according to Beegle, is the tendency to accept the hermeneutical methods of the NT apostles when they appropriate OT texts and apply them. Beegle does not accept this as a valid method for interpretation of the texts today; each generation encapsulated in the biblical documents must be allowed to speak for itself.

The problem identified by Beegle stems from a continuing desire to extend a legitimate short-term promise made in the OT context into a long-term messianic prediction. His solution is to let the prophet speak to his immediate context. Any subsequent appropriation must fit that context without forcing crossovers that are not explicit. Beegle's primary example of this principle is the text of Isaiah 7:14. The single element expressed in both Matthew 1:21–23 and Isaiah is the term *Immanuel*. The use of the term in Isaiah, according to Beegle, means something like this: Ahaz's son, who is among them, is a sign that God is with Judah. In contrast, Matthew's use of the term *Immanuel* means God is actually present in body with us. Other aspects of Matthew's appropriation of the prophecy—such as the term *virgin* and the naming of the baby (in the former case by his mother and in the latter by Joseph)—are, according to Beegle, forced on the Isaiah text. Beegle's point is not that Matthew or Isaiah are mistaken; rather, each writer, he argues, is addressing completely different contexts. Efforts to harmonize the two accounts are not beneficial to honest inquiry.[61]

---

61. Beegle, *Prophecy and Prediction*, 42–46.

In another set of examples, Beegle takes issue with the evangelical stance on biblical inerrancy by describing what he believes are historical predictions that never occurred (e.g., Ezek 26:7–13; Zech 6:12–13; Mic 3:12). When he describes specifically why he thinks these prophecies failed, his arguments are not wholly convincing.[62] Even so, his major point is to allege that the rigid commitment of conservative biblical scholars to a brand of "supernaturalism" does not make room for human culture and errors. Beegle denounces this type of conservatism for treating prophecy as another piece in a jigsaw puzzle that must by some means be fitted together.

Using the prophecies concerning Zerubbabel as exemplars, Beegle demonstrates his version of the evangelical "prophetic criticism" method. He argues that only a scattered few pieces of the Zerubbabel puzzle fit into the Persian period; others are deferred to the time of Jesus, the millennial kingdom, or even the final judgment. This method of interpretation, as critiqued by Beegle, illustrates a supernaturalism bordering on the magical. It represents a system presupposed to be perfect.[63] The irony in Beegle's argument is that he approves of the same type of dissecting procedure when applied as literary-source criticism. These methods often draw the ire of evangelicals and the accolades of anti-supernaturalists. Beegle does not conclude that all liberal or historical-critical conclusions are correct; rather, he chastises evangelical Christians for rejecting the work of thousands of scholars working over a 150-year period. He believes the conclusions of these scholars should be given due consideration. Beegle is correct on this point. As demonstrated below, the engagement of the evangelical and scholarly worlds with various critical methodologies has increased significantly.

Joseph Fitzmyer: The One Who Is to Come

Joseph Fitzmyer's insightful work, *The One Who Is to Come*, is an excellent treatment of the messianic concept. It contains key thoughts and components for those handling messianic prophecy. Its methodological proximity to the present study, in cooperation with a balanced critical procedure, marks a major step forward in messianic studies. Fitzmyer examines OT texts that Christians have traditionally believed to express messianic content. His approach to these texts is to ground them in both their literary and

---

62. Beegle does not give any attention to the interpretive principle set out in Jeremiah 18:7–10. This text contains a promise that *Yahweh* will relent of the either prophesied disaster or prosperity if the nation fails to listen and act. This principle must be considered before declaring a specific prophecy as failed.

63. Beegle, *Prophecy and Prediction*, 61–62.

historical contexts in order to understand the meaning in the same way as the first recipients of those texts.

The problem with Christian messianic titles such as *Son of Man*, *Son of God*, and *Servant of the Lord*,[64] according to Fitzmyer, is not that Christians use them, since NT writers have predicated these titles of Jesus. Rather, the problem is "whether these titles were used in a messianic sense in pre-Christian Judaism in the Old Testament or other pre-Christian Jewish writings."[65] Employing this methodology requires that the texts themselves be examined in canonical order. The result is that some display messianic overtones from the period of their original composition, while others gradually acquire messianic implications through a process of supplementary oracles added to the Hebrew prophetic writings. Still other texts acquire messianic import through the interpretation afforded them by Jewish commentators over long periods of history.

The progressive development of messianic prophecy works in genetic and teleological connection with the course of the history of the OT kingdom of God. The genetic connection is due to the influence of the historical relations just mentioned. The teleological connection surfaces because history, as much as prophecy, was interpreted as preparing and educating Israel for its destiny and for the reception of the messianic blessing.[66]

The rare feature of a chapter devoted to the analysis of the allegedly messianic OT texts as they are presented in the Septuagint also distinguishes Fitzmyer's work. This important and early translation of the Hebrew *Tanakh* into Greek is not a monolithic work composed during one brief period sometime during the third century BC; rather, it is a composite work, reflecting, in part, the thoughts and influences of early Christian scribes. As a result, it may reflect some Christian interpretations of OT texts. In short, the Septuagint is—to some degree—a commentary on the *Tanakh*, and, as such, provides valuable insight into the interpretation of OT prophecy.

The importance of Fitzmyer's work for the present study cannot be overemphasized. Methodologically, he has approached the OT messianic texts with the same initial goal as that informing the current study. He seeks to understand how the texts were originally understood. A second element, in congruence with the current study, is seen in his attempt to follow how the meaning of texts evolved. Fitzmyer is by far the most critically accepted source in this Literature Review. He interacts with other critical

---

64. Fitzmyer, *One Who Is to Come*, viii.

65. Fitzmyer, *One Who Is to Come*, viii.

66. Several of the biblical texts addressed by Fitzmyer are included in the current study, as are many of the extra-canonical writings from the second temple period and later rabbinic writings.

works effectively and often comes to conclusions that are at variance with traditional Christian interpretation.[67]

The weakness of Fitzmyer's approach, which the present study hopes to buttress, is that he fails to sufficiently bring the various lines of argumentation together, assimilate the evidence, and reduce the evidence to factual statements. When completed effectively, these additional steps should find acceptance with a broad spectrum of scholars with relevant expertise. Stated differently, if the conclusions offered by Fitzmyer were melded with the more traditional conclusions, the contradictions discarded, what facts would remain?[68]

Section 3. The Possibility of Miracles

Elements in and Rationale for Section 3 of the Literature Review

Until this point in the current work, no attempt has been made to demonstrate the possibility of miracles. Further, no attempt has been made to differentiate between spectacular acts of healing or the less spectacular—but just as miraculous—act of predictive prophecy. Both expressions of the miraculous, if they are critically evidenced, are undeniably beyond the capabilities of unaided human agents. The position taken thus far in the work is that the *a priori* rejection of miracles is unwarranted. To reject the possibility of miracles without investigating the relevant data requires omniscience. Omniscience itself is supernatural and thus a miracle if attained by a human being. That fact alone renders the entire concept of *a priori* rejection incoherent. However, this logical conclusion may not satisfy the skeptic. Therefore, this section of the current work seeks to disclose additional rationale for not rejecting miracles *a priori*.

---

67. For example, Fitzmyer's treatment of Psalm 2 does not give adequate treatment or place to the term begotten (ילד) and appears to rely on an undemonstrated adoption motif that has questionable application in Jewish history and little—if any—verbal correspondence to the psalm itself. In addition, despite the intertestamental evidence, he gives no place for a messianic interpretation of the psalm, stating his agreement with other scholars who hold "that Psalm 2 is not 'messianic' in any sense" (Fitzmyer, *One Who Is to Come*, 20).

68. Cf. Mowinckel, *He that Cometh*; Satterthwaite et al., *Lord's Anointed Interpretation*; Charlesworth, *Messiah*; and Day, *King and Messiah*.

Hume's Arguments against Miracles

David Hume's *An Enquiry Concerning Human Understanding* is the *locus classsicus* for the conviction that miracles do not occur and cannot be historically verified. This conviction emerged during the Enlightenment and is still embraced by many among skeptical and critical historians. In order to address this Hume-based conviction as relevant to the current work, several quotations from Hume are required. In doing so, it is important to note that much has changed since 1748, when Hume penned this particular treatise. Hume's conclusions were based on experience and information gleaned from that age. His arguments were flawed then, even as they are now. However, exposing these flaws and understanding why they are present is currently facilitated by globalization and the digital era. The scope of knowledge, experience, and verifiable data available to individuals far exceeds anything Hume could have imagined.

Hume's basic argument consists of several key points addressed as they occur in Section 10 of his treatise, "Miracles." First, because no current eyewitness is available to verify the miracle accounts in the NT, Hume levels the assertion that the "truth of the *Christian* religion is less than the evidence for the truth of our senses."[69] All Christians subsequent to those eyewitnesses of Jesus' works are thus handicapped by their inability to adjudicate the miracles claimed in the NT. The "authority, of either scripture or tradition," Hume avows, is founded "merely in the testimony of the apostles."[70]

The flaw in this portion of Hume's logic consists of a failure to grasp the entire system of Christian belief adequately, resulting in seven distinct errors. First, Hume commits his first error by thinking that Christians anchor their belief system exclusively on the testimony of the apostles. The apostolic testimony comprises but one link in a chain of evidence. Moving retrogressively, that chain of evidence, at the least, includes personal experience and observation as a first premise. Often contemporary personal experience and observation carry the weight of eyewitness testimony to marvelous or even miraculous events. Second, individuals regularly report innate experiences with something numinous that they characterize as the immediate operation of the Holy Spirit. Hume mentions that his experience is absent of the internal work of the Holy Spirit. Perhaps, however, his lack of experience does not disallow the possibility for the remainder of mankind.[71] Third, both currently and historically beginning with the era of

---

69. Hume, *Enquiry Concerning Human Understanding*, 114. Emphasis in the original.

70. Hume, *Enquiry Concerning Human Understanding*, 114.

71. Hume may fall into the all-or-nothing fallacy or the suppressing-evidence

the apostles, Christians have reported multitudes of healings or other acts that they believe are the direct intervention of the supernatural into the normal course of cause and effect. Fourth, no scholarly rationale permits the discarding of the apostolic witness as captured in the NT documents *a priori*. Fifth, prior to and subsequent to the NT era, some independent, non-canonical Jewish writers verify the expectation that a miracle-working messianic figure would arise: a figure with characteristics remarkably like those recorded of Jesus. Sixth, the OT witness of the prophets and nation of Israel must be considered. These records give reason to believe that what the NT records was specifically and miraculously predicted. Seventh, the Christian religion is able to explain origins coherently; why *something* rather than *nothing* exists. In response to Hume, the composite evidence for the Christian religion emerges from personal and corporate experience, history, independent documentation, and philosophical rationale—not "merely" the apostolic testimony.

Hume's well-known statement disregarding any and all testimony as sufficient to establish a miracle claim (unless the falsification would be more miraculous) is also problematic.[72] The basis for Hume's unwillingness to accept human testimony for miracle claims is fourfold. First, he does not believe that any miracle has the requisite number of witnesses who possess the following virtues: good-sense, education, learning, undeluded perspective, integrity, credit, reputation, and potential for loss. In addition, the event in question must have been performed in public and "in so celebrated a part of the world, as to render the detection unavoidable."[73] Second, Hume argues that the "most usual is always most probable; and that where there is an opposition of arguments, we ought to give the preference to such as are founded on the greatest number of past observations."[74] Third, Hume holds the presumption against miracles reported by citizens of undeveloped third-world nations.[75] Fourth, he objects to the evidential use of miracles to establish the truth of religions whose ideologies are in conflict.[76] In short, Hume contends that human testimony regarding miracles is untrustworthy and always attended by mistake, delusion, or fraud. Therefore, Hume's argument is epistemological. One simply cannot know if a miracle happened.

---

fallacy on this point. Either everyone confirms the same experience or it must be disallowed.

72. Hume, *Enquiry Concerning Human Understanding*, 121.
73. Hume, *Enquiry Concerning Human Understanding*, 122.
74. Hume, *Enquiry Concerning Human Understanding*, 122–23.
75. Hume, *Enquiry Concerning Human Understanding*, 125.
76. Hume, *Enquiry Concerning Human Understanding*, 127–28.

Undeniably, Hume's analysis is partially correct. No serious scholar doubts that miracle testimony can be tainted. Nevertheless, Hume does not adequately address several issues, including the two addressed below, which leaves open the possibility for genuine miraculous activity. First, it must be acknowledged that the probability an event has occurred must be weighed against the probability that the event did not occur, given the extant testimony. J. P. Moreland and William Lane Craig argue this point cogently.[77] Using the purported resurrection of Jesus as a case in point, Moreland and Craig reason that it is beyond incredulity to disbelieve that the evidence in our possession would be the same if the resurrection did not occur. An event described as a miracle may be attended with multiple independent witnesses—including postmortem appearances—and physical evidence, such as the empty tomb. In such cases, what is the probability that the event in question did *not* happen? The point of the illustration is to demonstrate that both the positive testimony for the event and the probability of the event *not* happening need to be considered in light of the available evidence. Soberly considered, given the overall scope of the evidence, little probability exists that all of the witnesses to the resurrection suffer from delusion or integrity problems. The same types of evidence can be gathered from other miracle claims. Some of these are captured for scrutiny in Craig Keener's two-volume work on miracles.[78] The probability that the bulk of the miracle accounts Keener investigated and reported are overladen with mistakes, delusion, or fraud is minute to such a degree as to make it incredible. Furthermore, reports of miracles are not limited to under-developed, third-world countries.

Second, the *a priori* rejection of miracles based on naturalistic assumptions is neither a scientifically-grounded nor philosophically-sound approach to history. Historicity is established by applying a set of rules or usually accepted criteria to historical claims.[79] An appeal to the laws of nature or the argument that necessity and causation uniformly arise from operations of nature is also misguided. The scientific method and its conclusions change and evolve as knowledge increases. In this context, Habermas

---

77. Moreland and Craig, *Philosophical Foundations*, 570.

78. Keener, *Miracles*.

79. The criteria for establishing historicity are as follows: (1) eyewitness sources; (2) the superiority of early sources over latter sources; (3) multiple attestation by independent sources; (4) multiple attestation by different forms or genres; (5) discontinuity of the source with the prevailing culture; (6) possible embarrassment resulting from the contents of the source; (7) surprise elements contained in the source; (8) attestation by enemies or former enemies of the source; (9) coherence of the terminology and style with the source; and (10) the presence of an Aramaic substrata in NT sources.

acknowledges the inability of science to "postulate absolutes."[80] None of the conclusions of science are inviolable. As such, an appeal to inviolable laws of nature serve only as empty rhetoric. The so-called "laws of nature" describe what happens in regular and predictable ways. However, the existence of the regular and the predictable can never rule out the irregular or unpredictable event. Richard Swinburne establishes that a non-repeatable occurrence, counter to a law of nature, is logically compatible with the existence of the law.[81] When the conceptually impossible happens (something irregular or unpredictable), it highlights the difference between a law (something regular and predicable) and something universally true (inviolable).[82] As such, methodological naturalism and historical naturalism consisting of the unwarranted exclusion of supranatural or supernatural explanations fails as a scientific methodology.

Philosophically, the basis for historical naturalism is usually linked to the *principle of analogy*. Stated in simplest terms, this principle maintains that, "on the analogy of the events known to us we seek by conjecture and sympathetic understanding to explain and reconstruct the past."[83] As utilized by Ernst Troeltsch, *the principle of analogy* is flawed and often misapplied. Moreland and Craig maintain that ancient myths, legends, illusions, and the like are dismissed as unhistorical not because they are unusual but rather because they have no objective referent—no historical reality.[84] They are analogous to modern myths and dismissed casually. This clearly demonstrates the flaw in the *principle of analogy* as applied to historical investigation. It is not the *absence* of an analogy that demonstrates something unhistorical but rather the positive *presence* of the analogy containing imaginary thought forms.[85] Reality, consisting of unpredictable, irregular, or even conceptually impossible events, may not have a direct analogy, yet may still be a real historical event.

Hume's Argument and Predictive Prophecy

How do the arguments presented above apply to predictive prophecy and fulfillment? Hume made no distinction between other types of miracles and prophecy, asserting: "What we have said of miracles may be applied,

80. Habermas, *Historical Jesus*, 59.
81. Swinburne, "Violation of a Law of Nature," 78.
82. Swinburne, "Violation of a Law of Nature," 80.
83. Troeltsch, "Historiography," 6:718.
84. Moreland and Craig, *Philosophical Foundations*, 572.
85. Craig, *Reasonable Faith*, 153–54.

without any variation, to prophecies."[86] This statement is particularly incorrect in the case of prophecy. The species of miracle in which accurate predictions of future events are made—predictions meeting the critical criteria for fulfillment—are of a different nature than isolated events springing from supernatural or suprahuman sources.

When applied to prophecy, both of Hume's major arguments fail for four key reasons. First, the miracle of prophecy and its later fulfillment is sometimes verifiable historically. Predictive prophecy and fulfillment may manifest in two distinct phases. Critical criteria can be applied to confirm or disconfirm both phases. This evaluative process might entail an event universally acknowledged to have occurred,[87] an event attested by several witnesses, or an event supported by other types of evidence.

Second, prophecy and its fulfillment are not necessarily bound to second-hand testimony. Eyewitnesses might be present or the prophecy may be recorded at one time and place, while the fulfillment is recorded at an entirely different time and place. Each aspect of the event might be verified by eyewitness testimony. Third, it is even possible that first-hand observation of prophecy and fulfillment occur today. Nothing limits genuine prophetic activity with a corresponding fulfillment to the historical past. Fourth, prophecy and its corresponding fulfillment do not require a violation of a law of nature. No appeal to so-called laws of nature impact the process of determining whether a prophecy is authentic.

Peter Harrison has argued persuasively from a variety of sources that Hume's arguments were not accepted in the eighteenth and nineteenth centuries when they were applied to prophecy. Harrison states, "'Miracles alone . . . are 'not sufficient confirmation of a true prophet.' Nor, it was widely admitted, could miracles convince an atheist. Together, however, miracles and accomplished prophecies could give a moral certainty of the truth of Christianity to the contemporary believer."[88] This is why historical investigation of credible evidence is so crucial to establish in the case of prophecy.

---

86. Hume, *Enquiry Concerning Human Understanding*, 138.

87. Harrison, "Prophecy," 242.

88. Harrison, "Prophecy," 243. Harrison cites Cudworth, *True Intellectual System*, 700, to support his statement that miracles alone are not enough to confirm a true prophet. Further, he cites the following list of sources to support his assertion that miracles alone will not convert an atheist: Bacon, *Advancement of Learning*, 2:vi; Boyle, *Christian Virtuoso*, 5:514; Stillingfleet, *Origines Sacrae*, 116; Fleetwood, *Essay upon Miracles in Two Discourses*, 13; Bentley, *Works*, 3:125. Cf. Aquinas, *Summa theologiae* 2a.2ae. 6, 1; Sykes, *Brief Discourse*, 43; and Lemoine, *Treatise on Miracles*, 359, 365. On the acknowledged limitations of the argument from miracles and the linking of the arguments from miracles and prophecy, see Burs, *Great Debate*, 109–110.

Employing the proper hermeneutical and historiographic methodology, verification of prophetic prediction and fulfillment is possible.

Conclusion

This review has sought to delineate and comment on a select group of published works from among the masses treating OT prophecy and alleged NT fulfillments. The works selected, with the exception of Hume, contain both a messianic component and a definite apologetic appeal. The evaluation of their content has highlighted significant lacunas in current OT and NT messianic scholarship that, at some level, is represented in each of the works reviewed. Each suffer from one or more shortcomings: (1) approaching the topic uncritically, (2) presupposing some form of divine inspiration, (3) offering sparse historical evidence, (4) providing little interaction with textual difficulties or historical context (i.e., both OT and NT contexts), and (5) offering little interaction with the objections of critical scholarship. These shortcomings often result in the rejection of the conclusions offered.

The most difficult presupposition to remedy exposed by this review is the concept of divine inspiration. If one adopts a skeptically extreme position, abandoning divine inspiration illegitimates any attempt to read either the OT or the NT as unified works. Readings that allow the various biblical books to illuminate or to intertextually inform one another must be reconsidered developmentally and diachronically. This approach may lead to discarding canonical readings in favor of viewing the texts as isolated oracles. Conversely, critical scholarship also posits a final redactive process after the Babylonian exile for the OT and the well-documented history of the establishment of the NT as a developing unified body of thought. In light of these insights, it is possible to argue for a canonical reading of both: the OT in light of the historical-cultural intent of the final OT redactor and the NT in light of the historical-cultural understanding of the first-century authors. No treatment of these issues will be problem free. Even so, the aim of this dissertation is to fill the lacuna exposed with facts that are well-attested and accepted by the majority of scholars.[89]

Concordant with the arguments offered above, one further conclusion is indicated by the literature. The position remains that no *a priori* rejection

---

[89]. In the "Statement of the Problem" section above: "This investigation envisions the existence of three possible outcomes for each prophecy examined: (1) Jesus directly fulfilled the prophecy and sufficient historical evidence establishes the claim as probable, (2) Jesus directly fulfilled the prophecy, but the available historical evidence is insufficient to establish the claim as probable, and (3) sufficient historical evidence exists to refute the claim that Jesus directly fulfilled the prophecy."

of miracles is warranted for the historian. Epistemological certainty is never possible with historical investigations. This does not, however, exempt the responsible historian from a methodological and philosophical obligation to approach the task with an open mind and to draw conclusions from all relevant data. The obligation to treat data fairly holds true whether or not the event or phenomena in question is analogous to current data and whether or not it is consistent with one's own experience.

Part II

Exegesis Analysis and Synthesis

Introduction to Part II

BEFORE BEGINNING THE WORK with various texts, it is proper to remind ourselves that demonstrating the probability of a historical event is very difficult. Origen remarked, "that the endeavour to show, with regard to almost any history, however true, that it actually occurred, and to produce an intelligent conception regarding it, is one of the most difficult undertakings that can be attempted, and is in some instances an impossibility."[90] Without minimizing the daunting task this dissertation has undertaken, it is possible to show the probability of many historical events. Although exhaustive knowledge of them is beyond human capacity, adequate or even substantial knowledge is still possible.

It is no less difficult to establish facts about authorial intent when interpreting ancient literature. It is possible to show the likelihood that the gist of interpretations is correct, although exhaustive knowledge of the author's intent is unattainable. In sum, adequate explanations are possible.

With these issues in view, the present study approaches the subject texts from a historical-evidential orientation. The method of argumentation during the exposition, the "plausible historical-evidential conclusions," and "facts" presented at the end of each text investigated are not intended to be understood as *minimal facts*. They represent the present author's style and personal conclusions. Other scholars may or may not agree. Only those items specifically labeled *minimal facts* meet the criteria and will be treated in chapter 8.

---

90. Origen, "Origen against Celsus," 1.42.

Chapter 3

The First Group of Biblical Texts

Introduction to the First Group of Biblical Texts

THE FIRST GROUP OF texts to be investigated are sometimes referenced to substantiate the claim that the *terminus ad quem* for the coming of the Messiah must be before Israel loses its status as self-governing and before the destruction of the temple in AD 70. The OT texts chosen for evaluation cover virtually the entire era for the writing of the OT (Gen 49:10; Ps 118:26; Hag 2:7, 9; Mal 3:1). If plausible conclusions or *minimal facts* can be ascertained from either the literary or the historical contexts of the OT prophecies and the NT witnesses, these texts are the place to begin the research.

Genesis 49:10

Literary and Textual Analysis

Two Key Questions for Understanding this Study of Genesis 49:10:
what do the Terms Scepter (שבט) and Shilo (שילה) Mean?

Genesis 49:10 contains problematic elements for exegetes. This part of the poem—directed to Jacob's fourth son—is uncertain with reference to both its wording and its meaning. These ambiguities make any broad statements about historical facts or interpretations tenuous. The primary difficulty, for most exegetes, lies in the term שילה (šylh) or שִׁילוֹ (šîlŏ). According the *Hebrew Aramaic Lexicon of the Old Testament* (HALOT), the meaning and spelling of this term remains a disputed question. The latter spelling is translated predominantly with one of three senses: (1) "until the one comes to whom it (the sceptre) belongs," (2) "the one to whom it (authority) belongs," and (3) "until the Messiah comes to whom the kingdom belongs."[1] In addition, Rydelnik includes the long-standing views that Shiloh (if the former spelling is correct) is either a place name or a personal name of the Messiah.[2] Neither of Rydelnik's options, however, have any conclusive support. Shiloh as the personal name of the Messiah has limited support from later Jewish literature.[3] This later support notwithstanding, neither the *analogia Scriptura* nor lexical evidence dispels the difficulties of this translation. Similarly, Briggs flatly states that this view was not introduced into the Christian church until the sixteenth century.[4]

If *Shiloh* is translated as a place name, the text would read, "until he comes to Shiloh" with a focus on the Judah's role in the conquest of Canaan. Rydelnik rejects this possibility based on the MT's (Masoretic Text) consistently different spelling for the place Shiloh (שילו) in relation to the word appearing in Genesis 49:10 (שילה). However, in light of Joshua 18:1, regardless of spelling irregularities or if the text is rightly translated as a place name, any suggestion that it does not relate to the conquest of Canaan can be dismissed. These observations make any alleged connection to the Messiah for both the personal name and place name translations indefensible.[5]

All three of the remaining possible translations might be interpreted as predictive of the Messiah, David, or the Davidic dynasty. The most frequently chosen of the possibilities is something similar to "he whose it is," or "that which belongs to him."[6] As will be demonstrated below, wording similar to these examples is indicated as the most likely translation.[7]

The answer to the other crucial interpretive question lies in solving two problems. First, what is meant by the "*scepter*" (שבט) and the "*ruler's staff*" (מחקק)? Second, when were these emblems *de facto* removed from a representative of the tribe of Judah? The importance of this second question arises because some Christian interpretations of Genesis 49:10 contend it

---

1. Koehler et al., *Hebrew and Aramaic Lexicon*, 1478. Cf. Swanson, *Dictionary of Biblical Languages*, 8869.

2. Rydlelnik, *Messianic Hope*, 48–49.

3. For example, see, *b. Sanh.* 96B which Brown, Driver, and Briggs describe as "groundless" (Brown et al., *Hebrew and English Lexicon*, 1010).

4. Briggs, *Messianic Prophecy*, 95.

5. Cf. Schley, "Traditions and History of Biblical Shiloh," 185–201.

6. Brown et al., *Hebrew and English Lexicon*, 1010.

7. With slight variations, see the Syriac Version (Sa Sw), Targum Onkelos, the Ephraimitic source or the Old Latin Version. The Septuagint has two variants τὰ ἀποκείμενα αὐτῷ and ᾧ ἀπόκειται. Cf. Geisler and Howe, *When Critics Ask*, 61, and Archer Jr., *Encyclopedia of Biblical Difficulties*, 107–8.

demands a continuous succession of kings from the tribe of Judah—or at least self-governance by a Judahite—until the Messiah comes.[8]

The scepter is an emblem of royal authority. In Genesis 49:10, *scepter* and the *ruler's staff* are in synonymous parallelism. Together, they denote the vesting of rulership in the tribe of Judah over the other tribes. This assertion is not controversial; however, the tribe of Judah is not currently in a leadership role in Israel and has not been for more than 2000 years. These preliminary observations lead to one of three conclusions: (1) the text does not demand a continuous succession of Judahite rulers, (2) the prediction has been realized, or (3) both one and two are true.

When examined diachronically, the recorded history of Israelite leadership quickly exposes the inconsistency of maintaining that Genesis 49:10 prophesies an unbroken line of Davidic kings or, at least, that the internal affairs of the Jews be governed by a Judahite leader until the advent of the Messiah.[9] This approach has several historical problems to overcome. First, neither Moses nor Joshua was Judahite. Second, the office of the king of Israel was initially occupied and divinely ordained to Saul from the tribe of Benjamin (1 Sam 9:16). Third, a considerable amount of historical contortionism is required if one hopes to demonstrate an unbroken line of Israelite leaders (official or unofficial) from the tribe of Judah (even when allowances for beginning with David are granted) until the birth of Jesus. Subsequent to the destruction of Jerusalem in 587 BC, it is doubtful that the succession of *bona fide* Jewish monarchs from the tribe of Judah can be mustered. For the vast majority of Israel's post-exilic history, it existed as vassal state, answerable to a non-Israelite king. When the nation was sovereign for short epochs—such as the Hasmonean period (circa 144–63)—Judean ancestry of its leaders is possible, but uncertain.[10] Newman proposes to address this problem by making the reference to Judah in Genesis 49:10 a geographical designation. If correct, this interpretation would place the location of Israelite kings in the land of Judah, with the last king being Herod Agrippa I.[11] Newman's approach solves the succession problem by

---

8. Keith, *Evidence of the Truth of the Christian Religion*, 26. Cf. Klayman, *What the Rabbis Know*, 26–27, and Henry, *Matthew Henry's Commentary*, 92.

For a slightly nuanced conclusion, see Newman, *Jesus*, 162–76. J. L. Dagg turns the usual interpretations of the prophecy upside down by contending that the Messiah must come while the scepter is departing from Judah. See Dagg, *Evidences of Christianity*, 106. Cf. Hengstenberg, *Christology of the Old Testament*, 1:1003–821.

9. Keith, *Evidence of the Truth of the Christian Religion*, 26. Cf. Klayman, *What the Rabbis Know*, 26–27.

10. Myers, *Eerdmans Bible Dictionary*, 465.

11. Newman, *Jesus*, 176.

simply reframing the question to one of geographical origins rather than of specific tribal ancestry. This approach, however, ignores the personal language and character traits the author of the Testament of Jacob applies. It also potentially allows for a Reubenite born in Judea to become king. Moreover, Newman's topographical maneuver cannot satisfactorily explain how the scepter did not depart during the exile or those eras when the kingdom of Judah was a vassal state.

The reasonable way to understand the prophecy, whether originally penned in the patriarchal period or during the early monarchy, requires using the same general approach reflected centuries later in the text of the Dead Sea Scrolls:

> The sceptre [shall not] depart from the tribe of Judah . . . [Gen 49:10]. Whenever Israel rules, there shall [not] fail to be a descendant of David upon the throne. For the ruler's staff is the covenant of kingship, [and the clans] of Israel are the divisions, until the Messiah of Righteousness comes, the Branch of David. For to him and his seed is granted the Covenant of kingship over his people for everlasting generations.[12]

Adela Collins and Harold Attridge concur with this understanding, concluding that "it is likely that the figure declared to be 'son of God' and 'son of the Most High' in a controversial Aramaic fragment from Qumran is also the Davidic messiah."[13] The fragment they are referencing reads as follows:

> The Lord declares to you that he will build you a House (2 Sam 7:11c). I will raise up your seed after you (2 Sam 7:12). I will establish the throne of his kingdom [forever] (2 Sam 7:13). [I will be] his father and he shall be my son (2 Sam 7:14). He is the Branch of David who shall arise with the Interpreter of the Law [to rule] in Zion [at the end] of time. (4Q174 Frags. 1 i, 21, 2)

The theme of Genesis 49:10, then, is not a promise of an unbroken chain of leaders from or situated in Judah. It is not even a promise that can be explained by sporadic Judean kings. The only reasonable way to understand the text is to accept that it is primarily a declaration that the divinely appointed ruler of Israel is from the tribe of Judah. Secondarily, if later texts are allowed an interpreting voice, the universal eschatological rule of Israel will be vested in a king from the tribe of Judah. This interpretation

---

12. Vermes, *Dead Sea Scrolls*, 302. 4Q252 Col. v. Cf. Martínez and Tigchelaar, *Dead Sea Scrolls Study Edition*, and Collins, *Scepter and the Star*, 70. Collins quotes the Vermes translation exactly as rendered.

13. Collins and Attridge, *Mark*, 65.

aligns well with the overall development of the messianic concept in the OT; it also aligns well with the insights of historical criticism while avoiding anachronism.

Genesis 49:1b and 49:10 Redacted Insertions?

Historical critical scholars assert that Genesis 49:1–27 is a poem and is not a part of the original Patriarchal narrative that constitutes the body of Genesis. They argue it is *vaticinia ex eventu;* the poem has been inserted into the narrative of the Priestly (P) or the Yahwist (J) source[14] by a later redactor, leaving the reader with the impression of a prophetic utterance by Jacob.[15] Hermann Gunkel agrees with this position, describing the poem as very old and originally part of the J corpus.[16] The basis for his claim lies partly with the identifiable parallels in the characteristics of the tribal sayings in Genesis 49:10 with those of Deuteronomy 33 and Judges 5:14–18.[17] Claus Westermann contends that these tribal sayings originate during era of the Judges—with the exception of those concerning Judah, which must come sometime after the establishment of the monarchy. The specific attributions concerning the tribes of Israel in the Testament of Jacob are reflective of internally known and discussed characteristics of the tribes arising from

---

14. Skinner, *Critical and Exegetical Commentary on Genesis*, 509. For the purpose of this dissertation, the Yahwist source (J) is dated tenth century BC; the Elohist (E) ninth century BC; the Deuteronomist (D) seventh century BC; and the Priestly source (P) sixth century BC.

15. Mazar, *Archaeology of the Land of the Bible*, 224–26. Amihai Mazar takes issue with the total invention of the patriarchal narratives. He contends that the cultural environment of the Middle Bronze Age II "provides the most suitable background for the patriarchal sagas in the Book of Genesis." Further, the prosperous urban culture, pastoral clans, and the four-hundred-year chronology for the time in Egypt, all point to the seventeenth century BC as the time of Jacob. Other informative points of interest include, (1) Joseph's place in Egypt could fit the Hyksos period, (2) most cities mentioned were occupied (e.g., Shechem, Bethel, Jerusalem, and Hebron), (3) Abraham's journey from Ur to Haran and on to Canaan are explained by the general movements of people during the era, and (4) personal names used in Genesis are of "West Semitic form known from the first half of the second millennium BCE." These apparent parallels with the Middle Bronze Age II do not dismiss the probability that later redactors (perhaps during the time of the Judges or monarchy) modified the stories, whether in written or oral form, but this does imply the probability that there is some historicity to the underlying stories.

16. Gunkel, *Genesis*, 453.

17. Deuteronomy 33 also contains a list of blessings directed to the tribal groups. Similar to Genesis 49:1–27, this list includes images drawn from nature (particularly animal life) set in prophetic prose. The parallels in Judges 5:14–18 are not as pronounced.

tribal meetings and battles on various occasions after entering Canaan; these extend to the period of the judges.[18]

Important for this discussion is Westermann's contention that a second redactor, inserting verse 1b into Genesis 49, is purposely imposing prophetic eschatological meaning on verses 8–10. This later redactor understood verses 8–10 as designating a ruler of the last days.[19] This is indicated by the phrase: "Gather yourselves together, that I may tell you what shall happen to you in days to come" (Gen 49:1).[20] Barfield tacitly affirms this position by indicating that the phrase "in the last days" (KJV) (באחרית הימים) "generally speaks of a time when the Jewish kingdom would be judged by God and replaced with a new kingdom and covenant."[21] If this interpretation is accurate, according to Barfield, scholars customarily locate the period of judgment and replacement in the decades prior to the destruction of Jerusalem in AD 70. Johnston, however, is more cautious, noting that the phrase "in the days to come" is a technical expression of the eschatological future in the prophets—although it does not necessarily point toward an eschatological event in the Pentateuch (e.g., Deut 4:30; 31:29).[22] Conceptually, then, given the passage's prophetic nature, it is possible that this pericope intends to project a judgment and replacement motif present in the mind of the redactor of 1b or his peers. The only constant that may be asserted is the focus on Judah and a probable extension to the Davidic monarchy.

Numbers 24:14 and following is particularly informative in relation to Genesis 49:1–27. It originates from approximately the same period or earlier and inarguably contains import that later Jewish interpreters considered as pointing to the ideal Davidic scion.[23] The initial concept was probably a *vaticinia ex eventu* affirmation of the subjugation of Moab and Edom by

---

18. Westermann, *Genesis 37–50*, 222.

19. Westermann, *Genesis 37–50*, 223.

20. ESV. Westermann cites Hermann Gunkel in this regard, noting that several other biblical texts use the same type of eschatological language. Even the most conservative view of the phrase "in the days to come" indicates a long-term perspective. However, when other texts are allowed to inform the reader, the messianic eschatological understanding appears the most reasonable.

21. Barfield, *Prophet Motive*, 126–27. The difference of wording lies in the English translation, not the Hebrew text. Other occurrences of similar phrases in the OT prophets support this interpretive approach (e.g., Num 24:14; Isa 2:2; Jer 48:47; 49:39; Mic 4:1).

22. Johnston, "Messianic Trajectories in Genesis and Numbers," 41.

23. Numbers 24:17 is referenced with probable messianic overtones in 4Q175, CD 7:19–20 (4QDa 3 iii 20–21), and 1QM 11:6–7. Lim et al., *Dead Sea Scrolls in Their Historical Context*, 113–14.

David.²⁴ If so, a further intertextual relationship emerges in prophecy of a particular ideal Davidic scion (2 Sam 7:12–16). Relating these affirmations to Genesis 49:1–27 as the work of monarchial or later redactors leaves open the possibility that Numbers 24:17 is the earliest biblical mention of rulership coming from Jacob. The bulk of the Balaam oracles are attributed to J and E. However, if these oracles derive their basis from historical events, as Martin Noth contends, they are necessarily from an earlier tradition; they easily could pre-date the introduction of the Testament of Jacob into the patriarchal narrative.²⁵ This possibility makes it more likely that Genesis 49:10 was originally pointing toward more than Judah's role in the conquest of Canaan, or a *vaticinia ex eventu* affirmation of the Davidic monarchy. Genesis 49:1–27 may have formed a type of messianic commentary on the Balaam oracle. With this additional evidence, it is probable (given redaction) that the text of Genesis 49:10 was (1) intended to affirm the role of Judah and the perpetuity and "inviolability"²⁶ of Davidic monarchy and (2) perhaps even point toward the nascent ideal of a scion of David, as implied in Numbers 24:17.

Conversely, if Genesis 49:10 is read in its traditional patriarchal context—and not as a later redaction—the meaning was probably not overtly messianic. The messianic interpretation, according to Fitzmyer, came about through a process. He contends that Genesis 49:10 is meant to emphasize the "ascendancy of the tribe of Judah among the twelve tribes."²⁷ While acknowledging the problematic aspects of the last half of the verse and its reference to *Shiloh*, Fitzmyer understands the verse to be an oracle pointing to the tribute that will eventually be paid to Judah through David and his descendants. This honor will continue until the dissolution of the monarchy that ended with the reign of Zedekiah. In his view, to interpret the text otherwise is anachronistic. Similarly, Johnston notes the openness of the text, adding that this text "initially conceived the role the tribe of Judah would play in the conquest and settlement of Canaan to fulfill God's ancient promise."²⁸ Even so, a latent and progressive messianic potential exists in the text.

24. Fitzmyer, *One Who Is to Come*, 99.

25. Scholar Martin Noth believes that the region from which this story originates is East of the Northern end of the Dead Sea. Balak was probably a "petty" king and underlies the character of Balaam who was a real historical figure. The story as a whole is also thought to have a historical basis, from which it was handed down from one generation to the next. Noth, *Numbers*, 172.

26. Roberts, "Old Testament's Contribution to Messianic Expectations," 41.

27. Fitzmyer, *One Who Is to Come*, 29–30.

28. Johnston, "Messianic Trajectories," 41.

Briggs also evaluates the text as a progressive promise after treating the textual issue surrounding the term *Shiloh*. Briggs makes the cogent point that claiming this term as the name of the Messiah disturbs the flow of the progressive unveiling of the messianic promise. Viewed as the next step in the revelation given to Abraham regarding the promise of a seed, the natural way to understand the promises made to Jacob's son Judah is that of headship during the conquest of Canaan.[29] As was the case with Fitzmyer and Johnston, however, Briggs does not end his exegesis with the conquest of Canaan. This prophecy, he argues, transcends the era of Joshua and Caleb or even David and Solomon, pointing toward a final realization "at the end of the world."[30]

These assertions by Fitzmyer, Johnston, and Briggs are logical deductions. More importantly, they allow "in the days to come" (1b) to bear the same prophetic and eschatological meaning (of a permanent, ideal Davidic monarch), whether it was inserted by a redactor or not. None of these scholars omits David or the Davidic monarchy as part of the progressively included meaning. Temporally, rather than beginning with David and the monarchy, they simply regress one step further back in time to the initial conquest of Canaan.

If the Testament of Jacob is a product of later redactions, as Westermann claims, it presupposed, at a minimum, the monarchy and probably contained connotations of Jewish prophetic eschatology (in the sense of a permanent ideal Davidic monarch) from its first insertion into the narrative.[31] However, given the lack of any historical data that clearly establishes the date of writing or any redactive process to which the text has been subjected, an examination of how the text was interpreted in exilic and post-exilic Judaism is warranted.

The Interpretation of Genesis 49:10 in Exilic and Post-exilic Judaism

Old Testament Evidence

Regardless of whether the Testament of Jacob or the Balaam oracles are earlier, sometime before the chronicler recorded his books (1 Chr 5:2), the

---

29. Briggs, *Messianic Prophecy*, 97n3.

30. Briggs, *Messianic Prophecy*, 98.

31. The Genesis Rabbah on 49:1–26 (XCVII:II. 7) specifically ties the phrase "in the days to come" (1b) to eschatological Gog and the end of days; (XCVIII:VIII. 1) connects the term Shiloh to the Messiah

text of Genesis 49:10 was understood as delineating a Davidic leader from Judah. Subsequently, it received additional messianic interpretation. This assertion is supported by two key conclusions: one from the OT, discussed in this section, and the second from intertestamental literature, discussed in the following section.

The exilic oracle of Ezekiel 21 (with focus on 21:27) manipulates what seems to be a commonly accepted messianic understanding of the promise made in Genesis 49:10. Ezekiel's "sinister reinterpretation"[32] intends to bring attention to the humiliation of Judah and Zedekiah. The removal of the royal symbols from Zedekiah—including the turban, crown, and (implicitly) the scepter—indicate his impending judgment. The implication is that Nebuchadnezzar temporarily possesses the ruler's scepter. The phrase "until he comes, the one to whom judgment belongs, and I will give it to him" (Ezek 21:27b) is effectively a reversal of the traditional understanding, replacing the meaning of משפט (mišpāt), understood as *right* or *claim*, with connotations of judgment on Israel.[33] Ezekiel's appropriation of the expression "until he comes, the one to whom judgment belongs" directly correlates with several translations of the term שילה in Genesis 49:10. This correlation indicates not only the correctness of the conclusions made above but also implies that Ezekiel may be thinking beyond localized terms toward the ideal eschatological Davidic king. Walther Zimmerli provides several of the translations of the term שילה proposed by critical scholars that support an understanding in general agreement with this observation:

> 'For whom it is fitting' (Smend), 'who has a claim (to it)' (Kraetzschmar, Ziegler, Ezechiel), 'who has a right to it' (Fohrer), 'who is right' (Herrmann), 'to whom the right belongs' (Cooke), 'die er recht op heeft' (van den Born), 'die het recht heeft' (Aalders), 'cui est jus (debitum)' (Knabenbauer).[34]

As indicated above, these translations can be construed as denoting either the Messiah or simply a Davidic king. The phrase appearing in Ezekiel 21:27b, however, actually marks the end of formal Judahite rule in Israel. For the first time since the establishment of the monarchy, there is a clear break with the Davidic line. A promise accompanies this break by appropriating Genesis 49:10 in reference to a specific future individual, "until the one comes whose judgment it is (עד־בא אשר־לו המשפט)."[35] It seems that Ezekiel

---

32. Satterthwaite et al., *Lord's Anointed Interpretation*, 167.
33. Satterthwaite et al., *Lord's Anointed Interpretation*, 167–68.
34. Zimmerli, *Ezekiel*, 447.
35. The author's translation.

was thinking in terms of a single eschatological judge to whom the scepter will be given.[36] Sigmund Mowinckel affirms that Ezekiel probably "alludes to the expected righteous scion of David."[37] Perhaps, adds Mowinckel, the prophet is thinking about the texts mentioned and several royal psalms that contribute to the overall idea of the Messiah.

Intertestamental Evidence

The locus of the second line of argumentation, supporting the gradual accruing of a messianic interpretation for Genesis 49:10, emerges in the Testament of Judah, second-century BC. The Testament of Judah reasserts the idea that the posterity of Judah is the tribe from which the rulers of Israel will come (22:3 and perhaps 1:6). Similarly, the Dead Sea Scrolls also address the issue of Genesis 49:10. 4Q252, a commentary on Genesis, explicitly interprets Genesis 49:10 as a messianic prediction of the Messiah who is the branch of David (4Q252 Col. v). The *Targum Onkelos* is another example of Jewish interpretation stemming from about the first century AD, which also explicitly interprets Genesis 49:10 in messianic terms. Tom Huckle translates the *Targum Onkelos* as follows: "The transmission of dominion shall not cease from the house of Judah, nor the scribe from his children's children, forever, until the Messiah comes, to whom the kingdom belongs, and whom nations shall obey."[38] The *Targum Pseudo Jonathan* reads much the same way, as do some fragmentary Targum and several midrashic texts.[39]

---

36. Robert Henry Charles argues that Ezekiel and those subsequent, post-exilic writers who thought in similar ways conceived of judgment in terms of purging Israel of evil and preparing individuals for the establishment of the eternal Messianic kingdom. Charles, *Critical History*, 101.

37. Mowinckel, *He that Cometh*, 175.

38. Huckel, *Rabbinic Messiah*, Gen 49:10.

39. In addition to those listed above, the Midrash Rabbah that Huckel identifies as having import for understanding Jewish interpretation of Genesis 49:10 are as follows: (1) Genesis 97; (2) Proverbs 19:21; (3) Genesis 99; (4) Lamentations 1:16, 51; (5) Genesis 98:8–9. Huckel, *Rabbinic Messiah*, Gen 49:10. The Eagle vision of 4 Ezra is also probably a reference to the Davidic Messiah by the lion image associated the tribe of Judah and Genesis 49:10. See Neusner et al., *Judaism and Their Messiahs at the Turn of the Christian Era*.

New Testament Evidence

This study has not discovered any NT evidence that demands Genesis 49:10 be interpreted as a *terminus ad quem* either for Israelite sovereignty or for the advent of the Messiah.[40]

Summary

In summary, it has been demonstrated that from as early as the monarchial period, some Jewish interpreters may have believed that Genesis 49:10 pointed beyond the immediate context and toward the ideal Davidic king. Although indemonstrable, the possibility that the Testament of Jacob has a historical basis cannot be wholly dismissed. If it did have such a basis, that work was probably intended to designate Judah as the tribe from which the leaders of the conquest of Canaan and the kings of Israel would arise. This tradition was further developed during the early monarchy, with the resulting fully messianic interpretation coming gradually.

If Numbers 24:17 has a historical basis, as asserted in the current work, it could not have been far from the mind of the monarchial author/redactors of Genesis 49:10. The messianic interpretation becomes increasingly obvious in Ezekiel, continuing through to the intertestamental period. More interpretations are added in the Qumran literature and later rabbinic writings.

The preceding conclusion leaves unaddressed the question of *when* Genesis 49:10 was first interpreted as a reference to the Messiah. In contrast, the question of *how* the text has been understood is clear. For as long as relevant records exist, they interpret Genesis 49:10 as containing the dictum that the Messiah and other divinely installed kings of Israel will be from the tribe of Judah. No *terminus ad quem* can be established from Genesis 49:10. Israel's status as self-governing may come and go, but when

---

40. Although indemonstrable, Nils Alstrup Dahl argues that Paul, as someone steeped in the Jewish understanding of the OT, had concluded that Jesus was the τὸ σπέρμα ᾧ ἐπήγγελται (Gal 3:19b, NA27). Dahl ties the Abrahamic covenant and Abraham's seed in Genesis 12:7 (to Jesus) and connects Genesis 49:10 to 2 Samuel 7:12. The claim is that Paul is using a form of rabbinic exegesis that involves inference by analogy, whereby the promise related to "your offspring" made to Abraham (Gen 12:7) and to David (2 Sam 7:12) are fulfilled by one and the same person—Jesus. Dahl further argues that Paul employs a free exegesis of Genesis 49:10 with its reference to שׁילה as designating an individual according to birthright. This individual is the offspring "to whom the promise had been made" (Gal 3:19b). Three promises (Gen 12:7; 49:10; 2 Sam 7:12) are fulfilled in one offspring—Jesus. Dahl, *Studies in Paul*, 130–31. Cf. Whitsett, "Son of God, Seed of David," 667.

a king is seated, he rightfully should be from the tribe of Judah. These assertions align well with the criteria for justifying historical descriptions established in chapter 1.[41]

Plausible Historical-Evidential Conclusions Related to Genesis 49:10

1. Presupposing a monarchial insertion into the Patriarchal narrative, Genesis 49:10 is intended to denote the perpetual ascendancy of the tribe of Judah as the bearer of the ruler's scepter.
2. Presupposing a monarchial insertion into the Patriarchal narrative, the intent of the author/redactor affirms permanent rule for Judah.
3. Presupposing a monarchial and later (Genesis 49:1b) insertion into the Patriarchal narrative, the passage reflects the prophetic eschatological expectation of a Davidic king and permanent rule over the kingdom.
4. Presupposing that Genesis 49:10 is part of the original narrative, it is intended to denote the ascendancy and rulership of the tribe of Judah and permanent rule over the kingdom.
5. Presupposing that Genesis 49:10 is part of the original narrative, it was imbued with increasingly specific eschatological messianic import subsequent to the original writing.

Historical-Evidential Facts Related to Genesis 49:10[42]

1. No *terminus ad quem* for the advent of the Messiah can be established from Genesis 49:10.

Psalm 118

Literary and Textual Analysis

The NT writers regularly explain parts of the ministry and life of Jesus by referencing Psalm 118. Leslie Allen communicates this observation in a slightly different but informative way. Psalm 118 is used by the NT writers

---

41. McCullagh, *Justifying Historical Descriptions*, 19. See "Overview of Methodology" in chapter 1 for the full description of the criteria.

42. These facts and those presented throughout the remainder of the paper should not be confused with the *minimal facts* (defined in chapter 1) presented in chapter 8.

to "exegete the work of Jesus in theological terms, in connection with both the royal manifestation of the triumphal entry and the great twin themes of Christ's humiliation and exaltation."[43] When the claims and life of Jesus are read back into Psalm 118, as the four evangelists did, the Psalm reflects: (1) their understanding of Jesus' relationship to Israel; (2) Israel's institutions, such as the temple; and (3) the eschatological themes of salvation, healing, and righteousness. All four evangelists use either verse 25, 26, or both in their Triumphal Entry narrative (Matt 21:9; Mark 11:9; Luke 19:38; John 12:13).

Allen contends that Psalm 118 is a thanksgiving song offered in a "festival procession that is on its way to the 'portal of *Yahweh.*'"[44] In this processional context, Jesus enters Jerusalem in a manner consistent with intentionally acting out the messianic promise associated with Zechariah 9:9. It is probable that Jesus deliberately acts out the prophecy by riding on the foal of a donkey; it is also probable that the writers of the synoptic texts organized their material to highlight messianic functions accomplished by Jesus. Darrell Bock describes one aspect of this organizational emphasis in light of Psalm 118, noting its placement between two other symbolic events. Just prior to the Triumphal Entry is the healing of Bartimaeus, and immediately subsequent to it is the cleansing of the temple. These events, according to Bock, are best understood as both prophetic fulfillments and eschatological messianic signs; signs possibly invoking thoughts of *Shemoneh Esreh* (specifically benediction 14) among the recipients.[45]

There is little doubt that prophecy related to the riding of a donkey and cleansing of the temple are specifically staged as fulfillments of prophecy, but those fulfillments are not at issue. The issue is whether Psalm 118 indicates that the Messiah must enter the second or rebuilt temple. If this is the case, it is reasonable to conclude that this must have preceded the destruction of said temple in AD 70. It is, after all, impossible to enter a non-existent temple.

Prior to the first century and the events transmitted in the NT accounts, the overall significance of Psalm 118 was certainly understood in relation to a specific individual,[46] possibly a king,[47] leading the participants in the ascent to the temple. John J. Collins affirms the kingly identity of

---

43. Allen, *Psalms 101–150*, 168.

44. Kraus, *Psalms 60–150*, 395.

45. Bock, "Identity of Jesus as the Christ," 451.

46. Gunkel, *Introduction to the Psalms*, 199.

47. Allen, *Psalms 101–150*, 164. Allen cites Dahood as holding the position that a king is in view.

the individual based on the "nations" of verse 10 being set in opposition to the celebrant.[48] Psalm 118 is part of the "gate liturgies" that include Psalms 15 and 18, both ostensibly authored by David the king. If the individual is a king, he is symbolically leading the nation as a whole. The liturgy is clearly a communal event, and part of it may have been sung antiphonally or perhaps even with multiple individual parts. The Babylonian Talmud confirms this probability:

> He said, "[I learned this] from what I saw the great rabbis do. When reciting in public [the Hallel on a festival or the new moon], one [group] recited, 'Blessed is he that comes,' and another [group] answered, 'In the name of the Lord'" [Ps. 118:26].[49]

In the Psalmist's historical context, the notion is plausible that the stone the builders rejected may be national Israel or, more likely, the king as representative of Israel (see below, within this section).[50] However, a third and more contextually suitable option exists. Gregory R. Lanier has argued convincingly that the stone is best understood in relationship to the stone metaphor as it is consistently applied in the OT. Lanier's research indicates that the stone metaphor contains a "two-fold significance: for some it is a stone of strength or upbuilding; for others, it is a stone of stumbling."[51] The metaphor, according to Lanier, first appears in Deuteronomy 32:4, 37 in relation to *Yahweh* as the true God against false gods. In one verse, Isaiah 8:14 presents a prime example of the two-fold aspect of the stone metaphor. If Israel will fear *Yahweh*, he will be a sanctuary; if not, he will become a stone of stumbling: a trap and snare.

Isaiah 28:16–17 is even more striking in that it employs construction language related to true and plumb structures in combination with the stone metaphor closely related to Psalm 118. Once again, *Yahweh* is the one laying the stone (a corner stone) pictured in contrast to a covenant made with Egypt. The implication in this passage is that those who express trust in him by obedience are secure, while those trusting in Egypt will be destroyed. Further, Lanier notes two key pieces of evidence that personify the stone in Isaiah 28:16. First, the Aramaic Targum replaces the crucial

---

48. Collins, *Scepter and the Star*, 155.

49. Neusner, *Babylonian Talmud*, y. Ber. 8:8, I.2.G.

50. Bratcher and Reyburn, *Translator's Handbook on the Book of Psalms*, 993. Bratcher and Reyburn think the reference to the rejected stone is a proverbial saying applied to the nearly defeated king or to the insignificance of Israel when compared to world empires. In either case, the image is of rejection, defeat, and near death with a sudden reversal of fortune because of *Yahweh*'s intervention.

51. Lanier, "Rejected Stone in the Parable of the Wicked Tenants," 746.

word *stone* with *king*; second, most codices of the LXX include the dative pronoun *in him* (αὐτῷ) in reference to the stone.[52]

The trajectory of the stone metaphor in exilic and post-exilic literature shifts from an emphasis on Israel's unbelief to its eschatological deliverance, to a messianic kingly image.[53] Philip E. Satterthwaite, Richard S. Hess, and Gordon J. Wenham confirm that the cornerstone image from Isaiah 28:16 and the "tent peg" image from Isaiah 22:20–23 have strong royal associations and are translated as "king and messiah" respectively in the Aramaic Targum.[54] Lanier concludes his essay by identifying the stone as originally meaning *Yahweh*, but later identified a messianic kingly figure. This kingly figure fulfills one of two functions: either building up the faithful or crushing unbelievers. Both functions apply to Jew and Gentile alike.[55]

The cogent point to be grasped from Lanier's work is that the conceptually interconnected images of *Yahweh*, his Davidic king, and the Messiah in relation to the stone metaphor are no late accretion or invention of the NT writers. The stone has a history as long as the canon itself and is consistently presented as both a source of refuge for the faithful, and a source of destruction for the unbelieving—all of which depends on the faithfulness of *Yahweh*.

Interpreting the stone in Psalm 118 as the nation of Israel while isolating this occurrence of the metaphor from other OT uses inflicts little damage to the current study.[56] From the nation comes the Davidic king, and from the Davidic line comes the Messiah. In this case, the stone metaphor could only be applied to the faithful of Israel and would still require the faithfulness of *Yahweh*. Another similar approach that nets little dam-

---

52. Lanier, "Rejected Stone in the Parable of the Wicked Tenants," 747. Cf. Isaiah 31:9; 51:1.

53. Other significant uses of the stone metaphor that Lanier includes are: Zechariah 3:9, where the stone bears an inscription relating to forgiveness of Israel's sin; Zechariah 4:7, where the stone very quickly reappears as the headstone for the rebuilding of the future temple; and again in Zechariah 12:3 as a heavy stone against which the nations of the earth will gather. Daniel 2:34 portrays a stone cut out by no human hand that destroys the nations.

In the Qumran literature, Isaiah 28:16 is referenced in relation to the Qumran community and as the stone. The "tested rampart, the precious cornerstone whose foundations do not shake or tremble [from] their [place]," with the apparent implication that the foundation stone does not shake or tremble, but is a "most holy dwelling." Martínez and Tigchelaar, *Dead Sea Scrolls Study Edition (Translations)*, 89.

54. Satterthwaite et al., *Lord's Anointed Interpretation of Old Testament Messianic Texts*, 271–72.

55. Lanier, "Rejected Stone in the Parable of the Wicked Tenants," 748.

56. The attribution of the stone metaphor as a reference to Israel in Psalm 118 is common. Hossfeld and Zenger, *Commentary on Psalms 101–150*, 232.

age to the current argument is that located in the Aramaic Psalter. This text prefers to understand the stone that the builders reject as the "lad" David.[57] If this conception is accurate, the most that could be said of the original meaning in relation to the alleged NT fulfillment is that in contains some typological significance.

The stone metaphor notwithstanding, the objective of this portion of the study is to determine if the implied but unnamed celebrant is the Messiah and, if so, whether he must enter the second temple. The conclusions drawn from Lanier's work assure that the messianic implication was early. Given an exilic or post-exilic date for Psalm 118, the messianic implication may have been part of the original conception. Allen confirms at the least a gradual messianic recognition of this psalm. He believes it is placed at the beginning of Book V in the Psalter because of its gradual imbuement with messianic import. This arrangement occurred in the pre-Christian era perhaps as early as Ezra, but certainly no later than the translation of the LXX.[58]

Scholars such as Frank-Lothar Hossfeld and Erich Zenger argue that the psalm contained eschatological (and not necessarily messianic) motifs from its origin. These commentators observe that the motif of rescue by *Yahweh* is a major theme of the psalm, with direct quotations from Exodus 15 and textual ties to Isaiah 12. They note "striking commonalities" with the thanksgiving song in Isaiah 12:1–6, which closes the composition in Isaiah 1–12. These commonalities are especially visible in Psalm 118:14/Isaiah 12:2 and Psalm 118:21/Isaiah 12:1–2. These commonalities, then, further relate to the theme of rescue from Exodus 15:2 with connection to Isaiah 12:2b.[59] The importance of this observation is heightened when the processional images and worship encapsulated in this psalm are understood as spanning the period from the exodus from Egypt to the eschatological restoration or second exodus. Hossfeld and Zenger argue that the procession toward the temple is:

> Imagined in such a way that this event is tied into the history of YHWH with his people Israel—and indeed with the whole world of the nations—and placed within a time horizon extending from Israel's beginnings to the completion of its history. This powerful spatial and temporal horizon in the psalm is constituted primarily by intertextual links to the book of Exodus (the past) and the book of Isaiah (the future).[60]

---

57. Evans, "Aramaic Psalmer and the New Testament," 82–83.
58. Young, *Introduction to the Old Testament*, 306.
59. Hossfeld and Zenger, 235. These authors highlight several other links to Isaiah.
60. Hossfeld and Zenger, 234. Hossfeld and Zenger also note the striking parallels

There is little doubt that Psalm 118 contains a combination of poetry and liturgy set in a cultic celebration with the temple as its center. This does not mean, however, that the historicity of any specific event or king can be established. Conceptually, the central message of Psalm 118 is eschatological deliverance. The petitioner depicted in the Psalm may be the reigning king, but just as easily could be an individual expressing thanksgiving for some type of deliverance.

Critical scholars suggest that the text of the Psalm is the result of a post-exilic author/redactor. John Day confirms this probability, observing that the present form of the psalm refers to the "'house of Aaron' which makes best sense as a reference to the post-exilic priests, who were known as 'the sons of Aaron' (in the pre-exilic era the priests were the Levites)."[61] If this dating is accurate, for the present form of the psalm, there was no temporal king on the throne and the second temple (house of *Yahweh*) is the setting. The historical period proposed for the composition of the psalm is during the construction and dedication of the rebuilt temple (520–515 BC). Dating the composition of the psalm to this period, or even to time of the Maccabees, renders any other possibility moot. The psalmist is depicting a procession with strong eschatological overtones led by an individual (possibly a king) who enters the temple and participates in the salvation and blessing of Israel by *Yahweh*.[62] Only two plausible alternatives from the second temple setting exist. First, one might appeal to the poetic genres of Psalms, thereby relegating the "house of the LORD" setting to the status of a lyrical prop rather than the location of a real event. This possibility seems unlikely. Second, one might posit the original form of the psalm as pre-exilic and David or another *davidid* are in view. This makes any direct correlation of the Psalm with the Messiah highly unlikely and direct fulfillment by Jesus impossible.

---

between Psalm 116 and 118: "(a) Crisis as 'distress/constriction': 116:3; 118:5; (b) Power of the name of YHWH: 116:4, 13, 17; 118:10–12, 26; (c)YHWH's intervention as 'rescue/salvation': 116:6, 13; 118:14, 15, 21, 25; (d) 'Thanking'(ritual thanksgiving): 116:17; 118:1, 19, 21, 28, 29; (e) Mortal threat/rescue from death/return to life: 116:3–4, 7–9, 15; 118:17–18; (f) Cry for help: 'O YHWH!': 116:4, 16; 118:25'" (244). If the Jewish people generally recognized these motifs, it is clear why the disciples, writing after the fact, quoted Psalm 118 in reference to the Triumphal Entry.

61. Day, *Psalms*, 106.

62. Herman Gunkel affirms several verses of Psalm 118 as part of the smaller genres of "blessings." Gunkel, *Introduction to the Psalms*, 222–35.

Intertestamental and Extra-Biblical Literature

References to Psalm 118 in the intertestamental literature are limited in the extreme. Fragmentary mention of Psalm 118:20 and 27 is found in Q173a 1, 3, from which nothing of value can be gleaned. The OT pseudepigraphal text of the Psalms of Solomon 23:4 mentions Psalm 118:22 in the context of a nonsensical account about the building of Solomon's temple. This text also renders nothing of value for the current study.

Other evidence from post-biblical Judaism sporadically surfaces in Talmudic texts such as y. Meg 2:1, I.2.H, I, and J. In these verses, Psalm 116; 118:27, 28 are interpreted as speaking of the Messiah, Gog and Magog, and the age to come, respectively.[63] These texts confirm that at least some Jewish rabbis' considered the psalm to contain eschatological and messianic elements:

> [I] "I love the Lord, because he has heard my voice and my supplications" (Ps. 116)—this refers to the days of the Messiah.
>
> [J] "Bind the festal procession with branches" [Ps. 118:27], [refers to the future events of] the age of Gog and Magog. [The word "Bind" is an allusion to the time following the festival. Bind over or hold over the festival to celebrate it in the future.]
>
> [K] "Thou art my God and I will give thanks" [Ps. 118:28], [the use of the future tense refers to] the future age [after the messianic conflict and triumph].[64]

These texts neither provide support for any conclusive historical understanding of Psalm 118 nor do they demonstrate any reliable counter-evidence for an alternative interpretation.

New Testament Evidence

As noted earlier, all four evangelists narrate their version of the Triumphal Entry (Matt 21:1–17; Mark 11:1–11; Luke 19:28–48; John 12:12–15). John calls Jesus the "King of Israel," Matthew identifies Jesus as the "son of David," and Luke uses the phrase, "The King who comes in the name of the Lord!" Mark provides two key statements: the attribution that Jesus has come in the name of the Lord and that he is the representative of

---

63. Cf. y. Ber. 2:4, II.1.I–K. Strack and Billerbeck affirm much the same thing. See Strack and Billerbeck, *Kommentar zum Neuen Testament*, 1:847.

64. Neusner, *Jerusalem Talmud*. Cf. y. Meg. 2:1, I.2.J. This messianic import is also detected by the authors of the NT (Acts 4:11; Eph 2:20–21; Heb 13:6; 1 Pet 2:4–8)

the kingdom of David (Mark 11:9–10). The phrase, "Blessed is he who comes in the name of the Lord" (Mark 11:10), according to R. T. France, is the conceptual focus of all four of the Triumphal Entry accounts.[65] France also notes that all of the evangelists—except Luke—record the cry "Hosanna."[66] During this event, the people of Jerusalem are depicted as openly attributing messianic status to Jesus: more importantly, Jesus in no way discourages the acclamation of the crowd during the procession. Mowinckel admits as "fact" that Psalm 118:25ff was interpreted messianically by this time[67] and that prayers in the psalms related to the restoration of Israel may generally be assumed to have included prayer for the coming of the Messiah.[68] These same NT texts give reason to believe the procession included the traditional lining of the way with green branches, meant to give special royal significance to the procession.[69]

Three streams of thought by critical scholars also affirm the historicity of the basic story line of the Triumphal Entry and cleansing of the Temple. The first is provided by Bart Ehrman. Ehrman, dealing with this specific issue, believes that either immediately after his entry into Jerusalem or the next day, Jesus entered the city and engaged in the symbolic action of cleansing the temple. He calls this event a "mild ruckus."[70] Ehrman is skeptical of the overall historicity of the gospel narratives with respect to Jesus' entry into the city and the fanfare that would have required his immediate arrest. However, he does admit a historical basis for the events, predicated on multiple attestation (Mark and John). In fact, Ehrman concedes that Jesus probably did come to Jerusalem for the Passover celebration and may have entered the city on a donkey. He describes the incident in the temple as "exaggerated" but also acknowledges that the event's historicity is "almost certain."[71] Presenting a second stream of thought, E. P. Sanders allows for the historicity of Jesus' entry into Jerusalem on a donkey (although, like Ehrman, he is not able to explain why Jesus was not immediately arrested) and his symbolic action of cleansing the temple.[72] Finally, more than two-thirds

---

65. France, *Gospel of Matthew*, 779–80.

66. France, *Gospel of Matthew*, 779–80.

67. Mowinckel, *He that Cometh*, 468. Cf. Strack and Billerbeck, *Kommentar zum Neuen Testament*, 1:849–876; 2:256; and 3.

68. Mowinckel, *He that Cometh*, 341.

69. France, *Gospel of Matthew*, 779.

70. Ehrman, *Jesus*, 208.

71. Ehrman, *Jesus*, 212.

72. Sanders, *Historical Figure of Jesus*, 252–54.

of the fellows of the Jesus Seminar answered affirmatively to both of the following questions:

1. Did Jesus perform some anti-temple act?
2. Did Jesus speak against the temple?[73]

The likelihood that Jesus intentionally did these things is functionally beyond dispute.

Jesus acted against the existing temple and then, in the Parable of the Tenants (Matt 21:33–43pp), interprets the stone as the vineyard owner's son. N.T. Wright observes that the Aramaic word for *stone* as it appears in Daniel 2 is *eben* and is perhaps a pun on the normal Hebrew word *ben* (e.g., 2 Samuel 7). Wright contends that Jesus intentionally links the stone metaphor to the new eschatological temple (the people of *Yahweh*). He admits that he is not aware of any specific attribution of Psalm 118:22–23 to the new eschatological temple/people of *Yahweh*. Even so, "Jesus' own varied use of scriptural rock/stone imagery in relation to the building of the new Temple, interpreted apparently as the new community of the people of YHWH, makes it quite likely that this was his intention here as well."[74] These findings confirm much of the previously reported OT research and result in the following conclusions: (1) Jesus did enter the second temple, (2) no other temple or messianic candidate fitting the processional image of Psalm 118 exists, (3) Jesus considered himself to be the stone and directly related to the vineyard owner (*Yahweh*).

Summary

In summary, it is virtually certain that Jesus intentionally acted out the fulfillments associated with Zechariah 9:9 and the processional entry into the temple and its symbolic cleansing. It is also likely that he intentionally invoked messianic images of the *son of David* and the eschatological restoration of Zion present in Psalm 118. Wright captures this thought with clarity when he writes, "Someone doing what Jesus did was indicating that Israel's history had reached the point of decisive destruction and rebuilding, and that his own actions were embodying that moment."[75] The temple is the central feature appearing in this decisive moment; neither the OT context nor the NT utilization of Psalm 118 allows for the dismissal of the

---

73. Funk and Hoover, *Five Gospels*, 97–98.
74. Wright, *Jesus and the Victory of God*, 499.
75. Wright, *Jesus and the Victory of God*, 492.

temple structure as inconsequential, and yet, certainty about the specific temple is allusive.

The evidence indicates a possibility that Israel's eschatological King/Messiah is depicted as entering a Jewish temple in a festal procession in Psalm 118 with the consequence that a fundamental reformation of the structure takes place. The rejected stone (the faithfulness of *Yahweh*) is reset (same stone personified) as the Messiah/cornerstone, where the faithful of *Yahweh* have always found refuge. This conclusion is supported by multiple OT texts referencing the stone metaphor (above), extra-biblical literature (above), and also attested by the NT in the narratives.[76] The temple that these actions were directed toward was most likely the same temple that either existed or was under construction during the composition of Psalm 118. No other temple has existed since its destruction in AD 70. Nevertheless, it is uncertain as to whether the Psalmist envisioned the temple built by Solomon, the rebuilt second Temple, or a fundamentally altered eschatological counterpart of some form. In addition, there is no historical-evidential way to demonstrate that the celebrant of the psalm or the stone metaphor, as it appears in verse 22, directly and exclusively identifies with the Messiah. Anyone attempting to make such a claim bears the burden of proof and that proof is wanting.

Plausible Historical-Evidential Conclusions Drawn from the Study of Psalm 118

1. The temple existing during the composition of Psalm 118 was probably the rebuilt temple.
2. It is probable that Psalm 118 originally included eschatological elements.
3. Jesus intentionally invoked the processional images related to Psalm 118.
4. The temple (*house of Yahweh*) in Psalm 118 is the central cultic feature.
5. An extant temple is not necessary to the central meaning of Psalm 118; the temple may be incidental to the cultic setting.

---

76. For example: the Triumphal Entry (Matt 21:1–11), the cleansing of the Temple (Matt 21:12–17), and the Parable of the Tenants (Matt 21:33–43).

PART II: EXEGESIS ANALYSIS AND SYNTHESIS

Historical-Evidential Facts Drawn from the Study of Psalm 118

1. No *terminus ad quem* for the advent of the Messiah can be established from Psalm 118.

2. The rebuilt temple is the one Jesus entered, then spoke and acted against.

3. No other temple (*house of Yahweh*) exists.

4. The Triumphal Entry and Jesus' entry into the temple have multiple NT attestations.

Haggai 2:1–9

Literary and Textual Analysis

Old Testament Evidence

The text of Haggai 2:1–9 has a long interpretive history within Christian thought. If this text is isolated from its Jewish contextual origins, the reader might believe its connotations have always been interpreted messianically. Conversely, Jewish as well as many non-Jewish modern interpreters understand the key word חמדת (ḥemdat) (Hag 2:7) as a metonym, impersonally referring to the wealth of the nations that the Lord will cause to flow into the rebuilt temple. These interpreters also argue that כבוד (kābōwd) is the resplendence of the temple from the acquisition of this material wealth. This resplendence will make the glory of the latter temple greater than that of Solomon's.

The core exegetical issues in the subject text center on how to understand three terms laden with ambiguity. First, the reference to "this house" (את־הבית הזה) appears three times in the first nine verses of chapter 2. Second, the interpreter must determine what is intended by the term "treasures" or "desired one" (חמדת)? Third, the interpreter must also determine what "glory" (כבוד) means in each of its three near occurrences.

Treating the term "this house" (Hag 2:3) begins with the observation that the splendor of the first temple in terms of tangible wealth far exceeded the initial splendor of the second temple. This much seems certain. The second temple's decor was not initially impressive, even though its latter state will be greater than its beginnings. This straightforward reading of the text seems difficult to escape. It is not problem-free, however. The former glory of "this house" is obviously a reference to Solomon's temple. This means no less than two structures are in view. Another problem with simply assuming that the latter glory of "this house" means the second temple lies in the apocalyptic tone and vocabulary used in the passage. The eschatological nature of the prophecy is evident; Meyers and Meyers affirm that it envisions a time when Jerusalem is more than the capital of Yehud (as it was then). They infer that the scope of the prophecy entails a time when Jerusalem is the capital of the nations and riches flow into it.[77]

Ray Taylor and E. Ray Clendenen attempt to provide clarity on the meaning of "this house" by contending that Haggai 2:9 refers to only one temple: "The Hebrew reads literally, 'Great will be the glory of this house the latter.'"[78] Their analysis places the modifying adjective *latter* as attached to *glory* rather than *house*, based on the Hebrew world order. This makes the proper reading "the latter glory of this house." Taylor and Clendenen argue that this understanding is confirmed by Haggai 2:3, which speaks of "this house in its former glory."[79] It seems the rebuilt temple and the former temple are held to be distinct in glory, but not distinct as the cultic center of Israel and the house of *Yahweh*, even though they are two different structures. If this same approach is applied to the former and latter glory, "this house" may be yet another structure (worship center) with greater glory.

The textual-historical ground for understanding *treasures* (חמדת) in a personal messianic sense is largely based on the perception that Jerome properly translated the reading of the Masoretic Text as "*et veniet Desideratus cunctis gentibus.*" The same thought is reflected in the Authorized Version "and the desire of all nations shall come" (Hag 2:7a). This interpretation sees correspondence between Haggai 2:21b–23 and 2:6–7. This understanding is doubtful for at least two reasons. The basis for Haggai's exhortation is to motivate the constructors of the new temple. Their sparse resources and the meager appointments available for the rebuilt temple tempted them to compare the state of the new temple negatively to the splendor of the first. The disparity between the two temples, as Haggai speaks, is visually obvious to his listeners. Second, the term חמדת is used sixteen times in the OT and is translated in four distinct ways:

1. As *treasure* or *wealth* in a material sense on seven occasions (2 Chr 32:27; 36:10; Jer 25:34; Ezek 26:12; Dan 11:8; Hos 13:15; Hag 3:7).

2. As *desire*, as a personal statement of feelings, on four occasions (1 Sam 9:20; Isa 2:16; Dan 11:37; Nah 2:6).

---

77. Meyers and Meyers, *Haggia, Zechariah 1–8*, 54.
78. Taylor and Clendenen, *Haggai, Malachi*, 167.
79. Taylor and Clendenen, *Haggai, Malachi*, 167.

3. As *pleasant*, in the sense of fruitful, on four occasions (Ps 106:24; Jer 3:19; 12:10; Zech 7:14).

4. As *regret*, in the sense of an absence of sorrow, on one occasion (2 Chr 21:20).[80]

This term never means Messiah. *Treasure* not only makes the best sense in context, but it agrees with the majority of uses in the OT.

The term *glory* (כבוד) is more complex because it appears three times in close proximity (verses 3, 7, and 9) in this prophecy and may denote more than one thing. The former כבוד may not mean the same as to fill the house with כבוד which, in turn, may not mean the same as the latter כבוד of this house being greater than the former. This term, translated as *glory*, appears approximately 200 times in the OT and is understood in the following nine senses:

1. As a state of *high honor* on ninety-six occasions.
2. As reflective of the *presence of God* on forty-seven occasions.
3. As something being in a highly honored or *revered state* on thirty occasions.
4. As a *manifestation of power* on eight occasions.
5. As *personal glory* on six occasions.
6. As *wealth* on five occasions.
7. As the quality of *being honorable* on three occasions.
8. As *God* as the personification of glory on two occasions.
9. As a member of the *ruling class* in a city or town on one occasion.[81]

The lexical data demonstrates that the semantic range of the term translated as "glory" overlaps, making absolute claims of its meaning impossible. Verse 3 makes the best sense if *glory* is defined in the context of material wealth.[82] Conversely, "fill this house with glory" (Hag 2:7) makes the best sense if it includes the visual phenomena associated with the presence of *Yahweh*. Alfred Edersheim remarks, about the obvious absence of the ark of the covenant, the tables of the law, the book of the covenant, Aaron's rod that budded, and the pot of manna. Also missing were the fire from heaven and the visible Shekhinah of *Yahweh*.[83] Wright cogently

---

80. Logos Bible Software produced the word study of חמדת.
81. Logos Bible Software produced the word study of כבוד.
82. Wolff, *Hosea*, 78–81.
83. Edersheim, *Temple*, 61–62.

notes: "The geographical return from exile, when it came about under Cyrus and his successors, was not accompanied by any manifestations such as those in Exodus 40, Leviticus 9, 1 Kings 8, or even (a revelation to an individual) Isaiah 6."[84] Including the visual phenomena does not mean divorcing material wealth from the context; these are not mutually exclusive concepts. The mention of silver and gold immediately after כבוד confirms that something like this approach is most probably the correct interpretation. In verse 9, the former and latter glory again must, at least in part, be a reference to material splendor. However, if the latter glory exceeds the former in every way, it is very difficult to exclude some type of recognizable divine presence from the meaning.

The prophecy may be contrasting the glory of Solomon's temple with the rebuilt temple, and then the initial state of the rebuilt temple with its finished state. Alternatively, verse 9 may be making some vague prophetic reference to an eschatological temple. In either case, it is virtually certain that the phrase "fill this house with glory" demands the presence of some recognizable supernatural phenomena and great material wealth.

Intertestamental and Extra-Biblical Evidence

The Babylonian Talmud takes two different approaches to interpreting Haggai 2:7. It does this by first claiming that the second temple was greater in size, and second, by claiming it stood longer than the first temple.[85] The Jewish historian Josephus approaches the issue from another angle by mentioning Herod the Great's expenditures and embellishment of the temple: "He laid out larger sums of money upon them than had been done before him, till it seemed that no one else had so greatly adorned the temple as he had done."[86] Tim Shenton nuances his understanding of this text in a slightly different manner:

> "And I will fill this house with glory." This is not a reference to Christ's physical presence in the temple (cf. Matt 21:12–14); nor is it a picture of the splendour of Herod's renovated temple or the Shekinah glory of God. Rather, it points to the treasures of foreign nations that would be brought to God's temple, thus making it materially glorious.[87]

---

84. Wright, *Jesus and the Victory of God*, 621.
85. Neusner, *Babylonian Talmud*, b. Bat. 1:1, III.5.C-6.C. y. Meg. 1:12, I.11.R.
86. Josephus and Whiston, "Antiquities of the Jews," 396.
87. Shenton, *Haggai*, 50.

Shenton's approach implies that the text is describing the eschatological rule of *Yahweh;* his rule entails the monarchy of Israel and the collection of tribute from the nations. This line of reasoning parallels the interpretation offered by Caroll Meyers and Eric Meyers. They note the "universalistic dimension"[88] to Haggai's prophecy and the collection of tribute, but hold that filling the house with glory signifies the immanence and resplendence of God in the temple.

Running contrary to the modern critical interpretation of the text, some historical evidence exists that demonstrates an early Jewish understanding of Haggai 2:7 and 2:9 that included a messianic stream of thought. In the Testament of Benjamin (second century BC), the writer affirms that the latter temple will exceed the first in glory, adding that: "The twelve tribes shall be gathered there and all the nations, until such time as the Most High shall send forth his salvation through the ministration of the unique prophet."[89] The text immediately ensuing includes references to the "Lord being raised up on wood . . . being abused . . . the temple curtain shall be torn . . . ascending from Hades." These additional comments are surely later Christian interpolations, but, as H. C. Kee notes, a genuinely predictive element may have existed in the original text. The expectation of an eschatological prophet is not unique to the Testament of Benjamin, a concept built on Deuteronomy 18:15. This same eschatological idea was prominent in the writings of the community at Qumran (1QS IX 10–11; 1QSa II 11–12). The prophet is mentioned in 4QTestimonia I 5–8 and in what appears to be a reference to the star in Balaam's oracle from Numbers 24 and also referenced Acts 7:37. One who is the star, scepter, and prince interprets the Law according to CD-A VII 15–20.[90]

The author of 2 Baruch 32:1–4, writing from a thoroughly Jewish and messianic perspective, seems to defer the greater "glory" of the temple to the eschatological future. This text may or may not be alluding to Haggai 2:7 and 2:9, but it appears that the author was familiar with both the prophecy and the expectation of the Jewish people. Wright explains that the Jewish people had the genuine expectation and desire that *Yahweh* would return to Zion. From their own historical stories, the people of the second temple period would have known about the glory of *Yahweh* and what his presence meant for them. Even so, Wright observes the following:

> Never do we hear that the pillar of cloud and fire which accompanied the Israelites in the wilderness has led the people back

---

88. Meyers and Meyers, *Haggia, Zechariah 1–8*, 54.
89. Kee, "Testament of the Twelve Patriarchs," 827. T. Benj 829, 822.
90. Kee, "Testament of the Twelve Patriarchs," 827nc.

from their exile. At no point do we hear that *YHWH* has now gloriously returned to Zion. At no point is the house again filled with the cloud which veils his glory. At no point is the rebuilt Temple universally hailed as the true restored shrine spoken of by Ezekiel. Significantly, at no point, either, is there a final decisive victory over Israel's enemies, or the establishment of a universally welcomed royal dynasty.[91]

Wright goes on to explain that it should be no surprise, then, to see the hope of "glory" continued as a theme in the post-biblical writings. The predicted return of *Yahweh* and the accompanying glory is still awaited.[92] These obvious ocular absences lend credence to the interpretation that sees the glory and wealth of the nations as recognizable features of a future manifestation of *Yahweh* (Rev 21:24).

From both a Jewish and a Christian perspective, Michael Brown challenges non-messianic interpretations: "'to fill with glory' refers to the manifest presence of God and not to physical splendor . . . 'to fill with glory' always refers to the divine manifestation in the Bible."[93] Although material splendor cannot be excluded from the context, several OT passages clearly illustrate the concept of the glory of God and the filling of the temple or tabernacle (Exod 40:34; 2 Chr 5:14; 7:1–4; Ezek 43:5; 44:4). Given the repeated image in which the presence of God and visible phenomena are associated with His glory, completely eliminating this as a concomitant meaning for the text is unjustifiable.

M. Brown also takes stock of the Talmudic citations (above) and the disagreement among the ancient Jewish sages as to the meaning. In summary, he labels their arguments "weak" and refuted by opponents of Christianity:

> If the promise was merely one of physical glory and splendor—which, as we have noted, falls far short of the description of being filled with God's glory—why then is an additional promise offered in Haggai 2:9, namely, that in the Second Temple God would appoint peace?[94]

---

91. Wright, *Jesus and the Victory of God*, 621.

92. Wright, *Jesus and the Victory of God*, 621–22.

93. Brown, *Answering Jewish Objections to Jesus*, 3:146.

94. Brown, *Answering Jewish Objections to Jesus*, 3:147. Citing *Batei Midrashot* 2, 24:11, Brown lists five things missing from the Second Temple that must return to the final temple based on their exegesis of Haggai 2: "The fire of the Shekhinah, the ark, the kapporet and cherubim, the Holy Spirit, and the Urim and Thummim" (Brown, *Answering Jewish Objections to Jesus*, 3:148n300).

Based on these brief representations offered by historical documents and modern scholars, it seems impossible to allow an interpretation of the passage that does not include some form of eschatology, material splendor, and the visible presence of *Yahweh*. The personal presence of *Yahweh* and His glory may or may not include the presence of the Messiah, but the text does not make the presence of the Messiah a necessity.

New Testament Evidence

As established above, the historicity of Jesus' entry into Jerusalem and the temple is certain. Some Christian interpreters have identified his presence in the temple as fulfilling the prophecy of Haggai.[95] Recognizing the ambiguities of the terms discussed above, others contend for a view involving multiple temples.[96] The biblical historical-evidential data confidently portrays Jesus as symbolically declaring himself as the Messiah and King of Israel by his manner of entry into Jerusalem and the temple. Despite this historical evidence, it is difficult to assert dogmatically that his presence constitutes *Yahweh*'s promise to "fill this house with glory." Was Jesus' physical presence, even granting his divinity, more glorious than the divine presence in Solomon's temple? This certainly cannot be the case if the divine glory requires visible theophanic phenomena. That his presence added glory, making the latter glory of the rebuilt temple greater than its former, could be granted, if that is Haggai's intent.

The day of Pentecost is another pressing aspect to consider in relation to the phrase, "fill this house with glory," and its theophanic implication of God's manifest presence. The argumentation regarding Haggai 2:1–9 has thus far demonstrated that the latter glory of the temple cannot be pressed into forcing a delimitation on the time for the Messiah's coming. If Haggai were intentionally speaking in prophetically ambiguous terms, *glory* could have implications for the phenomena witnessed on Pentecost morning. Taking the description offered in Acts 2 as historical,[97] the visible tongues of fire

---

95. Meldau, *Prophets Still Speak*, 10. Brown, *Answering Jewish Objections to Jesus*, 3:148.

96. Walvoord, *Every Prophecy of the Bible*, 315.

97. Hans Conzelmann contends that Luke's Pentecost narrative is the result of two (or even more) sources, which have been combined. It is possible that these sources included accounts of "mass ecstasy" or the "original substratum" may have included "miraculous speech in many languages." Conzelmann asserts that the basis for the account "is clearly not a naive legend." Conzelmann, *Acts of the Apostles*, 15. In addition, Craig Keener comments on the historicity of the events described. See the next footnote.

and audible sound like mighty wind, in combination with tongues-speech and the other miraculous events, would fit the criteria of greater glory.

This supernatural event may have started either in the temple or in a private dwelling; the temple is the logical place for the overtly public manifestation within the hearing of the crowd.[98] Significantly, the theophanic activity on the day of Pentecost is said to have "filled the entire house" (Acts 2:2). Keener highlights the ambiguity of Luke's use of the term *house* and its reference to both private houses and the temple; the evidence is inconclusive.[99] Nevertheless, the appearance of phenomena such as fire, wind, and noise—combined with the ambiguity of the word *house*—creates a context more closely suited to the images of Haggai 2:1–9 than any other known possibility.[100]

In Christian theology, many believe that the day of Pentecost denotes the inauguration of that kingdom whose full and future glory is yet to be realized. This inaugural event is eschatological, and when considered in light of other biblical data, it signifies a reversal of human disunity, the new creation, and the full recognition of redeemed man as the temple of God.[101] Pentecost is both present and future; it is thoroughly eschatological and the most probable fulfillment of Haggai 2:1–9 available for consideration.[102]

---

98. Keener, *Acts*, 796. Keener also contends that the evidence for the initial gathering place of the believers is about evenly split between a room in the temple and a private house. Importantly, however, he highlights the fact that the only place large enough to accommodate 3,000 people for Peter's sermon is the area immediately around and in the courts of the temple. Keener addresses the historicity of the account by acknowledging that some scholars are skeptical about the event. Keener argues, however, that even though Acts is the only historical narrative of the early church, the pouring out of the Holy Spirit is mentioned by other NT writers (e.g., Rom 5:5; Tit 3:5–6) and in other settings within the book of Acts (Keener, *Acts*, 787).

99. Keener, *Acts*, 798–99.

100. At a minimum, the ἑτέραις γλώσσαις manifestations apparently continued as the Christian message spread across the Roman Empire. It is also possible that the peace (Hag 2:9) prophesied to come during the period of the second temple's latter glory was inaugurated by Jesus (Luke 1:79; 2:14; 19:42; Acts 10:36), but will find it eschatological fullness in a latter temple, just as the former glory referenced the first temple.

101. Pervo, *Acts*, 61–62.

102. The primary difficulty for allowing or insisting on a future eschatological temple such as that prophesied by Ezekiel is that unfulfilled prophecy cannot be evaluated evidentially. How these prophecies will be realized is uncertain. There may or may not be a literal eschatological temple filled with the treasures of the nations and the visible presence of *Yahweh*. Perhaps Ezekiel is speaking symbolically. If such a temple is built, it may or may not be as Ezekiel envisioned.

Summary

In summary, it is not possible to affirm that the latter glory prophesied by Haggai is a specific reference to the Messiah or in some way delimits his debut in Israel to the second temple period. Ample evidence supports the notion that after the renovation begun by Herod the Great (ca AD 19) was finished (ca AD 62), the material splendor of the temple had been greatly enhanced—perhaps even exceeding Solomon's. In addition, the inescapable association of the phrase "fill this house with glory" with visible theophanic phenomena makes the day of the Pentecost a stronger argument for fulfilling Haggai 2:1–9 than the mere physical presence of Jesus or even the Triumphal Entry. Finally, the first nine verses of Haggai 2 reflect a distinct eschatological apocalyptic tone. This fact makes the terminology "this house" ambiguous; one cannot dismiss the possibility of a double entendre or *sensus plenior* meaning that remains unrealized.

Plausible Historical-Evidential Conclusions Drawn from the Study of Haggai 2:1–9

1. After the renovation by Herod, the second temple possessed great material splendor.
2. The meaning of the phrase "this house" in the first nine verses of Haggai 2 is ambiguous.
3. The phrase "fill this house with glory" implies theophanic phenomena.
4. Luke describes theophanic phenomena associated with the day of Pentecost that meet the criteria of "fill this house with glory" if "house" (Acts 2:2) refers to the temple.[103]

Historical-Evidential Facts Drawn from the Study of Haggai 2:1–9

1. No *terminus ad quem* for the advent of the Messiah can be established from Haggai 2:1–9.

---

103. The objection that Haggai or Malachi (below) perceived continuity between the first, second, and a future or eschatological temple, such as that described in Ezekiel 40–48, is speculative. It cannot be demonstrated that either Haggai or Malachi understood that the rebuilt second-temple would be destroyed or that the temple described by Ezekiel was a literal future structure. The temple vision of Ezekiel may be an extended holiness and purity metaphor.

Malachi 3:1

Literary and Textual Analysis

The text of Malachi 3:1ff and the identity of its objects and referents generate controversy among biblical scholars. The key issue for the current work is whether the second temple or another temple was specifically in the mind of Malachi. A secondary issue is whether the historical-evidential findings point toward the identities of the characters in Malachi's prophecy. Christians sometimes interpret the reference to the temple in Malachi 3:1 as mandating that the Messiah appear in the second temple prior to its destruction.

Malachi's Use of the Terms "Behold I Send" and "Suddenly"

Malachi appears to mix apocalyptic language with more immediate nomenclature by using the terms "Behold I send" and "suddenly" in contrast to the arrival of some long-desired or anticipated forerunner. Even though Malachi does not state that the Lord will come into his temple immediately, there is no exegetical rationale for moving the perceived era of fulfillment to the distant (and currently more than 2000 years) future. In fact, the opposite is evident. The apocalyptic undertone generated by the phrase "Behold I send" and "suddenly" is present, but subdued. Bruce K. Waltke and Michael Patrick O'Connor specifically tie the syntactical construction הנני שלח (*hinnî šōlēha*) consisting of the interjection and participle translated "Behold I send" to "exclamations of immediacy ... the here-and-now-ness, of the situation."[104] Andrew E. Hill emphasizes the notion of immediate circumstances or "future circumstances with immanency—the so-called *futurum instans* participle."[105] It seems clear that Malachi does not envision a far-distant but rather sudden, fulfillment. That would force radically foreign ideas upon Malachi's *sitz en leben* and construction of his message. He is writing to his contemporaries, intently focused on the cultic, priestly, and legal traditions of Israel and the failure of priesthood to live and act faithfully. The second temple is the religious center of all these functions within Israel. M. Brown argues: "The entire context of the Book of Malachi makes it clear that there was to be a time of divine judgment and visitation for the people who worshiped and served *at the Second Temple*."[106] "The temple is the Temple in Jerusalem rather than a heavenly temple,"

---

104. Waltke and O'Connor, *Introduction to Biblical Hebrew Syntax*, 675.
105. Hill, *Malachi*, 200.
106. Brown, *Answering Jewish Objections to Jesus*, 1:78n15.

declares David Clark and Howard A. Hatton.[107] When arguing that the second temple is being referenced, E. Pocock uses the decisive terms "no doubt" to describe his convictions.[108]

Ralph L. Smith rightly observes that Malachi's work was not primarily concerned with the eschatological future (this does not mean completely uninterested). Malachi has "no 'full-blown' system of eschatology."[109] The ground for the message of Malachi is his observation of contemporary problems and solutions that require swift implementation. Mark J. Boda cogently observes that the language of Malachi will not bear the eschatological weight sometimes placed on it. "The timing and arrival of YHWH is not specified, but it is related to his return to fill the *Second Temple*."[110]

In addition, Malachi neither employs the ambiguous language related to the temple (e.g., "this house") as did Haggai (see Hag 2:3, 7, 9 above), when referring to it, nor does the language suggest that Malachi is experiencing a visionary episode, pointing toward an hypothesized eschatological temple such as that depicted in Ezekiel. There is no conflating of temple structures, and no other textual indications requiring a double entendre. In fact, little, if any, early historical-evidential documentation emerges that indicates Malachi's intended referent is anything other than the second temple.

Richard H. Heirs places the emphasis of Malachi squarely in its contemporary *sitz en leben*: "The writer of Malachi promised his contemporaries that they could look for an end to famine and pestilence and the beginning of blessedness if only the sons of Jacob would keep God's statutes, especially those concerning tithes and proper offerings in the Temple."[111] Heirs further remarks that, in a generalized way, some of the biblical literature construes the temple reform and renewal that was contemporary with Haggai, Zechariah, and Malachi as representing the "inauguration of a new era."[112] In context, Heir clearly means inauguration of the new era in that place at that time. This information and its context are critical for the current study. It is very likely that the second temple period establishes the *terminus ad quem* associated with Malachi 3:1.

It is also improbable that Malachi was envisioning (1) the judgment of *Yahweh* directed exclusively to Gentiles, or (2) a means of rescuing Jerusalem without judgment. James Pohlig confirms the import of the term "suddenly"

---

107. Clark and Hatton, *Handbook on Malachi*, 430.
108. Pocock, "Doctrinal and Ethical," 20.
109. Smith, "Shape of Theology in the Book of Malachi," 26–27.
110. Boda, "Figuring the Future," 71.
111. Heirs, "Purification of the Temple," 86.
112. Heirs, "Purification of the Temple," 86.

(פתאם) as associated with "ominous conditions or imminent calamities."[113] S. R. Driver and Walter F. Adeney affirm that the text contains the concept of judgment at an unexpected moment.[114] The priestly context and lexical data simply do not allow for "suddenly" to mean something expected but occurring quickly, or something that excluded Israel. The intent of the passage is to give notice that *Yahweh* will make an unexpected but imminent coming into the temple for the purpose of judgment and purification.[115]

The context of Malachi 3 implies that it is Lord himself, האדון (*hā' ādôn*), who must come to the temple. This Hebrew term, a synonym for *Yahweh*, appears more than 400 times in the OT. The most prominent aspect of the prophesied coming of the Lord is to render judgment. When the historical context of Malachi is strictly isolated from the NT, the identities of "my messenger" and of the "messenger of the covenant" could be either angelic or human. These two statements, as far as they go, are uncontroversial. Following the interpretive process further, G. Mitchell Hinckley, John Powis, and Julius Brewer contend that the "messenger of the covenant" cannot be identical with "my messenger" (hereafter "the forerunner").[116] This interpretation requires that the two occurrences of the term *messenger* (מלאך) refer to different individuals. *Yahweh* and the messenger of the covenant (not the forerunner) apparently arrive simultaneously, sometime after the forerunner has made his appearance. These observations are logical and generally uncontroversial. They do, however, leave open to investigation the question of whether the messenger of the covenant is the Messiah.

The Structure of Malachi

The chiastic structure of Malachi 3:1 makes it difficult to distinguish between the messenger of the covenant and the Lord. Taylor and Clendenen claim the two are identical and illustrate the structure of verse as follows:

> a—*See, I am sending my messenger.*
> *And he will clear a path before me.*
> *And suddenly he will come to his temple,*
>
> > b—the Lord *whom you are seeking* [*ʾăšer-ʾa*[*attem mĕbaqšîm*].

---

113. Pohlig, *Exegetical Summary of Malachi*, 132.
114. Driver and Adeney, *Minor Prophets*, 318.
115. Cf. Boda, "Figuring the Future," 70–73.
116. Hinckley et al., "Haggai, Zechariah, Malachi, and Jonah," 63.

> b´—And the messenger of the covenant *in whom you delight* [*ʾăšer-ʾhăttem ḥăpēṣîm*],
>
> a´—*see, he is coming.*
> says *Yahweh* of hosts.[117]

Critical confirmation of how closely linked the *messenger of the covenant* and the Lord are in this verse is demonstrated by the observations in the *International Critical and Exegetical Commentary*.

> This "messenger" can hardly be identical with the forerunner, viz. "my messenger," at the opening of the verse; for his coming is here made simultaneous with that of "the Lord," who can hardly be other than *Yahweh* himself, and the coming of 'my messenger' is explicitly announced as preceding that of *Yahweh*. It is not at all unlikely, indeed, that "the messenger of the covenant" is here confused with *Yahweh*.[118]

Andrew Malone, after criticizing the less-than-critical evaluations of some scholars, concludes much the same thing. First, Malone observes five potential characters in the verse: (1) the first-person speaker, "I"; (2) "my messenger"; (3) "the Lord" (*haʾadon*, not YHWH "the Lord"); (4) "the messenger of the covenant" (*malʾak habberit*); and (5) "YHWH Sabaoth."[119] Second, he reduces the number of characters to two, based on their overlap. The first is *Yahweh* Sabaoth and the second is most likely a human messenger. The coming of *Yahweh* is equivalent to the coming of the LORD and the messenger of the covenant.[120] Malone is confident that this assessment captures the intent of the passage, something he argues is confirmed by the application of the prophecy to Jesus by the NT writers. They believed that Jesus represented the coming of *Yahweh*.[121]

The decisive factor in determining whether the terms *the Lord* and the *messenger of the covenant* are one in the same person is, according to Hill, a grammatical choice. Hill concludes that regardless of which of two possible options the exeget adopts, the lexical work amplifies how closely *Yahweh* and the messenger are associated. Option one understands the conjunction (ו) placed before מלאך as serving "epexegetically, specifying the identity of 'The Lord' (*hāʾ ādōwn*) who is coming, by restating the previous

---

117. Taylor and Clendenen, *Haggai, Malachi*, 384.
118. Hinckley et al., "Haggai, Zechariah, Malachi, and Jonah," 63.
119. Malone, "Is the Messiah Announced in Malachi 3:1?," 217.
120. Malone, "Is the Messiah Announced in Malachi 3:1?," 227–28.
121. Malone, "Is the Messiah Announced in Malachi 3:1?," 227–28.

clause which would mean 'that is', 'yea' or 'even.'"[122] Option two understands ומלאך הברית as a third eschatological figure, which Hill deems likely. In this case, "the *waw* functions as a simple conjunction ('and')."[123]

From the foregoing examples of current critical scholarship, it is clear that the "messenger of the covenant" is so closely aligned with *Yahweh* that the two are virtually identical; any distinction between the two appears to hang on a *waw*. An exact parallel to the Hebrew syntax does not exist elsewhere in the OT. Still, Hill notes several similar phrases, for example, *mal' ak 'ĕlōhîm*, meaning an angel or messenger of God (Gen 21:17; Exod 14:19) and *mal' ak Yahweh*, meaning the angel of *Yahweh* (Zech 1:11) or the messenger of *Yahweh* (Hag 1:13). As is common knowledge, the Hebrew *mal' ak* means messenger, but not necessarily a messenger of a specific type. The messenger could be human, angelic, or divine; it is not always clear which type of messenger is denoted. Various scholars have suggested all three types, and no consensus exists. Nevertheless, this mysterious messenger, whether human, angelic or divine, is to come into *Yahweh*'s temple. The temple is central to Malachi's book and cannot be dismissed as window dressing in this specific oracle.

The following section of the work highlights the NT evidence for a supposition about the identity of the *messenger of the covenant* and his presence in the temple for the purpose of purification and judgment. Before addressing that evidence, it important to observe that no temple was standing after the Romans razed Jerusalem. The temple building was torn down, stone-by-stone, to retrieve the molten gold that had oozed between the stones as the temple burned.[124] If Malachi did not envision a third temple or the destruction of the second, as suggested above, very little doubt remains that the temple Malachi believes is *Yahweh*'s, and the one *the messenger* will enter, is the second temple. If one should argue for a typological understanding of Malachi, including both near and far referents, the current argument is not fatally damaged. Although unlikely, if a typological understanding is correct, it would still require the initial historical actualization of the prophecy during the second temple period.

---

122. Hill, *Malachi*, 269.

123. Hill, *Malachi*, 269. The grammatical reasons for Hill's choice can be seen in Waltke and O'Connor, *Introduction to Biblical Hebrew Syntax*.

124. Wood, *Bible and Spade*, 7:45.

New Testament Evidence

The NT evidence of importance for the question at hand is whether Jesus is the probable fulfillment of Malachi 3:1. In order to answer this question, six related questions must be posed:

1. Is there a probable identification of Jesus with Malachi 3:1?
2. Did Jesus enter the second temple during his life?
3. Does a plausible forerunner exist?
4. Is it credible to assert that Jesus ontologically constitutes the coming of *Yahweh*?
5. Did Jesus enter *Yahweh's* temple for the purpose of purification and judgment?
6. Is Jesus the messenger of the covenant?

Is there a Probable Identification of Jesus with Malachi 3:1?

Fitzmyer provides the first strand of evidence to demonstrate that Jesus is the best identifiable candidate to fulfill Malachi 3:1. He contends that the "One who is to come" is the title of a messianic figure derived from Malachi 3:1 (ἰδοὺ ἔρχεται LXX). Fitzmyer links this prophecy with Matthew 11:3 and Luke 7:19, both of which contain the phrase, "One who is to come" (ὁ ἐρχόμενος). He then notes that a connection to Malachi 3:1 may also be apparent in the knowledge of the coming one as expressed by the Samaritan woman (Μεσσίας ἔρχεται). Both NT examples use the same verb as Malachi 3:1. According to the gospel writers, Jesus' reply in each instance was affirmative. The reconstructed Q document contains these connections as found in the Synoptic Gospels (Q 7:18–19, 20–21, 22–23); however, John is a separate and distinct witness to a connection of Jesus with Malachi 3:1. Given the context of JTB's question posed to Jesus (Matt 11:3), it is also quite probable that JTB's own statement (as recorded in Matthew 3:11, ὁ δὲ ὀπίσω μου ἐρχόμενος) stands in the background and at least implies a connection to Malachi. Even the language employed by Mark 1:2b to describe the ministry of JTB probably sources Malachi 3:1 (ἰδοὺ ἀποστέλλω τὸν ἄγγελόν μου πρὸ προσώπου σου).[125] No exegetical leap is necessary to ascertain that the NT depicts JTB as the forerunner of Jesus, and that his task was to prepare Israel for judgment. A significant affirmation of these statements comes from France, who asserts that the language of Mark 1:2–8

---

125. Collins and Attridge, *Mark*, 136.

appears "to leave no room for a human figure in the eschatological drama other than John himself."[126] The rest of the book of Mark—especially the heavens being torn open (ἰσχυρότερος) in Mark 1:2—explains how this remarkable set of circumstances could possibly be the case. France's exegesis implies not only that Jesus and JTB are associated with Malachi 3:1 but also that Jesus is more than merely human.

Did Jesus Enter the Second Temple During His Life?

The second strand of evidence for Jesus as the fulfillment of Malachi 3:1 is his presence in the second temple. There is substantial NT evidence that Jesus actually entered the second temple on multiple occasions during his life. All four canonical gospels confirm his presence in the temple. Multiple attestation comes via five of the six recognized gospel sources (including Q). Representative samples of these attestations are found in Matthew 21:12; Mark 12:35; 14:49; Luke 2:22ff, 46; 19:47; John 7:14; 10:23). An important confirmation of Jesus' presence in the temple surfaces in the hypothetical Q document. As critically reconstructed, Q makes a reference to the temple that must be understood in light of Jesus' judgment on Jerusalem, his interaction with the religious leaders, and his entering the temple proper (Q 13:35). These observations indicate an affirmative answer to questions one and four. Jesus did enter the temple, and one of his purposes was to declare its impending judgment.

Does a Plausible Forerunner Exist?

The third strand of evidence stems from the first. As indicated above, JTB is the most probable historical-evidential candidate to fulfill the role of the forerunner in Malachi 3:1. The earliest gospel places JTB in the role of the forerunner (*my messenger*) predicted in Malachi 3:1 (Mark 1:1–2; Luke 1:17, 76; 7:27). This claim is also reflected in slightly modified forms in Matthew (Matt 11:10) and in Luke (Luke 3:4–6). JTB dressed in the same clothing as Elijah (Mark 1:6; 2 Kgs 1:8) and ate food associated with the ascetic prophet; both actions denote his self-designation as a prophet in the OT tradition. Mark cites Isaiah 40:3 with the implication that JTB is *the voice*, an assertion with which all four evangelists agree. In a section of Luke (Luke 1:16–17),

---

126. France, *Gospel of Mark*, 62.

whose origin is independent of either Mark or Q, JTB is identified using language from Malachi 3:1 and 4:5–6.[127]

More evidence surfaces in the reconstructed text of Q. Q 3:16b–17 treats JTB as *the forerunner* and Jesus as the superior who exacts judgment.[128] John also affirms these traditions by highlighting the inferior status of JTB in relation to Jesus. According to John, JTB was a witness to the light, while Jesus was the light (John 1:7–8). JTB was before Jesus, as his forerunner, yet was after Jesus because of Jesus' preexistent deity (John 1:15, 30). The baptism in water offered by JTB is inferior to Jesus' baptism with the Holy Spirit (John 1:33).[129] JTB's ministry decreases while Jesus' ministry increases (John 3:30). Correspondingly, two of Paul's speeches, both separated historically and literarily from the gospels, place JTB in the role of forerunner (Acts 13:23; 19:4). Even those skeptical of the historicity of the specific relationship between JTB and Jesus depicted in the NT admit that JTB was a historical person, he preceded Jesus as teacher, and his message was a call to repentance.[130]

Is it Credible to Assert that Jesus Constitutes Yahweh Entering His Temple?

The fourth strand of evidence consists of the claims of Jesus and his followers to his equality with God and as the Messiah. The assertion that Malachi 3:1 is a prophecy that *Yahweh* will enter the temple possesses "almost universal agreement among both Jewish and Christian interpreters."[131] Perhaps the earliest written examples of the claim that Jesus is *Yahweh* are those contained in the verses penned by the apostle Paul. Paul routinely uses terms such as Χριστός, κύριος, and υἱοῦ τοῦ θεοῦ to describe Jesus. These attributions are present in Galatians (perhaps the earliest letter of Paul), written

---

127. Among Jewish interpreters, the references to Elijah in Malachi 4 are usually thought of in literal and eschatological terms. For example, in Justin Martyr's *Dialogue with Trypho*, Trypho the Jew contends: "We Jews all expect that Christ will be a man of merely human origin, and that Elias will come to anoint Him. If this man appears to be the Christ, He must be considered to be a man of solely human birth, yet, from the fact that Elias has not yet come, I must declare that this man is not the Christ." Falls and Martyr, *First Apology*, 221. Many Christians also believe in a literal return of Elijah before the day of *Yahweh*.

128. Robinson et al., *Critical Edition of Q*.

129. Q adds the element of fire to Jesus' work of baptizing. Both Matthew and Luke include this element in their accounts.

130. Funk and Hoover, *Five Gospels*, 132, 135.

131. Hill, *Malachi*, 287.

approximately twenty years after the life of Jesus.[132] In the book of Romans, one of Paul's most theologically mature works, Paul so closely aligns Jesus with *Yahweh* that they become virtually indistinguishable. Romans quotes from Joel 2:32: "For everyone who calls upon the name of the Lord shall be saved" (Rom 10:13). Clearly, "the LORD" in Joel is *Yahweh*. For Paul, however, "the Lord" is clearly Jesus. In Joel, salvation is for an Israelite remnant; for Paul, salvation is for anyone who confesses Jesus as Lord. James Dunn explains these apparent conflations and resolves them by concluding: "So the fact that Paul refers the same verse to the exalted Jesus presumably means for Paul either that Jesus *is Yahweh*, or, more likely, that *Yahweh* has bestowed his own unique saving power on the Lord who sits on his right side, or that the exalted Jesus is himself the embodiment as well as the executive of that saving power."[133]

In another of Paul's works, the alignment of Jesus and *Yahweh* is brilliantly illustrated. Philippians 2:5–11 shows close correspondence with Isaiah 45:23, with knees bowing and tongues confessing. In Isaiah, the confession is that there is only one God and no other. Paul appropriates this language and applies it to Jesus. Paul so clearly believes that *Yahweh* is glorified by confessing Jesus as Lord that an unequivocally monotheistic OT passage becomes the foundation for a virtual fusion of *Yahweh* and Jesus.[134]

One of the NT's sharpest claims to Jesus' deity and messiahship is recorded as Jesus' own words (Mark 14:62). Jesus' reply to the high priest when directly questioned about his relationship to God leaves little doubt about his claim to sonship, messiahship, and his eschatological role as Israel's judge. Most critical scholars allow for the historicity of the trial of Jesus before the Sanhedrin. Some controversy attends, however, how the gospel writers could know Jesus' reply to his interlocutors. None of them were actually present during the trial. Based on the absence of eyewitnesses, the fellows of the Jesus Seminar ignore or depreciate the available evidence. They describe Jesus' responses to Caiaphas as "undoubtedly the work of the evangelists."[135]

At the least, it must be acknowledged that the gospel writers could have gathered this information from Nicodemus. John portrays Nicodemus

---

132. Hurtado, *How on Earth Did Jesus Become God?* 33.

133. Dunn, *Did the First Christians Worship Jesus?*, 105.

134. The current work is not suggesting that Jesus and *Yahweh* are identical economically, but are identical essentially and ontologically. See also 1 Corinthians 8:6. Colossians 2:9 (one of the disputed books) also makes the claim that Jesus is God in all his fullness.

135. Funk and Hoover, *Five Gospels*, 123.

as well-disposed to Jesus (John 7:50–52).[136] It is likely that others within the council were also sympathetic to Jesus (John 12:52). In Acts, the historian Luke provides skeptics reason to believe that knowledge of Jesus' answer to the high priest was not beyond the knowledge of the gospel writers: "A great many of the priests became obedient to the faith" (Acts 6:7).

Paul (Saul of Tarsus) is another source of information concerning the testimony of Jesus. The NT portrays him as a student of the council member Gamaliel (Acts 22:3). Kaufmann Kohler, the Pauline critic of the nineteenth century, admits the possibility of a historical "kernel" in the story of the conversion of Saul of Tarsus. Kohler notes that Saul was "commissioned with the task of exterminating the Christian movement antagonistic to the Temple and the Law."[137] Commissioned by whom? It must be the Sanhedrin. Max Seligsohn never challenges the historicity of either the person of Stephen, his death by stoning, or that Paul is acting on his commission from the Sanhedrin when consenting to the stoning of Stephen.[138] There is no other plausible conclusion. Paul may well have been present during the inquisition of Jesus and related his account to the disciples after his conversion.

Additional early evidence supporting the supposition that Jesus claimed to be and was considered ontologically equal with *Yahweh* surfaces in Q. Q contains the narrative of Jesus' baptism. Although the exact words are uncertain, what has been reconstructed implies that "the voice from heaven" attributed the status of God's son to Jesus (Q 3:21).

---

136. Bauckham, "Nicodemus and the Gurion Family," 28–32. Bauckham makes five cogent points related to how knowledge of Jesus' answer could have been transmitted to the gospel writers. First, he contends that the name Nicodemus is "sufficiently" rare among Palestinian Jews of the first century to allow for the possibility that the account in John has a historical base. Bauckham argues that the family of Nicodemus is part of the ruling aristocracy of Jerusalem (ἄρχων, John 3:1; 7:26, 48; 12:42). Josephus, he notes, uses the term (βουλή: *Ant* 20:11) to refer to the council, but it is probable that this included not only the chief priests but also leading citizens and other powerful men. Historical persons of the Gurion family (probable relatives of Nicodemus) appear to fit within these categories. Second, Nicodemus is a Pharisee (John 3:1), but not in the general sense. He is part of a small group of wealthy aristocratic Pharisees who belonged to the ruling elite. Bauckham believes that this may be why John uses the terminology the chief priests and the Pharisees (7:32, 45; 11:47, 57; 18:3). Third, the research conducted by Bauckham lead to the conclusion that two probable members of Nicodemus's family (the Gurion family) were teachers of the law, as was Nicodemus (John 3:1). Fourth, Nicodemus is portrayed as very wealthy, something that is confirmed by the weight (approx. 65 lbs.) of spices provided for Jesus' burial (John 19:39). Other extravagant claims about the wealth of the Gurion family are present in rabbinic traditions. Bauckham notes that the traditions may be exaggerated. This does not disqualify them as having a historical basis, however. Fifth, although controversial, Nicodemus became a Christian.

137. Kohler, "Saul of Tarsus," 81.

138. Seligsohn, "Stephen," 548.

The apostle John likewise makes several claims that align the ontological status of Jesus to be essentially indistinguishable from *Yahweh*. In John 12:41, the writer ambiguously and with multifaceted implications contends that Isaiah saw the glory of Jesus in the throne vision leading to his commissioning (Isa 6:1ff). Other texts in John which unambiguously attribute Jesus' equality with God include John 1:18, 10:30, and 20:28.

Did Jesus Enter Yahweh's Temple for Purification and Judgment?

The fifth strand of evidence is the role of Jesus as Judge. Judgment is the primary thrust of Malachi 3, and the emphasis of the text is not pleasant greetings, but refining, cleansing, and removing the evildoer. If Jesus is the fulfillment of this prophecy, he must have acted as judge.

Jesus unmistakably declared his role of judge in Mark 14:62, as argued above. However, this is not the only text to substantiate his claim to be the judge of Israel. The Q source also picks up the motif of Jesus as judge with a saying that references the coming condemnation of Israel by the Queen of Sheba and by the Ninevites because Jesus' presence (though unrecognized) was greater than either Solomon or Jonah (Q 11:31–32). Matthew places Jesus in the judge's seat in relation to an eschatological and, apparently, final judgment (Matt 25:31–46). John 5:22–29 designates Jesus as the judge by the delegated authority given to him by God. John 9:39 makes judgment the explicit reason for Jesus' coming into the world. In addition, the Triumphal Entry and the cleansing of the temple—with the resulting condemnation of Jerusalem—is recorded in all four of the gospels. This repetition gives the exegete every reason to believe that the NT writers believed the temple cleansing was an important event. That Jesus both spoke against and acted against the temple is beyond dispute. More than two-thirds of the ultra-critical fellows of the Jesus Seminar affirm this position.[139] John's reference (John 2:13–17) probably had Zechariah 14:21 in mind, but "equally," according to D. A. Carson "John may be alluding to Malachi 3:1, 3" to denounce the impure worship.[140] Andreas J. Köstenberger and Richard H. Heirs also cite this same Malachi connection.[141] Tim

---

139. Funk and Hoover, *Five Gospels*, 97–98.

140. Carson, *Gospel According to John*, 179.

141. Köstenberger, *John*. Heirs, "Purification of the Temple: Preparation for the Kingdom of God," 87–88. Josephus attributes the destruction of the temple and Jerusalem to ancient prophecy. He does not provide any explicit reference, but he does mention these oracles of destruction twice. In both cases, he writes as though these

LaHaye and Ed Hindson explicitly cite John 2:13-22 and what may be a later event as recorded in the synoptic texts (Matt 21:13; Mark 11:15-18; Luke 19:45-47) as fulfillment of Malachi 3:1.[142]

Finally, consider the possibility that no NT historical evidence supported the idea that "the messenger of the covenant" entered the temple or was associated with the Messiah.[143] Even if this was true, or if JTB or any other second-temple person is the referent, Malachi's prophecy is still most probably exclusively directed to the second temple. As controversial as Daniel 9:24-27 is with regard to messianism, one observation seems difficult to refute. Prior to their destruction, the second temple and Jerusalem are in view. Neither Daniel, Malachi, nor the records of Israel's readers indicate that another temple is in view. No other conclusion even approaches the same level of plausibility.

Extra-Biblical Evidence

In addition to the above evidence, some early church writings interpret Malachi 3:1 in relation to Jesus. Cyril of Jerusalem writes:

> The Lord heard the prayer of the Prophets. The Father disregarded not the perishing of our race; He sent forth His Son, the Lord from heaven, as healer: and one of the Prophets saith, *The Lord whom ye seek, cometh, and shall suddenly come.* Whither? *The Lord* shall come *to His own temple*, where ye stoned Him.[144]

Although this text from Cyril of Jerusalem is not without difficulties, what is obvious is the intent to place Jesus in the role of healer of Israel

---

prophecies of judgment were common knowledge. Josephus and Whiston, "Antiquities of the Jews," 4.388 and 386.109.These citations from Josephus alone do not prove that Malachi envisioned the second temple or that "the messenger of the covenant" is Jesus. Malachi does not refer to the destruction of the temple. However, given the possibility that this is the case, it is significant to find a decidedly non-Christian voice declaring OT prophecy (probably Daniel 9:26) to be fulfilled by an attack against the temple and Jerusalem in what almost certainly must be accepted as judgment.

142. LaHaye and Hindson, *Popular Bible Prophecy Commentary*, 317. Cf. Payne, *Encyclopedia of Biblical Prophecy*, 473.

143. F. B. Huey notes that the messenger preceding the messenger of the covenant has been identified by scholars as Malachi, Elijah, Nehemiah, the angel of the Lord, or as a figurative embodiment of all prophets. The NT interprets the messenger as John the Baptist (Matt 11:10; Mark 1:2; Luke 7:27). The statement rests on the prophecy of Isaiah 40:3-5, which describes one who will prepare the way for the coming of the Lord. Huey, "Exposition of Malachi," 17.

144. Cyril, *Catechetical Lectures of S. Cyril*, 74.

and representative of *Yahweh* (if not *Yahweh* himself) coming to the temple. Cyril is writing long after these events; his interpretive judgment reflected in the quotation above demonstrated his understanding of history.[145]

Another instance of this same process is found in chapter 17 of Origen's commentary on the Gospel of John. Origen identifies John and his baptism as the forerunners of Jesus and his superior baptism.[146] Irenaeus removes all the ambiguities from his position, writing: "Truly it was by Him, of whom Gabriel is the angel, who also announced the glad tidings of his birth: [that God] who also had promised by the prophets that He would send His messenger before the face of His Son, who should prepare His way, that is, that he should bear witness of that Light in the spirit and power of Elias."[147] Thus, Irenaeus contends that John, sent in the power of Elijah, was sent directly by *Yahweh* to testify of the Light, and the light is the Son. The Talmud also provides a brief reference to the Messiah in association with the "day of the Lord" in the immediate context of Malachi 3:2.[148]

Summary

In summary, the available historical evidence suggests that the most plausible conclusion is that JTB and Jesus are the best historically identifiable candidates for fulfilling Malachi 3:1. No one has suggested a more probable conclusion based on historical evidence or exegesis. Historically and evidentially, JTB is most likely the *forerunner* and Jesus is "the messenger of the covenant." This is the answer to the sixth question (see New Testament Evidence above). No other candidates meet the criteria and it is extremely unlikely that any future pair of figures will do so. Furthermore, the relation of the second temple to Malachi's intent is virtually certain. To escape this fact, the exegete historian must resort to speculation or allegorization. It is

---

145. Augustine interprets the passage allegorically, citing or alluding to several texts in Malachi within just a few sentences. Augustine cites Malachi 1:10–11 in relation to the worship and sacrifice offered God in every place, from the rising of the sun to its going down, through Christ's priesthood. He comments that the Jews' sacrifices have ceased and cannot be accepted, so why do the Jews still look for another Christ? When they read this prophecy, Augustine reasoned, they should know that it could not be fulfilled except through Jesus. Citing Malachi 2:5–7 analogously, Augustine then applies the title "the messenger of the covenant" to Jesus and the temple to his physical body, his flesh. The coming in judgment is reserved for the Second Advent. Augustine, *City of God*, 2:381.

146. Origen, "Commentary on the Gospel of John," 367.

147. Irenaeus of Lyons, "Irenæus Against Heresies," Adv haer 3.11.14.

148. Neusner, *Babylonian Talmud*, b. Shabb. 16:12, II.17.B.

impossible for *Yahweh* or his covenant messenger, if they are distinct individuals, to enter a temple for judgment if a temple does not exist.

The related positions argued herein are: (1) this OT text requires the messenger of the covenant to be present in the second temple, and (2) no candidate other than Jesus as the incarnation of *Yahweh* adequately fits the facts.

Plausible Historical-Evidential Conclusions Drawn from the Study of Malachi 3:1

1. The historical-evidential data indicates that JTB is the best identifiable candidate fitting the image of the forerunner.
2. The NT gospels and Paul claim that Jesus is the Jewish Messiah and judge of Israel.
3. The NT gospels and Paul claim that Jesus is equal with *Yahweh*.

Historical-Evidential Facts Drawn from the Study of Malachi 3:1

1. Malachi 3:1 depicts *Yahweh* as coming into his temple for judgment.
2. Malachi provides no indication that he envisions a temple other than the one standing during his lifetime.
3. The historical-evidential data indicate that if the LORD (*hāʾādôn*) and *the messenger of the covenant* are different individuals, Jesus is the best identifiable candidate for the latter role.
4. If the LORD (*hāʾādôn*) and *the messenger of the covenant* are the same individual, Jesus is the best identifiable candidate known to historians.

Chapter 4

The Second Group of Biblical Texts

Introduction to the Second Group of Biblical Texts

THE SECOND GROUP OF biblical texts probe the claim that the Messiah would spring from the linage of King David and that, correspondingly, Jesus is a descendant of King David. The passages examined are 2 Samuel 7:13, Isaiah 11:1–2, Jeremiah 23:5–6, Ezekiel 34:23–24, Hosea 3:4–5, Matthew 1:1–17, and Luke 2:4, 3:23.

2 Samuel 7:13

Literary and Textual Analysis

Old Testament Evidence

2 SAMUEL 7:1–17

The Davidic Covenant is an integral element in the theology of the OT. The textual basis for the idea that *Yahweh* made a particular covenant with King David and his descendants is found in 2 Samuel 7:1–17. In this pericope, four things are promised to David. First, *Yahweh* will make David's name great (7:9b). Second, *Yahweh* will establish the kingdom of David's physical offspring (7:12). Third, this particular offspring will build a house for *Yahweh*'s name (7:13a). Fourth, the kingdom of David's offspring will last forever (7:13b).

Within this pericope, verses 13 and 16 both use the term עַד־עוֹלָם (*'d' wlm*) to describe the perpetuity of the Davidic dynasty. Subsequent statements by David and Solomon confirm *forever* as the correct understanding of the term (2 Sam 22:15; 1 Kings 2:45; Ps 18:50). Johnston highlights the fact that Abijah, king of Judah, and a later descendant of

David, also claimed the promise made to David as a covenantal basis for a perpetual dynasty (2 Chr 13:5).[1]

Significant for this discussion is the term ממעיך (*from the bowel/body of you*) in verse 12. This term unambiguously indicates that the promised son of David must be the physical offspring of David. The LXX translation agrees, stating that the promised son must be from the κοιλίας (*belly*) of David.

The Role of Isaiah 11:1 in Relation to 2 Samuel 7:13

The text of Isaiah 11:1 is definitely set in the future; it is a prophecy of an ideal ruler stemming from the house of Jesse. This text is almost universally recognized as reaffirming the promise made previously to David. Writers differ, however, in their explanation of the enigmatic reference to Jesse rather than David. Arnold Fruchtenbaum contends that referencing Jesse means the "Messiah would not be born until the House of David had once again returned to the state of poverty which it was in during the days of David's father, Jesse. [The] Messiah will be born into a house of lowliness."[2] Hans Wildberger, citing Geo Widengren, suggests that the selection of an image of the tree (stump) was because the tree of life served as a symbol for the Israelite monarchy.[3] History, in fact, depicts this monarchy as literally cut down. Fitzmyer notes that the MT of Isaiah 11 contains a promise of the continuation of the Davidic dynasty, but this promise gradually evolved into something more. Later interpreters understood Isaiah 11:1 as an explicit promise of a (distant) messianic king, as reflected in the Targum of Isaiah. Bruce Chilton translates Isaiah 11:1 in the Targum as follows: "And *a king* shall come forth from the *sons* of Jesse, and *the Messiah* shall *be exalted* from *the sons of* his *sons.*"[4]

Regardless of the time for fulfillment envisioned by the writer, no doubt remains about the overall import of Isaiah 11:1. It is a reaffirmation by a writer coming well after the life of David (and probably before the exile) of the promise made to David in 2 Samuel 7.

---

1. Johnston, "Messianic Trajectories," 67.
2. Fruchtenbaum, *Messianic Christology*, 43.
3. Wildberger, *Isaiah 1–12*, 470.
4. Cathcart et al., *Aramaic Bible*, 11:28.

The Role of Jeremiah 23:5–6 and Ezekiel 34:23–24 in Relation to 2 Samuel 7:13

Despite the well-documented disobedience of the Davidic kings, texts such as Jeremiah 23:5–6 and Ezekiel 34:23–24 confirm a continuing hope for a renewed Davidic leader and kingdom. The historical circumstances of the Babylonian exile were not favorable to the sustainability of such a hope. There is little doubt that the Jewish people's messianic hope did not suddenly spring into existence because of the exile. Rather, it continued to develop, despite the exile, during the occupation of their homeland and the deportation of their people.

In light of the failure of the Davidic kings, another paradox is that the hope for an archetypical Davidic king seems to have grown more prevalent as time progressed. For example, Jeremiah 23:5, indisputably written after the fall of Jerusalem, employs *tree*-related terminology reminiscent of Isaiah 11:1. Jeremiah speaks of a righteous branch of David. The term צדיק צמח (*ṣaddîq ṣemaḥ*), translated as "righteous branch" or "rightful scion" by William Lee Holladay, if not technically meaning Messiah at the time of Jeremiah, was indisputably taken as such by the time of Zechariah. According to Holliday, the term contains a technically messianic meaning in Zechariah 3:8.[5] Ezekiel 34:23–24 speaks again of the hope for the reestablishment of the Davidic dynasty with a sitting king acting as shepherd of Israel.

The Role of Hosea 3:4–5 in Relation to 2 Samuel 7:13

The bulk of the book of Hosea is uniformly recognized as pre-exilic, probably written during the reign of Jeroboam II. Hosea 3:1–5 may be the work of a later redactor. For the current purpose, however, as will be demonstrated below, this makes little difference. Hans Walter Wolff argues for the originality of the passage based on genre. He contends that the acting out portrayed in the passage is *memorabile*, which is neither parable nor allegory. *Memorabile* depicts a historical event in one central point and demonstrates a concern for facts expressed in symbolic action.[6] If Hosea 3:1–5, particularly verses 4–5, is part of the original prophecy, these verses represent a strong affirmation of the Jewish people's hope for a Davidic king during the pre-exilic period. Other texts (such as 1 Chronicles 22:6–10) support this assertion. If Hosea

---

5. Holladay, *Jeremiah 1*, 618.
6. Wolff, *Hosea*.

3:4-5 reflects the work of a later redactor, this passage represents the continuation of a pre-existing messianic hope that extends into the post-exilic period. It is doubtful that Hosea originated such hope.

In either case cited above, the text of Hosea 3:4-5 is not difficult to interpret. The text postpones the realization of the appearance of the Davidic king into the distant eschatological future. It also provides strong evidence for the pervasive expectation of the restoration of the Davidic line and that the ideal Davidic ruler would be the physical offspring of David (2 Samuel 7:13).

Intertestamental Evidence

The historical understanding of the extra-biblical texts, as conveyed by Jewish scribes, expresses the same hope for a coming Davidic scion. For example, during the intertestamental period, the belief that the messiah would be of Davidic decent is articulated in the Psalms of Solomon, "Ἰδέ, κύριε, καὶ ἀνάστησον αὐτοῖς τὸν βασιλέα αὐτῶν υἱὸν Δαυιδ εἰς τὸν καιρόν, ὃν εἵλου σύ, ὁ θεός, τοῦ βασιλεῦσαι ἐπὶ Ισραηλ παῖδά σου."[7] In context, this psalm is a lament over the Hasmonean usurpation of the title *king*. Apparently, many pharisaic Jews considered the Hasmoneans to be sinners without a legitimate claim to the throne.[8] The rightful king could only be a *davidid*.

Other evidence temporally proximate to this era is found in the writings of the Qumran Essenes. The messianic expectation of the Essenes included two messiahs; one Davidic and the other an interpreter of the law. In 4Q174 (Frags. 1 i, 21, 2:10-13), the Essene Midrash of 2 Samuel 7:12-14, the Davidic messiah is described as the "branch" (צמח) who raises the fallen hut of David (Amos 9:11). Another similar pesharim (4Q161 Frags. 8-10:11-25) interprets Isaiah 10:33-34 and 11:1-5 in light of a Davidic messiah: "See! The Lord YHWH of Hosts will rip off the branches at one wrench.... [A shoot will issue from the stump] of Jesse and [a bud] will sprout from [its roots]" (4Q161 Frags. 168-110:111).[9] Further evidence arises in 1Q28b Col. v: 20-28. This text echoes the images of Isaiah 11, applying them to their hope for messianic rule.

---

7. *Septuginta*, Ps 17:21.

8. Josephus records that a great numbers of Jews were slain in the battle against Alexander Janneus and on one occasion approximately 800 Pharisees were crucified. Josephus and Whiston, "Antiquities of the Jews," Antiquities 13.379.

9. Martínez and Tigchelaar, *Dead Sea Scrolls*, 317. Brackets indicate restored text.

Jewish liturgical material also indicates the desire and expectation that the throne of David would be reestablished. The *Shemoneh Esreh* (Eighteen Benedictions), numbers fourteen and fifteen, state:

> To Jerusalem Thy city return Thou in mercy and dwell in her midst as Thou hast spoken, and build her speedily in our days as an everlasting structure and soon establish there the throne of David. Blessed be Thou, O Lord, the builder of Jerusalem.
>
> The sprout of David Thy servant speedily cause Thou to sprout up; and his horn do Thou uplift through Thy victorious salvation; for Thy salvation we are hoping every day. Blessed be Thou, O Lord, who causest the horn of salvation to sprout forth.[10]

Mark. L. Strauss contends that the *Shemoneh Esreh* is the most important prayer in Judaism, with roots predating Christianity. Strauss suggests the Babylonian recension of the *Shemoneh Esreh* or *Tefillah* did not reach its final form until after AD 70. However, based on some textual similarities in the earlier Hebrew text of Sirach (Sir 51:12), textual dependence of the former on the latter may be argued. Strauss states: "The fact that references to the Temple and the Davidic messiah appear together and in the same order as the *Tefillah* suggests dependence of some kind; and it is not unlikely that the common tradition was an earlier version of the *Shemoneh Esreh*."[11] Strauss further identifies the phrase "horn of salvation" as common to Luke 1:69 and 2 Samuel 22:3. The author of the fifteenth benediction most probably was not dependent on Luke since the *Shemoneh Esreh* is a Jewish liturgical prayer, not a Christian prayer. The phrase "horn of salvation" in this benediction likely stems from an earlier source available to both Luke and the Jewish writers.[12]

Later Extra-Biblical Evidence

An apocalyptic glimpse of the messianic expectation is provided by the author of 4 Ezra who writes of someone from the posterity of David denouncing ungodliness, while judging and destroying enemies. The *davidid* 4 Ezra has in mind accomplishes the conquest while delivering a saved remnant (4 Ezra 12:31–34).[13]

---

10. Hirch, "Shemoneh Esreh," 271.
11. Strauss, *Davidic Messiah in Luke-Acts*, 49–50.
12. Strauss, *Davidic Messiah in Luke-Acts*, 50.
13. Charlesworth, *Old Testament Pseudepigrapha*, 1:550.

The early church father Augustine also accepted both the idea that the Messiah was to be the physical offspring of David and the tradition that Jesus was this particular descendant. In the classic work *The City of God*, Augustine exegetes Psalm 89: "I have sworn to David my servant that I will prepare his seed forever." He then affirms—in several ways—that Christ is the fulfillment of this ancient promise.[14]

Another representative example of the same thought process is located in Cyprian's claims that David was promised a seed from his own "bowels" that would build a house and have his throne raised forever.[15] These examples, though coming from Christian sources, have continuity with both the OT and intertestamental evidence regarding the key question of how the promise to David was interpreted. The evidence thus far demonstrates a consistent expectation that the seed of David would be a physical descendant. The evidence supports no figurative or symbolic interpretation.[16]

Davidic Thinking: A Significant Form of Jewish Messianism

Some scholars argue that no normative concept of Messiah existed in Judaism;[17] perhaps this assessment is correct, but the evidence suggests an alternative supposition. Fitzmyer, in the concluding remarks of *The One Who Is to Come*, notes that the messianic figure was not always conceived of as kingly. In some cases, he was priestly; in other cases, he was of Joseph. However, the "dominate expectation . . . was one that awaited a human kingly figure who was (and is) to bring deliverance, at once political, economic, and spiritual, to the Jewish people, and through them peace, prosperity, and righteousness to all humanity."[18] The significant characteristic of this kingly expectation is the messianic connection to David.

William Horbury provides important insight into the messianism of the OT and pseudepigraphal works. In one instance, he observes that the "Davidic monarchy forms a background against which a considerable unity [in messianism] can in fact be perceived."[19] Further, Horbury warns

14. Augustine, "City of God," 349–51.
15. Cyprian, "Three Books," 515.
16. A small body of Jewish polemical literature exists that denies that Jesus was either a descendant of David or born of a virgin (see below, "Evidence against a Contrived Birthplace"). None of these sources are contemporary with the NT data, with the possible exception of John 8:41. Cf. Origen, "Origen against Celsus," 1.38, and Bockmuehl, *This Jesus*, 14, 33.
17. Witherington, *Jesus Quest*, 213.
18. Fitzmyer, *One Who Is to Come*, 182.
19. Horbury, *Messianism among Jews and Christians*, 54.

that a "sharp division between Davidic and non-Davidic expectations is discouraged."[20] Why would this be so? The Jews traced their expectation not just to David, but to Genesis 49:10, which includes the whole series of Jewish kings. The Davidic monarchy, both in general and in particular, forms a background against which a unity of messianic expectation can, in fact, be perceived.[21]

Wright acknowledges the Davidic connection in the context of a discussion about the cultural milieu of the first century and the pervasive function and position of the temple in Jewish society. He argues thus:

> Dissatisfaction with the first-century Temple was also fuelled by the fact that, although it was certainly among the most beautiful buildings ever constructed, it was built by Herod. Only the true King, the proper successor of Solomon, the original Temple-builder, had the right to build the Temple . . . and whatever Herod was, he was not the true King. The last four prophetic books in the canon (Zephaniah, Haggai, Zechariah and Malachi), and in its own way the work of the Chronicler, all point to the restoration of the Temple under the leadership of a royal (Davidic), or possibly a priestly, figure.[22]

In another location, Wright acknowledges the existence of a "reasonably widespread Jewish messianic hope, including a belief that God would use a coming king to usher in divine rule. At least in one case that messianic hope took 'explicitly Davidic form.'"[23] Mowinckel affirms that the hope of the Jewish people was for a restored kingdom characterized by a tangible state in the present world, ruled by the scion of David: "The Messiah is the ideal king of David's line who reigns in the restored kingdom of his ancestor."[24]

The affirmation above does not suggest that messianism and Judaism were monolithic in nature. Neither does it suggest that the messianic hope instantly sprang *ex nihilo* into its full-orbed expression. This hope was characterized by variations, sects, and a long history of

---

20. Horbury, *Messianism among Jews and Christians*, 54.

21. Horbury, *Messianism among Jews and Christians*, 53–54. In these pages, Horbury provides a list of pseudepigrapha that attest to messianism as follows: "The Testaments of the Twelve Patriarchs in the second century BC, the Psalms of Solomon and relevant parts of the Third Sibylline book in the first century BC, and a series of apocalypses extending throughout and beyond the Herodian period, notably the Parables of Enoch, the apocalypses of Ezra (2 Esd 3–14) and Baruch (2 Baruch, the Syriac Apocalypse of Baruch), and the Fifth Sibylline book."

22. Wright, *New Testament and the People of God*, 225–26.

23. Wright, *New Testament and the People of God*, 308.

24. Mowinckel, *He that Cometh*, 157.

development—partially captured in the OT texts and partially within the historical records of the nation. Ben Witherington remarks on these variations that some specific Jews (the Sadducees) were not looking for a single Messiah figure to rescue them.[25]

Witherington's conclusion notwithstanding, the OT documents, the extra-biblical documents, and the history of the nation—as documented above—leave little doubt that the hope for Israel's ideal king was most often grounded in the royal line of David, particularly in the Davidic Covenant. Typically, a literal relational understanding existed between the messianic hope and the royal line of David, although some ideological elements are present. Physical descent was undeniably a significant aspect of the messianic hope from the inception of the Davidic Covenant. Even when the apocryphal and pseudepigraphical works describe messianic figures with superhuman characteristics, a steadfast connection to the historic Israelite kings remains.[26]

New Testament Evidence

THE PAULINE EVIDENCE

Employing the most gracious interpretation of the evidence, the careful exegete cannot press the succession of Davidic kings as the leaders of the Israelites beyond the time of Zerubbabel. Even granting Zerubbabel the status of king involves difficulties. He was more properly a governor of Judah (Hos 1:1) and, at best, a vassal of Persia. As discussed above, a broad range of OT texts support the idea that David's kingdom and throne would be reestablished (e.g., Isa 9:7; 11:1; Jer 23:5; 33:15–17; Ezek 34:23–24; 37:25; Hos 3:5; Amos 9:11). The early Christians believed that Jesus (*Christ, Messiah, or Anointed One*) fulfilled this promise as the ultimate descendant of David (Matt 27:11, 37; Mark 15:2, 26; Luke 23:3, 38; John 18:33–34; 19:19–22; Rev 17:14; 19:16). Thus, Christians contend that Jesus rules an eternal kingdom.

---

25. Witherington, *Jesus Quest*, 214.

26. Horbury, *Messianism among Jews and Christians*, 60. The superhuman features noted in the Apocrypha and Pseudepigrapha are frequent and diverse in nature. Is it more than coincidence that many of these characteristics are related to the representations of Jesus in the NT? These characteristics include: (1) pre-existence (2 Esd 13:26; 1 En 48:3, 6; 2 Bar 29:3; Sib Or 5:414); (cf. John 1:1; 8:23, 58; 1 Cor 8:6; Col 1:16–17); (2) Messiah coming from heaven (2 Esd 13:3; Sib Or 5:414; 1 En 48:4–7; 2 Bar 29:3); (cf. Mark 13:26; 14:62; 1 Thess 4:17; Rev 1:7); (3) annihilation of foes and establishment of kingdom (1 En 49:2; 2 Esd 13:9–13; 2 Bar 29:3–5; 39:7–40:3; Sib Or 5:414–28); (cf.1 Thess 5:3; 2 Thess 1:5–9; 2 Pet 3:7; Rev 19:11–21).

Dennis Duling, commenting on the Davidic concept in relation to Jesus' Davidic heritage, contends that two texts are primary: Romans 1:3–4 and Romans 15:12. Duling argues that Paul's use of 2 Samuel 7:12–14 in Romans 1:3–4, and the word play in 15:12, in which the "root of Jesse" is parallel to ὁ ἀνιστάμενος, is where the OT promise first enters Christian tradition.[27] This tradition includes a physical descendant of David ruling Israel and the nations, plus the OT impress of divine sonship.[28] It is Paul's belief in the physical (κατὰ σάρκα) descent that motivates his assertion that God's covenant-keeping righteousness is manifest in the flesh, through Jesus. God's faithfulness and Jesus' sonship are both proved by Jesus' resurrection and exaltation. Drawing from a list of metaphors used in the OT promise traditions, both canonical and non-canonical, Duling demonstrates the likelihood that Paul and the other NT writers were aware of and embraced the promise tradition that *Yahweh* would *raise up* (ἀνιστάμενος) a descendant of David. The emphasis of these metaphors is the raising up in the sense of a ruler ascending to the throne to rule over Israel and the nations.[29] However, the word play of ἀνιστάμενος also allows for the resurrection motif and the attribution of divine sonship in the same context.

These non-titular metaphors are of such quantity and their appropriation by Paul of such clarity that any attempt at dismissing the idea that God had promised David a seed—and that Paul believed that seed was Jesus—is untenable.[30] In Paul's mind, Jesus rules the kingdom and enjoys the status of having a father-son relationship with *Yahweh*.

Jesus' Genealogical and Family Data

The Davidic descent of Jesus was apparently a given in the early church. It is multiply attested in Matthew (SM) and Luke-Acts (SL) and affirmed by Mark (Mark 10:47–48; 12:35–37), in addition to the early, enemy attestation by Paul (Rom 1:3) mentioned above. Later (in what might be considered a satisfaction of the criteria of multiple forms), the author of 2 Timothy

---

27. Duling, "Promises to David," 70–77.
28. Duling, "Promises to David," 77.
29. Duling, "Promises to David," 77–78.
30. For example, Num 24:9, 17; Ps 79:25; Ps 132:17; Isa 9:10; Jer 23:5; 30:9; 33:14–15; Zech 3:8; 6:12; 4Qflor; T. Jud 24:1, 5b; T. Sim 1bf; T. Dan v. 10; Benediction 15; Targ. Isa 9:1; Ps 17:23.

2:8–9[31] and John of Patmos (Rev 3:7; 5:5; 22:16)[32] both specifically attribute a Davidic heritage to Jesus.[33]

To support a physical-descent claim beyond what the biblical witnesses overtly provide, it is important to note the mention of "brothers of the Lord" (1 Cor 9:5) in the context of apostles known to the Corinthians. Apparently, even the Gentile churches were aware of the apostolic ministry of Jesus' brothers, yet not a word refuting his Davidic descent can be identified in this passage. If the Gentile churches were aware of these relatives, it is certain that Jewish churches knew of them as well. The Jewish churches could have confronted those Gentile churches at any time regarding their false attribution of Davidic descent to Jesus. Richard Bauckham suggests that several relatives of Jesus were known and his four brothers were "well-known" in the first-century church.[34] These relatives include Joseph and Mary (his parents), James, Joses, Jude, and Simon (brothers in some familial sense); the possible inclusion of Salome and Mary as his sisters must also be considered. Jude has two grandsons, Zoker and James. Clopas and Mary are probably an uncle and aunt who have a son, Simon. In addition, it is probable that Clopas is Cleopas, one of the men mentioned on the road to Emmaus (Luke 24:13–27).[35]

The first-century work *Didache* provides further evidence that the early churches knew that the historical family of Jesus was rooted in the Davidic line. The text in 9:2 explicitly connects Jesus with the Davidic line.[36] The *Didache*'s later mention of "Ὡσαννὰ τῷ υἱῷ Δαβίδ" confirms that the author accepted Jesus' Davidic and divine sonship.[37] The authentic epistles of Ignatius contain several references to Jesus as a son of David, often in the context of his being the son of Mary and the son of God.[38]

---

31. "Remember Jesus Christ, risen from the dead, the offspring of David, as preached in my gospel, for which I am suffering, bound with chains as a criminal" (2 Timothy 2:8–9).

32. "I, Jesus, have sent my angel to testify to you about these things for the churches. I am the root and the descendant of David, the bright morning star" (Revelation 22:16).

33. Levin, "Jesus, 'Son of God' and 'Son of David,'" 417.

34. Bauckham, *Jude and the Relatives of Jesus*, 9. Bauckham provides an extensive list of references to support Jesus' Davidic descent (Mat 1:6, 17, 20; Mark 10:47–48; Luke 1:27, 32; 3:31; Acts 2:30; 13:23; 15:16; Rom 1:3; 2 Tim 2:8; Heb 7:14; Rev 5:5; 22:16; *Did* 10:6; *Asc Isa* 11:2; Ignatius, *Eph* 18:2; 20:2; *Smyrn* 1:1; *Trall* 9:1).

35. Bauckham, *Jude and the Relatives of Jesus*, 17–18, 97.

36. Hitchcock and Brown, *Teaching of the Twelve Apostles*, 16.

37. *Didache*, 10:6

38. See Eph 18, 20; Trall 9; Rom 7; Smyrnaeans 1; Antiochians 4.

Hegesippus reports a Palestinian tradition in which Roman authorities interrogated Zoker and James (the grandsons of Jesus' brother Jude) regarding their Davidic descent.[39] Julius Africanus attests that Jesus' relatives claimed Davidic descent in the *Letter to Aristides*.[40] Given the significant number of witnesses, it is impossible that the relatives of Jesus were unknown in the early church. Yet there is no record of them or Jewish polemicists ever attempting to refute their claim to be of the lineage of David.[41]

Rational Evidence Supporting the Davidic Heritage of Jesus

As Yeḥezkel Kaufmann observes, it may be impossible to *prove* Jesus' lineage using historical-critical criteria. Nonetheless, it is possible to identify other significant indicators of Jesus ancestry and how he was understood to be the son of David by his contemporaries. Kaufmann contends that Jesus' redemptive works would have identified him as Messiah, specifically his healing works. These curative acts would have been recognized as messianic behaviors, and the actor would be assumed to have a Davidic linage—a lineage stemming from Zerubbabel.[42] This conviction may surface in Nicodemus' affirmation that Jesus is a teacher sent from God (John 3:2), an affirmation based on his healing works. Duling describes these healing miracles as therapeutic in nature, especially as employed in Matthew's references to the title *son of David*. Specifically, Duling draws on the cry of Bartimaeus, who he believes stands in the background of Matthew's story

39. Eusebius, "Ecclesiastical History, Books 1–5," 3.11. (cf. 3.32.6; 4.22.4.)
40. Africanus, "Epistle to Aristides," 125–27.
41. Chapter 12 of the Epistle of Barnabas makes a puzzling statement about Jesus in relation to his ancestry. If that statement is taken at face value, it would seem to conflict with every other source that touches on the issue of Jesus' Davidic heritage: "Behold again: Jesus who was manifested, both by type and in the flesh, is not the Son of man, but the Son of God. Since, therefore, they were to say that Christ was the son of David, fearing and understanding the error of the wicked, he saith, 'The Lord said unto my Lord, Sit at My right hand, until I make Thine enemies Thy footstool.'" ("Epistle of Barnabas," 145). At the least, this pericope affirms that Davidic sonship was the prevailing view of the Messiah among the people. By its reference to Psalm 110, it also elevates Jesus' status beyond his human ancestry to one of divine sonship. The text, however, is not clear as to the author's intent. It seems likely that in a way similar to Mark 12:35–37, this is a subtle way of clarifying that Christians believed that Jesus was not merely the son of David but the son of God.
42. Kaufmann, "Messianic Idea," 141–50. Repentance is also linked with the coming of the messiah according to Neusner: "The Jerusalem Talmud indicates a second-century (AD) belief that repentance would bring the son of David, 'If Israel repents for one day, forthwith the son of David will come'" (Neusner, "Messiah in Rabbinic Judaism," 880–83).

of the healing of the two blind men (Matt 9:27–31).[43] The exegete must acknowledge that Jesus, in his encounter with Bartimaeus (Mark 10:46–52), did not reject, diminish the significance of, or display any disapproval of the title *Son of David*; rather, he responded affirmatively to it, asking what Bartimaeus wanted him to do.

Negatively, D. F. Strauss believes that the attribution of Davidic descent to Jesus was probably more dogmatic than historical. Even while employing a critical methodology, the skeptical Strauss seems forced to admit: "Jesus is universally represented in the New Testament, without any contradiction from his adversaries, as the descendant of David."[44] Akin to the conclusion of Strauss, Marshall Johnson argues that the claims of Davidic descent in the birth narratives are more works of art than history. The birth narratives, he maintains, are Midrash (a commentary on what should have been the case) and the historicizing of the unhistorical material. Apparently, Johnson believes the narratives are a type of *theologoumenon*.[45] However, other able scholars conclude differently, as indicated in the following three paragraphs.

Raymond Brown concludes that Jesus was from Davidic stock. He maintains that the majority of scholars still accept this position, naming Cullmann, Hahn, Jeremias, Michaelis, and Stauffer as examples.[46] Yigal Levin has thoughtfully answered the assertion that the genealogies are a *theologoumenon*. He did this by demonstrating that, although Davidic descent was an important characteristic for any messianic claimant, it was not of such universal significance that the gospel writers would resort to "invention."[47]

---

43. Duling, "Therapeutic Son of David," 399–400.

44. Strauss, *Life of Jesus*, 117.

45. Johnson, *Purpose of the Biblical Genealogies*, 254–56.

46. Raymond Brown cites the following as the reason for his conclusion against the *theologoumenon theory*: (1) In the early second century AD, Rabbi Aquiba hailed Bar Kochba (Simon ben Kosibah) as a messianic figure, even though he was not a *davidid*; (2) There were several types of messianic expectation in the first-century, (a) some looked for a hidden messiah with unknown origins, (b) at Qumran, they looked for both a *davidid* and a Messiah of Aaron; (3) The possibility that if Jesus were not a *davidid*, he would have been cast into one of these roles; (4) The author of the Epistle to the Hebrews apparently understood that Jesus' Davidic status and membership in the tribe of Judah was so well-known that presenting him as high priest needed significant explanation. See Brown, *Birth of the Messiah*, 505.

47. Levin, "Jesus, 'Son of God' and 'Son of David,'" 418. In support of this thesis, Levin cites Vermes, *Jesus the Jew*, 156–57; Noland, *Royal Son of God*, 64–71; Meier, *Marginal Jew*, 1:216–19; and Ankerberg and Weldon, *Handbook of Biblical Evidences*, 505–12.

Robert Gundry cogently argues that, through deeds and words, Jesus' ministry drove the attribution of OT fulfillments. The invention of history read back into prophecy is not characteristic of the NT accounts.[48] He further argues that the fabrication of stories are a part of the later apocryphal works. If the gospel accounts were manufactured, it would be logical to seek apocryphal literature surfacing concurrent with the gospel accounts. However, this study has not discovered any concurrent apocryphal works touching on the life of Jesus.

While concentrating on Matthew's use of the OT, Gundry provides several convincing reasons to believe that the NT accounts describing Jesus' fulfillment of OT prophesies are grounded in historical events. Some of these reasons are paraphrased below and can be applied with equal vigor to the any of the gospel documents:

1. Some texts to which the NT authors give messianic interpretation were not messianically interpreted in Judaism.
2. Matthew's account (and the other synoptic writers) sometimes receive independent attestation.
3. Some of Matthew's OT passages are obscure to the degree that no one would have thought to invent a fulfillment from them unless the tradition (event) came before the attribution of fulfillment;
4. Verisimilar details which cannot be ascertained from the OT prophecy are often present and in essential relationship to the NT context;
5. The NT texts demonstrate an absence of some elements found in the OT texts;
6. Invention is repugnant to Christian piety, yet the NT interpretation leaves the OT predictions open to contrary interpretation. Not every detail is covered.[49]

When thoughtfully weighed, the rational evidence indicates that it is highly improbable that Jesus or his disciples could lie about his ancestry and go undetected. Too many people knew too much about his family; further, too many people, both in the early church and throughout history, have scrutinized his life.

---

48. Gundry, *Use of the Old Testament*, 194–204.
49. Gundry, *Use of the Old Testament*, 204.

Jesus' Mother

Another conundrum to consider when discussing the ancestry of Jesus pertains to his mother. A suggestive strand of historical thought places her in the Davidic line. Luke 1:32 implies a possible link to the Davidic line through Mary.[50] Reasoned according to conventional thinking, if Jesus was from the seed of David, Mary must have been a *davidid*—it could be no other way. How can the exegete reinterpret the terms מִמֵּעֶיךָ (from bowel/body of you) or κοιλίας (belly) in reference to the original promise? This perceived need for a Davidic pedigree may explain why there are two different NT genealogies. It may also explain why the obvious discrepancies were allowed to remain a part of the texts. Persons with insider knowledge would have immediately recognized falsification in an attempt to harmonize the two accounts.

In contrast to the issue of Mary's lineage, the adoption of Jesus by Joseph has been one of the most prevalent ways to defend Jesus' messianic status.[51] If the adoption of Jesus into the family of David is a legitimate way for him to acquire a Davidic pedigree, the problems in the genealogies largely disappear. This tactic is problematic, however. M. Brown reminds his readers: "This whole argument [for Jesus' Davidic heritage] . . . is greatly weakened if the Messiah's descent cannot be traced through Miriam and if she is not, in fact, in the legitimate Messianic line from David."[52] M. Brown and Levin both remark that many New Testament scholars who believe that both Matthew and Luke give genealogies of Joseph find no contradiction in the idea that adoption is a legitimate way to place Jesus in the royal line. This would, require, however, some form of levirate marriage before reconciliation of the genealogies could even begin. The thesis of a levirate marriage, in this case, is indemonstrable. However, the simplest levirate-marriage

---

50. Based on her familial relationship with Elizabeth, there is probably also a Levitical association.

51. Levin lists the following scholars as holding to the adoption of Jesus by Joseph to obtain status as the son of David: Waetjen, "Genealogy as the key to the Gospel," 227; Beare, *Gospel According to Matthew*, 61; Davies and Allison Jr., *Gospel According to Saint Matthew*, 1:219–20; Richard, *Jesus: One and Many*, 146; Barnett, *Behind the Scenes of the New Testament*, 19; Green, *Theology of the Gospel of Luke*, 55–56; Schnackenburg, *Jesus in the Gospels*, 103; Senior, *Matthew*, 38; and Carter, *Matthew and the Margins*, 65.

52. See vol. 4 of Brown, *Answering Jewish Objections to Jesus*. David Stern contends that it is possible Luke intends to suggest that he is following Mary's genealogy because the definite article is absent before the name of Joseph, thereby separating it from the genealogical record. The implications of ἐνομίζετο (it was thought) is a further indication, according to Stern, that Luke intends to point out the mistake of readers who may be thinking in terms of Matthew's genealogy. Stern, *Jewish New Testament Commentary*, Luke 3:23.

hypothesis contends that Heli and Jacob were half-brothers; they had the same mother, but fathers of different names. Perhaps Heli died and Jacob married his widow.[53]

M. Brown flatly states, "I am not convinced . . . that Yeshua's Davidic descent can be maintained without Miriam herself also descending from that line."[54] Correspondingly, Levin argues persuasively that Joseph's adoption of Jesus is a non-Jewish concept: "Jewish law, both in antiquity and in the modern era, has no such legal institution."[55] If Matthew and Luke do actually record anything approaching Joseph's actual lineage, Mary's must be sought elsewhere. The notion that Mary is the source of Jesus' Davidic status is not novel and may well be necessary to fulfill the Davidic Covenant, but it is impossible to demonstrate.[56]

The Self-Understanding of Jesus and the Early Church

Approaching the problem of Jesus' alleged Davidic descent from another perspective, it is fitting to ask how Jesus or (allowing for critical scholarship) the early church understood his relationship to the house of David. Oscar Cullman treats this issue by examining Mark 14:61–65, Mark 15:2–5, and Mark 8:27–30 with their parallels. He also treats Mark 12:35–37 as perhaps the only text that provides information about whether Jesus designated himself the *son of David*. Cullman contends that the question posed to Jesus in Mark 14:61—and its parallel in Matthew 26:64—is not definitively answered in the affirmative. The ambiguity lies in Matthew's account. Cullman rightly finds much abstruseness in Jesus' σὺ εἶπας answer. The basis for Cullman's analysis is a presumed Aramaic original text in which the term in question does not mean *yes*.[57] As Matthew records the event, there is no disputing that Jesus does not flatly say *yes*. However, if one considers Mark's

---

53. Eusebius, "Ecclesiastical History, Books 1–5," 1.7.

54. Brown, *Answering Jewish Objections to Jesus*, 4:87n189.

55. Levin, "Jesus, 'Son of God' and 'Son of David,'" 423. David Lowery, commenting on Levin's work states: "The idea of Jesus' adoption may not be clear from available Jewish sources. But the issue of human and divine paternity in connection with the titles mentioned probably misses their point and to that extent makes the Roman comparison moot" (Lowery, "Review of Jesus, 'Son of God,'" 102). Lowery believes these titles should be understood functionally. If that is the correct interpretation, the entire quest to historically authenticate Jesus' Davidic status, his relationship to OT prophecy, and his divine relationship to *Yahweh* is futile.

56. Brown provides a brief survey of the problems with attributing Jesus' Davidic status to Mary along with some possible answers to the issues. Brown, *Answering Jewish Objections to Jesus*, 4:84–97.

57. Cullmann, *Christology of the New Testament*, 118–19.

version, Jesus does flatly say *yes* (ἐγώ εἰμι). In addition, if one observes the thoughts connected with the use of the term σὺ εἶπας (you have said so) in Matthew 26:25, Mark 15:2, and the hostility surfacing in Matthew 27:1, it is probable that an affirmative answer is implied. Jesus' elusive answer may have been an attempt to avoid overtly incriminating himself while appearing before those with inimical intentions.

Ulrich Luz notes that Jesus' vague response in Matthew 26:64 may be a result of his refusal to answer with an oath in combination with the already mentioned relational distance between him and his hostile interlocutors.[58] Immediately following his ἐγώ εἰμι answer in Mark 14:62, Jesus promises the Sanhedrin that they will see him "seated at the right hand of Power, and coming with the clouds of heaven." If this statement is historical, it leaves little doubt about whether Jesus answered Caiaphas's question affirmatively.[59]

Mark 8:29 provides another insight into Jesus' self-perception. Peter's answer to the question, "Who do you say that I am," was, "You are the Christ." The fact that Matthew does not depict Jesus denying or correcting Peter is often interpreted as Jesus' acceptance of the title. Conversely, Cullmann is technically correct when asserting that Jesus neither affirmed nor denied Peter's statement.[60] According to this line of argumentation, Peter and the other disciples (especially Judas) have a politically charged view of the Messiah. Peter's attempt to enforce such a view by rebuking Jesus (Mark 8:32) provokes Jesus' harsh reply: "Get behind me Satan" (Mark 8:33).[61] His unexpected reply leaves little doubt that Jesus' view of his task contrasts sharply with that of the disciples and the populist hope.

Embracing the politically charged perspective is, however, very different from assuming that Jesus rejected Peter's confession. Without question, Peter's confession of Jesus as the Messiah is often besieged with misunderstanding—even today. That alone, however, does not mean that such a confession is incorrect. Jesus did not reject the title; rather, he rejected Peter's attempt to intrude into his agenda. In fact, the synoptic evangelists, plus John and Paul, all clearly intended to support the idea that Jesus is the Messiah, not a mere human pursuing a political agenda.

Jesus himself may have intimated of something extraordinary when he asked the controversial question: "How can the scribes say that the Christ is the son of David"? (Mark 12:35). Clearly, Jesus did not say, *how can the scribes say I (Jesus) am the son of David?* His argumentation is more subtle.

---

58. Luz, *Commentary on Matthew 21–28*, 429.

59. See section entitled "New Testament Evidence" regarding Haggai 2:1–9 above.

60. Cullmann, *Christology of the New Testament*, 122.

61. Cullmann, *Christology of the New Testament*, 123.

It only touches on his Davidic status if one supposes that Jesus is tacitly claiming to be both a son of David and the Messiah. He certainly is not denying either; *a fortiori*, it is illogical to conclude that Jesus is denying such designations. That denial would render much of the NT incoherent. R. Brown notes two additional flaws in the proposition that Jesus is denying his or the Messiah's Davidic status. First, all three synoptic writers offer ample evidence that they believe Jesus to be a *davidid*. Second, in order to prove that the Messiah was foretold as a *davidid*, the scribes could have appropriated many texts and traditions.[62] Such denial would have revealed Jesus as a pretender and brought instant ridicule.

Cullmann is right to note that Jesus is not denying his Davidic status; rather, Jesus is demonstrating that this status is not the most significant component of his Christological work. Jesus is greater than David. Cullmann, however, overstates both his case and the NT texts when concluding that Jesus denied "any fundamental significance to Davidic sonship."[63] Instead, Jesus is asserting that the epithet *Son of David* alone is not adequate to depict his office: that designation is a descriptive prerequisite, but does not exhaust the qualifications of the Messiah. The Messiah is greater than any earthly king. This is the import of Psalm 8:6 and 110 when interpreted by the NT writers. Jesus, according to Mark 12:35, also implies the same thing.[64]

Rudolf Bultmann cogently addresses the import of Mark 12:35-37 by remarking that the passage is the product of a small community of primitive Christians who:

> *either* . . . intended to represent that the tension between faith in the Son of Man and hope in the Son of David (if, that is, it were not meant simply to refute the accusation that Jesus' Davidic descent could not be established). *Or* it comes from the Hellenistic Church, in which case it would be meant to prove that Jesus was more than a Son of David, viz. the Son of God."[65]

---

62. Brown, *Birth of the Messiah*, 509. William Lane correctly asserts that for the scribes: "This would be recognized as a Haggada-question, a question of exegesis concerned with the reconciliation of two seemingly contradictory points of view expressed in Scripture." Lane, *Gospel of Mark*, 436.

63. Cullmann, *Christology of the New Testament*, 131-32.

64. The question of authorship of Psalms 8 and 110 is irrelevant for the current argument in relation to Mark 12:35-37. The authors of the gospels and the Jewish people accepted these Psalms as compositions of David. Whether or not Jesus believed David was the author is irrelevant to his question.

65. Bultmann, *History of the Synoptic Tradition*, 136-37. Another issue arising in Bultmann's work on Mark 12:35-37 is his admission that it is "not impossible" that Jesus could have spoken the words attributed to him, but not in reference to himself. It seems that the reason for the question is to direct the listeners to understand him

Bultmann obviously desires to establish that the passage comes out of an early church and not from oral or written sources which pre-date Mark. In pursuing this desire, however, he overstates the demonstrable. Even so, Bultmann seems to have grasped the import of the passage as few others have. His dubious conclusion was that the pericope is the creation of an early church community based on the impossibility of a Davidic Messiah becoming fixed as dogma so early.

Bultmann's conclusion can be countered by briefly noting three things. First, scholars routinely place the date of Paul's conversion in the early to mid-part of the third decade, of the first century AD, perhaps as early as two to three years after the death and resurrection of Jesus.[66] If, indeed, Paul was the traveling evangelist portrayed in the NT, knowledge of Jesus as the son of David could have spread very rapidly. Key accounts in the book of Acts clearly indicate that Paul's first engagement in a new city was often in its synagogue (Acts 9:20; 13:5, 14; 14:1; 17:1, 10; 18:4). Acts 17:1 explicitly affirms that Paul customarily went to the synagogue to preach. It is beyond doubt that these Jewish listeners would have questioned Paul about Jesus' Davidic credentials; they doubtless carried, to every part of the Roman Empire, Paul's affirmation of Jesus as a son of David according to the flesh (Rom 1:3).

Second, as explained above, several of Jesus' family members were known and apparently had itinerate ministries of their own. Both the OT prophecies of a Davidic Messiah and Jesus' Davidic status would naturally have been components of their preaching.

Third, a significant portion of the Jewish world, like Paul (according to Bultmann), already presupposed a Davidic Messiah. Educating the masses as to the fulfillment of the ancient promise easily could have occurred within a couple of decades.

A Contrasting Opinion

The fellows of the Jesus Seminar present a contrasting opinion. They firmly reject the idea that Jesus asked Peter the question regarding his identity or that Peter answered it. They also reject the idea that Jesus answered Caiaphas's question affirmatively while on trial before the Sanhedrin.[67] In their

---

paradoxically; both as *son of David* and greater than David. If Jesus spoke these words, they almost certainly were of himself.

66 Copan, "True for You but Not for Me," 158. Cf., *Lexham Bible Dictionary*.

67 Funk and Hoover, *Five Gospels*, 75. Cf. Gospel of Thomas 13:1-8; John 1:35-45; 6:66-69.

collective opinion, both questions, and much of the speech attributed to Jesus in the NT, are examples of stylized Christian motifs—the work of the evangelists. Their view entails the idea that Jesus virtually never initiates any conversation about himself. His encounters are usually the result of questions directed to him or already developing situations. Their denials, however, do little damage to the historical textual evidence presented above. The opinion of this group of scholars is based on "generalizations"[68] and unofficially what "sounds like"[69] Jesus, rather than supplying any comparable evidence that contradicts the gospel witnesses. Admittedly, all written history is a reconstruction. Yet, the criteria of the Jesus Seminar, as applied to this issue, does not offer an alternative reconstruction of history. Their conclusion is, rather, a subjective assault on the evidence. Their problematic method rejects the reconstructions of others who were much closer to the events and historical contexts and who understood the rhythms of Jewish messianic expectations of the period. Devoid of supporting contrary documentation, the methodology of the Jesus Seminar irretrievably cascades out of the scholarly realm and into subjectivity.[70]

Even if one grants that Jesus never made an overt messianic claim, this does little damage to the argument and facts presented above. It is the Davidic status of Jesus that is the issue. To investigate this issue objectively, one must rely on historical sources. The sources that reflect the best historical information available contend, in a variety of ways, that Jesus was a *davidid*. These sources, stylized or not, consistently portray Jesus in this way.

Summary

In summary, there is ample reason to believe that the Davidic covenant and its promises were embedded in the Jewish messianic consciousness and gradually expanded from the time of the monarchy. These expectations survived—and perhaps intensified—during the exile. Integral to

---

68. Funk and Hoover, *Five Gospels*, 32.

69. Funk and Hoover, *Five Gospels*, 37.

70. Evan Fales also offers no historical counter-evidence directly refuting the historicity of the gospel accounts when he attacks them as "designed to exaggerate Jesus' visibility among contemporaries." He adds further that any historical core (especially of the crucifixion) has been "thoroughly obscured for the sake of the message." The basis for his critique is anthropological/sociological comparative studies leading to the contention that the genre of the gospels is myth, including the outright invention of many of the accounts. Fales notes that these accounts are symbolic in nature and that the meanings are readily understandable when understood symbolically. Fales, "Successful Defense?" 18–20.

this covenant was the idea that a messianic, kingly figure would be the physical offspring of the historical King David. Even when the apocryphal and pseudepigraphical works present messianic figures in a superhuman fashion, there is an identifiable connection to the historic Israelite Davidic kings. The NT and early church documents that address this issue uniformly place Jesus within the Davidic house. No early source attempts to refute this claim. Finally, even if the NT accounts of Jesus and his life are stylized works of the evangelists, that alone does not disqualify them as historically based facts. Stylization only proves that the early church universally understood Jesus as the Davidic Messiah.

Plausible Historical-Evidential Conclusions Drawn from the Study of the OT and NT Davidic Claim

1. The messianic expectation of the Jewish nation was rooted in the Davidic Covenant.
2. The messianic expectation was varied, but its chief characteristic was kingly.
3. The kingly aspect often contained a significant Davidic stream of thought.
4. Jesus' relatives were known in the early church.
5. Jesus was probably a descendant of King David.

Historical-Evidential Facts Drawn from the Study of the OT and NT Davidic Claim

1. No first-century evidence suggests that Jesus was not a descendant of King David.
2. Neither Jesus' adversaries nor his friends challenge his Davidic status.
3. Paul, a former enemy of the church, claimed Jesus was a physical descendant of King David.
4. Multiple NT and early extra-biblical sources attest Jesus' Davidic status.

Chapter 5

The Third Group of Biblical Texts

Introduction to the Third Group Biblical of Texts

THE ACTUAL BIRTHPLACE OF Jesus is an important issue because the OT prophecy, recorded in Micah 5:2, declares that a ruler will come from Bethlehem Ephrathah, later delineated Bethlehem of Judea. In John 7:42, the Jewish people are portrayed as giving assent to the idea that the Messiah must have genealogical roots in Bethlehem; this seems to accord with some known messianic expectations of the period.[1] According to Benjamin A. Foreman:

> The messianic interpretation of Mic 5:2 was not simply an overzealous Christological exegesis promoted by the early followers of Jesus to justify their belief that he was the messiah. The conviction that the messiah would be born in Bethlehem was also current in (at least some streams of) Jewish theology in the first and second centuries AD.[2]

The fact that Matthew mentions the knowledge of the chief priests and scribes in reference to the child's birth in Bethlehem indicates that some first-century Jews believed the Messiah would have roots in Bethlehem of Judea (Matt 2:6). Conversely, according to the Enlightenment philosopher John Locke, the Jewish people apparently questioned how someone passing for a Galilean could be the Messiah (John 7:42).[3] Matthew and Luke

---

1. Mayhew, "Current Trends In Messianology," 36. Leon Morris, *Gospel According to John*, 380. Although noting modern skepticism about the historicity of Jesus' birth in Bethlehem, R. Brown indicates that Matthew apparently believed that placing Jesus' birth in Bethlehem would be accepted by Jews as the birthplace of the Messiah. This, Brown notes, is partially supported by John 7:41–42. Brown, *Birth of the Messiah*, 182.

2. Foreman, "Matthew's Birth Narrative," s.v. "Matt 2:1–18."

3. See Mayhew, "Current Trends," 36, and Locke, *Reasonableness of Christianity*, 70.

both make the claim that Jesus was born in Bethlehem of Judea. What available evidence supports this claim? Is the evidence sufficient to make a factual statement regarding the birthplace of Jesus? As suggested above, the investigation to evaluate the claim that the Messiah would be born in Bethlehem of Judea begins with Micah 5:2. Additional texts investigated are those making the parallel claim that Jesus was actually born in this small village (Matthew 2:1–12; Luke 2: 1–7).

Micah 5:2

Literary and Textual Analysis

Old Testament Evidence

Although vague—and perhaps intentionally so—the text of Micah 5:2 is most often interpreted as prophesying the birth of a future ideal ruler, a ruler like David. He, in some fashion, springs from the house of Jesse and David[4] in the area of Bethlehem.[5] This Davidic ruler represents, according to Delbert Hillers, a David *redividus* who will reestablish the kingdom and end the exile.[6] Broadly conceived, this is still the opinion of the majority of scholars. Bethlehem of Judea is the predicted place from which the ruler comes.[7] The import is the same, whether dated to the eighth-century BC[8] and a prophecy of exile and restoration, or to the post-exilic era,[9] prophesying only the return from exile. J. J. M. Roberts suggests that Micah 5:2 and several other prophecies that foresee an ideal Davidic scion are more than predictive—they are also criticisms of the current king as an inadequate heir to David. He asserts that both Isaiah and Micah probably envisioned a time of cleansing and trial prior to the arrival of the new David; certainly, this is true for Isaiah and is probably true for Micah.[10] The dishonorable past and present conduct of the monarchy would be superseded by a glorious future ruler, one that Micah symbolically associates with the same geo-

---

4 Johnston, "Messianic Trajectories," 125.

5. Francis Schaeffer explicitly states his contention that the Messiah must be born in Bethlehem. Schaeffer, *Complete Works*, 2:337.

6. Hillers, *Micah*, 66.

7. Hinckley et al., "Micah, Zephaniah, Nahum, Habakkuk, Obadiah, and Joel," 102–6. Cf. Fitzmyer, *One Who Is to Come*, 53; Mowinckel, *He That Cometh*, 19; and Gundry, *Use of the Old Testament*, 91.

8. Barker, *Micah, Nahum, Habakkuk, Zephaniah*, 31.

9. Wolff, *Micah*, 135–36.

10. Roberts, "Old Testament's Contribution," 41.

graphic locale and to the same shepherd role (Micah 5:4)[11] as characterized David, the son of Jesse.[12]

Intertestamental Evidence

The first fragment of intertestamental evidence that must be considered is the Jewish cultural expectation building up to the first century. Many among the population expected a messianic figure. As noted in chapter 4, this expectation, however, was not monolithic in nature. The most prevalent characteristic among those looking for a messianic figure was the royal or kingly image. Messianism in general became increasingly important from the time of Herod the Great, as attested in the Parables of Enoch (1 En 37–71).[13] The messianic motif's historical development also included concepts such as "earthly warrior (1QM; Pss. Sol. 17–18), . . . preexisting and transcendent figure (1 Enoch; 4 Ezra)," and other relevant ideas.[14] Several later pseudepigraphical works also contain messianic components, some Davidic and some non-Davidic.[15] Evidence does emerge, however, to support the notion that some pre-Christian Jews believed the leader prophesied in Micah would be closely associated with Bethlehem.

Louis Ginzberg, Henrietta Szold, and Paul Radin associate Micah 5 with early rabbinic messianic expectations and the work of salvation.[16] Later, Jewish ideas that likely reflect pre-Christian interpretations of Micah—interpretations in concord with the messianic understanding—are recognizable in *Targum Jonathan to the Prophets* and *Midrash Rabbah* on Lamentations 1:16. Bethlehem is stated as the birthplace of the Messiah-king in the Jerusalem Talmud.[17] Origen alleges that, in a plot to discredit Christianity, Jewish teachers withheld information from the public about the birthplace of Jesus.[18] They did this despite knowing the prophecy of Micah and the truth about Jesus' birthplace.

---

11. McConville, "Micah," 548.
12. Jenson, "Models of Prophetic Prediction," 206.
13. Horbury, *Messianism among Jews and Christians*, 40.
14. Bird, *Are You the One Who Is to Come?*, 33.
15. Horbury, *Messianism among Jews and Christians*, 54.
16. "In allusion to Micah 5:4, it is asserted in the old rabbinic literature that when the Messiah is about to start his work of salvation, he will be furnished with a council of fourteen members to assist him." Ginzberg et al., *Legends of the Jews*, 99n142.
17. Neusner, *Jerusalem Talmud*, y. Ber. 2:4, II.3.N.
18. Origen, "Origen against Celsus," 1.51.

Extra Biblical Evidence

The extra-biblical witnesses to the birthplace of Jesus are several and varied. In the second-century work *Dialogue with Trypho*, Justin reiterates what by then must have been an established tradition: Bethlehem was the place of Jesus' birth. Interestingly, and in contrast to most modern depictions, Justin places the birth in a cave.[19] This detail, however, fits well with the known geography of the area and the habits of the local population; they still use the caves located on the outskirts of the city for the protection of livestock.[20] This detail may also reflect an independent line of attestation by relating facts not included in sources used by the biblical authors. Local tradition and the routine practices surrounding the care of animals often are trans-generational: they are practiced in the same way from generation to generation, using the same locations and techniques.

Origen wrote his tractate *Against Celsus* sometime in the first half of the third century AD. In this work, he asserts not only his understanding that Jesus was born in Bethlehem but also that evidence supports the claim:

> With respect to the birth of Jesus in Bethlehem, if any one desires, after the prophecy of Micah and after the history recorded in the Gospels by the disciples of Jesus, to have additional evidence from other sources, let him know that, in conformity with the narrative in the Gospel regarding His birth, there is shown at Bethlehem the cave where He was born, and the manger in the cave where He was wrapped in swaddling-clothes. And this sight is greatly talked of in surrounding places, even among the enemies of the faith, it being said that in this cave was born that Jesus who is worshipped and reverenced by the Christians.[21]

The evidence Origen speaks of is uncertain. Taken as written, however, Origen's text notes that even those who opposed the Christian faith could (and apparently did, since it was "talked of in surrounding places") journey to Bethlehem to see what was supposed to be the birthplace of Jesus.[22]

Ignatius, Bishop of Antioch, although not specifically mentioning "Bethlehem," is clearly drawing on the traditional material when writing to the church at Ephesus. He speaks of Jesus' miraculous birth being from the

---

19. Martyr, "Dialogue of Justin," 78.

20. The NT Apocryphal works are also in agreement with the historicity of Jesus' birth in a cave near Bethlehem. *Apocryphal New Testament: Being the Apocryphal Gospels, Acts, Epistles, and Apocalypses.* Prot. Jas. 17:11–18:11; Marias, "Gospel of the Nativity of Mary," 10. (cf. *Arabic Infancy Gospel*)

21. Origen, "Origen against Celsus," 1.51.

22. Origen, "Origen against Celsus," 1.51.

house of David and of the star that shone brighter than did all others. The letter is usually dated prior to AD 117 and virtually always before AD 138.

Documents such as those cited above affirm the earlier gospel witnesses who support the contention that Jesus was born in Bethlehem. All of the cited witnesses date from long before the Roman Empire was declared Christian and the Church of the Nativity sanctioned as the birthplace of Jesus. Constantine ordered the construction of the Church of the Nativity in AD 333. That imperial order essentially verifies the general belief that Bethlehem was the birthplace. It is even possible that the Romans correctly assessed the tradition and correctly designated the actual cave in which Jesus' was born. When objectively weighed, the probability that the main aspects of the story have a factual basis are well supported.

William Mitchell Ramsay mentions several issues that would support the thesis that Jesus was born in Bethlehem. First, Luke has unambiguously claimed to be writing history and to have gathered facts in order to compile a narrative of the things derived—at least in part—from first-hand observers; he did this for the stated purpose of helping Theophilus gain certainty about the things he had been taught.[23] During Luke's birth narrative, for example, the importance of these alleged first-hand observers initially emerges when Mary, on two occasions, is described as treasuring up things and events, pondering them in her heart (Luke 2:19, 51). The account describes details of which only Mary had firsthand knowledge. Ramsay is convinced that Luke intends the reader to understand that Mary is his source: "The historian, by emphasizing the silence and secrecy in which she treasured up the facts, gives the reader to understand that she is the authority."[24] Perhaps this is not an account directly delivered to Luke by Mary, but may have been handed down through one or more intermediaries. In either case, the intimate nature of the narrative comes through to even the most uniformed reader.

In contrast, Meier argues against the historicity of the account and disputes the participation of Mary, or someone close to the events, as a Lukan source. At least in part, Meier contends that Luke is either mistaken or conflates Mary's purification with Jesus' redemption. This error or conflation, according to Meier, is something of which no informed Jew would be guilty.[25] If Luke's purpose was to write about the intricacies of Jewish redemptive and purification rites, Meier could be correct. Nonetheless,

---

23. On the reliability of Luke as a historian, see Hemer, "Luke the Historian"; Utley, *Luke the Historian*; and Marshall, *Luke: Historian and Theologian*.

24. Ramsay, *Was Christ Born at Bethlehem*, 651.

25. Meier, *Marginal Jew*, 1:210.

Meier is unconvincing in his attack on the historicity of these events. It seems fallacious to critique Luke as though he is writing about the intricacies of the Mosaic Law, thereby conflating two completely different Jewish rites. The differences in the emphases of Matthew, Luke, and their respective audiences have already been noted.

The majority of scholars today conclude that Luke is writing in historiographical style appropriate to his period.[26] Ostensibly, he is writing to one individual, Theophilus, conveying basic facts and information in order to ground his research and conclusions. It is true that Luke does not mention that payment was made during Jesus' presentation and consecration at the temple. It is also true that his account contains the textually difficult term αὐτῶν (them) in Luke 2:22. Still these facts are probably not the result of Lukan legal incompetence. It is much more plausible that the whole event was viewed as a family affair, not the private purification of a single family member.

If Mary or someone very close to her is the source of Luke's infancy narrative, there could be no better verification for the historicity of Jesus' birth in Bethlehem. Who better to verify these events than Jesus' mother? Luke's account as the recollection of an eyewitness cannot be demonstrated, but it is clear that Luke expects his account to be accepted as credible. Indeed, when objectively judged by the canons of historical criticism and in accordance with the standards of his time, the Lukan account fairs well.

New Testament Evidence

In the NT book of Matthew, Micah 5:2 is interpreted by the author—and, ostensibly, by the scribes of Herod the Great's court—as referring to the Messiah (Matt 2:5-6). The Matthean text states flatly that Jesus was born in "Bethlehem of Judea." After the family's flight to Egypt, Joseph and Mary wanted to resettle in the same area; however, Joseph's fear of Archelaus motivated them to move on to Nazareth.

The Lukan account also flatly states that Jesus was born in Bethlehem (Luke 2:4-6), but the historical context provided by Luke includes an initial travel sequence from Nazareth to Bethlehem. Specifically Luke's account asserts that the travel is compelled by the first registration during the governorship of Quirinius (discussed below). Luke gives the reader the impression that the family spent only a few weeks in the area before moving back to Galilee. The difficulties in integrating the accounts of Matthew and

---

26. For a detailed treatment of Luke's approach and style, see Witherington, *Acts of the Apostles*.

Luke have led scholars such as Sanders to claim that the accounts present "irreconcilable" ways of moving the family from one place to another.[27] Ehrman doubts the historicity of the stories, but admits that "completely different"[28] accounts of historical events do not necessarily create problems. In another publication Ehrman states: "Now it may be that Matthew is simply telling some of the story and Luke is telling the rest of it, so that we are justified every December in combining the two accounts into a Christmas pageant where you get both the shepherds *and* the wise men, both the trip from Nazareth *and* the flight to Egypt."[29] Christoph Burger states, what is probably still the consensus of critical scholarship: *"Daß Bethlehem nicht der historische Geburtsort Jesu ist, wurde unter der erdrückenden Last der Gegeninstanzen zur communis opinio neutestamentlicher Wissenschaft."*[30] Often rejections, such as those offered by Sanders and Burger, are based on what is *not* present in the account rather than what is represented. A cursory reading of these biblical texts demonstrate that the two versions are not intended to be unadorned, banal historical recollections. Rather, they are intended to highlight specific motifs. If creatively read, most of the apparent difficulties are plausibly resolved by allowing for divergent authorial purposes and acknowledging that neither account is exhaustive. This does not establish the historicity of the whole nor of any individual element; it does, however, compel a closer examination of other evidence.

Where Did Mary and Joseph Live?

The Matthean account makes no assertion about where Joseph and Mary lived prior to the birth of Jesus. When Matthew identifies Bethlehem as Jesus' birthplace, in reference to the visit by the *Magi*, he provides no details on the previous geographical location of the couple.[31] Their previous living arrangement apparently was of no concern to this author and his purpose. Yet the possibility that Bethlehem was the home of Joseph's relatives is at least lexically possible, based on the incidence of the term καταλύματι in

---

27. Sanders, *Historical Figure of Jesus*, 85–86.
28. Ehrman, *Jesus Apocalyptic Prophet of the New Millennium*, 36.
29. Ehrman, *Jesus Interrupted*, 33.
30. Burger, *Jesus als Davidssohn*, 104.
31. Justin Martyr also claims that the Arabian Magi who had first visited Herod visited the family: "As soon as He was born in Bethlehem, as I previously remarked, king Herod, having learned from the Arabian Magi about Him, made a plot to put Him to death: and by God's command Joseph took Him with Mary and departed into Egypt." Martyr, "Dialogue of Justin," 250.

Luke 2:7.[32] It is even possible, if not likely, that Joseph lived in Bethlehem for most of his life before his formal betrothal to Mary required his presence in Nazareth. The term καταλύματι is just as likely to have designated a guest room in the family home as some public accommodation (Luke 22:11). In addition, the text of Luke states that the reason for the travel was Joseph's familial relationship to David; that relationship required him to go to Bethlehem. It is reasonable to think that Joseph would seek to stay with his family, if possible.[33] Elsewhere Luke designates public accommodation by the term πανδοχεῖον (Luke 10:34). Καταλύματι and πανδοχεῖον are clearly distinct terms with distinct meaning. How the author intends for them to be understood is not perfectly clear, however. If the hypothesis is valid that Luke is referring to a family guest-room, this may explain why there was no space for Mary and Joseph. Perhaps others of Joseph's family had already arrived for the census and the house was full. Mary and Joseph's journey from Nazareth may have been slowed by Mary's advanced pregnancy. It is also plausible to think that giving birth would require some level of privacy and the best accommodation the family could provide was a cave or structure attached to the property.[34] If the family of Joseph did own a home in Bethlehem, it also could explain why the *Magi* found the infant Jesus living in a house (Matt 2:11) sometime after his birth.

Sanders claims that Luke has the family returning directly to Galilee after the scene at the temple during Jesus' presentation. It is true that Luke does not mention the family's flight to Egypt or the events leading up to that episode. On the other hand, Sanders's analysis seems to place the burden of an exhaustive account on Luke rather than one that includes only essential details. If one assumes (1) the historicity of Herod's order to kill the children of Bethlehem under two years of age, and (2) that Luke was aware of the order, one must conclude that he chose to exclude it from his account for some unstated reason. How does this affect the gospel's historicity? If Luke was not aware of the event, the lacuna cannot be fairly characterized as evidence of a contrived narrative. A fair assessment suggests that this omission of details was more likely an irrelevant lacuna in Luke rather than an inventive, apologetic element of Matthew. Scholars such as France have acknowledged that the overall population of the area around Bethlehem would have been small and the number of deaths probably would have not

---

32. Arndt et al., *Greek-English Lexicon*, 521.

33. Witherington, "Nativity According to Luke," 7. Cf. Carlson, "Accommodations of Joseph and Mary."

34. Witherington, "Nativity According to Luke," 46–47

exceeded twenty.³⁵ This small number of deaths would not have attracted empire-wide attention. Large numbers of people were killed in battles and executed for various reasons on a routine basis. In the first-century Roman world, Herod (and many other royal figures) dealt harshly with sedition. Additionally, Josephus is silent on this particular matter, despite recording details of Herod's ruthlessness on several other occasions.

The Herodian order to kill the children under two probably entailed a small number of deaths. Even so, Matthew appears to be true to his form and intent by tying the episode to OT prophecy typologically (Matt 2:13–15). The alleged fulfillment of OT prophecy would have been of great interest to the Hebrew reader. Luke, on the other hand, is probably writing to a Gentile audience that may not have readily grasped Matthew's interpretive method.³⁶ Both Luke and Matthew place the birth of Jesus in Bethlehem and the family's final residence in Nazareth of Galilee. This fact is confirmed in multiple ways throughout the various written accounts. Both authors also seem to have selectively chosen the elements of the total story.

Which Bethlehem?

Both Matthew and Luke take pains to explain that Jesus was born while Joseph and Mary were in Bethlehem of Judea. This southern village has sometimes been confused with the northern village, "Bethlehem," located in Galilee and currently known as *Beit Lahm*. This northern Bethlehem was located about eleven kilometers northwest of Nazareth.³⁷ Chilton has argued for this northern city as the place of Jesus' birth. The rationale for his position is grounded in his rejection of the virgin birth and the proximity of the Galilean Bethlehem to Nazareth. The problem with Chilton's analysis is that he does not deal with the biblical texts or the claims made by its authors; instead, he summarily discards those claims as inventions. Chilton, in fact, provides no positive textual or historical evidence for his claim. As a result, his conclusions logically follow from presuppositions based on difficulties in the text and *a priori* dismissal of the supernatural.

---

35. France, *Gospel of Matthew*, 85.

36. Perhaps Matthew's logic and method are reflective of the belief that bridging the cultural and philosophical distance between Jew and Gentile worldviews would take some time. This distance is reflected later in polemical statements like those of Tertullian: "What indeed has Athens to do with Jerusalem? What concord is there between the Academy and the Church? what between heretics and Christians?" (Turtullian, "The Prescription against Heretics," 246).

37 Bockmuehl, *This Jesus*, 25. Cf. Joshua 19:15 and Neusner, *Jerusalem Talmud, y. Meg.* 1:1, II.3.F-G.

The textual and historical evidence for Bethlehem of Judea as the birthplace of Jesus, as noted above, begins with Matthew 2:1 and Luke 2:11, 15. These are the earliest extant tractates for the origins of Jesus. Luke claims to be writing from sources, at least some of which had provided eyewitness testimony. Evidentially, it is important to note that birth narratives of both Matthew and Luke are neither a part of the Q material nor are they of Markan origin. They both appear to be parts of distinct lines of source material: one unique to Matthew and the other unique to Luke. Support for this assertion arises in the work of Kim Paffenroff, who authored a widely-cited work dealing with Luke's unique contributions to the overall gospel data. Paffenroff does not place the birth narrative among her specially selected "L" group of material, as one might expect. The "L" material consists of all the material gathered into a single source prior to Luke's appropriation of the documents. Paffenroff contends that "much of the infancy narrative most likely derives from Luke himself."[38]

Regardless of where and how Luke gathered his information, his birth narrative delineates Bethlehem of Judea as the birthplace of Jesus. Further, that narrative contains wording and elements that come from distinct historical sources. Luke's affirmation of Bethlehem of Judea as the birthplace of Jesus must be counted as a distinct source using early material that agrees in several ways with the Matthean witness.

The Matthean birth narrative is also an original composition based on unknown sources. Although some common elements with the Lukan account are present (as detailed below), the apologetic purpose, content, and arrangement are distinctively Matthean. Any lacuna in the two accounts cannot fairly be judged to be a contradiction, at least not without an evidential basis. In fact, the distinctive nature of the two versions constitutes evidence that no collusion occurred between authors and that subsequent smoothing is minimal.

The integrity of many of the elements in the infancy narratives are further supported by R. Brown's research. He asserts two important points for consideration. First, the infancy narratives are late additions to the basic gospel material that is centered on the resurrection and the recognition that Jesus is the Messiah. These additions became necessary as Christological developments pressed the inquiries about Jesus back beyond his baptism, to his birth, and even to his preexistence. This observation makes sense if one considers the content of the Gospel of John.[39] Second, much

---

38. Paffenroth, "Story of Jesus," 44. Paffenroth footnotes that the birth narrative of Luke is thought by other scholars to be a free interpretation and arrangement of OT material with early Christian models.

39. Brown, *Birth of the Messiah*, 31.

of the material for the birth narratives, although affixed to the basic gospel proclamation, were of pre-Matthean and pre-Lukan origin.[40] More to the point, all three of the angelic dream appearances are among the material R. Brown places within the pre-Matthean designation: (1) 1:20–21, 24–25; (2) 2:13–15a; and (3) 2:19–21.

The total amount of material attributed to the pre-Matthean sources are significantly reduced from what is contained in the narrative. The remaining elements, however, give virtually all of the historically significant details, including Bethlehem of Judea as the birthplace of Jesus. The narrative elements in R. Brown's reconstruction are as follows: betrothal, pregnancy, birth during the reign of Herod the Great, expectation that the Messiah would be born in Bethlehem of Judea, search for the child, escape to Egypt, and later return to Israel.[41]

In his examination of Luke's narrative, R. Brown contends that 2:6–20 are not pre-Lukan in form; he maintains, however, that the interpretive reflection on Gen 35:19–21 and Micah 4–5, also found in Matthew 2, is of pre-Lukan origin. The rationale for this conclusion is complex, beginning with the annunciation to the shepherds being paralleled by the *magi* story in Matt 2:1–12.

> In both Matthean and Lukan infancy narratives, after a first chapter, which informs one parent of the forthcoming birth of Jesus, there is a similar sequence of events early in chapter 2: a brief mention of birth at Bethlehem; the revelation of that birth to a group who were not present (magi, shepherds); the coming of that group to Bethlehem under the guidance of the revelation.[42]

If R. Brown's deductions are correct, the outright invention of the material in the birth narratives, especially Mathew's version, is improbable. Simply too much of the content has its roots in the early history of the church and it's recollections of the birth of Jesus.[43]

---

40. Brown, *Birth of the Messiah*, 32.
41. Brown, *Birth of the Messiah*, 109.
42. Brown, *Birth of the Messiah*, 412.
43. A significant part of the argument below utilizes some of the same material and rationale as the section, "Rational Evidence Supporting the Davidic Heritage of Jesus," above. Most of the lines of argumentation for Jesus' Davidic heritage also support Bethlehem of Judea as his birthplace.

Evidence Against a Contrived Birthplace

When approaching the evidence for or against Bethlehem as the birthplace of Jesus, one must seek to understand the motives of the biblical writers. To explain Matthew's insistence on Judean Bethlehem as the location, one motive offered in the literature is that he created the account as a historicized *theologoumenon*. Many Jews expected that Messiah would have his roots in that city. Several problems attend this approach, however, parallel the alternate theory that insists the narrative is simply fictitious.

Four distinct lines of argumentation demonstrate the improbability that Luke or Mathew invented a fictitious account intended to make the masses believe something false. First, Jesus' relatives could not have remained unknown during the early years of the church. If Jesus was not born in Bethlehem, at the least several key people in the early church would have known. These include Jesus' immediate family (James and Jude), JTB, and the disciple John as Mary's caretaker. It is not plausible to believe that JTB would have accepted Jesus' claim had he been aware that Jesus did not fit the criteria. Even those present at the Jerusalem council (Acts 15) included James, the leader of the church of Jerusalem. He certainly knew the truth about the birthplace of Jesus, yet we hear no word of refutation from him. Further critical thought reveals that even Joseph's brother would have to be involved in a deception. Eusebius, in his ecclesiastical history, records that Symeon succeeded his cousin, James, the brother of Jesus, as leader of the church in Jerusalem.[44] Symeon was the son of Clopas (an extremely rare name, one of the men on the road to Emmaus); Clopas, according to Hegesippus, was the brother of Joseph.[45] Is it plausible to believe that Joseph's own brother did not know the truth? Would he not have warned his son not to become involved in a deception?

The second line of argumentation builds on the fact that many Jews were expecting a messiah born in Bethlehem of Judea. That thought was not universal, however; competing expectations are identifiable in the literature. For example, R. Brown notes a parallel expectation of a hidden messiah who would appear suddenly, seemingly from nowhere (John 7:27).[46] The Zealots, a revolutionary messianic movement opposed to Roman rule, represented another messianic philosophy present during Jesus' life.[47] And according to Robert Charles, the Zadokites were a fourth mes-

---

44. Eusebius, "Ecclesiastical History, Books 1–5," 3.11.
45. Bauckham, *Jesus and the Eyewitnesses*, 47.
46. Brown, *Birth of the Messiah*, 514.
47. McCown, *Promise of His Coming*, 140–41.

sianic movement composed of a priestly group. This movement accepted both prophetic and apocalyptic writings; they also expected the advent of the Messiah from the seed of both Aaron and Israel: "Messiah was to be a son of Mariamne and Herod (i.e., from Aaron and Israel)"[48] This Zadokite expectation may explain why Herod had three of his sons executed; the potential competition must be eliminated. However, if invention or deception is the goal of the NT gospel writers, toward which messianic group would they direct their fictions? It does not seem possible to invent a set of circumstances that would satisfy everyone.

A third line of argumentation against the invention of the Bethlehem story is the silence of the Jewish religious leadership. The Jewish polemic against Jesus included his alleged illegitimate birth, charges of blasphemy, and even an alliance with Satan. Despite the uproar, however, none of these diatribes challenged his alleged place of birth. As noted in detail below, Origen seemed to believe that even enemies of Christianity knew the place where Jesus was born. The absence of any polemic against Jesus being born in Bethlehem does not fully meet the criterion of enemy attestation. Nonetheless, it seems reasonable to conclude that their silence on the matter at least suggests that they believed he was born in Bethlehem.[49]

The fourth line of argumentation surfaces when attempting to understand why the authors of the birth narratives would risk stigmatizing Mary and shock the sensibilities of the first readers. An attempt to deceive the general population with a false birthplace would be indiscriminate and arbitrary, especially in light of the scandal of a nine-month pregnant, unwed Mary claiming a virgin conception and birth. Luke even places the couple on a seventy-mile journey from Nazareth to Bethlehem. Traveling while pregnant is something from which Mary did not shy away. On two previous occasions, she made a journey of similar distance (Luke 1:39–45, 54). If Matthew, Luke, or one of their respective sources was inventing the stories, these details could only serve to undermine their credibility.

Regardless of the mode of transportation for the journey, an unwed mother in first-century Jewish culture was no trifling matter. Such a pregnancy could mean death and virtually always meant a life ostracized from the main stream of Jewish life. The accusation that Jesus was illegitimate

---

48. Charles, *Pseudepigrapha of the Old Testament*, 2:785.

49. Some authors contend that Matthew depicts Bethlehem as the home of Joseph and Mary before the birth of Jesus. The text does not say this: it is an inference drawn from presuppositions that may not be accurate. Perhaps Joseph was a former resident and traveled to Nazareth, met Mary there, and so on. What the text does not say is important, and it does not say that Joseph and Mary lived in Bethlehem before traveling there from Nazareth.

was neither a trivial nor fleeting problem; as it may be intimated in John 8:41, it certainly was an issue for Celsus.[50] Centuries later, these allegations were still part of the Jewish polemic against Jesus' family and Christianity. Examples from the third century, documented by Bockmuehl, include references to Jesus as son of "Pandera" or "Pantera."[51] References such as these also appear in the *Toledot Yeshu* and may have been intended as a disparaging comment on, or corruption of, the term *parthenos* (virgin) as originally applied to Mary.[52] In addition, the idea of a virgin conception was not necessary to the messianic concept. The thought of a woman conceiving without the participation of a man was foreign to any Jewish understanding of the procreative process. God's activity in that process has several OT precedents, but in no case is virginity in view. These elements certainly meet the criteria of surprise and embarrassment, as established by critical scholarship,[53] and therefore point to the authenticity and unwashed character of the narratives. Something as banal as the place of Jesus' birth was most likely not contrived.

The Registration of Augustus

One of the primary arguments leveled against the authenticity of the Lukan birth narrative is the mention of the registration ordered by Augustus. The goal here is not to make any claim to have solved the historical problems associated with dating the registration. Rather, the goal in exploring this problem is to point out that allegations of invention overlook significant evidence that supports the basic historicity of the Lukan account.

Without recounting the entire history of the registration debate, it is noteworthy that Ramsay suggests that three scholars known to him discovered indictional cycles of fourteen years for "enrollment" in Egypt after it became part of the Roman Empire.[54] Ramsay also observes that the

---

50. Origen, "Origen against Celsus," 1.38.
51. Bockmuehl, *This Jesus*, 14, 33.
52. Bockmuehl, *This Jesus*, 14.
53. Bovon and Koester acknowledge the shocking aspect of what Luke records. They contend these elements are "difficult to justify even by recourse to the nature of engagement, which legally constitutes marriage." A "novelist," they assert, might argue that the necessity of her traveling may have been prompted by her family owning land in the area (Bovon and Koester, *Luke 1*, 85). It also could have resulted from her being from the Davidic linage.
54. Ramsay, *Was Christ Born at Bethlehem*, 132. Ramsay notes the following sources for his assertion: Kenyon, "Berlin Papyri," 110; Viereck, "Die aegyptische Steuereinschätzungs-Commission in römischer Zeit," 219; Wilcken, "Απογραφαι," 230–251.

same Greek word that Luke employs for "enrollment" (ἀπογραφή) occurs in the papyri discovered in Egypt. François Bovon and Helmut Koester, commenting on this Greek term, note that it should be distinguished from "ἀποτίμησις (both translate the Latin *census*)."[55] The ἀπογραφή mentioned in Luke and the Egyptian papyri, "is the official registration of every inhabitant (age, occupation, wife, children), in order to establish military service and head tax. The ἀποτίμησις, on the other hand, aimed at registration of goods and income."[56] Ramsay claims that actual papers verifying the enrollments in Egypt have been found for several of the cycles (AD 34, 62, 90, 104, 118, 132, etc.), until AD 230, with some indirect references to the census of AD 20 and 48.

The facts presented above inform the inference that another registration occurred in AD 6 and is likely the one mentioned in Acts 5:37. If the pattern held true to form, 8 BC would be a probable date for the registration Luke mentions in the birth narrative. Ramsay's citation of Kenyon clearly supports his conclusions. In addition, Adolf Deissmann and Lionel Richard Mortimer Strachan document that the alleged taxation requiring individuals to return to their own city was known in Egypt. They argue that the taxation made by Quirinius was "no mere figment of St. Luke or his authority, but that similar things took place in that age, is proved by an edict of G. Vibius Maximus, governor of Egypt, AD 104."[57] In a subsequent book, Ramsay emphatically maintains:

> What a series of distinguished and famous scholars have blindly assumed is that their inability to estimate historical evidence correctly was the final and sure criterion of truth. This we can now say freely, because the whole matter, so far as the census is concerned, has passed out of the sphere of speculation into the region of definite historical truth.[58]

A. T. Robertson, commenting on Ramsay's conclusions (and the census question), stresses the need to actually read the text. Negatively, it does not say "'that a single census should be held of the whole Roman world,' but 'there went out a decree from Cæsar Augustus that all the world should be enrolled.'"[59] The emphasis is on the present tense. Robertson further argues that current knowledge—information not available to Ramsay in

---

55. Bovon and Koester, *Luke 1*, 83. Bovon and Koester note that there is some instability in the usage; on occasion, ἀπογραφή denotes the taxation of goods and income.

56. Bovon and Koester, *Luke 1*, 83.

57. Deissmann and Strachan, *Light from the Ancient East*, 268.

58. Ramsay, *Bearing of Recent Discoveries*, 254.

59. Robertson, *Luke the Historian*, 121.

1898—demonstrates that Augustus's governmental plan for a census was successful. "We have evidence for its operation in both West and East, though most for the East."[60] Robertson positively recounts the arguments of Ramsay in general.

The evidence presented above would seem to vindicate Luke. Adding some certitude to this line of evidence is the work of Martin Hengel. Hengel observes that both Greek terms in question were employed in provincial census taking, however, given the use of ἀποτίμησις and ἀπογραφή (by Josephus and Luke), they must be considered interchangeable; the choice of which is driven by stylistic reasons.[61] For example, Josephus appears to employ both interchangeably in the span of a few sentences in one of his works.[62]

F. F. Bruce argues to the same conclusion from two documents known from the period. The first document is the *Titulus Tiburtinus*. This document provides information that leaves open the possibility that Quirinius was a political leader prior to AD 6. Quirinius may have been appointed to the position of governor or imperial legate in a province other than Syria several years prior.[63] Nikos Kokkinos ventures much futher when arguing that the evidence demonstrates that the *ignotus* (unbeknown) of the *Titulus Tiburtinus* can only refer to either Saturninus or Quirinius. He prefers Saturninus, but admits there is reason to believe it could be Quirinius. No other candidates meet the requirements.[64] If his conclusions are accurate, Kokkinos has removed the clutter from the field of history, making Luke's account even more probable.

The second document is the *Titulus Venetus*. This Latin inscription set up in Beirut by one of Quirinius's officers provides information about a census held in the Roman province of Syria. The information contained in the *Titulus Venetus* is consistent with a fourteen-year cycle for census taking during the reign of Augustus and continuing until at least the third century AD.[65]

---

60. Robertson, *Luke the Historian*, 122.

61. Hengel, *Zealots*, 128n271. (cf. Josephus, *Antiquities* 18:3; 18:4; Luke 2:2; Acts 5:37). See also Moehring, "Census in Luke," 149–60.

62. Josephus, *Antiquities* 18:3; 18:4

63. Bruce, *Jesus and Christian Origins*, 192–93. Some of the scholars Bruce cites as references are: Dessau, *ILS*, 918; Mommsen, *Res Gestae Divi Augusti*, 161; Dessau, "Zu den neuen Inschriften des Sulpicius Quirinius," 252; Ramsay, "Studies in the Roman Province of Galatia," 273–75; and Roos, "Die Quirinius-Inschrift," 306.

64. Kokkinos, "Titulus Tiburtinus," 65.

65. Bruce, *Jesus and Christian*, 192–93. In addition, Bruce reasons that if the Greek text of Luke is translated as "before that made when Quirinius was governor," the problem disappears.

Indisputable documentation to support the specific registration of Luke 2 does not exist in the known literature. However, the existence of such ἀπογραφή within the provinces of the Roman Empire lends credibility to the account. Even though no specific record of a general decree exists, charges of fabricating the story are excessively skeptical in light of (1) the positive data for provincial registrations, (2) the absence of any data capable of refuting the claim, and (3) empire-wide implications of what is known. The obligation of the historian is to evaluate with an open mind. The available evidence disallows the possibility that Luke is inventing his account simply to support a theological agenda. What Luke reports or something similar is probable.[66]

A Contradicting Historical Voice

In Origen's work *Against Celsus*, the accusation is made that Jesus was a product of a sexual relationship between Mary and a Roman soldier (Panthera). The text reads as follows:

> For he represents him disputing with Jesus, and confuting Him, as he thinks, on many points; and in the first place, he accuses Him of having "invented his birth from a virgin," and upbraids Him with being "born in a certain Jewish village, of a poor woman of the country, who gained her subsistence by spinning, and who was turned out of doors by her husband, a carpenter by trade, because she was convicted of adultery; that after being driven away by her husband, and wandering about for a time, she disgracefully gave birth to Jesus, an illegitimate child, who having hired himself out as a servant in Egypt on account of his poverty, and having there acquired some miraculous powers, on which the Egyptians greatly pride themselves, returned to his own country, highly elated on account of them, and by means of these proclaimed himself a God." Now, as I cannot

---

66. Elements that appear in both birth narratives: (1) a betrothed couple named Mary and Joseph, (2) Joseph's Davidic family heritage, (3) supernatural conception and birth without human intercourse, (4) angelic revelation of the name Jesus, (5) the baby's birth in Bethlehem during the reign of Herod the Great, (6) later residence in Nazareth.

Until further evidence is available, perhaps the overly skeptical position of Horst R. Moehring will prevail. He argues that the only certainty about the census is that "Luke's historical accuracy cannot be defended on the basis of the available evidence" (Moehring, "Census in Luke," 145). This conclusion, however, is skewed by historical skepticism in light of the positive evidence for Luke's overall narrative. The facts presented do indicate that the general practice of a periodic census on a fourteen-year basis throughout the Roman Empire was a regular part of provincial life.

allow anything said by unbelievers to remain unexamined, but
must investigate everything from the beginning, I give it as my
opinion that all these things worthily harmonize with the predictions that Jesus is the Son of God.[67]

This accusation is far-fetched considering the ethnicity of Mary and what is known about the family. Origen flatly denies that it is true. The idea certainly has an aura of fiction for three reasons. First, Panthera was a common way to refer to any Roman soldier.[68] Second, it would have been thought a double disgrace to have a young Jewish girl willingly participate in a sexual escapade with a Roman. The whole idea was likely a way to discredit Jesus and the Christian sect. Third, and more relevant for the current discussion, this particular accusation makes no attempt to discredit the alleged place of Jesus' birth. The focus is to discredit the possibility of a virgin conception and birth.[69] On another occasion, however, Origen specifically alleges that, in a plot to discredit Christianity, Jewish teachers withheld information from the public about the birthplace of Jesus.[70] They did this despite knowing the prophecy of Micah and the truth about Jesus' birthplace.

Summary

Clearly, some—and perhaps many—Jews during the first-century believed that the Messiah would have roots in Bethlehem of Judea (Matt 2:6; John 7:42), as prophesied in Micah 5:2. The obvious differences in the birth narratives of Matthew and Luke are problematic but are not contradictory. If all the details were known, and if those details were considered in light of the differing audiences and theological purposes of the authors, the accounts would not appear to be irreconcilable. Both narratives present evidence of being based on independent sources without collusion. Luke's accuracy, in particular, has often been vindicated by independent research. Even the decree of Caesar Augustus and the first registration when Quirinius was governor, perennial related problems, are supported by solid historical data that imply the accuracy of Luke's account.

Culturally, little reason can be found to doubt the biblical narratives. No Jewish leader contemporary with the events is known to deny that Jesus was born in Bethlehem. In fact, the stigma and shock factors attached to

67. Origen, "Origen against Celsus," 1.28.

68. Brown, *Birth of the Messiah*, 536n538. Brown notes the various spelling of the name *pntyr'*, Pantira, Pandera, Pantiri, and Panteri.

69. This work makes to attempt support the virgin conception or birth of Jesus.

70. Origen, "Origen against Celsus," 1.51.

a pregnant, unwed Jewish girl possess a degree of defamation and scandal that opportunistic critics certainly would have exploited. It is also certain that no Christian would have invented stories that placed Mary or the other living members of Jesus' family in a position susceptible to unjust ridicule. In total, a crucial lack of evidence exists for dismissing Bethlehem of Judea as the birthplace of Jesus. Skeptical scholars have little basis for claiming any other locality for this event.[71]

---

71. This footnote anticipates and answers questions about why this dissertation does not treat Matthew's presentation of Jesus' family fleeing Herod and living in Egypt. The typological elements of Hosea 11:1 as related to Matthew 2:15 make them unsuitable for the current purpose. In addition, this story is unique to Matthew's gospel. In context, Hosea 11:1 is almost universally recognized as referring to Israel as a nation, not to any single individual.

However, at least four pieces of evidence support the historicity of Matthew's account: these are summarized by Bockmuehl and France. See Bockmuehl, *This Jesus*, 34–36, and France, "Infancy Narratives," 266. Challenges to the historicity of the account are summarized by Paul Maier. He argues that a challenge to the historicity of the account usually employs three criteria: (1) the silence of Josephus; (2) Matthew's fulfill-prophecy construction; and (3) the argument from analogy. Maier, "The Infant Massacre," 99–102.

Without undue rehashing of longstanding controversy, a historian in search of explanations for these conditions does not need to search far. First, an argument from silence regarding a localized atrocity is not a convincing refutation. The second objection, Matthew's fulfilled-prophecy construction, is actually no objection at all. Few biblical scholars suggest that Matthew has no theological agenda in mind. The third objection (the argument from analogy) is based on Matthew's theological agenda. Those who apply this argument believe Matthew must contrive a baby-slaughter-and-rescue story if the Moses-and-exodus motif is to be successful. Maier makes the simple observation that "the premise here seems to be that no atrocity can happen twice." If this *principle of analogy* was valid, there could not have been two Asian countries internally at war, divided north against south. There could not have been more than one tragic school shooting the United States, nor any other evil scheme perpetrated on mankind more than once. In fact, the *principle of analogy* as a rule of historicism is usually applied by critical scholarship and has the opposite meaning and effect. It elevates present "experience and occurrence" as the criteria of probability. Krentz, *Historical-Critical Method*, 55.

For additional historical evidence possibly supporting Jesus' presence in Egypt, consult Justin Martyr and his mention of Acts drawn up under Pontius Pilate (First Apology 35, 48) See also Tertullian (*Apology* 21.24). Several references to Jesus, or at least to Jesus' presence in Egypt, are found in later rabbinic texts (e.g., Tosephta, *Hullin* II 22–23, and the Babylonian Talmud tractates Aboda Zara 40d and Sabbath 14d. See also b. Sanh 107b; b. Šabb 104b. Cf. the "Protevangelium of James," 22.21. "History of Joseph the Carpenter or Death of Joseph," VIII.

Luz contends the "only point that must be taken seriously is whether there is a 'kernel of truth behind the tradition of Jesus' sojourn in Egypt.'" He argues that in light of the Jewish sources familiar with the tradition, the "oldest formulation could not have been dependent on Matthew." Luz, *Matthew 1–7*, 120.

Plausible Historical-Evidential Conclusions Gathered from the Study of Micah 5:2 and the Birth Narratives

1. Matthew and Luke reflect independent sources for their birth narratives.
2. Matthew and Luke do not show evidence of narrative smoothing in an attempt to minimize the difficulties in the accounts.
3. Either Jesus was born in Bethlehem of Judea or both Matthew and Luke recorded erroneous sources or independently invented fictitious accounts.
4. There is insufficient evidence to support the charge of an invented narrative in Matthew or Luke.
5. The preponderance of the evidence points toward a historical basis for the birth narratives.

Historical-Evidential Facts Gathered from the Study of Micah 5:2 and the Birth Narratives

1. Both Matthew and Luke emphasize Bethlehem of Judea as the birthplace.
2. Both Matthew and Luke emphasize that Joseph's ancestor was David.
3. Both Matthew and Luke place Jesus' family in Bethlehem for an undesignated amount of time.
4. No written source earlier than Celsus denies that Jesus was born in Bethlehem.
5. Both Matthew and Luke place the final home of the family in Nazareth of Galilee.

Chapter 6

The Fourth Group of Biblical Texts

Introduction to the Fourth Group of Biblical Texts

IN THE FOURTH SET of passages, Jesus' miracles in relation to the expectations of the messianic age, the Messiah himself, and the predictions of the OT prophets are analyzed. Jesus' self-described *titular nomens* such as "prophet" (Luke 4:17–19), "son of man," "son of the Blessed" (Mark 14:61–62), and "son of David" (Matt 9:27; 12:23; 15:22; 21:9; Mark 10:47) all bear implications for his assertion of a future "seated at the right hand of God" (Mark 14:62). In fact, various people referred to Jesus as *Son of David* (Matt 9:27; 12:23; 15:22; 21:9; Mark 10:47). The best and perhaps only currently available means of verifying whether these titles attributed to Jesus are justifiable is an examination of whether Jesus performed the miracles that the OT prophets allegedly predicted would accompany the preaching of the good news in the messianic age (Deut 18:15–18; Isa 29:18; 35:5–6; 61:1–2; Matt 9:35; 11:4–6; Luke 7:22–23).[1]

Jesus the Miracle-Worker: A Synopsis

The purpose for this section of the work is not to provide exhaustive support for the thesis that Jesus performed miraculous acts. Rather, it is to offer the rationale for the presupposition that Jesus did so. A subsequent section of the work will then investigate whether the Messiah must perform such acts.

Miraculous acts attributed to Jesus are multiply attested in a variety of ancient books. Conversely, no sources touching on the issue of the miraculous in general, or the life of Jesus in particular, deny his miracle-working activity. The NT gospels affirm Jesus as performing various

---

1. The argument for not rejecting miracles *a priori* is presented in chapter 2, "Section 3: The Possibility of Miracles."

miracles in Q, Mark, special Matthew, special Luke, and John. Ostensibly, Peter also believed that Jesus was a miracle-worker (Acts 2.22). Beyond the NT, numerous reports of miracles performed by Jesus are extant; a few examples will suffice.

The church historian Eusebius records the words of a lost work written by Quadratus (circa AD 120) that describes the working of miracles during the life of Jesus:

> But the works of our Saviour were always at hand, for they were true, those who were cured, those who rose from the dead, who were seen not only when being cured and when rising, but also, being always at hand, not only when the Saviour was on earth, but even after he had departed, survived for a considerable time, so that some of them have even come down to our own time.[2]

Commenting on Quadratus, Habermas carefully points out that these miracles consist of people who were "both healed and raised from the dead, concerning which . . . some of the eyewitnesses to these events were still alive."[3]

The Epistle of Barnabas 5:8 (before AD 132) designates Jesus as both a teacher and miracle-worker. Justin (circa 150) avows Jesus as a miracle-worker in clear terms:

> And that it was predicted that our Christ should heal all diseases and raise the dead, hear what was said. There are these words: "At His coming the lame shall leap as an [sic] hart, and the tongue of the stammerer shall be clear speaking: the blind shall see, and the lepers shall be cleansed; and the dead shall rise and walk about."[4]

Justin mentions that Jesus fulfilled many OT prophecies during his life. Documentation of his contentions about Jesus are said to have been recorded in the lost document, *Acts of Pontius Pilate*. To clarify for the reader, this is not the same work as the apocryphal document mentioned in the footnote treating Hosea 11:1 and Matthew 2:15 in the current work. The apocryphal *Acts of Pilate* is a spurious document. In contrast, a genuine report from Pilate to the Roman Emperor Tiberius is historically probable. Tertullian (circa AD 200) also appears to make an allusion to such a document.[5]

---

2. Eusebius, "Ecclesiastical History, Books 1–5," 210.
3. Habermas, *Historical Jesus*, 239.
4. Martyr, "First Apology of Justin," 178–79.
5. Turtullian, "Apology," 21. Such records detailing events and acts by the Roman Senate and provincial leaders are known to exist. These records are of two types. The

Enemy attestation of Jesus' miracles appear in the work of Celsus titled *A True Discourse*. Although this work is lost, it is sufficiently quoted by Origen to establish that Celsus believed that Jesus performed miracles in accordance with miraculous powers acquired in Egypt.[6] These same allegations also appear in rabbinic literature, attributing miraculous power to Jesus through sorcery.[7]

Among modern scholars, a broad consensus exists that Jesus was a miracle-worker. Eric Eve verifies this assertion:

> First, there is a consensus among virtually all the scholars reviewed here that Jesus did indeed perform healings and exorcisms that his contemporaries thought remarkable, and that this can be regarded as virtually certain. There is also a growing consensus that this miraculous activity formed an integral part of Jesus' ministry, and should not be brushed aside to leave room for a Jesus who was almost entirely a teacher.[8]

Similarly, Graham Twelftree, after having done extensive research on the subject, concludes:

> The necessary conclusion, in light of our inquiry, is that *there is hardly any aspect of the life of the historical Jesus which is so well and widely attested as that he conducted unparalleled wonders*. Further, *the miracles dominated and were the most important aspect of Jesus' whole pre-Easter ministry*.[9]

Based on the data provided in this brief survey of the available evidence, ample historical and scholarly rationale exists for the current investigation to proceed from the presupposition that Jesus was a miracle-worker. In fact, the belief that Jesus performed miracles (healings and exorcisms) is

---

Acta Senatus are also called the *Commentarii Senatus* or *Acta Patrum*. They contain accounts of "matters brought before the senate, the opinions of the chief speakers, and the decision of the house" (Smith, *Dictionary of Greek and Roman*, 7). The other type of documentation archived by the Romans were the *Commentarii principis*. They were letters composed of the correspondence sent to the emperors from various parts of the empire. See Habermas, *Historical Jesus*, 215.

6. Origen, "Origen against Celsus," 1.38.

7. See *b. Sanh* 6:1h, II.1. The Jewish historian Josephus, at the least, makes mention of Jesus in the context of a virtuous life. The problems with the *Testimonium Flavianum* as a historical source are well-known. The attribution of "wonderful works" to Jesus is probably a Christian interpolation. Thus, little support for Jesus as a miracle-worker is evident in Josephus.

8. Eve, *Jewish Context of Jesus' Miracles*, 16–17. For a substantial list of modern scholars who concede that Jesus worked miracles, see Keener, *Miracles*, 23n12.

9. Twelftree, *Jesus the Miracle Worker*, 345.

widely supported and is rarely challenged. Yet to be established, however, is that the Jewish messianic expectation included a significant strand of thought requiring a miracle-working Messiah.

Did the Jews Expect a Miracle-Working Messiah?

The OT, NT, and modern scholarship provide ample reason to investigate if one aspect of the Jewish expectation for the messianic age included the working of miracles. From the perspective of the casual reader, it would seem axiomatic that the OT contains the expectation of miracles and miracle working in the context of the expected messianic restoration of Zion. This statement, however, conflicts with the negative assessment of this possibility by scholars such as Sanders and Keener. Sanders argues that the Jewish people were not expecting a miracle-working messianic figure. However, since Jesus did perform miracles, "many modern Christians think that first-century Jews looked for a Messiah who performed miracles, and that Jesus' contemporaries would conclude that a miracle-worker was the Messiah."[10] Sanders explicitly describes this view as "incorrect."[11] Keener similarly writes, "We lack substantial contemporary evidence that Jewish people expected a miracle-working messiah."[12] Conversely, M. Brown emphatically argues that the expectation of a miracle-working Messiah definitely existed in Israel. He describes those who doubt or dismiss this expectation as "misinformed"[13] and self-deceived.

The investigation of this important question will proceed by employing the same general methodology as utilized above. The most relevant OT texts, extra-biblical texts, and NT texts will be examined; additionally, any cultural-historical evidence available will be examined.

Old Testament Evidence Supporting a Jewish Expectation of a Miracle-Working Messiah

Deuteronomy 18:15–18 and Moses/Messiah Typology

In Jewish thought, Moses may be the most important person to have existed. Moses was the liberator, mediator of *Yahweh*'s revelation, miracle

---

10. Sanders, *Historical Figure of Jesus*, 132.
11. Sanders, *Historical Figure of Jesus*, 133.
12. Keener, *Miracles*, 1:27.
13. Brown, *Answering Jewish Objections to Jesus*, 1:98.

worker, and "absolute teacher" of the nation;[14] he was a divine prophet for the nation and the whole world (As Mos 11:16). In Deuteronomy 18:15–18 Moses asserts that *Yahweh* promised Israel that he would raise from among them another prophet like himself. Jeffrey H. Tigay's confident exposition of the passage takes the view that a succession of prophets is in view and that the preposition "like" indicates that no prophet could ever equal Moses.[15] Undoubtedly, one of the reasons for Tigay's assertion is the frequent presence of the miraculous in the OT accounts of the life of Moses. Ideologically, it is difficult to imagine a Moses without the miracles before and after the exodus from Egypt. These elements flow together as two threads in a single story. Any individual's claim to be a prophet, *a fortiori* a prophet like Moses, logically carries the burden of requiring miracle-working activity. Without the miracles to verify such a lofty title, rapid dismissal of the assertion would soon follow. Matthew 11:56 and Luke 4:18–19 provide reason for the biblical exegete to believe that Jesus self-identifies as the prophet predicted in Deuteronomy 18:15–18. In addition, John 1:21 and 6:14 portray the coming of a specific prophet as a common understanding of the Jewish people. The implication of the question posed by the crowd, recorded in John 6:14b "οὗτός ἐστιν ἀληθῶς ὁ προφήτης ὁ ἐρχόμενος εἰς τὸν κόσμον," is that they were expecting a specific eschatological prophet, not simply another cult prophet within the succession of OT prophets. Modern readers approaching these texts from a canonical reading conceptually grasp the connection between (1) Jesus' related claims of setting Israel free, and healing the nation, (spiritually and physically), and (2) Moses, the Exodus, and the expectation of the coming prophet (cf. Isa 11:10–16). Historically, however, the parallels between the succession of prophets, the prophetic office, and the coming of the Messiah are not unilineal. The Moses/Christ typology certainly exists; similar to other aspects of messianism; the typological aspects appear gradually, however, as did the latter technical use of the term *Messiah*.

In context, the promise of Deuteronomy 18:15–18 is debated. The majority of scholars today argue for a non-messianic referent. For example, S. R. Driver maintains that no single prophet is intended: the reference is to a permanent institution. The need for the prophet was recurring; to avoid the pagan diviners, *Yahweh* supplied Israel with a succession of prophets.[16] Conversely, interpretations exist that attach fulfillment of this prophecy to individual prophets such as Joshua, Jeremiah, and several other well-known prophetic figures of the past.

14. Jeremias, "Μωυσῆς," 4:867.
15. Tigay, *Deuteronomy*, 175.
16. Driver, *Commentary on Deuteronomy*, 227.

Interpretations have also arisen which place the antitypical prophet—who would be like Moses—in an eschatological role. In early Jewish thought, according to J. Jeremias, the eschatological prophet is not necessarily the Messiah. That eschatological prophet, in some instances, inflicts plagues reminiscent of those in Egypt to secure the freedom of Israel. In other literature, he arises in the manner of other prophets, or represents the return of one of the old prophets. However, at least in the early literature Jeremias references, the prophet's role is limited to a messianic forerunner who acts alongside Elijah and the Messiah.[17] Nevertheless, he judges as "extremely likely"[18] that later Judaism and the Samaritans knew of a messianic interpretation of Deuteronomy 18:15, 18.

The Moses typology within the OT cannot be arbitrarily limited to an eschatological Messiah. Several OT prophets are variously portrayed with actions intended to bring events related to the life of Moses to mind. The text of Deuteronomy 34:9–12 is of particular importance to this discussion. The prophet that Moses promises to Israel will be like him (Deut 18:15, 18). The Hebrew term כמו (kĕmô), translated "like," has a broad semantic range that includes ideas of *similarity*, but not necessarily *equality* or of two identical things. In Deuteronomy 34:9–12 Joshua's endowment with the spirit of wisdom to lead Israel is described with reference to Moses' unsurpassed status in Israelite thought. Joshua, as the designated successor to Moses, receives a promise in Joshua 1:5 that *Yahweh* would be with him as he was with Moses. Clearly, Joshua's designation and *Yahweh's* promise constitute the raising up of a prophet "like" or similar to Moses to lead Israel into the promised land. During Joshua's period of leadership, several miracles are manifest (e.g., Josh 3:7, 6:20, 10:13) that affirm his anointed position. Significant among the miraculous events recorded in relation to Joshua is the crossing of the Jordan River. It is noteworthy that in the language employed in Joshua 3:7, *Yahweh* promises to be with Joshua "as" with Moses. The Hebrew term used contains the same basic preposition as found in Moses' promise (Deut 1:15, 18), and the ensuing stoppage of the Jordan River is reminiscent of the parting of the Red Sea. In addition, after crossing the river, Joshua leads Israel in a covenant renewal that includes circumcision and observance of the Passover.[19]

An exhaustive exposition of the second Moses typology in the OT is beyond the scope of this work; even so, several scholars have noted that the

---

17. Jeremias, "Μωυσῆς," 4:857.

18. Jeremias, "Μωυσῆς," 4:859.

19. Beale, *Right Doctrine from the Wrong Texts?*, 341. Cf. La Sor et al., *Old Testament Survey*, 142–43.

OT portrays several prophets with some second-Moses themes. In addition, to Joshua these include Ezra,[20] Elijah,[21] and David.[22]

In contrast, Michael Rydelnik is among the few current scholars espousing the view that Deuteronomy 18:15-18 is originally messianic. Arguing from the perspective that the Tanakh is rightly read as canon, he analyzes the textual/lexical data. In his estimation, the overall import of the Pentateuch is that Deuteronomy 18:15-18 refers exclusively to the Messiah.[23]

Jeremias agrees that the kind of reductionism that isolates Deuteronomy 18 from the rest of the Tanakh is improper. However, his contention is that exclusive use of later Jewish exegesis of Deuteronomy 18:15-18 cannot govern the extent of the Moses/messiah typology. As demonstrated above, several additional OT passages (i.e., Isa 11:11; 48:21; Mic 7:15; Hos 2:16; 12:10) typologically connect Moses and messianic redemption with a second Moses motif. These texts do not specifically reference Deuteronomy 18, yet they do contain images related to Moses.[24] Strack and Billerbeck elevate the second-Moses concept to a position of near primacy in Jewish redemptive thought. They state:

> *Der Heranziehung von Hos 11, 1 liegt der Gedanke zugrunde, daß die Erlösung Israels aus Ägypten ein Typus der messian. Erlösung sei, ein Gedanke, der (vom AT angeregt Jes 11, 11; 48, 21; Hos 2, 16; 12, 10; Micha 7, 15) wie kein anderer neben ihm die Ausgestaltung des Lehrstücks von der Enderlösung schon frühzeitig in umfassendster Weise bestimt hat.*[25]

Strack and Billerbeck affirm that, in multiple contexts, the Talmud and other rabbinic literature correlate the foretold prophet with the Messiah. This was especially prominent in the thinking of the Israelites in the period just prior to AD 70.[26]

Much disparity of opinion exists about early Jewish interpretation of Deuteronomy 18:15-18 and how the text was originally understood.

---

20. According to Paul Ferguson, the Jewish Talmud considers Ezra as the second Moses, describing Ezra as second father to biblical Judaism, while providing solidarity and spiritual unity. Ferguson, "Ezra," 235.

21. Anderson, *Contours of Old Testament Theology*, 46. Cf. Wiseman, *1 and 2 Kings*, 184.

22. Selman, *2 Chronicles*, 365.

23. Rydlelnik, *Messianic Hope*, 59.

24 Jeremias, "Μωυσῆς," 4:859.

25 Strack and Billerbeck, *Kommentar zum Neuen Testament*, 1:85. Cf. 1:68-69; 2:284, 293.

26. Strack and Billerbeck, 591. Cf. 2:626

Nonetheless, it is certain that at least some later Jewish and Christian exegesis inculcated the passage with messianic elements. This conclusion is evidenced in the teachings and actions of the Qumran community authoring 1QS Col. ix:11 and 4Q175, the NT authors,[27] Origen's work *Against Celsus* (1.57), and Eusebius's *Theophania* (Bk 4, 35). The Jewish historian Josephus also confirms the conceptual connection between the promised prophet and the Messiah. He mentions two self-described prophets: Theudas (Ant 20, 97) and an unnamed Egyptian (20, 169); both promised the working of miracles on behalf of those that followed them.

Collectively considered, it is probable that the correct understanding of Israel's expected salvation must include some form of second Exodus, including miracles performed by the Messiah, whose antitypical role is the prophet like Moses. This eschatological role is predicated on Deuteronomy 18:15-18. The prophetic connection may be either direct (the original intent of the oracle), typological, or as indirect as an ultimate prophet who stands within the succession of prophets. In either case, no prophet could credibly lay claim to either an individual or successive fulfillment without the miracles to attest his claim.

Isaiah 29:18

During his analysis of the messianic concept, Mowinckel makes this important observation: the eschatological sayings of prophetic books, in a strict sense, all belong to later strata. These strata all presuppose the catastrophe inflicted by the Babylonians. His analysis, although controversial in light of Amos 5:18, makes a cogent point. The expectation of Israel regarding the Day of *Yahweh* gradually developed from one centered on national and cultic experience to something that required more than national restoration. Individual and cosmic elements were infused into the eschatological vision alongside the nationalist vision.[28] Isaiah 29 is a case in point. The presence of several proto-apocalyptic elements in this chapter show affinity with the work of Deutero-Isaiah or his disciples. These elements include the voice of a ghost, a visit by the LORD, thunder, an earthquake, and a great noise. Other elements that cannot be ignored include a whirlwind and tempest, a devouring fire, a dream, a vision, wonder upon wonder, and gloom and darkness.

These proto-apocalyptic elements contribute to the lack of consensus among scholars as to the dating of Isaiah 29 and to whether it is the work

27. Matthew 11:56; Luke 4:18-19; John 1:21; 6:14.
28. Mowinckel, *He that Cometh*, 132, 270-79.

of Isaiah or a later redactor. For example, Payne places the entire chapter in the period concerning Sennacherib's advance into Israel. The thrust of Isaiah 29:18, according to Payne, is that "divine restoration brings true illumination."[29] Dating the chapter prior to the exile makes tenuous any attempt to attach a miracle-working messianic expectation to this chapter. However, if the dating of critical scholarship remains the predominate view, as presupposed in the current work, artificially imposing a meaning from the period of Sennacherib is not only anachronistic but also self-defeating.

Working from another strand of argumentation, the question arises: is the healing described in Isaiah 29:18–19 physical or spiritual? The text's reference to the healing of the blind, deaf, meek, and poor, in light of other Isaianic texts, give reason to conclude that the description includes a mixture of literal and spiritual states. The language is reminiscent of Isaiah 35:6, 42:7, and 43:8, all of which are closely related to the inability of Israel to hear and see the truth (Isa 6:10), and to the promise of a coming scion of David (Isa 11). Likewise, present in these verses is the reversal of the people's vision being shrouded by darkness and gloom (Isa 8:22). Wildberger comments that the deaf being enabled to hear the words of a book is unique to this passage. It is probable that this is the result of *Yahweh*'s acting again on behalf of Israel, reversing the perceptive stupor described in Isaiah 29:9–11. The idea that the deaf will be enabled to hear the words of the writing may mean that history and contemporary events will speak, thereby demonstrating the accuracy of *Yahweh*'s message.[30]

The overall import of the passage is summed up well by John D. W. Watts: "The *deaf*, the *blind*, the *meek*, and the *humble* have suffered much in a world that honors power and cunning. But their day will come when God changes all the rules to work to their advantage."[31]

These observations suggest a key question: is there any physical element in view? If Watts's summary is correct, the answer must be yes. Given the ideological affinities with other texts in Deutero-Isaiah, the "blindness" of verse 18 must have some correlation with the blindness of 35:5–6; 42:7; and 42:16. Further, the "poor" (אביון) in verse 19 is very similar in nature to the content of Isaiah 61, where physical helplessness cannot be excluded.[32] In point of fact, a restoration that leaves individuals infirmed is only partial and does not fit with the overall idea of Isaiah 29. Nevertheless, the physical aspect of the passage takes a subordinate role to its spiritual import. Israel's

---

29. Payne, *Encyclopedia of Biblical Prophecy*, 309–10.
30. Wildberger, *Isaiah 28–39*, 111.
31. Watts, *Isaiah 1–33*, 389.
32. Isaiah 61:1–2 are treated in relation to David Stern and Luke 4:18 below.

problem, in context, is not limited to physical infirmities. *Spiritual* blindness and deafness make the nation poor and weak; in Isaiah 29, both are miraculously reversed.

The text likely contains restorative elements that are best described as miraculous and, thus, related to the messianic era. Even so, any direct messianic implication is difficult to establish. The passage bears verbal correspondence with several elements of Isaiah 11 and the Servant Songs. Verbal parallels alone, however, will not support the needed weight. Thus, it is not possible to find a clear-cut expectation of a miracle-working Messiah in Isaiah 29. More likely, Isaiah 29 is part of a cadre of texts that imply eschatological restoration for Israel.

Isaiah 35:1-5

The thrust of Isaiah 35 is the healing of infirmities and the breaking forth of life-giving water in the wilderness. Other prominent themes are peace, safety, and purity, all of which are enjoyed by the redeemed of *Yahweh*. These pleasant themes are set in stark contrast to *Yahweh's* perpetual judgment on Edom (Isa 34:10).[33] This judgment was executed so thoroughly as to make Edom the haunt of wild animals and the resting place of demons. Chapter 35 and the realization of its images ostensibly occur at the institution of the messianic era. Despite the exalted language, however, George Adam Smith argues that the return of the exiles from Babylon may partially be in view. Smith contends that the infliction of vengeance on Edom, described in Chapter 34 and the opening two verses of 35, transitions with the remaining text, addressed to a people still in captivity. From Smith's perspective, verses 3-4 and 10 markedly betray this quality.[34] This conclusion is questionable, however, given the numerous reasons cited by critical scholars to date the text as part of the Deutero-Isaiah corpus (see below).

A line of argumentation that yields reason to believe that the messianic era is in view is visible in the detailed work of R. B. Y. Scott. Scott contends that the "central theme of Deutero-Isaiah is the announcement of the imminent, supreme, and final theophany of *Yahweh* . . . demonstrated by the return of the Jews to Zion, the judgment of the nations, and Israel's exaltation among them, of which 'His Anointed' is to be the agent."[35] Scott perceives

---

33. The four-fold repetition of terms indicating the unending ruin of Edom—*night and day, forever, generation to generation, and forever and ever*—offer no reason to reject the implication that the judgment is the preliminary preparation for the messianic age.

34. Smith, "Book of Isaiah," 726.

35. Scott, "Relation of Isaiah," 185.

that Isaiah 35 and 40:1–5 contain the basic thoughts of Deutero-Isaiah: thoughts further illuminated in the rest of Deutero-Isaiah. Scott identifies these "unit ideas" as follows:

1. The rejoicing of the wilderness (Isa 35:1; 42:11; 51:3; 52:9)
2. The blossoming of the desert (35:1–2; 41:19)
3. Lebanon as a symbol of magnificence (35:2; 40:16)
4. The glory of *Yahweh* manifest (35:2; 40:5)
5. A command to encourage the weak and fearful (35:3–4; 40:1–2; 40:29; 41:10, 13–14; 43:1, 5; 44:2; 51:7; 54:4, 14)
6. The vengeance and recompense of God (35:4; 40:10; 49:25–26)
7. God will come to save (35:4; 45:17; 46:13; 49:25)
8. The physically afflicted to be healed (35:5–6; 42:7, 16)[36]
9. Streams in the desert (35:6–7; 41:18; 43:19–20; 44:3)
10. Wild beasts no longer present (35:7, 9; 43:20)
11. The holy way (35:8; 40:3; 43:19; 49:11)
12. The unclean excluded (35:8; 52:1, 11)
13. The joyful return of the redeemed (35:9–10; 48:20; 52:8–9)
14. The banishment of sorrow and pain (35:10; 49:10; 51:22; 54:14)[37]

The point made from these observations is that miracles of some nature are in view. The anointed agent of *Yahweh* is the actor; the concomitant implication is that the messianic age is the period the author is describing.

Another line of argumentation emerges in the work of H. G. M. Williamson. In the context of a discussion of whether an early date is appropriate for Isaiah 32:1–5, Williamson detects that 35:5–6 provides evidence for a movement from metaphorical healing of blindness and deafness to the physical healing for blindness and deafness. He argues that the progression from the metaphorical (Isa 6:10) to the literal (Isa 35:5–6) indicates that this transition is a later addition to the thought of the narrative and introduces concepts from Deutero-Isaiah or even later to the earlier texts (cf. Isa 29:18). For Williamson, the scene in Chapter 35 is set in the eschatological future; his position is strongly influenced by Isaiah 6 and 11.[38]

---

36. Scott notes here that his interpretation is without prejudice toward metaphorical interpretations of the healing language.
37. Scott, "Relation of Isaiah," 185–88.
38. Williamson, "Messianic Text of Isaiah 1–39," 267.

Paul D. Hanson specifically places Isaiah 34–35 among the works of the disciples of Deutero-Isaiah. For Hanson, the increasingly prominent apocalyptic elements of the pericope are evidence that the particular and concrete elements of plain history are gradually supplanted in favor of the mythic. Restoration is in view without doubt, but the restoration according to Hanson, like Mowinckel mentioned above, is not as firmly attached to Israel's nationalistic hopes as it was in the earlier literary strata.[39]

J. Barton furthers the discussion by arguing that chapters 34–35 are not a part of Isaiah's original work. Whether the two chapters originally were penned together or as separate works, Barton concludes they should be understood as eschatological in nature. These two chapters, he argues, are of the genre *apocalyptic prediction* and contain a mixture of literal and metaphorical language. Key for the present analysis is when the oracle of salvation, depicted in Chapter 35, was written and what salvation event is intended. Barton states:

> Commentators have usually seen the chapter as "deutero-deutero-Isaianic," much like Isaiah 56–66: the work of a disciple, close in time but probably already back in Judah, rather than, like Deutero-Isaiah himself, still in Babylon, awaiting the return. Isa 35:10, it should be noted, is a quotation from Isa 51:11—which implies that the author of Isaiah 35 knew Deutero-Isaiah's work, and hence wrote at a later time.[40]

If Barton's assertion is correct, the oracle could not be both a prophetic prediction and have any reference to the return of the Babylonian captives. It must have the eschatological future in mind. This is the logical conclusion and one that Barton shares when closing his excursus on these chapters. He maintains: "Whatever the origin of the 'Little Apocalypse', its contribution to chs. 1–39 is to focus attention on Israel's eschatological hope."[41]

The question of whether the prophet is speaking figuratively or spiritually in Isaiah 35 appears to be answered decisively by Hans Wildberger. He identifies Matthew 11:5 as a loose quotation and notes the phrase "lame leap like a deer" in Isaiah 35:6a. Wildberger's comments, especially those related to verse 6a, indicate that he understands the text as a literal promise in which diseases and other calamities now commonly affecting mankind will find no place in the future messianic age.[42] There is no denying the physical aspect of the prophecy; however, a clear line of argumentation is

---

39. Hanson, *Dawn of Apocalyptic*, 128–29.
40. Barton, *Isaiah 1–39*, 94.
41. Barton, *Isaiah 1–39*, 95.
42. Wildberger, *Isaiah 28–39*, 351.

evident that attaches spiritual blindness and deafness to Israel. The text of Isaiah 6 reads as though the infliction of these conditions on the nation came as a result of (1) the prophet's preaching and (2) the people's continued rejection of *Yahweh*. In light of the overall context, both spiritual renewal and the healing of physical infirmities are probably in view

Extra-Biblical Data

An Overview of Miracles and the Messiah in the Pseudepigrapha

As previously established, Jewish messianic hopes were not monolithic in nature. The several OT texts discussed above demonstrate that miracle language in relation to the messianic era is more than an isolated anomaly. Further support for this relationship is presented in the extant Jewish apocryphal and pseudepigraphical works.

According to Mark Saucy the Pseudepigrapha do not contain explicit statements "for or against" a miracle-working Messiah.[43] The Pseudepigrapha portray the messianic age as a time of miracles, including a strong Moses typology and a Messiah bearing the power of the miracle-working Holy Spirit (e.g., 2 Baruch 51:7).[44] However, this nuanced statement by Saucy should not lead one to assume the obscurity of a miracle-working Messiah in the Pseudepigrapha. The Messiah is referenced in various contexts with several exalted functions. J. Collins identifies the title "Son of Man" with "Messiah" in the Similitudes (Parables) and describes his several exalted functions. He "casts down kings" from thrones and kingdoms, "takes his seat on the throne of glory," receives worship, and "seems to be assimilated to deity."[45] In another work, A. Collins and J. Collins remark that the word *messiah* "is used unambiguously with reference to a heavenly judge."[46] Robert Henry Charles demonstrates: "The Messiah in the Parables is (1) Judge of the world, (2) Revealer of all things, (3) Champion and Ruler of the righteous."[47] In a directly miraculous claim, the Messiah raises the dead in 1 Enoch 51:1 and 61:5.

The Messiah in the narrow technical sense of the term is mentioned on several occasions in the Pseudepigrapha (1 En 48:10; 52:4; Pss Sol 17:36;

---

43. Saucy, "Kingdom-of-God," 180n117.
44. Saucy, "Kingdom-of-God," 180n117.
45. Collins, *Scepter and the Star*, 203–4.
46. Collins and Collins, *King and Messiah*, 94.
47. Charles, *Commentary on the Pseudepigrapha*, 2:214.

18:6, 8; 4 Ezra 7:29; 12:32; 2 Bar 29:3). In other contexts, the messianic age is in view, with the actions of a messianic figure implied. For example, the book of Jubilees 23:29–30 describes days of healing and blessing in the context of eschatological restoration and greatly increased human lifespans. These states of affairs are a miraculous turnabout from the previously described condition of Israel.[48]

An Overview of Miracles and the Messiah in Qumran, First-Century Thought, and Later Talmudic Evidence

Another strand of argumentation emerges in the work of Paul J. Achtemeier, Joel B. Green, and Marianne Meye Thompson. They note that in the first century, miracles were often associated with prophets. Some of these prophets promised signs, especially acts of deliverance, like those carried out by Moses or Joshua.[49] Achtemeier, Green, and Thompson concede that while few Jewish texts speak of the hope for a "wonder-working" messiah, it is possible that the concept had developed by the NT period (John 6:15; 7:31; Mark 13:22).[50] This appears to be an understatement, given the known texts of the NT and the existence of 4Q521 directly linking miraculous deeds with the messianic era:

> [The heavens] and the earth will listen to His Messiah, and none therein will stray from the commandments of the holy ones.
>
> Seekers of the Lord, strengthen yourselves in His service!
>
> All you hopeful in (your) heart, will you not find the Lord in this?
>
> For the Lord will consider the pious (*hasidim*) and call the righteous by name.

---

48. Interestingly, there is one mention of an eschatological Melkisedek [sic] bearing significant messianic resemblance: "And afterward, in the last generation, there will be another Melkisedek, the first of 12 priests. And the last will be the head of all, a great archpriest, the Word and Power of God, who will perform miracles, greater and more glorious than all the previous ones" (2 Enoch 71:34–35). The original documents are lost and the dating and recension history of 2 Enoch are difficult to establish. Even so, Charlesworth notes that 2 Enoch's portrayal of Enoch as God's chosen and exalted agent is incompatible with Christian belief. This does not mean the document is Jewish, but it does provide reason to think that an early sectarian group equated eschatology with miracle-working. Charlesworth, *Old Testament Pseudepigrapha*, 1:208.

49. *Antiquities*, 20.5.1; 20.8.6. Cf. *Wars*, 2.13.5

50. Achtemeier et al., *Introducing the New Testament*, 227.

> Over the poor His spirit will hover and will renew the faithful with His power.
>
> And He will glorify the pious on the throne of the eternal Kingdom,
>
> He who liberates the captives, restores sight to the blind, straightens the [bent].
>
> And [for] ever I will [cleave to the hopeful] and in His mercy . . .
>
> And the [fruit] . . . will not be delayed for anyone
>
> And the Lord will accomplish glorious things which have never been as [He] . . .
>
> For He will heal the wounded, and revive the dead and bring good news to the poor . . .
>
> He will lead the uprooted and knowledge . . . and smoke (?)[51]

Fitzmyer may be overly cautious when he warns against reading 4Q521 with such dogmatism that it necessitates a miracle-working messiah. His objection is two-fold. First, he argues that the text is better understood as including miraculous works and the resuscitation of the dead, rather than the resurrection. Second, the agent of the miracles may or may not be the Messiah. The messianic eschatological agent of *Yahweh* is clearly in view in the first three verses, but in verse four the actor appears to be the *Lord*. Conflating the two images may not be the correct way to understand the text.[52] Whether the actor instigating the miraculous acts is *Yahweh* or the Messiah, the people of Qumran clearly expected miracles to accompany the age and work of the Messiah. This is an important detail. The messianic age, according to the sect living at Qumran, would be marked by miracles. Strack and Billerbeck demonstrate how this was a normative thought in latter Judaism,

> *In der messian. Heilszeit erwartete man Heilung aller Krankheiten. Man nahm an. daß der Messias seinem Volk Israel alle jene Güter wiederbringen werde, die durch Adams Fall verloren gegangen waren; dazu gehörte natürlich auch die Beseitigung von Krankheit u.Tod. Diese Erwartung hatte übrigens für das jüdische Denken nichts Exorbitantes. Die Tage des Messias erreichten damit nur die Höhenlage der Zeit der Gesetzgebung am Sinai; denn auch damals war Israel frei vom Kranken u. Sterben.*[53]

51. Vermes, *Dead Sea Scrolls in English*, 244–45.
52. Fitzmyer, *One Who Is to Come*, 97.
53. Strack and Billerbeck, *Kommentar zum Neuen Testament*, 1:293.

A confirmation of the investigation above is located in the work of Jewish scholar M. Brown. He cites the *Genesis Rabbah* to support his argument that the signs associated with Isaiah 35:5–6 indicate the arrival of God's kingdom. When these signs are present, it is understood to be an affirmation of the presence of the messianic era: the visitation of *Yahweh* to his people.[54] The *Genesis Rabbah* 95:1 confirms these assertions by specifically mentioning that the blind, lame, and dumb are healed, as Isaiah 35:5 promises.[55] Later works, such as the Babylonian Talmud (Sukkah 52a), also associate miracles with the Messiah (e.g., Messiah ben David raising Messiah ben Joseph from the dead). In addition, M. Brown notes that the messianic pretenders Honi the Circle Drawer and Hanina Ben Dosa were thought especially favored by God because of miracle-working power.[56]

New Testament Evidence

Additional evidence for a pronounced strain of Jewish messianism that included miracles emerges when one examines the NT documents. The evidence begins with the hypothesized Q source and recurs in Matthew 11:3–6 and Luke 7:18–23. These pericopes consists of JTB messengers questioning Jesus concerning his messiahship and Jesus responding to them. His answer is undeniably intended to demonstrate to JTB and the disciples of JTB that he is the Messiah. "Go and tell John what you hear and see: the blind receive their sight and the lame walk, lepers are cleansed and the deaf hear, and the dead are raised up, and the poor have good news preached to them" (Matt 11:4b–5). In this case, fulfillment of OT prophecy is directly associated with proof for Jesus' messianic status. David Stern remarks that the book of Isaiah provides six signs that the Messiah will give to authenticate his person:

> He will make the blind see (Isaiah 29:18, 35:5), make the lame walk (Isaiah 35:6, 61:1), cleanse lepers (Isaiah 61:1), make the deaf hear (Isaiah 29:18, 35:5), raise the dead (implied in Isaiah 11:1–2 but not made specific), and evangelize the poor (Isaiah 61:1–2 in the light of 4:23N above). Since he has done all these things ([Matt] chapters 8–9), the message should be clear: Yeshua is the one; Yochanan need not look for another.[57]

---

54. Brown, *Answering Jewish Objections to Jesus*, 1:99.
55. Neusner, *Genesis Rabbah*, 325.
56. Brown, *Answering Jewish Objections to Jesus*, 1:100.
57. Stern, *Jewish New Testament Commentary*, s.v. "Matt 11:13."

Although the details of Stern's assertions do not receive unanimous support from scholars, the grounds for the overall import of his comments are correct. The exegetical rationale for Stern's reference to Isaiah 61:1 and Luke 4:18, with reference to the cleansing of lepers and healing of the lame, entail that the "poor" (עֲנָוִים) in Isaiah 61:1 or "poor" (πτωχοῖς) in Luke 4:18 encompass more than the economically disadvantaged. The term עֲנָוִים (*'ănāwîm*) has the basic entomological meaning of bowed. However, the semantic range of the family of terms conceptually encompasses both poverty and emotional and physical affliction. According to Leonard J. Coppes, the slightly different term עָנִי (*ānî*) is more likely to specifically designate physical affliction,[58] yet the overall semantic range allows for some overlap. The translators of the LXX and Luke appear to agree that more than mere financial poverty is in view by employing exactly the same term (πτωχοῖς), which carries the expanded meaning. The lexical work by William Arndt, Fredrick Danker, and Walter Bauer clarifies: it is those who are oppressed, disillusioned, and in special need of God's help who are intended.[59] John N. Oswalt's comments on Isaiah 61:1 further reveal this semantic overlap in the meaning of the terms. He contends the connotation of the term is not restricted to financial, material conditions, or to an oppressed minority of righteous persons. He argues for a reference to "all who are distressed and in trouble for any reason."[60] Based on these findings, there is no reason to discard the idea that the translators of the LXX and the author of Luke intended their readers to understand "poor" with the expanded connotation of their overall circumstances, including physical afflictions. More than economic disadvantage is clearly in view.

Mark 1:44 contains additional support for the forgoing assertions. Jesus commands the healed leper to go and show himself to the priests for a proof (μαρτύριον) to them. What would this healing prove? The implication is that the cleansing of a person of what was normally an incurable disease was a messianic sign. The priests verifying the cleansing would tacitly be admitting the sign while contradicting themselves by rejecting as Messiah the one who had performed the miracle.

The witnesses to Jesus' life and ministry agree that Jesus did these things in accordance with what the OT prophets predicted. These miracles carry the implication that the messianic age had, in some sense, arrived. Roy Zuck observes that the sign of giving sight to the blind is especially

---

58. Coppes, "1652 עָנָה," 683.

59. Arndt et al., *Greek-English Lexicon*, 896.

60. Oswalt, *Book of Isaiah, Chapters 40–66*, 564–65. Cf. Jamieson et al., *Commentary Critical and Explanatory on the Whole Bible*, 499.

significant since it carries both physical and spiritual adumbrations. Giving sight to the blind was associated with the activity of *Yahweh* (Exod 4:11; Ps 146:8). It also carried connotations associated with the arrival of the messianic age (Isa 29:18; 35:5; 42:7) and the work of the Servant.[61]

The miracle-working strand of Jewish messianism and the current analysis of Isaiah 61:1 receives further support in Saucy's study of the kingdom of God motif in Matthew 1-10. Saucy correlates Jesus' preaching (κηρύσσων) the gospel (εὐαγγέλιον) with the healing of diseases and infirmities; this correlation "inherently" ties the kingdom motif to the hope for fulfillment of the OT promises. Saucy remarks that twice in the first nine chapters of Matthew, Jesus' ministry is "summarized as teaching in the synagogues, preaching the 'gospel of the kingdom,' and healing every disease and infirmity (4:23; 9:35)."[62] This particular insight is important for understanding why the Jews of the first century associated feats of power with the coming of the messianic age. Jesus and the people apparently understood this association and required both the preaching of the εὐαγγέλιον and the working of miracles to authenticate the coming of the Messiah and the messianic age. According to the synoptic writers, Jesus gave the disciples power to work miracles in combination with preaching the gospel. There is little doubt that both elements were intended to confirm the coming of the Messiah and messianic age.

Twelftree argues that the twin themes of Jesus as teacher (Matt 5-7) and the miracle stories associated with Jesus (Matt 8-9) as they are presented in Matthew form a two-part panel intended to highlight Jesus as the new Moses. Both Exodus 7-12 and Matthew 8-9, according to Twelftree's analysis, contain ten miracles.[63] Significantly, Twelftree, like Saucy (see above) correlates the coming of the kingdom with miracles, but not miracles alone. Miracles must be accompanied by the preaching of the good news. In fact, miracles are not the most prominent or important aspect of Jesus' "new Moses" persona. Without these deeds of divine power as witness to his status, the Jews generally would not have designated him *Son of David*.

Exorcism is widely recognized as a form of miracle. In the NT, exorcism directly correlates with the coming of the kingdom and the power of *Yahweh*. That Jesus was recognized as an exorcist by his contemporaries is acknowledged by a wide variety of scholars. Ehrman describes Jesus' exorcisms as "among the best-attested" of his deeds.[64] The incident recorded

---

61. Zuck, *Biblical Theology of the New Testament*, 177-78.
62. Saucy, "Kingdom-of-God," 179.
63. Twelftree, "Miracles and Miracle Stories," 597.
64. Ehrman, *Jesus Apocalyptic Prophet of the New Millennium*, 197.

in Matthew 12:22–32 is especially important because it consists of a total package of messianic healing elements. The man brought to Jesus was blind, mute, and demonized. The people witnessing Jesus' actions against the demons had one of two reactions. Some, particularly the religious elite, alleged that the power behind Jesus' ability to cast out demons was effected by the prince of demons (Matt 12:24). Others recognized the messianic implication of Jesus' deeds and asked, "Can this be the Son of David?" (Matt 12:23). The wording of this question demonstrates that the deeds Jesus performed were anticipated from the OT and had a direct mental correlation with the Messiah, Son of David, and perhaps even the Son of God in the popular conscience. James Brady forwards the work of several scholars who argue that exorcism was thought to be a keystone of Davidic royal power often associated with Solomon[65] as the "Son of David" and the only king to be called "God's son."[66]

M. Brown construes the meaning of the crowd's comments as a reminder that the title "Son of David" in that era meant "Messiah."[67] "Son of David" as a Christological messianic title is significant for Matthew (Matt 12:23; 21:9, 15) in that it is associated with healing miracles (Matt 9:27; 12:23; 15:22; 20:30–31; cf. Matt 1:1, 20; 21:9, 15) and exorcisms. Jack Dean Kingsbury has taken this concept further by demonstrating that for the author of Mark, the titles "Messiah/Christ" (Anointed One), "King of the Jews," "Son of David," "Son of the Blessed," and "Son of God" interrelate and inform one another.[68] He then argues that the title "Messiah" is interpreted by each of the other titles (1:1; 15:32; 12:35; 14:61).[69] The evidence indicates that all three function together—the titles, the preaching of the gospel, and the miracles that accompanied that preaching.

Summary

Jesus appears to have believed that the particular work of exorcism demonstrated that the kingdom of God had arrived (Matt 12:28), and that he was the Messiah and Son of David. Jesus' miracles, in combination with his

---

65. See *Antiquities of the Jews* 8.45
66. Brady, "Do Miracles Authenticate the Messiah?," 104.
67. Brown, *Answering Jewish Objections to Jesus*, 1:99.
68. Kingsbury, *Christology of Mark's Gospel*, 55. Further establishing this point is the fact that the titles "Son of God" and "Christ" are juxtaposed in Matthew 16:16 and 26:63. Kingsbury also notes several minor Christological titles in Mark (e.g., "bridegroom," "shepherd," "coming one," "prophet," "teacher-rabbi," and "Lord" (or "lord") (Kingsbury, *Christology of Mark's Gospel*, 53).
69. Kingsbury, *Christology of Mark's Gospel*, 55.

exorcisms and the preaching of the good news, affirm that his work and his self-understanding were, at least, the beginning of the eschatological fulfillment of the Jewish nation's messianic expectations, as foretold in the OT. In fact, Jesus' work as a fulfillment of OT prophecy is depicted in the NT as involving more than the individual miracles. The overall intention of the writers was to display Jesus' announcement and inauguration of a reordered kingdom of peace emerging out of the chaos of fallen humanity. Jesus fulfilled the OT prophecies of miracle-working not only by bringing individual relief from affliction but by bringing soundness, health, and peace to Israel as well.[70] In this way, he exemplified the image of the expected prophet like Moses pattern. This conclusion aligns seamlessly with the texts and ideas examined above and may be why many of the people desired to make Jesus king by force (John 6:15).

Plausible Historical-Evidential Conclusions Gathered from the Study of the Miracles in Relation to Jewish Messianism

1. Israel's expected salvation includes some form of second Exodus.
2. Israel's expected salvation includes miracles performed by the Messiah.
3. The Messiah's antitypical role is the prophet like Moses.
4. Isaiah 29 likely contains miraculous transformations related to the messianic era.
5. Isaiah 29 is part of a cadre of texts that imply eschatological restoration for Israel.
6. A pre-exilic date for Isaiah 35 is improbable.
7. Isaiah 35 primarily describes the messianic era.
8. Isaiah 35 contains images of miraculous activity.
9. Isaiah 35 contains elements of both physical and spiritual healing.

Historical-Evidential Facts Gathered from the Study of the Miracles in Relation to Jewish Messianism

1. The OT contains evidence to support the concept of a miracle-working prophet and messianic figure.

---

70. Brady, "Do Miracles Authenticate the Messiah?," 107.

2. The Pseudepigrapha, Dead Sea Scrolls, and later Jewish literature depict miracles in relation to the Messiah or the messianic age.
3. The NT depicts the expectation of a particular prophet.
4. The NT depicts miracles as an authentication of Jesus as the Messiah.
5. The NT records that Jesus performed miracles in accordance with the OT, certain sectarian, and proletariat Jewish messianic expectations.
6. Jesus believed he was the particular prophet and Messiah.
7. The Gospel writers believed Jesus was the particular prophet and Messiah.

Chapter 7

The Fifth Group of Biblical Texts

Introduction to the Fifth Group of Biblical Texts

THE FIFTH GROUP OF biblical texts include Psalm 2:1–12, emphasizing verse 7; Psalm 16, emphasizing verses 9–10; and Psalm 22:1–31, emphasizing verse 16. Psalm 2 is often interpreted as a description of the unique relationship Jesus claimed to have with God the Father. Psalm 22 is allegedly messianic, with some interpreters claiming it reports circumstances related to the crucifixion of Jesus. Psalm 16 contains language that may also be indicative of the resurrection of Jesus. As stated in chapter 1, this portion of the work will not deal in depth with the actual NT data concerning the reported resurrection of Jesus. The resurrection proper has been extensively treated by other scholars.[1]

Psalm 2:1–12, Emphasizing Verse 7

Literary and Textual Analysis

Old Testament Evidence

Psalm 2 is usually classified as a Royal Psalm, marking the enthronement of the king of Israel. Several scholars, both modern and ancient, have considered Psalm 1 and 2 a single unit that forms the introduction to the Hebrew Psalter.[2] The specific occasion for its writing is unknown, and no particular king or author is named in the Psalm. Some scholars argue this psalm may have been utilized on multiple occasions as part of the official liturgy for

---

1. See Habermas, *Historical Jesus*. Cf. Craig et al., *Jesus' Resurrection*; Licona, *Resurrection of Jesus*.

2. Waltke et al., *Psalms as Christian Worship*, 160–61. Whiting, "Psalms 1 and 2 as a Hermeneutical Lens," 247–62.

the installation of a new king or at an annual festival.³ Most scholars affirm something similar as the basis for interpretation. Further, it seems clear that the most controversial aspect of Psalm 2 is not about what letters or words are present. It must be acknowledged that a minor issue exists with the Aramaic loanword בר (son) in the MT and whether it needs emendation or is original to this psalm usually dated during the monarchy. The Aramaic word is clearly different from the one used in verse 7 (בן) when *Yahweh* is speaking to his king. However, the whole argument may be moot since the majority of manuscripts use the Hebrew term, not the Aramaic.

The most controversial aspect of the work is prophetic and eschatological in nature. Does the text in its current form refer to an eschatological messianic agent? The *crux interpretum* for the passage when viewed from this perspective is verse 7. For example, Peter C. Craigie states, "'I have begotten you' is metaphorical language; it means more than simply adoption, which has legal overtones, and implies that a 'new birth' of a divine nature took place during the coronation."⁴ Nonetheless, Craigie contends for a non-messianic original intent. How can the language be both metaphorical and actual divine intervention of some sort create a "new birth" of a "divine nature"? As will be further developed below, categorically ruling out the possibility that the referent of the psalm maintains a status beyond metaphorical adoption overstates the demonstrable. It is possible the psalm unveils some metaphysical relationship between the king and *Yahweh*. It seems inconsistent to argue, as Craigie has done, for both a metaphorical meaning and some actual change resulting in the impartation of a divine nature. However, Craigie has acknowledged that something more than purely metaphorical ideals is present.

Similarly, John T. Willis has documented four of the most often proffered arguments supporting an eschatological messianic understanding of Psalm 2. The third of his counter-arguments deals with the ambiguous phrase "You are my Son; today I have begotten you" (Ps 2:7).⁵ Willis rejects a messianic referent, arguing instead for an intimate relationship between the historically enthroned king and *Yahweh*. Conversely, other interpreters—including Augustine and some early Jewish documents—argue that "son" and "begotten" mean something more literal.⁶ Theologically, as most orthodox Christians would agree, even Jesus is not the son of God in the normal, procreative sense that literal begetting and sonship require. The

---

3. Kraus, *Psalms 1–59*, 126.
4 Craigie, *Psalms 1–50*, 67.
5. Willis, "A Cry of Defiance—Psalm 2," 33.
6. Bird, "The Psalms," 448.

troubling fact, however, is that, without justifiable warrant, one cannot dispose of the odd and infrequent application of begetting in relation to *Yahweh*. Allen P. Ross is on a slightly more consistent track when remarking that the phrase "You are my Son; today I have begotten you" is a reference to the Davidic Covenant (2 Sam 7:14) and "is appropriated by the king to show his legitimate right to rule. 'Today' then refers to the coronation day, and the expression 'I have begotten you' ... refers not to physical birth but is an extended metaphor describing his becoming God's 'son.'"[7] Even this explanation, like that proposed by Craigie, fails to adequately treat the unique use of "begotten." Psalm 2 is the only OT context where uncontested manuscripts evidence suggests that *Yahweh* begets (ילד) a son. However, Psalm 110, a verbally and conceptually similar passage according to one reading contains (Ps 110:3) the same implication.[8] As seen above, the "begotten" language of the psalm is usually explained as part of near-eastern coronation rituals and the concomitant adoption of the king by a deity. J. J. M. Roberts disputes this conclusion, however. While noting the ubiquity of this claim and its acceptance,[9] Roberts thinks the generally held assumption that the statement in Psalms 2:7, "You are my son, today I have begotten you," represents a legal formula of adoption is unsupported by evidence.[10] Citing the work of Martin David,[11] Roberts finds only three examples of an adoption formula in Akkadian texts, none of which contains the language "you are my son" as used in Psalm 2:7. Further, he observes that none of three examples are a second-person address as in Psalms 2:7. They are, instead, addressed to the nobles of the royal court. Most importantly for the current study, the language of begetting is completely absent in these formulas. Roberts explains that the Akkadian verb *walādu*, meaning to give birth, never appears in any Akkadian adoption formula. Yet the Hebrew equivalent of *walādu*, *yālad*, is present in Psalm 2:7. Roberts argues that adoption, if it existed at all in Judaism, was not a widespread practice; the explanation for the supposed metaphorical begetting in Psalm 2 is not from near-eastern adoption texts. Jeffrey Howard Tigay, Ben-Zion Schereschewsky, and Yisrael Gilat maintain that "the evidence for adoption in the Bible is so equivocal that some have denied it was practiced at all in the biblical period."[12]

7. Ross, "Psalms," 792.

8. *Yělidtīkā* means I have begotten you, whereas the MT reads *yaldutêkā*, meaning youth. Weil et al., *Biblia Hebraica Stuttgartensia*, s.v. "Psalm 110:3."

9. For an overview of the consensus opinion and related literature, see Kraus, *Psalms 1–59*, 129–32.

10. Roberts, *Bible and the Ancient Near East*, 147. Cf. Gunn, "Psalm 2," 432.

11. David, *Die adoption im altbabylonischen Recht*, 79.

12. Tigay et al., "Adoption," 415.

Evidence from Postexilic Redaction and Arrangement

Considering the probability that the current form of Psalms 2 is a product of a postexilic redactor provides additional reasons for questioning the currently held consensus that the term "begotten" and the concept of *sonship* do not contain a metaphysical element. According to Mowinckel, the final form of the psalms could be as late as 200 BC[13] and pointedly later than the demise of the last Davidic king. The composition of the psalter and its history are important to help understand the development of messianism in Israel. Joachim Schaper notes the work of H. L. Hossfeld and E. Zenger in demonstrating the likelihood that Psalms 2–89 are the result of combining two earlier collections (Ps 3–41 and 42–89) with Psalm 2 prefixed to the finished collection. Collectively, this constituted a "messianic psalter." Schaper thinks this psalter was probably edited during the period from Cyrus to Alexander.[14] Gerald Henry Wilson confirms these findings; he "examined the evidence for purposeful editorial activity in the Psalter and found confirmation for the reality of the five books as editorial divisions."[15] This approach suggests that by the postexilic period, the interpretation of God's Davidic promise was in relation to a future anointed one. This line of argumentation is particularly virulent when the eschatological connotations of both Psalms 1 and 2 are considered as a unit, in respect to their utopian, and not merely restoration, implications. For example, Bruce K. Waltke, James M. Houston, and Erika Moore detect several reasons supporting the notion that Psalms 1 and 2 were once separate and, subsequently, placed together, to form a literary unit introducing the psalter.[16] First, both psalms lack a superscription. Second, several of the early church fathers considered the two psalms as a single unit.[17] Third, the emergence of many verbal correspondences implies a thematic relationship:

> The first verse of Psalm 1 (1:1a) and the last verse of Psalm 2 (2:12b) begin with 'ašrê ('fortunate'), forming an inclusio framing the introduction. The introductory stanzas of both psalms use *hāga* ('to meditate,' 1:2; "to plot," 2:1). The last verses of both psalms use the metaphor of *derek* ('way') in connection

---

13. Mowinckel, *Psalms in Israel's Worship*, 2:199.
14. Schaper, "Persian Period," 10–11.
15. Wilson, "Use of Royal Psalms," 86.
16. Waltke et al., *Psalms as Christian Worship*, 160–61.
17. Waltke et al., *Psalms as Christian Worship*, 145. Among them are Clement of Alexandria, Justin Martyr, Origen, and Tertullian.

with *'ābad* ('perish,' 1:6; 2:12). Both Psalms also employ terms belonging to the semantic domain of 'mock' (*lēsîm*, 'mockers' [against *I AM*'s law], 1:1, and "*lā'ag*, 'derision' of [*I AM* against rebels to his rule], 2:4). Third, the two psalms expound a uniform message: the pious and righteous are fully rewarded, and in the time of judgment, they triumph over the wicked.[18]

Mark J. Whiting notes the long-standing recognition that Joshua 1:7 and Psalm 1 have connections. More particularly, Joshua 1:7 and Psalm 1:3 both contain encouragement and a promise of success if one meditates on the law day and night. Perfect adherence to the law guarantees success. "Perhaps," Whiting argues, the editors of the Psalter are echoing a concern for an ideal leader.[19] Such a leader would be a type of second-Joshua, an ideal king, who enjoys total (not partial) victory over all enemies because of his perfect faithfulness to *Yahweh* and Torah. The image of this ideal king receives further illumination in Psalm 2. Clearly, no historic king of Israel has fulfilled or brought to realization the full implications contained in these psalms.

Psalm 1 and 2 also contain an eschatological dimension. The identification of the wicked with chaff (Psalm 1:5) is a metaphor that elsewhere in the prophets "unambiguously reflects eschatological judgement (Isa 17:13; 41:15; Hos 13:3; Zeph 2:2)."[20] This theme receives further expansion in Psalm 2:8–12, when the victor triumphs over the "nations" and they perish in a universal judgment.[21] Jerome F. D. Creach suggests a close connection between the verdant tree of Psalm 1:3 and the tradition equating Zion and the temple with paradise, including the image contained in Ezekiel 47:12.[22] This image intimates that the agent of the judgment (Ps 2:8–12) is the righteous king/tree reappearing in Psalm 2:6.[23]

A compelling piece of evidence for questioning the rejection of a metaphysical relationship between *Yahweh* and the "begotten" son is the juxtaposition of the scoffers and their plotting council, from which emerges rebellion, and the righteous king sitting (not in the council of the wicked) in the council of *Yahweh*, from which emerges universal dominion. Robert Luther Cole identifies the individual who *sits* in the heavens (Ps 2:4a)

---

18. Waltke et al., *Psalms as Christian Worship*, 160–61.
19. Whiting, "Psalms 1 and 2," 255.
20. Whiting, "Psalms 1 and 2," 255.
21. Cole, "Psalms 1 and 2," 82. Cole thinks his exegesis on the concept of judgement in Psalm 1 and 2 is confirmed in Psalm 149 (Cole, "Psalms 1 and 2," 82n15).
22. Creach, "Like a Tree," 46.
23. Cole, "Psalms 1 and 2," 76.

not as *Yahweh*,²⁴ but אֲדֹנָי (*'ădōnāy*), as his "Anointed," who is identified in Psalm 110:1 as sitting in the heavens at the right hand of *Yahweh*. The rationale for this identification is that consonantally, אדֹנִי (*'dōnî*, Ps 110:1) and אֲדֹנָי (*'ădōnāy*, Ps 2:4a) are identical (אדני). In addition, the response to the scoffing of the unrighteous rulers seems best understood as an earthly activity responded to by the righteous, earthly, but exalted, king. The king, in both psalms, rules from Zion, a "holy hill" (Ps 2:6) and in "'holy array' . . . or more closely to the possible 'holy mountains'" (Ps 110:3).²⁵ This king is addressed by *Yahweh* with second masculine singular pronouns in both Psalms 2:7 and 110:4, with the common enemy expressed as the nations.²⁶ Citing David C. Mitchell, Cole contends that the "conflation"²⁷ of *Yahweh* and the king in Psalm 110 is intentional, designed to hearken the attentive reader back to אדני in Psalm 2:4 as the heavenly-seated one. The ambiguity is intentional, according to Cole, who amplifies his conclusions by noting the role reversal in Psalm 110:5, where אדני is at the right hand of the king. Consequently, according to Cole, he who "sits" and the divine name אדני are deliberate fusion of *Yahweh* and his anointed king.²⁸ Cole's conclusion, simply stated, is that the full integration of Psalms 1 and 2 function as the introduction to the entire psalter.

Evidence from the Genre of the Royal Psalm

This brief mention of the function of the Royal Psalm in the psalter also provides evidence to support the supposition that dogmatic denials of Psalm 2 as referring to a metaphysical relationship between the king and *Yahweh* go beyond what the evidence supports. Detailed treatment of the genre is beyond the scope of the current work, but some evidence emerges even when the function of royal psalms are broadly outlined. Concisely defined, the royal psalms affirm the Davidic Covenant and the promises it contains. M. L. Strauss summarizes these elements as follows:

> God's faithfulness to his 'covenant' (Ps 89:4, 29; 132:12) guarantees the perpetuity of David's line (Ps 18:50; 45:6, 16–17; 132:10–12, 17). The Davidic king's divine sonship is affirmed

---

24. BHS critical apparatus does identify one manuscript that contains the יהוה perhaps in an attempt to remove the ambiguity of the reference. Weil et al., *Biblia Hebraica Stuttgartensia*, s.v. "Psalm 2:4."
25. Cole, "Psalms 1 and 2," 84.
26. Cole, "Psalms 1 and 2," 84.
27. Mitchell, *Message of the Psalter*, 262.
28. Cole, "Psalms 1 and 2," 85.

(Ps 2:7), together with his enthronement on Mount Zion (Ps 2:4-6; 110:2), his reign in justice and righteousness (Ps 45:7; 72:1-4, 7), his victory over enemies through the Lord's power (Ps 2:1-9; 18:31-42; 20:1-9; 21:1-13; 45:5; 72:9-11; 110:1-2, 5-6) and material prosperity in the land (Ps 72:16). New features introduced include worldwide dominion (Ps 2:8; 72:8-11), a privileged position at the Lord's right hand (Ps 110:1), and a perpetual priesthood 'according to the order of Melchizedek' (Ps 110:4, nrsv). Though not of Levitical lineage, the Davidic king oversees the temple cult and serves as a priest in his own right.[29]

Gunkel affirms ten Royal Psalms, all of which deal with Israelite kings and their celebrations or festivals.[30] He contends that "often" (not always) the particular occasion is clear.[31] Other scholars expand the list substantially.[32] As articulated above, the division of the Hebrew Psalter into units is universally recognized. The five-fold division, as understood by Wilson, is the result of organization specifically directed to place royal psalms at the seams of the first three books of the Psalter (Ps 2; 72; 89).[33] Schaper agrees with the likelihood that Psalm 2-89 are the result of combining two earlier collections (Ps 3-41; 42-89), as discussed above, with Psalm 2 prefixed to the finished collection to create a "messianic psalter."[34] Wilson argues that Psalm 1 represents a late addition as an introduction to the whole Psalter, and that book one begins with Psalm 2. He also recognizes the connection to the David Covenant present in Psalm 2. Kaiser contends that Psalm 2 treats the institution of the Davidic Covenant; he also contends, as does Wilson, that the placement of Psalm 89 at the end of Book III of the psalter represents a lament over what appeared to be Yahweh's ultimate "(if in our view only a temporary)" rejection of the Davidic kingship.[35] This rejection and the failure of the Davidic kings may be reflected in the diminished role of Royal Psalms in books four and five of the Psalter.[36]

If due consideration is given to the context of the covenant promise contained in the text of 2 Samuel 7:13, 16 and the implication of "forever,"

---

29. Strauss, "David," 437.
30. Gunkel, *Introduction to the Psalms*, 99-100.
31. Gunkel, *Introduction to the Psalms*, 99-100.
32. Eaton, *Kingship and the Psalms*, 1-26.
33. Wilson, "Use of Royal Psalms."
34. Schaper, "Persian Period," 10-11.
35. Kaiser, "Psalm 72," 270; Wilson, "Use of Royal Psalms," 90.
36. Kaiser, "Psalm 72," 270.

why must Psalm 2 be arbitrarily limited to an historic enthronement? The psalm celebrates the institution of the Davidic covenant with an unnamed king, in an unidentifiable *sitz en leben*, with flawless idealistic imagery. The idealistic, ultimate Davidic scion may have been in view from the beginning. Perhaps the ideal of the promise preceded and was recorded before the flawed imperfect descendants of David appear on the historical scene as kings. David is clearly already enthroned in 2 Samuel 7 and has sons, none of whom become king.

These observations and possibilities based on OT literature and exegesis seem to cast a shadow on dogmatic rejections of the possibility of a metaphysical link with the "son" king of Psalm 1 and 2 and the certainty of a historical Davidic referent. Perhaps a future ideal utopian conception was present in the original versions of Psalm 1, 2, or both. If Psalm 2 can be legitimately restricted to metaphorical adoption in any sense, it must have originated in the covenants between *Yahweh* and Israel, and later with David.[37] Still, this explanation leaves at least four questions unanswered. First, since no historical king can be identified, what evidential ground mandates that Psalm 2 refer to a historical king? Second, since no other near-eastern royal-adoption formula contains the "begotten" language, what evidence mandates metaphorical adoption? Third, can all other relational possibilities be excluded, given the probable intentional arrangement of the psalms? Fourth, in light of the fact that Psalm 1 and 2 contain much the same imagery and ideals and have numerous textual parallels with Psalm 110, is it inconceivable that a metaphysical relationship exists between the king and *Yahweh*?

Intertestamental Evidence

Four of the most cited extra-biblical works that bear on the interpretation of Psalm 2 are 4Q174, 1QSa, 1 Enoch 48:10, and Psalms of Solomon 17. The first text, 4Q174 is among the several scrolls from Qumran that, in some way, employ the term משיח (*māšîaḥ*) in the narrow sense of an anointed eschatological agent of *Yahweh*. The inclusion of a reference to Messiah as a branch or scion of David, for whom *Yahweh* will be a father (and the branch a son), heightens the importance of this text. Fitzmyer laments that because

---

37. Tigay et al., "Adoption," 417. These authors appear to affirm that Psalm 2:7–8 contains adoptive language with a "declaration, 'You are my son,' a typical date formula, 'this day' (the next phrase, 'I have born you')." In this sense, the adoption carries the conception of new birth complete with the promise of an inherited empire. Waltke, Houston, and Moore contend that adoption was "well-known in the history of Israel" (Waltke et al., *Psalms as Christian Worship*, 171).

the beginning of the *pesher* is lost, "one will never learn how Psalm 2 was interpreted eschatologically."[38] A cogent point must not be lost here, however. The process of interpretation (*how*) is secondary to the fact that, according to Fitzmyer, Psalm 2 *was* interpreted eschatologically. It was so interpreted using the language of "the scion of David . . . who is to arise . . . in the last days" and "seed/son" language from 2 Samuel 7:11-14. If Fitzmyer is correct: it was not interpreted as pertaining to a historical king of Israel.

J. Collins emphatically stresses the futuristic intent of 4Q174. He states, "a future 'successor to the Davidic throne' in an apocalyptic or eschatological context is, by definition, a Davidic messiah."[39] Collins continues his exposition by vesting 4Q174 with exactly this type of messianic significance.[40] In fact, according to a later work authored by Collins, this text does not specifically delineate how sonship should be understood; in some sense, however, the future Davidic scion is the son of God.[41] L. H. Schiffman affirms the eschatological nature of the text by noting that the temple is eschatological in character and, at the end of days, a "shoot of David . . . the 'Davidic Messiah'" arises to save Israel.[42]

The second of the relevant texts, 1QSa, contains a reading that has stirred much controversy among Dead Sea Scrolls scholarship. J. Collins remarks that some scholars read "when God begets the messiah with them." Others have suggested various readings such as, "when God sends the Messiah to be with them."[43] Another reading includes "when God leads the Messiah." In a later work, coauthored by Adela Yarbro Collins, J. Collins affirms that most scroll scholars of the 1950s held to the "begets" reading, rather than the "leads" emendation.[44] Robert Gordis argues that the reading that identifies "God" as the begetter is virtually certain, based on normal Hebrew grammar. He reads the text as follows:

> This is the order of sitting for the men of renown invited to the convocation, to the counsels of the Community: When (God) begets the Messiah, with them shall come the Priest, head of all the Congregation of Israel and of all the elders of the sons of Aaron, the priests, invited to the convocation, men of renown. And they shall sit before him, each man according

38. Fitzmyer, *One Who Is to Come*, 98-99.
39. Collins, *Scepter and the Star*, 184.
40. Collins, *Scepter and the Star*, 185.
41. Collins and Collins, *King and Messiah*, 64.
42. Schiffman, "Messianic Figures," 125.
43. Collins, *Scepter and the Star*, 81.
44. See Collins and Collins, *King and Messiah*.

to his dignity. And afterwards the Messiah of Israel shall sit, and there shall sit before him the heads of the clans of Israel, each according to his dignity and his post, in their stations and according to their marchings.[45]

As Gordis highlights, it is of great importance to know if 1QSa does contain an affirmation of divine begetting in relationship to the Messiah. Vermes also confirms the translation of the problematic term יוליד as "engendered," the reading supported by computer enhancement.[46] Jan Willem van Henten directly associates 1QSa with messianism, "the end of time," Psalm 2, and God's begetting the messiah.[47]

The third important document is 1 Enoch 37–71 (the Parables or Similitudes). This text is a significant source for the study of Psalm 2. On at least two occasions, the Similitudes use the title *Messiah* in the narrow sense of the term (48:10; 52:4). This portion of 1 Enoch is a Jewish, probably pre-Christian, work usually dated after the final redaction of Daniel and before the late first century AD. The Similitudes contain what George W. E. Nickelsburg and James C. VanderKam identify as the first use of titular language such as *Son of Man/Chosen One*—titles drawn from biblical texts about the Davidic king—in combination or "together with the expression 'the kings of the earth' (and 'the strong'?) in 48:8a."[48] All of these titles and descriptions occur in the context of the eschatological Anointed One/Messiah. This allusion to Psalm 2:2 provides a second pre-Christian verification that Psalm 2 was understood eschatologically by some Jews.

Another of the Similitudes that requires a brief comment is 1 Enoch 52 and the reference to the Messiah/Anointed One in relation to "the earth" (52:4). Nickelsburg and VanderKam, in agreement with Fitzmyer, note the royal authority or kingly image adhering to this messianic figure.[49] However, Nickelsburg and VanderKam extend their analysis by observing the possible connection between the sovereignty of the Anointed One over "the earth" and similar words in Psalm 2: "The ends of the earth your possession" (52:8) and "O rulers of the earth" (52:10).[50] If a connection exists—which is likely—it serves to underscore again the eschatological nature of Psalms 2.

---

45. Gordis, "'Begotten' Messiah," 192–93.

46. Vermes, *Dead Sea Scrolls in English*, 120. Cf. Martínez and Tigchelaar, *Dead Sea Scrolls Study Edition (Transcriptions)*, 100.

47. van Henten, "Hasmonean Period," 22.

48. Nickelsburg and VanderKam, *1 Enoch 2: Chapters 37–82*, 176.

49. Fitzmyer, *One Who Is to Come*, 88.

50. Nickelsburg and VanderKam, *1 Enoch 2: Chapters 37–82*, 189.

None of texts in the Similitudes or 4Q174 and 1QSa permits a factual statement about precisely when Psalm 2 acquired a messianic eschatological interpretation. Pace Puech, however, delimits the *terminus ad quem* to the middle of the second century BC: "Je serai pour lui un père et il sera pour moi un fils', voir aussi Ps 2:7; 89:27-30; 110:3. Tous ces textes avaient certainement reçu vers le milieu du IIe siècle une interprétation messianique."[51]

The fourth significant text for our current purpose is the Psalms of Solomon 17. Kiwoong Son captures the essence of its relevance: "Psalms of Solomon 17 refers to the 'son of David' as the eschatological king who will judge the nations and purge Jerusalem. The iron rod in Psalm 2:9 is applied to him and he is described as a righteous king who will not rely on horse and rider and bow but rule with his word."[52] Max-Alain Chevallier surveyed the Psalms of Solomon, and concludes:

> L'hymne messianique de Ps Sal 17 dont dépend Ps Sal 18/6-10, manifeste l'autorité dont jouissait aux yeux de son auteur une tradition du Messie, fils de David, selon ES 11, de façon assez lâche et verbeuse pour l'adapter à ses vues personnelles.
>
> C'est ainsi qu'il a effacé comme dans un brouillage tout trace d'un salut universel, la désignation du Messie comme Rameau d'Israël les perspectives paradisiaques et d'une façon générale tous les traits qui pouvaient s'opposer à sa description d'un Messie terrestre et fort. L'Esprit même ne l'ensemble demeuré pourtant étroitement lié au texte de la tradition.[53]

Chevallier connects not only Isaiah 11, but the tradition of a strong earthly Davidic messiah with Psalms of Solomon 17. Other pre-Christian Jewish texts frequently associated with Psalms 2 are also among those analyzed by Chevallier. He includes the Parables of Enoch, Sirach, 4 Esdras, and Baruch. Whitsett translates Chevallier as contending: "Insofar as the Apocrypha and Pseudepigrapha represent Palestinian Judaism, . . . it developed its messianic beliefs from two or three foundational scriptures: Isaiah 11:1-10, Psalm 2,

---

51. Brooke et al., *Discoveries in the Judan Desert XXII*, 181. Fitzmyer affirms this quotation as a general statement (Fitzmyer, *One Who Is to Come*, 107n103). However, he disagrees with Peuch's statement and position: "Qui refuse une appellation messianique dans cette composition et même une lecture messianique de Ps 2:2 dans le judaïsme préchrétien, voir cependant Psaumes de Salomon 17" (Brooke et al., *Discoveries in the Judan Desert*, 181n40). Fitzmyer does not find a connection between Psalm 2 and Psalms of Solomon 17.

52. Son, *Zion Symbolism in Hebrews*, 114.

53. Chevallier, *L'esprit et le Messie*, 16-17.

and, interestingly, Isaiah 49:1–9, the second song of the Servant of YHWH, which already combines Isaiah 11 and Psalm 2 in its own original fashion."[54]

The medieval commentator Rashi affirmed that the "Sages" of the Jews interpreted Psalm 2:1 as referring to the King Messiah (b. Ber 7B). Rashi, however, thought it was proper to interpret it as referring to David (2 Sam 5:17).[55] Strack and Billerbeck reference several Talmudic eschatological interpretations related to Psalm 2. They contend that the messianic interpretation related to messiah ben David is the oldest and most common. They state:

> sie findet sich bereits in den Psalmen Salomos u. hat gewiß wesentlich dazu beigetragen, daß der messianische König kurzweg der „Gesalbte" מָשִׁיחַ u. der „Sohn" (Gottes) genannt wurde (s. Ps 2, 2 u. 7). Besonders gern ist der 2. Psalm auf die Empörung Gogs u. Magogs wider Gott u. seinen Messias bezogen worden.[56]

In addition, Strack and Billerbeck note the significant number of later messianic interpretations offered by rabbinic scholars in relation to Psalm 2, while demonstrating, in accordance with Psalms of Solomon 17, that the Targum on Psalms 2 is eschatologically and messianically oriented:

> Vermutlich hat auch der Targum Ps 2 messianisch gedeutet; denn die spätere Zeit hat bei dem „Gesalbten" Jahves kaum an etwas andres als an den messianischen König gedacht. Die Targumübersetzung lautet: Warum toben die Völker u. sinnen (lies מרנגין statt מרגנין) die Nationen Eitelkeit? Aufstehen die Könige der Erde, u. die Herrscher vereinigen sich, um sich vor Jahve zu empören u. um zu hadern wider seinen Gesalbten (= Messias).[57]

---

54. Whitsett, "Son of God, Seed of David," 678. According to Whitsett, of special value to Chevallier's analysis are Pss Sol 17:23–45; 1 Enoch 46:3–6; 48:2–5; 49:1–4; Sir 47:11. Whitsett further argues that Chevallier found the same OT texts (Isa 11; Ps 2; Isa 49) form the basis for messianic exegesis in the Sibylline Oracles, in Philo, and in the LXX texts of Numbers 24:7, 17 (Balaam's oracles). These texts all build an exegetical structure leading to Paul's work and the grounding assumption that Jesus is the Son of God, Messiah, and the σπέρμα.

55. Rashi, *Rashi's Commentary*, s.v. "Psalm 2." Cf. b. Sukk 52A

56. Strack and Billerbeck, *Kommentar zum Neuen Testament*, 3:675–80. Although Strack and Billerbeck contend the messianic interpretation is the oldest, it is not the only interpretation of Psalm 2 in the Talmudic and midrashic exegetical traditions. Psalm 2 has also been interpreted in relation to Aaron, David, and the people of Israel during the messianic age.

57. Strack and Billerbeck, *Kommentar zum Neuen Testament*, 3:675. Cf. Maimonides, *Commentary on the Mishnah Tractate Sanhedrin*. Maimonides contends that the "prophets desired and righteously yearned for the days of the Messiah" (Maimonides, *Commentary*, 148). Maimonides's translator Rosner remarks on two other

Considered as a whole, the extra-biblical evidence cannot demonstrate a direct and original messianic interpretation of Psalm 2. It does, however, demonstrate that the messianic understanding is no late entry into the interpretive stream. This messianic stream has a long history; given the ambiguities of the text itself, discarding any thought of an original messianic intent is unwarranted. At the least, a messianic perspective is possible, if not probable.

New Testament Data

Psalm 2 is quoted or alluded to on a number of occasions in the NT (e.g., Mark 1:11pp.; Acts 4:25ff; 13:33; 17:13; Rom 1:4; Heb 1:5; 5:5; Rev 2:26–27; 12:5; 19:15). In each instance, Jesus is an integral part of the reference with the implication that he is the anointed king/son. These multiple contexts and authors further heighten the likelihood that Psalm 2 is prophecy—not enigmatic poetry—that, by default, should be bound to a pre-exilic referent. The various NT contexts evoke images of anointing, sonship, resurrection, enthronement, and rulership that may contain better explanations than those offered by current critical scholarship. Most importantly, however, is the evocation of the unique relationship of Jesus with God (μονογενής) in John 1:14, 18: a relationship that conceptually intimates of another, just as unique relationship in Psalm 2:7 (γεννάω). That they are not the same term is obvious; they do not share the same etymology. However, both terms indicate that the subject enjoys a unique status in relationship to God. Whether the correct object is God, Son, or One is irrelevant for our purpose. The relationship of Jesus to the Father indicated in John 1:14 (and John 3:16) is one of an absolutely unique person entering the human condition from outside. The begetting in Psalm 2:7 and John 1:14, according

---

translator commentators of Maimonides (Maimonides, *Commentary*, 148n273). Rosner tacitly concurs with them, arguing that Maimonides takes sonship in Psalms 2:7 in the sense of kinship, nearness in the moral and spiritual senses and that "The Messiah is the son of God insofar as he is, humanly speaking, as near God as possible in possession of the highest virtues." This is another proof that many Jewish rabbis have historically understood Psalm 2:7 as messianic and not merely as adoptive of every Davidic king.

Williams, *Manual of Christian Evidences*, 2:121–28. Williams lists several Jewish and some critical Christians scholars who leave open the possibility that Psalm 2 is originally intended messianically.

The Genesis Rabbah 44:8 also contains traces of a historically viable messianic interpretation, "Said R. Johnathan, 'There are three who were allowed to ask, Solomon, Ahaz, and King Messiah.'" The OT reference cited in relation to King Messiah is Psalm 2:8. Jacob Neusner, *Parashiyyot Thirty-Four through Sixty-Seven on Genesis 8:15 to 28:9*, 131.

to J. MacArthur and R. Mayhue, "clearly refers to something more than the conception of Christ's humanity in Mary's womb."[58] MacArthur and Mayhue argue for an understanding of the eternal sonship of Jesus and a begetting that is not temporally located.[59]

Both Matthew and Luke also indicate the unique relationship of Jesus to God (Matt 1:18; Luke 1:35). The author of 1 Clement clearly ties the divinely begotten status of Jesus to Psalm 2 with the statement, "Ask of me, and I will give you the Gentiles for your inheritance, and the ends of the earth for your possession" (36:4).[60] This unique status is discussed by Spiros Zodhiates, who first points out the distinction between μονογενής and γεννάω. The former describes the unique class or kind of relationship of Jesus to God the Father, while the latter describes something that is the result of birth: "beget, engender or create."[61] Interestingly, the NT establishes that both apply to Jesus: it claims Jesus holds both a special economic and metaphysical relationship to God:

1. Economic as he fulfills his special positional, redemptive role as son.

2. Metaphysical as God incarnate, which implies begetting or engendering as indicated by the frequent references to his divine origin (Rom 1:3; 8:3; Gal 4:4; Phil 2:7, 8; Col. 1:22; 1 Tim 3:16; Heb 2:14; 1 John 4:2; 2 John 7).

The point here is that Jesus is Son of God by position (2 Sam 7:14; Matt 1:1), but, unlike the historic kings of Israel, he is the Son of God by nature (Matt 1:18; Luke 1:35; Acts 13:33; Heb 1:5).[62] The nature of an individual is, at least in part, inherited from his progenitors. This understanding of Jesus aligns better with the overall semantic range and implications of the term *begotten*, as it appears in Psalm 2 and possibly in Psalm 110, than it does with a metaphorical adoption. It also conforms more closely to an open-minded appraisal of the historical-evidential basis for the NT claims of Jesus' origin.

Craigie observes that the phrase "You are my son," from Psalm 2 is quoted or paraphrased "at a number of points in Jesus' life: (a) at his baptism (Matt 3:17); (b) at the Transfiguration (Matt 17:5), and (c) with

---

58. MacArthur and Mayhue, *Biblical Doctrine*, 239.
59. MacArthur and Mayhue, *Biblical Doctrine*, 239.
60. Holmes, *Apostolic Fathers*, 69.
61. Zodhiates, *Complete Word Study Dictionary*, s.v. "μονογενής."
62. Zodhiates, *Complete Word Study Dictionary*, s.v. "μονογενής." Cf. Arndt et al., *Greek-English Lexicon*, 658.

reference to the Resurrection (Acts 13:33)."⁶³ One such occasion is Mark's appropriation of Psalm 2 (Mark 1:11pp). Mark 1:11 appears to be designed to identify Jesus as the anointed son of *Yahweh*. Unlike the psalm, though, it contains no hint of a coronation, enthronement, or rulership in the traditional sense. Interestingly, Psalm 2 is written from the perspective that the king's anointing, begotten sonship, and exaltation to the throne are accomplished facts and public matters. Psalm 2 is not a private acknowledgment, but Mark 1:11 clearly pictures something less than a nation-wide public coronation complete with all the pomp usually associated with such occasions. Although a significant number of people must have been present to witness the identification of Jesus as God's anointed Son, Mark and the other NT authors' defer the more regal aspects of the king's public introduction to later texts (discussed below).

In Acts 4:25-26 the image of Jesus as the anointed of God surfaces again in relation to Psalm 2. This passage explicitly cites David as the author, but implied in the citation and application to Jesus is the statement that David is writing prophetically, not autobiographically (προώρισεν). In addition, the Acts 4 citation stops at a precarious place in the Psalm. It does not mention smashing the nations with a rod of iron or any activity designed to squelch a rebellion.

Paul's use of the sonship concept in Acts 13:33, Acts 17:31, and Romans 1:1-6 demonstrates not only the consistent messianic exegesis of Psalm 2 by the NT authors but also marks a transition to an explicit nation-wide and empire-wide declaration of Jesus' sonship, beyond those detailed in the gospels. For Paul, the declaration that Jesus is *Yahweh's* son is directly affixed to the resurrection and obedience of the Gentile nations.⁶⁴

Paul's use of Psalm 2:7 in Romans 1:4 requires some additional comments. For Paul, Jesus' resurrection marked the beginning of the large-scale fulfillment of God's promises to David. Whitsett describes his understanding of Paul's thought on the resurrection as the "royal investiture" of Jesus. The term ὁρισθέντος in Paul's works, according to Whitsett, encapsulates Jesus' exaltation and enthronement. In combination, themes such as *sonship* and *resurrection* point directly to Psalm 2.⁶⁵ In Romans 1:4, for example,

---

63. Craigie, *Psalms 1–50*, 69.

64. Acts 13:34 explicitly references Psalm 16:10 in relation to the resurrection of Jesus. Given this, there is some question as to whether Luke intends for the reader to understand the previous verse (33) as referring to the resurrection of Jesus, one of the earlier event in Jesus' life (Luke 1:32; 3:22; e.g., birth or baptism), or his emergence into the sphere of humanity. In any case, it is certain that for Luke and Paul the resurrection stands as a universal declaration of Jesus' divine sonship.

65. Whitsett, "Son of God, Seed of David," 676.

Jesus is declared ὁρισθέντος, the son of God. Interestingly, 1 Corinthians 2:7 uses the closely related verb προορίζω in a way reminiscent of Acts 4:28, in relation to a decree made beforehand. Whitsett concludes, "If Paul's use of προορίζειν in 1 Cor 2:7 is part of an interpretation of Ps 2, the probability of its use in Rom 1:4 is markedly enhanced."[66]

Whitsett's case relies in part on the work of Leslie Allen. Allen convincingly argued that ὁρίζειν and προορίζειν in the NT, especially in the speeches in Acts, occur in contexts proximate to affirmations of Jesus' sonship or in reference to Psalm 2:7.[67] Specifically addressing 1 Corinthians 2:7–8, Allen contends that Paul had the terms κύριον and δόξης, in mind from previous uses: both carry resurrection overtones, and both point toward Psalm 2.[68] This observation confirms that the conceptual tie between the divine decree in Psalms 2, the speeches in Acts,[69] and Paul's use of ὁρισθέντος (the language of marking out or appointment) is virtually certain.

On two occasions, the writer of the book of Hebrews affirms the OT exegesis of Paul. The text of Psalm 2:7 is applied to Jesus in both instances 1:5 and 5:5, probably as related to his exaltation. Harold W. Attridge and Helmut Koester remark that the affirmation of Jesus in relation to his exaltation is probably earlier than those related to his baptism.[70] This suggests the question as to when the sonship portrayed in the Psalm is affected. Attridge and Koester offer two possible solutions to the conundrum: (1) the term *Son* "is properly applied at the point of exaltation, but proleptically in other contexts"; and (2) the term *Son* applied "not as the creation of a new status but as the definitive recognition or revelation of what Christ is and has been."[71] In either case, the tension between the declarations of sonship at Jesus' baptism (Mark 1:11), his transfiguration (Mark 9:7), and his resurrection (Rom 1:4) are satisfactorily resolved.

The book of Revelation contains two references to Psalm 2 that clearly associate the psalm with Jesus (Rev 12:5; 19:15). In Revelation 12:5 Jesus is

---

66. Whitsett, "Son of God, Seed of David," 676.

67. Allen, "Old Testament Background." Other comments made by Allen are paraphrased below: (1) Acts 10:42, the resurrection of Jesus is closely associated with the decree, or his appointment (ὡρισμένος) as judge; (2) Acts 17:31 He, [God] has appointed (ὥρισεν) a judge and given assurance of this by raising him from the dead; and (3) Acts 4:25–28, in the context of group prayer, ostensibly led by Peter, is a slightly different matter. God predetermined (προώρισεν) or decreed beforehand the events according to His plan.

68. Allen, "Old Testament Background," 108.

69. Allen, "Old Testament Background," 106.

70. Attridge and Koester, *Epistle to the Hebrews*, 53.

71. Attridge and Koester, *Epistle to the Hebrews*, 54.

depicted from birth—to ascension—to parousia "in one fell swoop."[72] G. K. Beale concurs, adding that this kind of telescoping is consistent with other presentations of the life of Jesus (John 3:13; 8:14; 13:3; 16:5, 28; Rom 1:3–4; 1 Tim 3:16).[73] The primary image of interest to this study is that of ruling the nations with a "rod of iron." This citation from Psalm 2:9 is set in the eschatological future, as is Revelation 19:15, which again uses the image of the "rod of iron" in relation to the rulership of Jesus over the nations. Revelation 2:26–27 provides additional reason to believe that Psalm 2 should be understood eschatologically. In these verses, Jesus promises to delegate authority to rule the nations. Conspicuously, the image of the "rod of iron" is still the reference point connecting Psalm 2 with Revelation 2:26–27.

Three Additional Objections to the Eschatological Messianic Interpretation

As explained above, Willis addresses the four most proffered arguments supporting an eschatological messianic original intent for Psalm 2. In this section, the remaining three arguments, and Willis's objections to them, are examined for methodological errors and evidence allowing for an original eschatological messianic referent.[74] The first of these arguments is that the NT quotes and arbitrarily applies the text to Jesus as the Messiah. Willis objects to this type of canonical reading in which NT meanings are given priority over the OT contexts and meanings. For the current work, this objection is accepted, and the NT witnesses do not receive priority. The fact remains, however, that the NT writers are a legitimate source, and any demand that they be disregarded also constitutes a methodological error. The NT witnesses possessed insight into how the Hebrew Scriptures were traditionally understood, and that insight is not wholly accessible to the modern exegete. They were Jews and, at least in Paul's case, knowledgeable about traditional Hebrew exegesis. The incomplete transmission of the oral traditions of the Jews, the fragmentary nature of many historical manuscripts, and the frequent citation of now lost works all indicate the need for an inclusive evaluation of all relevant data. Given these factors, dismissing the exegetical contribution of the NT authors too quickly seems impetuous.

The second of Willis's objections addresses the argument that the universal scope of Psalm 2 (Ps 2:2, 7–8, 10) requires a messianic referent. Willis maintains that this argument constitutes a hermeneutical error that

72. Osborne, *Revelation*, 463.
73. Beale, *Book of Revelation*, 639.
74. Willis, "A Cry of Defiance—Psalm 2," 33.

interprets the text as messianic based on the limited scope of Israel's kingdom (at its largest) or one of the historically enthroned kings. The basis for this messianic argument is that Israel never enjoyed universal dominion. History supports this position, but such a simplistic approach fails to account for the poetic language and devices of the Royal Psalm genre. Psalm 2 includes a four-part synthetic parallelism (Ps 2:12) and perhaps twenty synonymous parallelisms that may not be intended as woodenly literal statements.[75] In addition, Gunkel asserts that the enthronement and dominionist poetry employed by Israel is idealistic to some extent. Although this idealism imitates, in a livelier and more diverse way, rites found in Egypt and Babylon, they remain imitations nonetheless.[76] The hyperbolic language seems appropriate for the occasion of a coronation requiring a significant amount of pomp.

James E. Smith provides an example of what seems to be a demand for an over-literalization of the language. He assumes Davidic authorship and then poses two significant arguments: first, that no mass rebellion of Gentiles against David occurred, and second, that David was anointed king at Bethlehem and Hebron, not on Mt. Zion. Therefore, David must be speaking "strictly as a prophet."[77] In response, rebellions of vassal states were commonplace in the ancient world. The Philistines did rebel against David when he was publically installed as king (1 Chr 14), and David somehow earned a reputation as a slayer of ten thousand (1 Sam 21:11). The second objection Smith records is his rejection of the notion that the Psalm is intended to describe an enthronement. The king in the Psalm is installed on Zion; simply stated, this could either refer to Jerusalem as a city or some part of the city, such as the Jebusite fortress conquered by David.

Gunkel affirms that the nations of the world never rebelled against any newly installed Israelite king. In fact, he refers to this language as "arrogantly presumptive" and "a concrete example of an imitation of a foreign pattern."[78] Perhaps, however, the universalistic and dominionist emphasis of Psalm 2 is, as Mowinckel asserts, due to the implicit promise that the king, as *Yahweh*'s anointed son, had a rightful claim to dominion over the whole world.[79]

J. Smith's approach to distinguishing between David and the king described in Psalm 2 is not satisfying. Still, a clear distinction must be made

---

75. Witthoff et al., "Psalm 2," s.v. "Psalm 2."
76. Gunkel, *Introduction to the Psalms*, 116–17.
77. Smith, *Wisdom Literature and Psalms*, s.v. "Psalm 2."
78. Gunkel, *Introduction to the Psalms*, 116.
79. Mowinckel, *Psalms in Israel's Worship*, 67.

between David's anointing and his coronation. George A. Gunn argues that, in the normal course of events, a king is anointed and coroneted on the same day.[80] In the particular case of David, however, years ensued between his anointing by Samuel (1 Sam 16:13), the beginning of his rule, and his subsequent anointing in Hebron (2 Sam 2:1–4). Even more years passed before he began ruling from Jerusalem. During this entire period, however, David was called God's king (1 Sam 16:1).

In the last of Willis's objections, he offers a counter-argument to the assertion that "there is no known historical setting which would fit the scene portrayed in Psalm 2; therefore, it must refer to the future coming of the Messiah."[81] This is perhaps the weakest of the four arguments, although it is not completely without merit. There is no specifically known historical setting for several psalms, including Psalm 22 (addressed below). That lack may contribute to a hasty messianic conclusion. The absence of a known historical setting does not necessitate a chronological leap into the eschaton, however. Conversely, the positive evidence for a historical fulfillment seems to entail the same truth. The presence of Psalm 2 in the Psalter is not evidence of, nor does it necessitate, a historical *sitz im leben*. Logically, a future realization is just as likely; other evidence must settle this question. Cohen remarks that "interpreters both ancient and modern differ as to whether the subject of the Psalm is the Messiah or historical king."[82] One cannot leap into the eschaton without evidence, but it is also methodologically improper to insist on a historical actualization for Psalm 2.

This brief synopsis of the arguments most often forwarded to support an original messianic referent for Psalm 2 leaves the question open. In each of the four objections documented above, questions remain that make the absolute rejection of an eschatological king as the original referent an overstatement of the facts. In addition, nothing this study has discovered has addressed the birth/begotten (ילד) nomenclature used in Psalm 2:7 as consistently as the NT data.

Summary

Data gathered from the various sources reviewed in this section conflict with the perspectives of most critical scholars. Johnston determined in his analysis of Psalm 2 that the best approach to interpreting the text was a

---

80. Gunn, "Psalm 2 and the Reign of the Messiah," 432.
81. Willis, "Cry of Defiance," 34.
82. Cohen, *Psalms*, 3.

"'both/and' rather than 'either/or' approach to its prophetic nature."[83] He prefers to interpret Psalm 2 typologically. Mowinckel rejects the idea that Psalm 2 (or any other OT passage) is a direct reference to the eschatological Messiah.[84] Fitzmyer and Gunkel steadfastly ground the entire psalm in the historical Israelite monarchy.[85]

The above perspectives notwithstanding, allowing for the genre of the Royal Psalm, the purposeful arrangement of the texts, and interpreted charitably, the prophetic features of Psalm 2 are not identifiable with any certain historical king or *sitz im leben*. This study agrees that the singular appearance of "Anointed"[86] in Psalm 2 cannot be tortured into meaning the eschatological Messiah. Even so, without historical or other types of evidence relevant to Hebrew culture, the rare appearance of the term "begotten"—in light of Psalm 110, the intertestamental literature, and the NT data—cannot be legitimately truncated to mean *adopted*. No other near eastern enthronement text provides an adequate parallel from which to judge the meaning. The current study concludes that Psalm 2 is probably eschatological in nature, not typologically or historically constituted. David cannot be demonstrated to be the type.

Three facts are evident in relation to Psalm 2: (1) no certain historical king or occasion can be assigned to the psalm, (2) the peculiar begotten language is found in no other near-eastern enthronement narrative and is never applied to a known historical Israelite king, and (3) the earliest documents that address Psalm 2, consistently interpret this psalm in an eschatological or messianic sense. It is certainly possible, if not probable, that Psalm 2 was originally written as messianic prophecy, rather than an account of the enthronement of a historical king.[87] The NT data does not even hint otherwise, and Acts 4:25–28 overtly supports this assertion. Perhaps Lange, Schaff, Moll, Briggs, Forsyth, Hammond, McCurdy, and Conant are correct when they state:

> The *prophetic* or *direct Messianic* explanation can alone explain this Psalm (all ancient Jewish and ancient Christian interpreters, with some from all periods); neither the *typical* (Hofmann), nor the *historical* (the later Jewish and many recent interpreters),

---

83. Johnston, "Messianic Trajectories in Psalm 2," 76.

84. Mowinckel, *Psalms in Israel's Worship*, 7.

85. Fitzmyer, *One Who Is to Come*, 107. Cf. Gunkel, *Introduction to the Psalms*, 99.

86. Gillingham, "Messiah in the Psalms," 210.

87. The results of this study appear to confirm that something similar to the "canonical process approach" of Waltke carries significant explanatory power in relation to the Royal Psalms. Waltke, "Canonical Process Approach to the Psalms," 3–18.

nor the *poetical* (Hupf., as a general glorification of the theocratic kingdom), nor indeed the explanation to be found in the transition from the typical to the prophetic (Kurtz) can suffice.[88]

Given the increasing pressure of critical scholarship for its exegetes to produce positive evidence for their positions, it seems only fair to ask the same in reply. Perhaps the accusations of eisegesis leveled at scholars who argue for the messianic interpretation[89] actually constitute a symptomatic response to their failure to produce or address all of the available evidence.

Plausible Historical-Evidential Conclusions Gathered from the Study of Psalm 2:1–12

1. It is possible that Psalm 2 was originally written as prophecy and not as an account of the enthronement of a historical king.

Historical-Evidential Facts Gathered from the Study of Psalm 2

1. No certain historical king or occasion can be assigned to Psalm 2.
2. The peculiar Hebrew term, ילד, translated as the English term *begotten*, is found in no other near-eastern enthronement narrative.
3. The Hebrew term ילד is never applied to a known historical Israelite king.
4. The earliest documents available consistently interpret Psalm 2 from an eschatological messianic perspective.

---

88. Lange et al., *Psalms*, 55.

89. Gillingham, "Messiah in the Psalms," 213. Gillingham directs his eisegetical claim toward Walter Kaiser. Cf. Kaiser, *Messiah in the Old Testament*.

Psalm 16, Emphasizing Verses 9–10

Literary and Textual Analysis

Old Testament Evidence

Scholarly Opinions

Traditional Christian teaching often interprets Psalm 16 as a prophecy of Jesus' resurrection. As is consistent with the methodology of this study, however, historical evidence about the text, the immediate context of Psalm 16, and its developmental history must first be considered before accepting this traditional view. The primary question is whether sufficient evidence exists to substantiate the claim that the author of the Psalm directly prophesied regarding the resurrection of Jesus. Several scholars have labored extensively on Psalm 16 and this section will reflect their efforts.

The general tenor of the psalm allows it to be broadly classified as a psalm of "confidence."[90] Several divergent interpretations have arisen based on differing views of the context, date, authorship, and theological development of the Jewish nation. Robert G. Bratcher and William David Reyburn contend that verse 10 is a declaration of confidence that *Yahweh* will protect the psalmist ("your Holy One") from an early death.[91] A number of scholars share this common view.[92]

William A. VanGemeren believes verse 10 speaks of David's (God's Holy One) confidence that after death and going into the grave, he will not "suffer eternal alienation." He also believes the reference to "decay" is a "metaphor for total isolation and abandonment from God's presence."[93] There exists, VanGemeren argues, no certainty about whether the psalmist thought in terms of some form of afterlife[94] or resurrection of the body.[95]

---

90. Craigie, *Psalms 1–50*, 155.

91. Bratcher and Reyburn, *Translator's Handbook on the Book of Psalms*, 146.

92. For example, see vol. 1 of Hengstenberg, *Commentary on the Psalms*. Benzinger et al. state: "Gegen die Deutung, dass der Verf. nur an ein langes Leben denke und sich vor dem Tode sicher fühle, lässt sich nicht einwenden, dass kein Mensch von sich sagen könne, er werde die Grube nicht sehen, da jeder Leser wusste, wie diese Sätze gemeint seien, mindestens ebenso gut, wie z. B. Der Wunsch 61 7 8. Diese Deutung ist aber der auf die Unsterblichkeit vorzuziehen, weil der Verf. schwerlich sagen konnte: weil ich unsterblich sein werde, wohnt mein Leib sicher" (Benzinger et al., *Die Psalmen*, 49).

93. VanGemeren, *Expositors Bible Commentary*, s.v. "Psalm 16:10."

94. For a brief exposition of the early Jewish understanding of the grave/pit, see Eichrodt, *Theology of the Old Testament*, 2:210–16.

95. VanGemeren, *Expositors Bible Commentary*.

Charles Augustus Briggs and Emilie Grace Briggs contend for the psalmist's security after death, but modify the way in which this security is envisioned. They interpret verse 10 as an expression of confidence that *Yahweh* will not allow the psalmist to be consigned to the cavern under Sheol: the "deeper place . . . Abaddon, the dungeon of Sheol."[96] The pit is for the wicked and the righteous ones will not go there. Thus, the path of life will lead him into the presence of *Yahweh*.[97]

Conversely, the Roman Catholic Church's official interpretation of Psalm 16 specifically denies that it concerns any person other than Jesus Christ:

> Is it right for a Catholic, especially after the authentic interpretation given by the Princes of the Apostles (Acts 2:24–33; 13:35–37) to interpret the words of Psalm 15:10 ff.: "Thou wilt not leave my soul in hell, nor wilt thou give thy holy one to see corruption. Thou hast made known to me the ways of life," as if the sacred author did not speak of the resurrection of our Lord Jesus Christ? Answer: In the negative.[98]

Based on this brief survey of opinions, it becomes clear that no consensus will emerge about the overall interpretation of the psalm. Nevertheless, it may be possible to narrow the number of possibilities somewhat by examining lexical and other evidence.[99]

---

96. Briggs and Briggs, *Book of Psalms*, 1:122.

97. Briggs and Briggs, *Book of Psalms*, 1:122.

98. Sutcliffe, "Replies of the Biblical Commission," 73. Sutcliffe references the Douay Rheims version of the Bible. Cf. Payne, *Encyclopedia of Biblical Prophecy*, 265–66. Payne contends that verse 9 expresses the psalmist's hope for life beyond death: a hope that applies to all the righteous. Verse 10 then changes and prophetically the psalmist speaks for the Messiah, as he does in Psalms 110:4. Mowinckel discounts any mention of a resurrection in Psalm 16:10. He holds that two texts from the Hellenistic era, Isaiah 26:19 and Daniel 12:2, contain the earliest mentions of resurrection in the OT. Mowinckel, *Psalms in Israel's Worship*, 205n203.

99. Trull divides the range of opinions concerning the meaning of the psalm into five categories: First Dahood is perhaps the only scholar to contend that the psalmist's hope is for a physical translation such as that experienced by Enoch and Elijah. Second, Trull names Briggs, Constant, and VanGemeren as advocates for the belief that the psalmist means communion with God after death. Third, Weiser and Aparicio are named as those who "interpret verse 10 as referring to unbroken fellowship (without clarifying the mode)." Fourth, Trull names a substantial list of scholars who contend that the author expected to be preserved from an untimely death. Fifth, he names some who hold to an interpretation that the verse in question prophesies of a personal resurrection from the dead. Trull, "Exegesis of Psalm 16:10a," 308.

Lexical Evidence

Unlike some of the other texts this study evaluated, Psalm 16 contains several lexical problems that potentially affect the meaning of verses 9 and 10. The first issue requiring clarification is authorship. It is not possible to categorically disallow the possibility that someone other than David wrote the psalm. However, the psalm bears the title לדוד (*lĕdāwid*) as do Psalms 56–60, which are also usually attributed to David. Additional support for Davidic authorship arises because Psalm 16 contains some verbal similarities with other Davidic psalms and a possible link to the covenantal language of 2 Samuel 7:22–23.[100]

Second, and key for the interpretation of the psalm, are the grammatical difficulties contained in verses 9–10. For example, some authors have argued that the Septuagint translators forced a meaning on the term לבטח (*lābeṭaḥ*) (in verse 9) that allowed for their theology of resurrection to be read into verse 10. The Seventy translated the Hebrew term as ἐπ ἐλπίδι. The difference lies in the fact that לבטח is usually understood as *security* or *confidence*, whereas ἐλπίς is most often understood as *hope* or *expectation*. The distinction seems negligible for the meaning of verse 10; what substantive difference exists? On one hand, Lange et al. remark, based on 9b, that the psalm "may indeed speak of the preservation and secure rest of the entombed body."[101] If so, the thought anticipates the Septuagint's κατασκηνώσει ἐπ' ἐλπίθε.[102] On the other hand, one could argue for a forced change in perspective from the present to the future. This charge is problematic, however, as it requires intimate knowledge of the psalmist's mind; it also fails to account for the future orientation of the next verse. For certain, verse 10 contains a future tone. Given the presence of the conjunction כי (*kî*) ("for or, because") that causally connects verses 9 and 10,[103] the alleged eisegesis makes little difference.[104] The psalmist describes the *prophetic protagonist*[105] as dwelling securely or expectantly *because* he was confident that Yahweh would not abandon him.

---

100. Trull, "Exegesis of Psalm 16:10a," 305. Dating Psalm 16 after the Babylonian exile or even the Maccabean period, as do many critical scholars, enhances the likelihood that the eschatology of Jewish people had developed a theology of resurrection.

101. Lange et al., *Psalms*, 126.

102. Lange et al., *Psalms*, 126.

103. Trull, "Exegesis of Psalm 16:10a," 309.

104. Bock, *Proclamation*, 174–75. Bock remarks that the change is not decisive for a new understanding of the text.

105. The current work uses the term "prophetic protagonist" as the referent of the psalm. No consensus exists on either authorship or the date of writing, it is

Third, although the conjunctive aspect of verse 10 is uncontroversial, scholarly opinions related to the meaning of other key terms often result in mutually exclusive conclusions. The verb עזב (ʿăzōb), for instance, is one of the focal points of the controversy surrounding Psalm 16:10. HALOT designates the basic concept as "to leave," which would support a translation similar to *desert* or *abandon*. The perception impressed on the reader's mind by the *yiqtōl* prefix reflects an action participated in, or seen from the inside of, the unfolding events.[106] The *prophetic protagonist* will not be *left* in Sheol. However, Mitchell Dahood, one of the most cited authors treating this text, disagrees. He offers instead a distinctive interpretation in which he used the English construction similar to *put* or *place*, "For you shall not place me in Sheol." He supports this reading by citing Ugaritic language similarities and his belief that תַעֲזֹב לִשְׁאוֹל (taʿ ăzōb liš'ôl) is not essentially different from the Ugaritic *db lars*, meaning placement in the *underworld*. Dahood connects the sentiment expressed in this psalm with those of Psalms 49:16 and 73:24, concluding: "These texts imply the assumption of the righteous by God to himself, a belief which developed more fully in later Judaism."[107] If Dahood's construction is correct, the fundamental idea does not support the idea that the *prophetic protagonist* was confident that he would not experience abandonment or being left in Sheol; rather, it indicates never being placed there at all. The psalmist's hope, if Dahood's exegesis proves correct, is an outright escape from death similar to that experienced by Enoch and Elijah.[108]

The difficulty with Dahood's analysis is that no parallel usage of the root עזב (or a different root that is a homonym from the biblical text) supports the meaning of *place* or *put* as it appears in Psalm 16:10. Most often, the sense of the passages containing the root עזב connotes *leave* or *abandon*; this usage often extends to *forsakenness*. Considering Dahood's work in particular, this study has encountered no other exegete supporting his analysis.[109] Holding

---

methodologically inconsistent to demand that the author be speaking of himself.

106. Heiser and Setterholm, *Glossary of Morpho-Syntactic Database Terminology*, s.v. "yiqtōl" (imperfect).

107. Dahood, "Root 'zb II in Job," 308n316.

108. Dahood, *Psalms 1–50*, 91.

109. Assuming the conclusions of critical scholarship and the late dating of Psalm 16, it is improbable that the psalmist is thinking in terms of bodily translation rather than death without the loss of relationship with *Yahweh* or outright resurrection. In addition, given Davidic authorship, it would be both inconsistent and contradictory for David to believe that he would escape death. The Davidic covenant predicted David's death and the rise of his offspring. Some critical scholars date the finished Psalter to the period of the postexilic diaspora. See Gunkel, *Introduction to the Psalms*, 319–32. Gunkel argues that material from the individual "psalms of confidence" such as Psalm 16 developed from "individual complaint psalms" over a long historical period. These

this view requires that עזב actually means *never put* or *never see*, rather than *not leave* or *abandon* permanently. The term עזב cannot support the meaning necessary for Dahood to be correct. Therefore, the psalmist's hope cannot be for the complete avoidance of Sheol.[110] There is little ambiguity remaining as to whether the psalmist intends to convey the idea that his hope for the *prophetic protagonist* is to never to be placed in Sheol in any sense—that is, not experiencing death by means of translation or immortality. The lexical evidence does not support this stance; further, David, the most plausible author, knew that he would die (2 Sam 7:12).

More likely is the approach employed by Philip S. Johnston, one that does not read implausible denials of immortality into the text. He argues that the psalmist had either experienced or believed that he would experience preservation from premature death inflicted by an imminent crisis. This is why the psalmist is not shaken, dwells securely, and will not be abandoned to Sheol, or see corruption.[111] Yahweh will see him through the imminent crisis and open up a way that leads to a continued enjoyment of life.[112] Craigie takes a similar approach, making the germane observation that if this interpretation reflects the "initial meaning of the psalm," the concluding section "should not be interpreted either messianically or in terms of individual eschatology."[113] Important to this interpretation of the psalm is that the identity of the *prophetic protagonist* חסידך (*ḥăsîděka*) would necessarily be contemporary to the psalmist at the time of original authorship. A direct prophecy of the Messiah would be excluded. This solution is not only possible but also reasonable. However, it does not answer all the questions raised by these verses, nor does it deal with the entire scope of the available data, especially if the "holy one" is not a contemporary of the author.

A fourth key issue for determining the interpretation of the text is based on how the noun שחת (*šāḥat*) is best understood. Psalm 16:10 is the only OT verse in which the ESV translates the term as "corruption." The overwhelming majority of its occurrences carry the meaning of *pit*. Part

---

psalms were first used in cultic settings before 587 BC (Gunkel, *Introduction to the Psalms*, 325) and then gradually became the stock of individual prayers (Gunkel, *Introduction to the Psalms*, 120–98, esp. 132–34). Some, or even much, of the original thought and lyric forms come from the monarchial period; however, by circa 500–200 BC, the genre declined (Gunkel, *Introduction to the Psalms*, 329). Cf. Feinberg, "Dating of the Psalms," 426–40.

110. Cf. Brown et al., *Hebrew and English Lexicon*, s.v. "עָזַב." Swanson, *Dictionary of Biblical Languages*, 6440.

111. Johnston, "Left in Hell?," 215.

112. See Goldingay, *Psalms 1–41*.

113. Craigie, *Psalms 1–50*, 158.

of the controversy involves the possibility that two Hebrew roots with two distinct meanings are at play within the Hebrew language. R. Laird Harris succinctly captures this discussion and its apparently irresolvable difficulties: "Quite possibly we are dealing here with two homonym-ous nouns, one from *šûaḥ* 'sink down' (not really 'dig') and the other from (*šāḥat*) 'go to ruin.'"[114] VanGemeren argues convincingly that the masculine form of שחת is found in Job 17:14 and Psalm 16:10 and that both mean *corruption*. In Job 17:14, the term personifies the masculine pronoun father as contrasted with the feminine term, רמה (worm), personifying mother. VanGemeren states:

> We may confidently infer, therefore, that שַׁחַת, personified as 'father,' is the masc. form, 'decay/corruption.' Moreover, it can be established that the masc. form, 'corruption,' not the fem. form, 'pit,' is in view in Ps 16:10 by the vb. to see (לִרְאוֹת). 'To see' expresses the ideas of 'experiencing,' 'enduring,' 'proving,' and the like, and takes for its object a nom. indicative of *state* of the soul or of the body.[115]

If the pit as Sheol was in view, Waltke claims, the psalmist would have employed a verb of motion rather than experience.

The distinction between the two possible roots is weighty: one meaning corruption, associated with death and decay, and the other associated with the pit (as associated with Sheol). This distinction may, however, be overstated. Conceptually, *the pit* and *corruption* intersect, thereby reducing any substantive difference to delaying the logical conclusion by one chronological step.[116] Regardless of whether "the pit" is in synonymous parallelism with "Sheol"[117] or is in synthetic parallelism[118] meaning *corruption*, the reader's attention should be drawn to the physical aspect (although the entire being of the prophetic protagonist is addressed during the course of the psalm, including his unending relationship with *Yahweh*). Physical corruption is a patent derivative of any discussion of souls existing in "the pit" or synonymously "Sheol." Likewise, physical corruption is just as certainly a conceptual and integral aspect of "the pit" as synthetically related to "Sheol" via the grave. The expressed faith of the prophetic protagonist consists of confidence that he will not be abandoned—whether to the corruption of the grave or to the corruption of the pit as Sheol. Preservation is the unavoidable idea of the psalmist: preservation of the whole being, including the flesh.

114. Harris, "2343," 911.
115. Waltke, "Psalms," 1113. Cf. Merrill, "שַׁחַת (*šaḥat*)," 93–95.
116. See Goldingay, *Psalms 1–41*.
117. Witthoff et al., "Psalm 16," s.v. "Psalm 16:10."
118. Trull, "Exegesis of Psalm 16:10a," 319.

Evidence supporting this preservation supposition emerges from the *Encyclopedia of Judaism*. Forcing the dichotomy of thought between שחת as either the corruption of the grave (literally a tomb or hole in which a body is buried) or the pit of Sheol is apparently unnecessary. Speaking from a Jewish perspective, Neusner reminds that Sheol, in and of itself, is considered to be a place "of maggots and decay (Job 17:13–16)."[119] David J. A. Clines also recognizes the putrescent nature of the connotations associated with שחת. He describes the condition of Job, whose expectation is descent into the pit as entering a new "macabre community" associated with death, worms, and corruption.[120]

A further distinction is evident, according to Robert A. Morey. He argues that the OT usually designates the *grave* by the word קבר (*qeber*). Sheol and קבר (*qeber*) are "never used in Hebrew poetic parallelism as equivalents."[121] Consider the images conjured in the human mind by the range of meanings possible in the Hebrew term; add to this the knowledge that no soul goes to the pit apart from a state of death involving physical corruption. Given this reality, completely separating the meaning of שחת from the corruption of the grave appears imbalanced and reductionist. Insufficient lexical support exists to enforce rigid limitations on the meaning of שחת to either that of physical corruption or the pit; both inferences are interconnected.

Attempting to blunt the force of the observation that the psalmist may be speaking of life after death by late-dating Psalm 16 or denying Davidic authorship actually reinforces this possibility rather than refuting it. During the post-exilic era, significant changes occurred in the way the Jewish people viewed death and Sheol. These changes included the development of a firm belief in (1) separate fates for the righteous and the unrighteous, and (2) the physical resurrection of the dead.[122] These changes did not arise *ex nihilo* and likely had a long period of development. They may have included ideas carried over from the monarchial period, but they were fully formed during the intertestamental period. Consequently, the later the psalm is dated, the more probable that it refers to resurrection.

---

119. Gillman, "Death and the Afterlife," 197–98. The Babylonian Talmud quotes Psalm 16:10 and lists the "pit" as one of seven names for Gehenna, but does not reference corruption or decay in relation to Psalm 16. Neusner, *Babylonian Talmud*, b. Erub. 2:1, I.19.D. The other six names are as follows: netherworld, destruction, tumultuous pit, miry clay, shadow of death, and underworld.

120. Clines, *Job 1–20*, 399.

121. Morey, *Death and the Afterlife*, 76.

122. For a review of the changes occurring during the exilic and post-exilic eras, see Jeremias, "Μωυσῆς," s,v. ᾅδης in Later Judaism.

Other OT evidence supporting resurrection as the original intent surfaces in the Septuagint. The Septuagint translation of Psalm 15 (English 16) is undoubtedly pre-Christian.[123] The fact that the translation of Psalm 15 is pre-Christian is evidenced by its abundant use in the NT and by the presence of portions of Psalm 15 in the scrolls of Qumran.[124] This important fact vanquishes arguments that the controversial term διαφθοράν appears because of Christian eisegesis and a Christological agenda. The Greek translators interpreted the Hebrew term in question as meaning corruption of the body.[125] Their choice of διαφθοράν to translate שחת demonstrates their conviction that bodily corruption is in view.

The OT evidence supports the notion that the import of Psalm 16 contains an expectant declaration that the *prophetic protagonist's* whole being will be preserved in a life-giving relationship with *Yahweh* outside "the pit" (despite his unavoidable physical death)—forever (verse 11). The allusions contained in the language of verse 11 point to something more than temporary escape from a threat: rather they point to something proximate to eternal security and life despite death.[126] Rolles, Plumber, and Briggs describe the emotive state of the psalmist as possessing a "calm view of death and the expectation of the presence of God and blessedness after death." They argue the text "[implies] an advancement beyond Isa 57:1–2; but prior to the emergence of the doctrine of the resurrection of the righteous Isa 26:19."[127] How can the life of the entire person beyond death be expressed without employing something conceptually similar to *resurrection*?

These data, complete with the implication of resurrection, indicate the possibility that the *prophetic protagonist* is not a contemporary of the author, but a future "holy one," who will experience preservation of his whole being without the corruption associated with death forever.

---

123. Dines and Knibb, *Septuagint*, 46.

124. For example, see 4Q85 Psalms c: Frg. 1: *Naḥal Ḥever Psalms*: Col. 7 (Frg. 4)

125. The third issue needing clarification is the identity of the חסיד (*ḥāsîd*) and perhaps the identity of the *prophetic protago*nist of the entire psalm. Although the term does not carry connotations either of divinity or of absolute moral perfection, it is difficult to read either the Hebrew term or the Greek term (ὅσιος) and accept this as a banal reference to the psalmist. This is possible, of course. The general meaning of the term conveys the idea of a person who accepts and fulfills obligations relating to his and the covenant people's relationship to God. The terms are used of God, the Israelites, groups within the nation of Israel, and individuals. Zodhiates, s.v. "ὅσιος." There is also according to Zodhiates, a group of ὅσιοι τοῦ θεοῦ (Ps 8:23; 13:10; 14:3, 10). In Psalm 4:23 φοβούμενοι τὸν κύριον οἱ, Psalm 4:25 οἱ ἀγαπῶντες θεόν, appear as likely synonyms and οἱ ἁμαρτωλοί, παράνομοι as antonyms in Psalm 14:6.

126. Keil and Delitzsch, *Commentary on the Old Testament*, 142.

127. Briggs and Briggs, *Book of Psalms*, 1:118.

Intertestamental Evidence

The intertestamental evidence that may be applied to help understand Psalm 16 is scarce. However, Roland E. Murphy does specifically address the issue of the *šaḥat* as employed in the Qumran Literature. Murphy argues that the people of Qumran associated *šaḥat* with corruption. He cites 1QS 9:16; 9:22; and 10:19 as examples in which the term means "moral corruption rather than pit or grave."[128] In 9:17 and 10:20, the terms *ʾnšy hʿwl* or *ʿwlh* respectively runs parallel with other words with the same implications. Murphy also cites the *Damascus Documenta* (CD 6:15; 13:14) adding that CD 15:7–8 is of the most evidential value because it specifically addresses an individual who "turns from his corrupt way."[129] Conversely, Murphy, as noted by Trull, also cites several texts in which the noun form seems to be a synonym for *Sheol* (1QH 3:19; 8:28–29; 3:18; 1QS 11:13).[130] Thus, the evidence from Qumran, like that of the OT, is inconclusive. Once again, the evidence indicates the Jewish conceptual overlap between the images of corruption in Sheol/the pit and the grave.

The work of John C. Poirier is significant for the study of Psalm 16. Poirier advances the possibility that the Jewish scholars translating the Septuagint correctly understood the psalmist to mean that the holy one would not see corruption (διαφθοράν) and thereby tacitly forecasting a resurrection. Extending the work of Douglas Hill, Poirier argues, from a small pool of extra-biblical and biblical texts, for the wide-spread Jewish belief that corruption of the body did not begin until approximately seventy-two hours (three days) after death.[131] He contends that this belief may be the key to connecting an OT text with Paul's nebulous reference to Jesus being raised after three days "according to the Scriptures" (1 Cor 15:4). Both Peter and Paul make reference to Jesus' flesh not seeing corruption (Acts 2:31; 13:35). The *three-day* tradition Poirier describes may stand behind these NT claims.

The third day in Jewish thought, according to Poirier, would be the maximum amount of time before corruption of the body would ensue. Support for this thesis arises from the work of R. Mach. Mach documents the Jewish belief that the soul and body are separated at death, yet a loose connection remains between them. This connection has been understood in three distinct ways. First, the soul "Drei Tage lang umschwebt die Seele den Körper im dem Glauben, sie werde in ihn Zurückkehren Können";

---

128. Murphy, "Šaḥat in the Qumran Literature," 61.

129. Murphy, "Šaḥat in the Qumran Literature," 61.

130. Trull, "Exegesis of Psalm 16:10a," 317.

131. Poirier, "Psalm 16:10," 160. Poirier contends that Zoroastrianism likely provides the origin of the belief that the soul remains near the body.

second, "Die Seele Trauert um den Menschen sieben Tage lang"; and third, "Die Verbindung dauert bis zur vollständigen Verwesung der Leiche, d. i. Zwölf Monate lang."[132] David Allison provides several additional historical records indicating the importance of the three-day period in ancient Jewish thought in reference to a deceased person and his or her soul. The angels attending the body of Abraham continue their work until the third day. The Testament of Job (5–7) indicates that Job was not placed into his tomb until after three days. The Apocalypse of Zephaniah 4:7 describes an angelic escort for the ungodly in terms of "servants of all creation" who fly around for three days with the souls of the dead before leaving them in the place of eternal punishment.[133]

Extra-Biblical Evidence

Other material from the NT era and the era just subsequent include those Richard Bauckham analyzes. He documents no less than twelve Jewish texts related to the martyrdom of Enoch and Elijah, all of which consistently demonstrate the belief that they would remain dead less than four days.[134]

Another important text is Genesis Rabbah 100.7. Section X states, "Up to the third day, the soul keeps returning to the body, thinking that it will go back in. When it sees that the features of the face have crumbled, it goes its way and leaves the body. This is in line with this verse: 'But his flesh grieves for him, and his soul mourns over him (Job 14:22).'"[135]

Other historical evidence lending support to the idea that the psalmist may have possessed a nascent theology of resurrection surfaces in 1 Enoch

---

132. Mach, *Der Zaddik*, 174.

133. Allison Jr., *Testament of Abraham*, 401. Cf. *y. Moed Qat.* 3.5, 82b and *Leviticus. Rabbah.* 18.1. 4 Baruch 9:12–14, reads as follows: "And behold, there came a voice saying, 'Do not bury one still living, for his soul is coming into his body again.' And because they heard the voice, they did not bury him but remained in a circle around his tabernacle for three days, saying, 'At what hour is he going to rise?' And after three days, his soul came into his body and he lifted up his voice in the midst of (them) all and said, 'Glorify God with one voice! All (of you) glorify God, and the Son of God who awakens us, Jesus Christ the light of all the aeons, the inextinguishable lamp, the life of faith!'"

134. Bauckham, *Jewish World*, 5, 17. Only one text, the Syriac (Clementine) version of the Apocalypse of Peter extends the length to four days. A closely related NT example is of the two unknown witnesses of Revelation 11 who are widely thought to be Enoch and Elijah lying in the street dead for three and a half days before being caught up to heaven.

135. Neusner, *Genesis Rabbah: Parashiyyot Sixty-Eight through One Hundred on Genesis 28:10 to 50:26*, 386.

22–27 (antedating 200 BC), 4Q521, and 2 Maccabees 14.[136] In addition, 1 Enoch 51:1 and 61:5 indicate a well-developed theology of a general resurrection. When this belief came into full-flower is not certain. However, as N.T. Wright explains, several indications can be identified in Genesis and other early OT books that some hope for continuing existence and fellowship with *Yahweh* was a part of the Jewish belief system.[137] Benedictions two and three in the *Shemoneh Esreh* also depict *Yahweh* as a raiser of the dead. Although finalized during or just after the first century, the first three benedictions in particular likely contain material handed down from early post-exilic sources.[138]

In addition, anticipating the NT section (below), the fact that Lazarus had been dead for four days and was exhibiting the obvious signs of corruption is perhaps by design (John 11:17). If the thesis of Poirier is correct, one of the reasons for the despair exhibited by both Mary and Martha was the passing of more than three days. In their minds, this may have made resuscitation of Lazarus impossible.

New Testament Evidence

EVIDENCE FROM ACTS 2

The text of Acts 2 is crucial for understanding the overall New Testament witness concerning the Christian belief in the resurrection of Jesus from the dead and his status as the Davidic/Messianic King. One of key texts offered as evidence for this affirmation is Psalm 16:10. As Trull observes: "If resurrection was intended by David, then Peter's argument in Acts 2 regarding resurrection did not rely on mistranslations, later fuller senses, or escalation of meaning."[139] The author of Psalm 16 would be speaking directly of the Messiah. Given the paradigmatic significance of the book of Acts for the theology of the NT (and chapter 2 in particular), it is essential (1) to under-

---

136. Charlesworth et al., *Resurrection*, 12–15. Charlesworth also notes that the author of 1 Enoch 92–105 portrays a time of judgment for the righteous and the wicked, including eschatological rewards that may be understood as after a resurrection (1 Enoch 104:13).

137. Wright, *Resurrection of the Son of God*, 86. Wright acknowledges that many scholars believe the history of the Israelites in relation to the resurrection divides into three broad stages: "Absence of hope beyond death; hope for blissful life after death; [and] hope for new bodily life *after* 'life after death'" (Wright, *Resurrection of the Son of God*, 86).

138. Lipson, *Blessing the King of the Universe*, 74. Hirch, "Shemoneh Esreh," 277.

139. Trull, "Exegesis of Psalm 16:10a," 316.

stand how and why Peter arrived at his conclusion, and (2) to determine if Psalm 16:10 is a direct prophesy of the Messiah.[140]

Peter's argument in Acts 2:24-31 for the resurrection of Jesus follows a five-point outline drawn entirely from the LXX. Robert J. Kepple condenses these points as follows:

> God raised up Jesus, (1) having loosed the bonds of death (a necessary prerequisite); (2) this was done because death was not able to hold Jesus; (3) but how does Peter know this? Because David had foretold it! The prophecy of David (Ps 16:8-11), Peter argues, could not possibly refer to David himself since he obviously had seen corruption and remained in Hades (you can still see his tomb!); (4) therefore, David spoke of the resurrection of the Messiah.[141]

Peter contends that David comprehended, based on the Davidic Covenant and Psalm 16:10, 110, and 132:11, that one of his descendants would rule Israel and be raised from the dead (John 13:22; Luke 1:32-33; Acts 13:23). This declaration is dramatically more significant than merely asserting that David possessed knowledge of his descendant's royal messianic status. By uttering the phrase Δαυὶδ γὰρ λέγει εἰς αὐτόν, Peter unambiguously identifies Jesus as the particular descendant of David, prophesied as ruler, and the one raised from the dead. In Acts 2:25-32, Peter corroborates his claim by demonstrating why the prophecy could not speak of David. The presence of David's tomb and a body provide convincing rationale for eliminating him from consideration and arguing that Jesus is the only possible referent in Psalm 16:10.[142] Trull proffers five points as evidence for the latter argument, as transmitted by Peter:

> First, Peter referred to the presence of David's tomb as proof that David could not have been speaking of his own physical resurrection. Second, David could speak of the future Messiah because David was a prophet. Third, David could speak of the Messiah because the Davidic Covenant involved a messianic hope. Fourth, David had prophetic insight into the future appearance

---

140. Both the historicity of Peter's speech, its early date, and the accuracy of it fundamental message will be assumed for the current work. A sample of sources justifying these assumptions are: Dunn, *Beginning from Jerusalem*; Hemer, *Book of Acts*; Keener, *Acts*, 788; Witherington, *Acts of the Apostles*, 46; Stronstad, *Charismatic Theology*, 61.

141. Kepple, "Hope of Israel," 237. Cf. Dupont, *Salvation of the Gentiles*, 106-16.

142. Most of the same points could be made of any historical person. Peter specifically attributes authorship to David; however, if any other person wrote Psalm 16, they too died and their body suffered corruption.

THE FIFTH GROUP OF BIBLICAL TEXTS 199

of the Messiah. Fifth, Peter asserted that David spoke of the Messiah's resurrection in Psalm 16, specifically verse 10b.[143]

Peter's use of Psalm 16:10 as applied to the resurrection of Jesus is a clear affirmation of Jesus' status. Even so, Luke's method of recording Peter's words goes further. Conzelmann detects that "Luke means 'leave in Hades,' that is, in death" when interpreting the problematic meaning of Psalm 16:10.[144] This insight is consistent with the concept of not being abandoned, as it appears in the OT data. Conzelmann seems intent to represent Luke as not affirming a pre-existing Jewish "journey to Hades" motif.[145] Luke, however, must be referring to more than death followed by resurrection. The Jewish audience present on the Day of Pentecost already believed in the resurrection of the dead (Isa 26:19; Dan 12:2). Luke via Peter is arguing for something completely unique to human experience: death and subsequent resurrection before corruption.[146] Bock captures the weight of the

---

143. Trull, "Views on Peter's Use of Psalm 16:8–11 in Acts 2:25–32," 439. Trull explains these five points by demonstrating that David's tomb and a monument erected by Herod the Great were likely well-known landmarks in Jerusalem. In addition, Peter's argument attempts to establish that David had prophetic gifts and prophesied (προϊδών) of the greater king (Psalm 110) from his own descendants (Psalm 132:11), and that God gave him special insights and instruction (Psalm 16:7). Further, that David was considered to have prophetic gifts by the Jewish people is confirmed from Qumran (11QPsa 27:2–11); by Josephus *(Ant.* 6:166); and both the OT and NT documents. Cf. Fitzmyer, "David," 332–39. Fitzmyer is more cautious and does not argue for a certain date to establish when David was widely held to be a prophet. However, he affirms that in Qumran or earlier the references to David in Psalm 18:51, 2 Sam 22:51 and 23:1 may have begun to be understood as indicating that he was a prophet (Fitzmyer, "David," 338).

144. Conzelmann, *Acts of the Apostles*, 21. This probability casts further doubt on Dahood's analysis of Psalm 16.

145. Conzelmann, *Acts of the Apostles*, 21. Conzelmann may be referring to legends such as those depicted in Homer's *Odyssey*, Plato's *Republic*, or *1 Enoch* 17–19.

146. Germane support for the thesis that Luke via Peter is actually attempting to demonstrate that Jesus directly fulfills the prophecy of Psalm 16:10 and that he is in some sense divine are found in his citations of other OT texts (Joel 2:28–32 in Acts 2:17–21 as does Paul in Romans 10:13). The concept of calling on the name of the Lord (κυρίου) connects the three texts, with the added feature of the appearance of this connection in reference to Joel 2:32, where the LORD is *Yahweh*. This language appearing in Acts 2 and an early creedal formula adopted by Paul confirms that the nascent church overtly declared the divinity of Jesus.

Even more convincing is the quotation of Psalm 110:1 in Acts 2:34–35. It is a part of the earliest Christian teaching; it is present in both Mark 12:36 (likely the earliest gospel) and 1 Corinthians 15:25. Dunn believes Psalm 110:1 plays a key role "across the board," whether by explicit quotation or allusion because it provided the clearest answers to the questions about what the resurrection declared about Jesus. Not only does Dunn tie Psalm 110 into the tradition of Mark 14:62, a very-well attested text, but its pervasive presence throughout the New Testament demonstrates its key role (e.g.,

NT evidence and perspective of the apostolic community by avowing: "A clearer presentation of a direct prophecy fulfilled could not exist. . . . David prophesied ultimately concerning both of the immediate resurrection and the bodily resurrection of his seed, Christ."[147] Bock's conclusion is a strong affirmation of the suggestion that evidence from Acts 2 indicates a single plausible interpretation of Psalm 16:10.

Evidence from Acts 13

Acts 13:26-36 consists of a complex unit of OT quotes and references employed by Paul to support his contention that the resurrection of Jesus is the fulfillment of the Davidic Covenant. Paul cites Psalm 16:10 in this speech and several elements therein are similar to those used by Peter in Acts 2. Particularly important are those elements dealing with the mortality of David. Paul, however, goes well beyond David's mortality to emphasize the everlasting nature of the Davidic Covenant and the physical immortality of its king. He appears to intentionally prioritize Psalm 2:7 and Isaiah 55:3 before treating Psalm 16:10. The order of the OT texts may provide a logical sequence to justify his conclusion. The force of Paul's argument suggests that he believed Jesus was not only the uniquely begotten Son, but was also eternal, never to see corruption. No temporally bound man could fulfill or enjoy eternal promises or everlasting dominion such as was given to David (2 Sam 7:13, 16).[148] The loyal or sure mercies of David (חסדי דוד הנאמנים) in Isaiah 55:3 are an "everlasting covenant" (ברית עולם), apparently the same covenant described in 2 Samuel 7:8-16.[149] Evald Lövestam's analysis of the

---

Mark 12:36; 14:62; Acts 2:34-35; Rom 8:34; 1 Cor 15:25; Eph 1:20; Col 3:1; Heb 1:3). See Dunn, *Beginning from Jerusalem*, 218-19.

G. E. Ladd understands the import of Peter's citation of Psalm 110:1 when affirming that "the exaltation of Jesus to the right hand of God means nothing less than his enthronement as messianic King" and "because of the resurrection and ascension of Jesus, Peter transfers the messianic Davidic throne from Jerusalem to God's right hand in heaven" (Ladd, *Theology of the New Testament*, 373). Dunn exclaims, "How could the first believers have come to such a conclusion without Ps 110:1?!" (Dunn, *Beginning from Jerusalem*, 219). It seems they could not have, and they would never have understood Psalm 110:1 without Psalm 16:10.

147. Bock, *Proclamation from Prophecy and Pattern*, 180.

148. The authors of the NT documents attest the divinity of Jesus in a variety of ways (Mark 14:62; Matt 1:23; 28:19; Luke 1:35; 2:11; John 1:1-2, 18; 3:13, 31; 5:17-18; 6:4-42, 62; 8:58; 12:40-41; 13:3; 14:16; 16:28; 17:5, 24; Rom 1:3-4; 9:5; 9:33; 10:9, 13; 11:36; 1 Cor 8:6; 2 Cor 4:5; Eph 1:13-14; 2:18, 22; 3:14-17; 4:4-6, 8; Heb 1:8; Phil 2:6, 9-11).

149. Lövestam, *Son and Saviour*, 72.

relationship between Acts 13:34 and the relevant OT texts notes that from very early (2 Sam 23:5), the promise made to David is viewed as both a covenant and a divine decree. Both ideas stress the eternal character and irrevocability of the promise (e.g., 2 Sam. 7:13–16; Ps 89:30; Sir 47:11; 1 Macc 2:57; Pss 17, 4; Luke 1:32–33). Both are based on God's faithfulness.[150] Logically, these elements in the Davidic covenant can be realized only through a Messiah who is risen, who would never see corruption, and who is thus the inheritor of a permanent and universal dominion. The resurrection thus guarantees that the loyal or sure mercies of David (Isa 55:3) are not partially but rather completely fulfilled. Conzelmann adds support for Lövestam's exegesis by maintaining that he understands τὰ πιστά in Acts 13:34 as the equivalent of "sure," with the connotation of "'imperishable'—thus the word cannot refer to David."[151]

Summary

At a minimum, this section confirms the psalmist's belief that the *prophetic protagonist's* existence in the realm of the dead would not be permanent. First, the lexical evidence convincingly supports this assertion. Second, the entire effort to somehow dissect the term שחת and segment its meaning and implications is fruitless. Regardless of whether the psalmist's intent is to portray the term as synonymous with Sheol, or it exists in a synthetic relationship that means *corruption*, the reader's attention should be drawn to the physical aspect of the *prophetic protagonist*. Nevertheless, both the material and immaterial aspects of the person are included in relation to *Yahweh*.

Conceptually, the unavoidable idea of preservation of the whole being inherently arises from the text. This understanding does not allow for the meaning of *pit* to be reduced to *grave* (literally a tomb or hole in which a body is buried). However, it is impossible to discuss the pit/Sheol without the attendant image of death, involving a dead body and a burial. As confirmed by the lexical evidence, the most viable interpretation is that the *prophetic protagonist* will not be permanently *left* in Sheol. This is not the same as having no contact with Sheol. The critical assessment of the text by several major commentators reflects an expectant declaration that the prophetic protagonist's whole being will be preserved in a life-giving relationship with *Yahweh*. This special relationship seems to indicate something

---

150. Lövestam, *Son and Saviour*, 73.
151. Conzelmann, *Acts of the Apostles*, 105.

more than temporary escape from a threat: something proximate to eternal security and life despite death. However, this conclusion is not unassailable.

If David wrote the Psalm, it may be possible to speak of anachronism in relation to resurrection, but only remotely so. If critical dating and scholarship are correct, the existence of a developing doctrine of the resurrection and blessed state of the righteous become certain.

The evidence from Qumran is inconclusive: although informative, it offers little to establish facts concerning Psalm 16. Other sources of intertestamental and extra-biblical evidence do establish the existence of a social-cultural belief that the soul of the dead remained near for approximately seventy-two hours after death; during this period, a resuscitation or resurrection was thought possible. After this three-day period had expired, however, the person was dead beyond all hope. This belief may have played a significant role in the thoughts of the Jewish nation as its theology developed.

The entire effort related to Psalm 16 ultimately hinges on authorship and referent (the identity of the "holy one"). Was the author David, a post-exilic prophet, or another unknown person? Did this author write of the "holy one" as his hope or the hope of a contemporary—or the Messiah? The NT unambiguously attributed Psalm 16 to David. It teaches that verse 10 is a direct prophecy of the resurrection of Jesus. Jesus was the particular son of David promised by the Davidic Covenant. He was the only person who, according to Acts, was able to fulfill an eternal covenant with eternal promises. According to the NT, neither David nor any other human could be the referent; all are dead, buried, and subject to corruption. If the NT evidence is allowed to settle the issue, David wrote of the Messiah.

Plausible Historical-Evidential Conclusions Gathered from the Study of Psalm 16:9–10

1. The lexical evidence from the OT and Qumran allow for the probability that שחת in Psalm 16:10 is best translated as "corruption."

2. The lexical evidence does not betray a significant change in the interpretive trajectory when לבטח (*security* or *confidence*) is translated as ἐλπίς (*hope* or *expectation*).

3. The lexical evidence allows for the possibility that Psalm 16 is a direct prophecy of a human resurrection before decay.

4. A widely-held belief existed among the Jewish people that the soul remained near a dead body for approximately three days.

*Historical-Evidential Facts Gathered
from the Study of Psalm 16:9–10*

1. Psalm 16 speaks of the preservation of an individual from the corruption associated with death.

2. The individual depicted in Psalm 16 believes he will be preserved based on his relationship with *Yahweh*.

3. The earliest available Jewish documents (LXX) support the interpretation of Psalm 16:10 as messianic prophecy.

4. The NT documents uniformly interpret Psalm 16:10 as a direct messianic prophecy.

Psalm 22:1–31, Emphasizing Verse 16

Literary and Textual Analysis

Old Testament Evidence

Psalm 22 is a controversial piece of literature. Little consensus exists regarding the import of these thirty-one verses. For example, Payne argues that the "Messiah speaks forth the entire composition."[152] In direct opposition to Payne, Mowinckel states: "If they may be applied to Christ at all, it is by typological interpretation and not because they are directly messianic prophecies." Mowinckel further contends that Psalm 22 is not "prophecy but prayer."[153] Fitzmyer takes note of the NT use of the Psalm despite the absence of the term משיח (*māšîaḥ*), and questions whether its use is appropriate.[154] Compounding the exegetical difficulties is the infamous textual problem of verse 16, and the impossibility of certitude when ascribing a date, authorship, or *sitz-im-Leben* to the Psalm. Suggested periods range from the era of King David to that of the Maccabees.[155] The title attributes it to David; however, as Keith Campbell points out, the originality of psalm titles is sometimes disputed.[156] The only thing most scholars agree upon is

---

152. Payne, *Encyclopedia of Biblical Prophecy*, 266.
153. Mowinckel, *Psalms in Israel's Worship*, 12.
154. Fitzmyer, *One Who Is to Come*, 46–47.
155. Patterson, "Psalm 22," 214–15.
156. Campbell, "Matthew's Hermeneutic," 48. Campbell observes, "A further complication lies in the prepositional interpretation of לדוד. Does it mean 'for David,' 'by David,' 'to David,' or 'with reference to David'?"

that Psalm 22 describes the suffering and subsequent victory of an individual supplicant.

Three reasons emerge as the basis for the continued Christian messianic interpretation: (1) the absence of a known, pre-Christian individual to whom this psalm might be appropriately applied, (2) the NT use of the psalm, and (3) the historically well-documented suffering of Jesus. Adding weight to this Christian interpretation is its consistency with Jesus' prophesied, yet future (i.e., eschatological), victory over his enemies. However, putting Christian interpretations aside for the moment, the interpretive history of Psalm 22 prior to the Christian era is the basis from which this study must proceed.

Evidence about how these verses were historically understood emerges in the LXX. Rick Brannan and Israel Loken observe that the majority of the extant texts read verse 16 as: "Like the lion, they are at my hands and my feet." However, the rendering of the LXX, ὤρυξαν, agrees with other Hebrew manuscripts: "They have pierced my hands and my feet."[157] Lexically, the two Hebrew terms at the center of the controversy are almost identical כָּאֲרִ֗י (kā' ărî), a noun meaning "like a lion" and כארו or כרו (k' rû or kārû) a verb rendered "pierced."[158] Though the "pierced" reading is in the minority, the oldest evidence available from the LXX, Qumran, the Syriac, the Vulgate, and some other Hebrew manuscripts uses the "pierced" verbal form.[159]

Mark H. Heinemann, commenting on the term *pierced*, thinks pre-Christian readers would have dismissed the language as an obscure figurative expression or exercise of poetic license by the author.[160] Nevertheless, on the unlikely chance that the other reading is closer to correct, and judging from the continuing lexical debate, not much of Heinemann's statement is lost, regardless of the correct terminology. The nomenclature probably was enigmatic and, in some ways, it remains so.

Addressing more directly with whether Psalm 22 was originally understood as a messianic text, Lange et al. mention that, in the ancient synagogue, a "direct Messianic interpretation" of Psalm 22 existed that excluded David.[161] The source of this claim is not cited, which poses a serious problem

---

157. Brannan and Loken, *Lexham Textual Notes on the Bible*, s.v. "Ps 22:16."

158. For insight into questions and proposed solutions to this textual problem, see Swenson, "Psalm 22:17," and Strawn, "Psalm 22:17b."

159. Brannan and Loken, *Lexham Textual Notes on the Bible*, s.v. "Psalm 22:16." Cf. Got Questions Ministries, *Got Questions?*, s.v. "What Is the Correct Translation of Psalm 22:16?" The reading of the MT is not incomprehensible and one could make an argument for it even if it may not be the preferred reading.

160. Heinemann, "Exposition of Psalm 22," 297.

161. Lange et al., *Psalms*, 168. Emphasis added.

from an evidential perspective. In fact, no evidence confirming a messianic interpretation of Psalm 22 from an OT source clearly pre-dating the LXX exists—although the Dead Sea Scrolls do provide some additional support for the idea. A fair evaluation must also conclude that, given the repeated use of animal imagery (dogs, lions, and oxen in verses 16, 20, 21a, 21b, respectively), a clear representation of crucifixion cannot be established. Even if *pierced* is the correct English term, this still does little evidentially to establish this psalm as messianic prophecy.

Intertestamental Evidence

Psalm 22 is partially preserved in three of the Dead Sea Scrolls (4QPs^f, 4QPs^w and 5/6HevPs). The key terms are missing from the first two manuscripts. The only scroll from Qumran to preserve the controversial key text is the *Nahal Hever* Psalms Col. 11 (Frgs. 8 + 9). Peter W. Flint speaks decisively when stating: "The verse in question—reads '*they have pierced* my hands and my feet,' thus confirming that the Hebrew text used by the Septuagint translator contained this reading, not the one in the MT."[162] This assertion is probably correct, as confirmed by the present study. The term employed by the *Nahal Hever* Psalm is כארו (*k' rû*.

Harvey D. Lange's analysis of several hymns of thanksgiving (*Hodayot*) from Qumran lead away from a messianic interpretation. Several of the phrases and words of Psalm 22 arise again in the work of a psalmist of Qumran. Lange argues that this particular psalmist knew the Scriptures, used them in his personal prayer life, and identified with the sufferer of Psalm 22. The sufferer in Qumran found the language of Psalm 22 appropriate to his own suffering. He speaks of forsakenness, his tongue cleaving to his mouth, being poured out like water, having bones out of joint, strength being dried up like a potsherd, and a heart melted like wax.[163] This personal appropriation, in combination with the absence of any indication that the psalmist of Qumran considered the text as predictive of his or messianic suffering, would argue against a directly predictive original intent. Another indicator militating against a predictive messianic interpretation according to Lange, is that several elements present in the *Hodayot* are absent from Psalm 22. These include:

---

162. Flint, "Dead Sea Scrolls Psalms," s.v. "The Variant Readings in Psalm 22:17b (English 22:16b) and New Testament Exegesis."

163. Lange, "Relationship of Psalm 22," 611–12.

1. The sinfulness of man (1 QH IV, 27, 29–30, 33–35; 1 QH XII, 18–20; 1 QH XIII, 13–17; 1 QH XVIII, 18–30).

2. Divine punishment via chastisement (1 QH I, 31–34; 1 QH V, 15–18; 1 QH IX, 23–28; 1 QH XI, 8–14).

3. Apocalyptic salvation involving condemnation of the wicked and rescue for the chosen (1 QH IV, 20–22; 1 QH VI, 29–33).

4. Specific identification of threatening enemies (1 QH V, 23–25), and new emphases in the expressions of praise (1 QH II, 13–15; 1 QH IV, 27–28; 1 QH XVIII, 6–12).[164]

The combined weight of these observations indicates that the psalmist of Qumran was likely familiar with, freely used, and appropriated the language in Psalm 22. This evidence also indicates that this psalmist was not directly verbally dependent on the psalm and was not bound to a messianic interpretation. Lange concludes that this is the same method that allowed Jesus to appropriate Psalm 22 to describe his own torment during his passion. Thus, Jesus identified with Psalm 22, but Psalm 22 did not specifically identify Jesus.

Richard D. Patterson obseves that some literature outside of Qumran during the intertestamental period also demonstrates a knowledge of the Psalter (e.g., Jubilees, 3 Maccabees, Pseudo-Philo, and the intertestimental portion of the Sbyllbine Oracles). However, neither the pseudepigraphical works nor the Apocrypha (e.g., Judith and Ecclesiasticus) give extensive attention to Psalm 22.[165]

Early Church Evidence

In stark contrast to the intertestamental literature, much extra-biblical literature from the early church attests an abiding conviction that Psalm 22 was both prophetic and messianic. Several works of St. Augustine, Tertullian, and other writers quote Psalm 22 in this way.[166] One of the earliest extra-biblical attestations of the church connecting Psalm 22 with Jesus as Messiah is the citation of verses 6–8 in 1 Clement. The author states:

164. Lange, "Relationship of Psalm 22," 612–13.

165. Patterson, "Psalm 22," 227. Patterson notes a possible allusion to Psalm 22:7 in Ecclesiasticus and the description of a man's enemies.

166. Letters of St. Augustine 76:1; 140:16; 199:50. See also, *De civ. Dei* 17:1, 17:17; *De fide* 4:7; *Tractates on the Gospel of John* 86.1–2; *Expositions on the Book of Psalms* 22:17; *Constitutions of the Holy Apostles* 5:14; Novation, *Trinity* 28:12; Tertullian, *Answer to the Jews* 8, 10; Tertullian, *Against Marcion* 3:19.

And again he himself says: "But I am a worm and not a man, a reproach among men and an object of contempt to the people. All those who saw me mocked me; they 'spoke with their lips'; they shook their heads, saying, 'He hoped in the Lord, let him deliver him; let him save him, because he takes pleasure in him.'"[167]

The Epistle of Barnabas, another early text, contains even more striking examples of the early church's interpretation:

> But he himself desired to suffer in this manner, for it was necessary for him to suffer on a tree. For the one who prophesies says, concerning him: "Spare my soul from the sword,"[168] and "Pierce my flesh with nails, for bands[169] of evil men have risen up against me." (Barn 5:13)[170]

> What, then, does the prophet again say? "A band of evil men have surrounded me, they have swarmed around me like bees around a honeycomb,"[171] and "for my garments they cast lots." (Barn 6:6)[172]

> For the Lord says again: "And with what shall I appear before the Lord my God and be glorified? I will confess you in the congregation of my brothers, and I will sing to you in the midst of the congregation of the saints." Therefore we are the ones whom he brought into the good land. (Barn 6:16)[173]

In summary, ample evidence exists to support the assertion that the early church interpreted Psalm 22 as directly messianic and considered Jesus to be the Messiah. Dissimilarly, sparse evidence exists to support the notion that those familiar with the Scriptures prior to the life and passion of Jesus understood the psalm as messianic prophecy.[174]

---

167. Holmes, *Apostolic Fathers*, 47.

168. Ps 22:20 (LXX 21:21).

169. According to Holmes *bands*, or perhaps *synagogues*.

170. Holmes, 287. Cf. Ps 119 (LXX 118); 120 (LXX text form only); 22:16 (LXX 21:17).

171. Ps 22:16 (LXX 21:17); 118 (LXX 117); 12.

172. Holmes, *Apostolic Fathers*, 289. Ps 22:18 (LXX 21:19).

173. Holmes, *Apostolic Fathers*, 291. Cf. Ps 42:2 (LXX 41:3); 22:22 (LXX 21:23).

174. Edersheim, *Life and Times of Jesus*, 2:718. Edersheim accepts a messianic interpretation. He observes that in the *Yalkut Shimeoni* (a compendium of older and lost works), a comment on Psalm 22:7 (8 in the Hebrew) in relation to Isaiah 40 is applied to the Messiah (the second, or son of Ephraim). According to Edersheim, the *Yalkut Shimeoni* uses words remarkably similar to those in the Psalm and those used by the NT writers to describe the reaction of people at the cross of Jesus. The same text also gives

New Testament Evidence

There is little doubt that the suffering supplicant in Psalm 22 exhibits characteristics that reflect a desperate physical and emotional state, as well as some striking parallels with what the NT accounts record. Heinemann unnecessarily assumes a typological interpretation, but his observation is still cogent. He reminds interpreters:

> Even if one holds to the reading, "Like a lion my hands and my feet," the prefiguring is only weakened in its directness; it is not disposed of entirely. It is important to note that there would still be a strong correspondence between David's enemies doing something harmful to his hands and feet and the fact that Jesus' enemies did something harmful to His hands and feet when they crucified Him. The connection and thus the prefiguring remains intact because of the specific and unusual mention of David's hands and feet.[175]

The NT authors claimed that Jesus was in just such a state during his crucifixion; as a result, they directly cite Psalm 22 on no less than fourteen occasions.[176] Licona, in a comprehensive study of the resurrection of Jesus, lists eight things present in both Psalm 22 and the accounts of the crucifixion:

> (1) The possibly historical statement from Jesus while on the cross, citing Psalm 22:1: "My God, my God! Why have you forsaken me?" (2) dividing and casting lots for his garments, (3) sneering at the victim, wagging their heads and saying, "Let God deliver him," (4) intense thirst or dry mouth, (5) being surrounded by dogs, (6) a band of evil men surrounding him, (7) piercing his hands and feet, and (8) exposed bones."[177]

---

a messianic interpretation to Psalm 22:15 (16 in the Hebrew).

175. Heinemann, "Exposition of Psalm 22," 296n293. The typological stance is unnecessary because historians do not know who the original supplicant may have been or if it is intended to describe a specific historical individual to the exclusion of all others.

176. Patterson, "Psalm 22," 228. According to Patterson, the following are direct quotations of Psalm 22 in the NT: Ps 22:1 in Matt 27:46 and Mark 15:34; Ps 22:5 in Rom 3:5; Ps 22:7 in Matt 27:39 and Mark 15:29; Ps 22:8 in Matt 27:43 and Luke 23:35; Ps 22:18 in Matt 27:35; Mark 15:24; Luke 23:34; John 19:24; Ps 22:22 in Heb 2:12; Ps 22:23 in Rev 19:5; Ps 22:31 in John 19:30.

177. Licona, 310. Licona lists the following texts as evidence: (1) Ps 22:1 in Matt 27:46 and Mark 15:34; (2) Ps 22:18 in Matt 27:35; Mark 15:24; John 19:23–24; (3) Ps 22:7–8 in Matt 27:39–43; Mark 15:29–32, 35–36; Luke 23:35–39; (4) Ps 22:15 in John 19:28; (cf. Matt 27:47–48; Mark 15:36–37; Luke 23:36); (5) Ps 22:16: according to

Even such a detailed investigation of the crucifixion of Jesus cannot make a certain historical connection to the expectation of a future suffering messiah and Psalm 22. Licona, however, finds "no reason to question the historicity of the crurifragium and piercing," and appears to accept much of the passion accounts as historical. Even so, he chooses to describe the NT account as reflected in Psalm 22 as "history prophesized."[178] Sheldon Tostengard leaves the same impression when stating: "The Messiah as future King of Salvation is not directly prefigured in this psalm. However, Jesus' use of the psalm denotes a substantive connection between the Godforsakenness of our beleaguered psalmist and what happened at Calvary."[179] Conclusions such as those reached by Licona and Tostengard make sense and carry the additional benefit of aligning well with the historical data.

Summary

This study did not discover a significant amount of historical evidence directly applicable to Psalm 22. Further, little consensus exists regarding the import of these thirty-one verses. Even what appears to be the likely confirmation of the "pierced" reading does little to confirm a pre-Christian messianic intent. The *Yalkut Shimeoni* provides support for a messianic reading, but this source alone is not sufficient for making this claim. The undocumented assertion of an early direct messianic interpretation, exclusive of David, as presented by Lange et al. also does little to provide evidential support.

Dissimilarly, the weight of the evidence against a directly messianic intent for the original work is compelling. First, the free personal application of the text by the psalmist of Qumran, with no messianic implication must be considered. Second, the paucity of clearly identifiable references attributable to Psalm 22 in the Pseudepigrapha and Apocrypha must be considered. None of those references thus far identified in the current study are both pre-Christian and messianic.[180]

Licona "The 'dogs' could refer to the animal or to Gentiles"; (6) Ps 22:16: perhaps this refers to those supporting or participating in the crucifixion or the two thieves placed on either side of Jesus (Matt 27:38; Mark 15:27; Luke 23:32–34; John 19:18); (7) Ps 22:16, as referencing piercing his hands and feet; Ps 22:17; Jos, *Wars of the Jews* 6.304.

178. Licona, *Resurrection of Jesus*, 309–11.
179. Tostengard, "Psalm 22," 170.
180. For example, see *Odes of Solomon*, 28, 31:9

The opposite is true for extra-biblical literature from the Christian era. Much literature attests the messianic interpretation of Psalm 22. This literature spans the period from the late first century until the present day.

The NT authors claim in multiple texts and sources that Jesus was the fulfillment of Psalm 22, citing the text on no less than fourteen occasions.[181] Even the statement placed on the lips of Jesus from Psalm 22:1: "My God, my God! Why have you forsaken me?" (Mark 15:34) may be historical. If this statement is historical, it is another strong affirmation of Jesus' personal identification with Psalm 22.

Despite these differing lines of evidence and argumentation, no certain historical connection to the expectation of a future suffering messiah and Psalm 22 is demonstrable. The crucifixion of Jesus is certain and many of the details of the passion account are accepted by scholars. However, the ground is firmer for understanding the NT accounts in relation to Psalm 22 as "history prophesized," rather than prophecy realized.[182] For certain, Psalm 22 describes the suffering and subsequent victory of an individual supplicant, and the NT authors correlated those images with the passion of Jesus. As appealing as this may be to the Christian reader, it does little to establish original messianic intent.

Plausible Historical-Evidential Conclusions Gathered from the Study of Psalm 22:1–31

1. The text of verse 16 likely should read "pierced."
2. Several items plausibly connected to crucifixion are present in the psalm.
3. Little pre-Christian support exists for a messianic interpretation.
4. Jesus probably identified with the supplicant in Psalm 22.

Historical-Evidential Facts Gathered from the Study of Psalm 22:1–31

1. The text records the pleas of an individual supplicant.
2. Much Christian literature attributes the fulfillment of the psalm to the passion of Jesus.

---

181. Patterson, "Psalm 22," 228.
182. Licona, *Resurrection of Jesus*, 309–11.

3. All four of the NT evangelists correlate Jesus' suffering with the supplicant of Psalm 22.

Summary of Chapters 3–7

Chapters 3 to 7 contain the argumentation and available evidence generated by analyzing the five groups of biblical texts chosen for this study. Modern interpretations of these texts often contain assertions that they are prophesies concerning the Jewish Messiah, which the NT authors equate with Jesus of Nazareth. A wide range of early, first-century, and post-apostolic historical and literary sources were examined in an attempt to verify or refute these claims. The results emerging from the data suggest that some assertions of both original messianic content and an original messianic referent are well-supported, while other assertions are either ambiguous or unsupported.

Chapter 8 presents the collated results of the study and briefly treats the available evidence. In addition to the final formulation of the *minimal-fact* statements, the criteria for justified historical descriptions will be applied to the results.

Part III

Conclusions

Chapter 8

The Results of the Study and Recommendations for Future Research

Introduction

THE PURPOSE OF THIS chapter is to collate and summarize the findings of this study. The investigation sought to establish if critically acceptable historical-evidential reasons exist for believing that Jesus Christ is the direct fulfillment of the specific OT messianic texts examined in the study. The methodology proceeded in three interrelated steps. First, the work was narrowly focused on specific, allegedly-predictive OT messianic texts and their alleged NT fulfillment texts. Second, exegetical analysis of relevant biblical and historical data isolated relevant evidence. Some of this evidence met the *minimal-facts* criteria. Third, the conclusions gleaned from the evidence were applied to and weighed against any plausible competing hypotheses proposed by other scholars.

This investigation envisioned the existence of three possible outcomes for each prophecy examined: (1) Jesus directly fulfilled the prophecy and sufficient historical evidence establishes the claim as probable, (2) Jesus directly fulfilled the prophecy, but the available historical evidence is insufficient to establish the claim as probable, and (3) sufficient historical evidence exists to refute the claim that Jesus directly fulfilled the prophecy.

Results of the Study

The First Group of Biblical Texts

The first group of texts investigated the claim that the *terminus ad quem* for the coming of the Messiah must occur before Israel loses its status as self-governing (Gen 49:10) and before the destruction of the temple in AD 70 (Ps 118; Hag 2:7, 9; Mal 3:1).

Genesis 49:10

Genesis 49:10 yielded no evidence able to validate an affirmative *minimal-facts* statement. The information gathered does not meet the *minimal-facts* criteria. Any claim to have established a *terminus ad quem* for the advent of the Messiah based on this passage is unsupported. Outcome category three best fits the evidence: "Sufficient historical evidence exists to refute the claim that Jesus directly fulfilled the prophecy."[1]

A second datum did emerge, however. Regardless of when the pericope known as the Testament of Jacob was written, the author intended to denote the perpetual ascendancy and rulership of the tribe of Judah within Israel.

Another plausible conclusion emerging from the study is that either from its original context or gradually, Jewish interpreters endued the passage with messianic import. This messianic interpretation included the prophetic eschatological expectation of a Davidic king and his permanent rule over the kingdom.

Psalm 118

Psalm 118 also did not generate the evidence required to attach to the second temple period a *terminus ad quem* for the advent of the Messiah. The rebuilt temple is surely the one that existed when the psalm was authored; accordingly, it is probable that some messianic and eschatological meaning was originally intended. Similarly, little doubt exists that Jesus intentionally invoked the processional images related to Psalm 118 when entering the temple during his Triumphal Entry (Matt 21:1–17; Mark 11:1–11; Luke 19:28–48; John 12:12–15).

One of the significant difficulties encountered during the exegetical process is the incidental nature of the temple to the meaning of the psalm. The temple serves only in a supportive role: it is not the essential element or focal point of the psalm. Therefore, its existence or destruction cannot bear the weight needed to establish a single, specific historical fulfillment.

---

1. Each time an outcome category is established below, refer to "Statement of the Problem" in chapter 1.

Outcome category three best fits the evidence: "Sufficient historical evidence exists to refute the claim that Jesus directly fulfilled the prophecy."

Haggai 2:1–9

The investigation of Haggai 2:1–9 also failed to produce a *terminus ad quem* for the advent of the Messiah. The nomenclature, particularly the terms "glory" and "house" are ambiguous. As a result, any assertion of direct fulfillment remains indemonstrable. Haggai does not indicate that any other structure ("house") except the original and rebuilt temples are in view during his speech. This limits the time for fulfillment to the period before AD 70. However, in light of the probability that the term "glory" includes theophanic phenomena, possible historical fulfillments may not be limited to a single event. Fulfillment could include aspects of the finished temple of Herod the Great, the Day of Pentecost, or other, less well-attested events. The second temple, when fully adorned by Herod, possessed great material splendor. Further, if the events of the day of Pentecost occurred in the temple precincts, the events described in Acts 2 did have theophanic portents, possibly fulfilling the prophet's expectation.

In the final analysis, the question about whether a *terminus ad quem* for the advent of the Messiah exists based on evidence associated with three of the four passages in the first group of texts must be answered negatively. Genesis 49:10, Psalm 118, and Haggai 2:1–9 are best placed in the third possible outcome category: "Sufficient evidence refutes the claim that Jesus directly fulfilled the prophecy." There is considerable circumstantial evidence of fulfillment that may be properly applied by another hermeneutical method, but direct fulfillment cannot be demonstrated (see Recommendations for Further Research below).

Malachi 3:1

Malachi 3:1 is the only text among the first group that exegetically produces the possibility of a *terminus ad quem* for the advent of the Messiah. The rebuilt temple is a central feature in the book of Malachi; this prophet never indicates or even implies that any other temple is in view. Sufficient evidence indicates the following:

1. Malachi 3:1 depicts *Yahweh* as coming into his temple for judgment.
2. The only temple Malachi envisions is the one standing during his lifetime.

3. As a logical consequence, it is possible that the *terminus ad quem* for *Yahweh*'s coming into his temple (and the sending of both the forerunner and the messenger of the covenant/Lord) was at or before the destruction of the second Jewish temple.

Outcome category two best fits the available historical evidence: "Jesus directly fulfilled the prophecy, but the available historical evidence is insufficient to establish the claim as probable."

It may also be plausibly asserted that JTB is the best known candidate if the messenger (forerunner) foretold in Malachi is human. This conclusion is based on the fact that some Jews of Malachi's period (Mal 4:5)—and some later Jews and Christians—believed that Elijah would appear before the prophesied judgment of *Yahweh*. JTB is specifically identified as such in the Synoptic Gospels (Matt 11:14; 17:10–13; Mark 9:11–13; Luke 1:17) and implied to be a forerunner (John 1:22–23). A straight-forward reading of Malachi 3:1 distinguishes between the messenger, the messenger of the covenant/Lord, and *Yahweh*: these appear to be three distinct individuals. The research demonstrated that the messenger of the covenant and the messenger of the Lord are most likely the same individual. The historical person of Jesus is the only viable candidate for fulfilling the prophecy. No other historical person exhibits both a forerunner, a covenant message, and multiple independent witnesses claiming his deity *a fortiori*—no other person living before AD 70. These are the claims of the best witnesses, as captured in the NT gospels and the writings of Paul, all of which evidence that Jesus is the Jewish Messiah, judge of Israel, and essentially equal with *Yahweh*.

The Second Group of Biblical Texts

The second group of texts probed the claim that the Messiah would spring from the linage of King David and, correspondingly, that Jesus is a descendant of King David (2 Sam 7:13; Isa 11:1–2; Jer 23:5–6; Ezek 34:23–24; Hos 3:4–5; Matt 1:1–17; Luke 2:4; 3:23f; Rom 1:3).

2 Samuel 7:13

The evidence for affirming both the expectation that the Messiah would be a *davidid* and the physical descent of Jesus from the historical King David is substantial. The Davidic Covenant (2 Sam 7:1–17) acts as the paradigmatic promise for this expectation; verses 13 and 16 specifically require the offspring to be established forever. It is possible that verses 13 and 16 did not originally refer to a single individual. However, the incongruity of this prophecy with history and the Davidic household is most readily resolved by the NT authors referencing the incarnation and the resurrected immortality of Jesus.[2]

The Role of Isaiah 11:1, Jeremiah 23:5–6, Ezekiel 34:23–24, and Hosea 3:4–5, in Relation to 2 Samuel 7:13

Univocally, each of the other investigated texts, as they relate to the 2 Samuel 7:1–17, support the specific idea that the prophesied offspring would be from the ממעיך (body/bowel) of David. The text of Isaiah 11:1 offers a reaffirmation, after the death of King David, that a perpetual dynasty will emerge from house of Jesse. This text is almost universally recognized as reaffirming the promise made previously to David. Paradoxically, in light of the failure of the Davidic kings and the successive rule of foreign powers over Israel, the hope for an archetypical Davidic king seems to have grown more prevalent as time progressed. Jeremiah 23:5 recounts the Davidic promise by employing *tree*-related terminology: a "righteous branch" is used to describe the coming scion of David. The later prophet Zechariah clearly uses the terms in relation to the Messiah (Zech 3:8). Ezekiel 34:23–24 places the hope for the reestablishment of the Davidic dynasty on the coming shepherd. Whether Hosea 3:1–5 (particularly verses 4–5) is part of the original prophecy or the work of a later redactor changes little. Either way, the passage represents a strong affirmation of the Jewish people's anticipation of a Davidic king. It describes a king whose advent occurs in the distant eschatological future, but who is, nonetheless, a *davidid*.

These OT passages are reaffirmed in the intertestamental literature, the NT, and writings of the early church. These observations endure even if the indictment is conceded that the gospel accounts are the stylized works of the evangelists. Stylization only proves that the early church universally understood Jesus to be the Davidic Messiah.

Outcome category one fits the data: "Jesus directly fulfilled the prophecy and sufficient evidence establishes the claim as historically probable."[3] With that stated, the evidence falls short of establishing Jesus' Davidic

---

2. Micah 5:2 implies the eternality of the coming ruler and the authors of the NT documents attest this by declaring the divinity of Jesus in a variety of ways (Mark 14:62; Matt 1:23; 28:19; Luke 1:35; 2:11; John 1:1–2, 18; 3:13, 31; 5:17–18; 6:4–42, 62; 8:58; 12:40–41; 13:3; 14:16; 16:28; 17:5, 24; Rom 1:3–4; 9:5, 33; 10:9, 13; 11:36; 1 Cor 8:6; 2 Cor 4:5; Eph 1:13–14; 2:18, 22; 3:14–17; 4:4–6, 8; Heb 1:8; Phil 2:6, 9–11).

3. Prophecy that meets the criteria established in chapter 1 is miraculous. See "Key Elements" and "Reasons for Including Each Element" in chapter 1.

descent as a *minimal fact*. The facts emerging from the data this study established do, however, lend support to the claim. No first-century evidence stated that Jesus was not a descendant of King David. The absence of such refutation includes works penned by adversary and friend alike. Positive, early affirmations of Jesus as a descendant of King David span all four NT Gospels, the work of Paul, and the *Didache*, along with several other later documents. Concrete statements beyond these might be possible if the NT genealogical evidence were ever conclusively unraveled.

Nevertheless, several other plausible affirmations also emerged from the study. The messianic expectation of the Jewish nation was rooted in the Davidic Covenant, and the most significant characteristic was a royal/kingly stream of thought. Further, it is likely that the Jews or Jesus' relatives would have become confrontational about the messianic deception if his Davidic descent were not a fact. In short, Jesus is probably a descendant of King David.

The Third Group of Biblical Texts

The third group of texts relates to the geographical locations associated with the birth and early life of the Messiah. Micah 5:2 was examined to substantiate the claim that the Messiah would be born in Bethlehem of Judea and the parallel claim that Jesus was born in this small village (Matt 2:1–12; Luke 2: 1–7).

Both this group of texts and the outcome of the investigation are mixed and prove difficult to categorize. The facts leave many questions unanswered. Broad support among scholars is indicated for the supposition that Bethlehem of Judea is the place from which Israel's predicted ruler emerges (Mic 5:2). In addition, the common view among many Jews during the first-century was that the Messiah would have roots in Bethlehem of Judea (John 7:42) as they interpreted Micah 5:2.

The NT evidence indicates that Matthew and Luke reflect independent sources for their birth narratives. Based on the points of discontinuity, collaboration is also ruled out. This finding indirectly adds to the credibility of both accounts. Moreover, the unlikely possibility that both authors created independent fictitious accounts or used two separate, but erroneous, sources is evidentially unsupported. Too many points of continuity in their accounts exist to support such contentions.

This study has demonstrated that the preponderance of evidence points toward a historical basis for the birth narratives. The best, earliest, and majority of available evidence indicates that Jesus was born in Bethlehem of

Judea. The evidence best fits outcome category one: "Jesus directly fulfilled the prophecy and sufficient evidence establishes the claim as historically probable." This conclusion, however, does not enjoy the needed consensus of scholarly opinion to be classified as a *minimal fact*.

The facts emerging from this part of the study demonstrate the underlying continuity in the gospel accounts. First, both NT authors emphasize Bethlehem of Judea as the birthplace of Jesus. Second, his ancestor was David. Third, both NT authors place Jesus' family in Bethlehem. How long they dwelled there is uncertain, however. Fourth, both accounts place the final home of Jesus in Nazareth of Galilee. In addition, no written source earlier than Celsus denies that Jesus was born in Bethlehem. To dismiss Bethlehem of Judea as the birthplace of Jesus requires that these accounts—the best and earliest historical sources available—be discounted as mistaken or deceptive.

The Fourth Group of Biblical Texts

In the fourth set of passages, Jesus' miracles were analyzed in relation to the expectations of the messianic age, the Messiah himself, and the predictions of the OT prophets. Jesus' self-described *titular nomens*, such as "prophet" (Luke 4:17–19), "son of man," "son of the Blessed" (Mark 14:61–62), and "son of David" (Matt 9:27; 12:23; 15:22; 21:9; Mark 10:47), all bear implications for his assertion of a future position "seated at the right hand of God" (Mark 14:62). The best, and perhaps only currently available, verification of whether these titles attributed to Jesus are justifiable, lies in an examination of whether Jesus performed the miracles that the OT prophets allegedly predicted would accompany the messianic age (Isa 29:18; 35:5–6; 61:1–2; Matt 9:35; 11:4–6; Luke 7:22–23).

This section of the work features the presupposition that Jesus was a miracle worker. His miracles are among the best attested aspects of his ministry. The data answering the question of whether the Jewish people expected a miracle-working Messiah is ambiguous, according to current scholarship. However, the data analyzed in this study points toward a more definitive conclusion. Isaiah 29, 35, and 61 contain references to restorative activity best described as miraculous. In addition, the promise of Deuteronomy 18:15–22, with its connotations of exodus and miracles, consistently arose in the literature. Collectively considered, the probability that many within Israel expected miracles in association with the advent of the Messiah is high. Even so, the majority of current scholarship argues for a non-messianic referent for Deuteronomy 18:15–22. A non-messianic referent is possible and the depiction of several OT prophets as participating in activities that might be characterized as a second-Moses motif supports this interpretive opinion. Despite the stance of current scholarship, some later Jewish and Christian exegetes did inculcate the passage with messianic elements. These gradually accruing interpretations are witnessed among the community of Qumran, and in Josephus, the NT authors, and the Talmud.

The text of Isaiah 29 (29:18 in particular) displays ambiguous restorative activity. The text undoubtedly refers, in part, to physical elements (blindness and deafness); however, the obvious ideological affinities with other texts in Deutero-Isaiah in relation to blindness and the poor (Isa 35:5–6; 42:7, 16) place emphasis on the spiritual aspects of restoration. The physical aspects assume a subordinate role. Isaiah 29 clearly contains reference to miraculous activity, but no direct messianic link. What is probable is that Isaiah 29 is part of a cadre of texts that point Israel toward eschatological restoration.

Similarly, Isaiah 35:1–5 contain a mixture of literal and metaphorical language. Unlike chapter 29, however, the physical aspect of healing miracles comes to the fore and the spiritual aspect assumes a subordinate role. The miraculous nature of the language of that chapter supports the conclusion that it describes circumstances obtained at the institution of the messianic era. The anointed agent of *Yahweh* is clearly the actor.

These OT texts, as they connect with the Pseudepigrapha, Dead Sea Scrolls, and latter Jewish literature, depict miracles in relation to the Messiah or to the messianic age. Later, the NT also clearly depicts the expectation of a particular prophet, with Jesus' miracles authenticating his identity as this prophet. Jesus appears to have performed his miracles with reference to the implications of the OT and the expectations of a broad range of sectarian and proletariat Jewish groups.

There is little doubt that Jesus believed he was the particular prophet and Messiah, and no doubt that the gospel writers believed Jesus was the particular prophet and Messiah. Outcome category two best fits the available evidence: "Jesus directly fulfilled the prophecy, but the available evidence is insufficient to establish the claim as historically probable." Oddly, only two things prevent this conclusion from rising to the first level or even to the level of a *minimal fact*: (1) the somewhat ambiguous nature of the concurrent OT contexts, and (2) an OT identification of the intended referent of Deuteronomy 15:18–22 as directly eschatological. Something more direct evidentially than a chronological or typological raising up of another prophet to succeed Moses.

The Fifth Group of Biblical Texts

Psalm 2:1–12, Emphasizing Verse 7

The data gathered from the various sources treating Psalm 2 conflicts with the perspectives of several critical scholars. These scholars either opt for a typological interpretation, ground the text in the historic Israelite monarchy, or otherwise deny any original messianic intent.

Objectively considered, the prophetic features of Psalm 2 are not identifiable with any certain historical king or *sitz im leben*. This study does however, conclude that the singular appearance of "Anointed" in Psalm 2:7 is not sufficient to establish the term as meaning an eschatological Messiah. Even so, without historical or other types of evidence relevant to Hebrew culture, the rare appearance of the term "begotten" in light of Psalm 110, 1QSa, and other, intertestamental literature cannot be arbitrarily truncated to mean *adopted*. No other near-eastern enthronement text provides an adequate parallel from which to form a judgement.

Supplementing these assertions is the fact that the NT data explicitly declares the unique metaphysical relationship of Jesus to the Father, citing Psalm 2 (Acts 4:25–28) in reference to Jesus as the anointed one. For these reasons, the conclusion that Psalm 2 is eschatological prophecy, not an account of the enthronement of a historical king is more likely than any other conclusion. This assertion is both reasonable and consistent with the evidence demonstrating the unlikely connection with a historical king. It does not, however, contain the scope of positive evidence required to meet the criteria for placement into the list of *minimal facts*. Nonetheless, outcome category two best fits the evidence: "Jesus directly fulfilled the prophecy, but the available evidence is insufficient to establish the claim as historically probable."

Psalm 16, Emphasizing Verses 9–10

This study confirms the psalmist's belief that (1) the prophetic protagonist's existence in the realm of the dead would not be permanent or (2) the less likely possibility that he believes he will escape an imminent threat. In either case, this prophetic protagonist would escape decay. Plausible lexical conclusions suggest the possibility that שחת in Psalm 16:10 is best translated as "corruption" rather than "pit." The charge of Christian interpolation or the intrusion of later Jewish ideology related to the resurrection of the righteous was demonstrated as unlikely by showing that the lexical trajectory does not change significantly when לבטח (*security* or *confidence*) is translated as ἐλπίς (*hope* or *expectation*). In addition, the perspective of the psalmist gives reason to suggest that the scope of the language employed exceeds the natural human lifespan of the prophetic protagonist. The earliest and best Jewish documents support a direct messianic interpretation, as do the related NT documents.

This conclusion should instill confidence in the probability that Jesus directly fulfilled the prophecy of Psalm 16:10. A problem arises, however, in that the authorship and referent of Psalm 16 are not demonstrable unless the exegete employs a canonical reading of the data. If David authored the passage, the probability is high that the referent is Jesus. If the author (whoever he was) did not speak of himself, but of another, the probability is also high that the referent is Jesus. If, on the other hand, the author wrote only of his personal hope without any prophetic intent, Jesus is not the referent. On balance, the preponderance of the evidence points toward outcome category two: "Jesus directly fulfilled the prophecy, but the available historical evidence is insufficient to establish the claim as probable."

Psalm 22, Emphasizing Verse 16

Although much Christian literature attributes Psalm 22 to the crucifixion of Jesus, the facts established by the study in relation to Psalm 22 are few and general in nature. The text of Psalm 22 records the pleas of an individual supplicant. The NT authors—and apparently Jesus himself—then identify his sufferings with those of the psalmist. This identification is related by the NT authors no fewer than fourteen times.

The evaluation of Psalm 22 did not identify any original or even intertestamental messianic intent. The textual and interpretive problems, in conjunction with the personal application of Psalm 22 by a psalmist in Qumran, makes any claim to direct fulfillment by Jesus dubious. No clear representation of crucifixion can be established in the text, despite the likelihood that *pierced* is the correct translation. All indicators point toward a placement in outcome category three: "Sufficient evidence exists to refute the claim that Jesus directly fulfilled the prophecy." Licona correctly assigned the phrase "history prophesized," rather than prophecy realized, as the proper understanding of the text.[4]

---

4. Licona, *Resurrection of Jesus*, 309–11.

Minimal-Fact Statements as Related to the Statement of the Problem

The statement of the problem cited in chapter 1 reads: This study will seek to establish if critically acceptable historical-evidential reasons exist for believing that Jesus is the direct fulfillment of the specific OT messianic texts included in the study. As stated earlier, three possible outcomes exist for each prophecy examined in this investigation: (1) Jesus directly fulfilled the prophecy and sufficient historical evidence establishes the claim as probable, (2) Jesus directly fulfilled the prophecy, but the available historical evidence is insufficient to establish the claim as probable, and (3) sufficient historical evidence exists to refute the claim that Jesus directly fulfilled the prophecy. The evidence generated by this study was then assigned to one of these three categories.

Due consideration was given to the contextual and historical information related to all the texts examined during the study. Through a process of reflection and inductive reasoning, fifteen historical-evidential *minimal facts* emerged; the following statements constitute the principle products of this study, as they directly resolve the question posed in the problem statement. Since, direct fulfillment of OT prophecies is specifically eliminated in outcome category three, only historical-evidential *minimal facts* related to outcome categories one and two are included.

Historical-Evidential Minimal Facts in Textual Group One

In this group, only the text of Malachi 3:1 produced a possible direct historic fulfillment of a prophecy by Jesus. This conclusion embodies three *minimal facts*.

1. Malachi 3:1 depicts *Yahweh* as coming into his temple for judgment.

2. Malachi provides no indication that he envisions a temple other than the one standing during his lifetime.

3. The historical-evidential data indicates that whether the LORD (*hā' ādôn*) and *the messenger of the covenant* are different individuals or the same individual, Jesus is the best identifiable candidate for both roles.

Historical-Evidential Minimal Facts in Textual Group Two

In textual group two, the plausible conclusions (and their supporting data) lead to the identification of three additional *minimal facts*.

4. 2 Samuel 7:13, 16 contain a prophecy of a perpetual dynasty of the descendants of King David.
5. None of Jesus' adversaries, friends, or any other first-century evidence challenged his Davidic status.
6. The NT and early extra-biblical sources multiply attest Jesus' Davidic status.

Historical-Evidential Minimal Facts in Textual Group Three

In textual group three, the plausible conclusions (and their supporting data) lead to the identification of two additional *minimal facts*.

7. Micah 5:2 is a prophecy naming Bethlehem of Judea in association with the origins of the eschatological ruler of Israel.
8. The overwhelming majority of evidence indicates that Jesus was born in Bethlehem of Judea and was believed, by the NT authors, to be the fulfillment of the prophecy in Micah 5:2.

Historical-Evidential Minimal Facts in Textual Group Four

In textual group four, the plausible conclusions (and their supporting data) lead to the identification of one additional *minimal fact*.

9. The NT records that Jesus performed miracles in accordance with the OT, certain sectarian, and proletariat Jewish messianic expectations.

Historical-Evidential Minimal Facts in Textual Group Five

In textual group five, the plausible conclusions (and their supporting data) lead to the identification of six additional *minimal facts*.

10. No certain historical king or occasion can be assigned to Psalm 2.
11. The peculiar Hebrew term ילד, translated as the English term *begotten*, is found in no other near-eastern enthronement narrative and is never applied to a known historical Israelite king.

12. The earliest documents available consistently interpret Psalm 2 from an eschatological messianic perspective.

13. Psalm 16 speaks of the preservation of an individual from the corruption associated with death.

14. The individual in Psalm 16 believes that he will be preserved based on his relationship with *Yahweh*.

15. The earliest available Jewish documents (LXX) and the NT documents uniformly interpret Psalm 16:10 as a direct messianic prophecy.

Applying the Criteria for Justifying Historical Descriptions

The final step in this study is to apply the seven criteria discussed in chapter 1 for justifying historical descriptions to the *minimal facts* identified above.[5] Do these *minimal facts* do justice to the texts? Are they the best explanation of the texts?

---

5 McCullagh, 19. See chapter 1, "Overview of Methodology, Key Terms, and Presuppositions."

1. The statement, together with other statements already held to be true, must imply yet other statements describing present, observable data. (We will henceforth call the first statement 'the hypothesis', and statements describing observable data, 'observation and statements'.)

2. The hypothesis must be *of greater explanatory scope* than any other incompatible hypothesis about the same subject; that is, it must imply a greater variety of observation statements.

3. The hypothesis must be *of greater explanatory power* than any other incompatible hypothesis about the same subject; that is, it must make the observation statements it implies more probable than any other.

4. The hypothesis must be *more plausible* than any other incompatible hypothesis about the same subject; that is, it must be implied to some degree by a greater variety of accepted truths than any other, and be implied more strongly than any other; and its probable negation must be implied by fewer beliefs, and implied less strongly than any other.

5. The hypothesis must be *less ad hoc* than any other incompatible hypothesis about the same subject; that is, it must include fewer new suppositions about the past which are not already implied to some extent by existing beliefs.

6. It must be *disconfirmed by fewer accepted beliefs* than any other incompatible hypothesis about the same subject; that is, when conjoined with accepted truths it must imply fewer observations statements and other statements.

7. It must exceed other incompatible hypotheses about the same subject by so much, in characteristics 2–6, that there is little chance of an incompatible hypothesis, after further investigation, soon exceeding it in these respects.

The fifteen *minimal facts* statements generated by this investigation (the "hypothesis," according to McCullagh) are supported by the present observable data. They also align well when the criteria for justifying historical descriptions are applied.

After AD 70 a future historical fulfillment for Malachi 3:1 became speculative at best. Even those who argue that a future temple will be constructed do not anticipate that (1) the Jewish nation will be dissolved, (2) the city of Jerusalem will be ravaged to the same extent as when Titus razed the it, and (3) the bulk of the remaining population will be deported. In addition, there were those among the first-century and later Jewish and Gentile populations who believed that God was judging the Jewish nation.[6]

One might object that *minimal fact* three implies that Jesus must be divine or metaphysically unique among humanity. This objection is moot, however. The *minimal facts* identified above report only the historical evidence—they do not pass judgment on metaphysical or ontological matters. The available historical documentation supports the uniqueness of Jesus, his birth in Bethlehem of Judea, and his Davidic decent.

In every remaining category for justifying historical descriptions, the elucidation offered by these *minimal facts* meet the seven criteria. These fifteen *minimal facts* do not require *ad hoc* speculation, the discarding of currently held beliefs, or the acceptance of novel theories. Historical descriptions are inherently less than certain, yet these *minimal facts* do not require the historian to abandon any aspect of the currently accepted body of historical knowledge. They are consistent with and emerge directly from an objective weighing of the available evidence.

The fifteen *minimal facts* presented above appear as a meager few when contrasted with the scope of the investigation. This effect is partially due to the strict hermeneutical criteria allowed by the study and the acceptance of many of the insights of historical critical scholarship. However, these fifteen are more than sufficient to establish the probability that the OT, on at least two occasions (2 Samuel 7:13, 16; Micah 5:2), directly prophecies regarding some aspect of Jesus' life and ministry. On three other occasions (Psalm 2:7; Psalm 16:10; Malachi 3:1), a distinct possibility exists that these texts directly prophesy regarding some aspect of Jesus' life and ministry. To reject this final conclusion, one must reject the available evidence.

Admittedly the available evidence is limited, partially because of the dearth of primary sources contemporary to the original writings of the OT; this fact contributes significantly to the exegetical difficulties identified

---

6. See Josephus and Whiston, "Antiquities of the Jews," 20.166; Charlesworth, *Old Testament Pseudepigrapha*, Sib Or 4.115–114.118; "Epistle of Barnabas," 4; Neusner, *Babylonian Talmud*, b. Yoma 39B.

throughout this work. The study of the OT would be bolstered substantially if additional extra-biblical primary sources from the pre-Maccabean and pre-exilic periods were available for comparison. Perhaps useful discoveries will be made in the future. Until then, the scholar must work with the available materials.

Recommendations for Future Research

While conducting research for the current work, several texts discussing the discipline of hermeneutics were consulted. The proper method for interpreting OT prophecy remains an open dialogue among scholars. The current work dealt with direct prophecies of Jesus in his role as Messiah. Other hermeneutical methods identified, but not employed include: Jewish Hermeneutics, *Sensus Plenior*, Canonical Approach, Typology, and Single Message.[7]

At this point, it is not certain that any one hermeneutical method will emerge as the most prevalent or most widely accepted. As a preliminary observation, based on the current study, it seems likely that a given prophecy, located in particular literary and historical context, may require a particular hermeneutical approach to arrive at the proper understanding of the author's intent.

This prediction should not, however, be understood as an endorsement of an *ad hoc* methodology designed to arrive at a predetermined conclusion. In light of the diverse contexts providing the OT prophetic material, further research on how OT messianic prophecies are alleged to have obtained fulfillment is warranted. It is possible that each of the methods listed above are appropriate to one or more OT prophetic contexts. Isolating specific prophecies and identifying, applying, and justifying the hermeneutical methodology employed for each prophecy would constitute a significant advancement in the study of messianic prophecy.

---

7. Trull, "Exegesis of Psalm 16:10a," 198. Cf. Gundry, *Use of the Old Testament*; Corley et al., *Biblical Hermeneutics*; Beale, *Handbook on the New Testament*; and Terry, *Biblical Apocalyptics*.

Bibliography

Achtemeier, Paul J., et al. *Introducing the New Testament: Its Literature and Theology.* Grand Rapids: Eerdmans, 2001.

Africanus, Julius. "The Epistle to Aristides." In *Fathers of the Third Century: Gregory Thaumaturgus, Dionysius the Great, Julius Africanus, Anatolius and Minor Writers, Methodius, Arnobius.* Vol. 6 of *The Ante-Nicene Fathers*, edited by Alexander Roberts, et al., 125–27. Buffalo, NY: Christian Literature, 1886.

Allen, Leslie C. "The Old Testament Background of (Προ-)Ὁρίζειν) in the New Testament." *New Testament Studies* 17.1 (1971) 104–8.

———. *Psalms 101–150.* Word Biblical Commentary 21. Rev. ed. Dallas, TX: Word, 2002.

Allison, Dale C. Jr. *The Testament of Abraham.* Commentaries on Jewish Literature. Berlin: de Gruyter, 2003.

Anderson, Bernhard W. *Contours of Old Testament Theology.* Minneapolis: Fortress, 2011.

Ankerberg, John, and John Weldon. *Handbook of Biblical Evidences.* Eugene, OR: Harvest House, 1997.

Archer, Gleason L. Jr. *Encyclopedia of Biblical Difficulties.* Grand Rapids: Zondervan, 1982.

Arndt, William, et al. *A Greek-English Lexicon of the New Testament and Other Early Christian Literature.* 3rd ed. Chicago: University of Chicago, 2000.

Attridge, Harold W., and Helmut Koester. *The Epistle to the Hebrews: A Commentary on the Epistle to the Hebrews.* Philadelphia: Fortress, 1989.

Augustine. "The City of God." In *St. Augustin's City of God and Christian Doctrine.* Vol. 2 of *A Select Library of the Nicene and Post-Nicene Fathers of the Christian Church*, edited by Philip Schaff, 9–511. Buffalo, NY: Christian Literature Company, 1887.

Barfield, Kenny. *The Prophet Motive.* Nashville: Gospel Advocate, 1995.

Barker, Kenneth L. *Micah, Nahum, Habakkuk, Zephaniah.* The New American Commentary 20. Nashville: Broadman & Holman, 1999.

Barnett, Paul. *Behind the Scenes of the New Testament.* Downers Grove, IL: InterVarsity, 1990.

Barton, John. *Isaiah 1–39.* London: T&T Clark, 1995.

Bateman, Herbert W. IV, ed. *Three Central Issues in Contemporary Dispensationalism.* Grand Rapids: Kregel, 1999.

Bateman, Herbert W. IV, et al. *Jesus the Messiah: Tracing the Promises, Expectations, and Coming of Israel's King*. Grand Rapids: Kregel, 2012.

Bauckham, Richard J. *Jesus and the Eyewitnesses: The Gospels as Eyewitness Testimony*. Grand Rapids: Eerdmans 2006.

———. *The Jewish World around the New Testament*. Grand Rapids: Baker Academic, 2010.

———. *Jude and the Relatives of Jesus in the Early Church*. London: T&T Clark, 2004.

———. "Nicodemus and the Gurion Family." *The Journal of Theological Studies* 47.1 (1996) 1–37.

Beale, Gregory K. *The Book of Revelation: A Commentary on the Greek Text*. Grand Rapids: Eerdmans, 1999.

———. *Handbook on the New Testament Use of the Old Testament: Exegesis and Interpretation*. Grand Rapids: Baker Academic, 2012.

———. *The Right Doctrine from the Wrong Texts?: Essays on the Use of the Old Testament in the New*. Grand Rapids: Baker Academic, 1994.

Beare, Francis Wright. *The Gospel According to Matthew: Translation, Introduction and Commentary*. Peabody, MA: Hendrickson, 1981.

Beegle, Dewey M. *Prophecy and Prediction*. Ann Arbor, MI: Pryor Pettengill, 1978.

Benzinger, I., et al. *Die Psalmen*. Leipzig, Germany: Mohr/Siebeck, 1899.

Bird, Michael F. *Are You the One Who Is to Come?: The Historical Jesus and the Messianic Question*. Grand Rapids: Baker Academic, 2009.

Bird, T. E. "The Psalms." In *A Catholic Commentary on Holy Scripture*, edited by Bernard Orchard and Edmund F. Sutcliffe, 442–73. Toronto: Thomas Nelson, 1953.

Blaising, Craig A., and Darrell L. Bock. *Progressive Dispensationalism*. Grand Rapids: Baker, 1993.

Bock, Darrell L. *Proclamation from Prophecy and Pattern: Lucan Old Testament Christology*. Journal for the Study of the New Testament Supplement Series 12. Sheffield, UK: Sheffield Academic, 1987.

———. *Studying the Historical Jesus*. Grand Rapids: Baker Academic, 2002.

Bockmuehl, Markus. *This Jesus: Martyr, Lord, Messiah*. London: T&T Clark, 2004.

Boda, Mark J. "Figuring the Future: The Prophets and Messiah." In *The Messiah in the Old and New Testaments*, edited by Stanley E. Porter, 35–74. Grand Rapids: Eerdmans, 2007.

Bovon, François, and Helmut Koester. *Luke 1: A Commentary on the Gospel of Luke 1:1–9:50*. Minneapolis: Fortress, 2002.

Brady, James. "Do Miracles Authenticate the Messiah?" *Evangelical Review of Theology* 13. 2 (1989) 101–9.

Brannan, Rick, and Israel Loken. *The Lexham Textual Notes on the Bible*. Bellingham, WA: Lexham, 2014.

Bratcher, Robert G., and William David Reyburn. *A Translator's Handbook on the Book of Psalms*. New York: United Bible Society, 1991.

Briggs, Charles Augustus. *Messianic Prophecy: The Prediction of the Fulfillment of the Redemption Through the Messiah*. Edinburgh: T&T Clark, 1886. Reprint. London: Forgotten Books, 2015.

Briggs, Charles Augustus, and Emilie Grace Briggs. *A Critical and Exegetical Commentary on the Book of Psalms*. International Critical Commentary on the Holy Scriptures of the Old and New Testament 1. Edinburgh: T&T Clark, 1906.

Brooke, George J., et al. *Qumran Cave 4, XVII. Discoveries in the Judan Desert 22.* Oxford: Clarendon, 1996.

Brown, Francis, et al. *Enhanced Brown-Driver-Briggs Hebrew and English Lexicon.* Oak Harbor, WA: Logos Research Systems, 2000.

Brown, Michael L. *Answering Jewish Objections to Jesus: General and Historical Objections.* 4 Vols. Grand Rapids: Baker, 2007.

Brown, Raymond E. *The Birth of the Messiah: A Commentary on the Infancy Narratives in the Gospels of Matthew and Luke.* Rev. ed. New York: Yale University Press, 1993.

Bruce, F. F. *Jesus and Christian Origins Outside the New Testament.* Grand Rapids: Eerdmans, 1974.

Bultmann, Rudolf Karl. *History of the Synoptic Tradition.* Translated by John Marsh. New York: Harper & Row, 1963.

Burger, Christoph. *Jesus Als Davidssohn: Aine Traditionsgeschichtliche Untersuchung.* Göttingen, Germany: Vandenhoeck & Ruprecht, 1970.

Callahan, Tim. *Bible Prophecy Failure or Fulfillment.* Altadena, CA: Millennium, 1997.

Campbell, Keith. "Matthew's Hermeneutic of Psalm 22:1 and Jer. 31:15." *Faith and Mission* 24. 3 (2006) 46–52.

Carlson, Stephen C. "The Accommodations of Joseph and Mary in Bethlehem: Κατάλυμα in Luke 2.7." *New Testament Studies* 56.3 (2010) 326–42.

Carroll, Robert P. *When Prophecy Failed.* New York: Seabury, 1979.

Carson, D. A. *The Gospel According to John.* Grand Rapids: InterVarsity, 1991.

Carter, Warren. *Matthew and the Margins: A Sociopolitical and Religious Reading.* Maryknoll, NY: Orbis, 2000.

Cathcart, Kevin, et al., eds. *The Isaiah Targum.* Translated by Bruce D. Chilton. The Aramaic Bible 11. Collegeville, MN: Liturgical, 1990.

Chadwick, Henry. *Lessing's Theological Writings.* Stanford, CA: Standford University Press, 1957.

Charles, Robert Henry, ed. *Commentary on the Pseudepigrapha of the Old Testament.* Vol. 2. Oxford: Clarendon, 1913.

———. *A Critical History of the Doctrine of a Future Life: In Israel, in Judaism, and in Christianity.* London: Adam and Charles Black, 1899.

———, ed. *Pseudepigrapha of the Old Testament.* Vol. 2. Bellingham, WA: Logos Research Systems, 2004.

Charlesworth, James H., ed. *The Messiah: Developments in Earliest Judaism and Christianity.* Minneapolis: Fortress, 1992.

———. *Resurrection: The Origin and Future of a Biblical Doctrine.* New York: T&T Clark, 2006.

Chevallier, Max-Alain. *L'esprit Et Le Messie Dans Le Bas-Judaïsme Et Le Nouveau Testament.* Études D'histoire Et De Philosophie Religieuses 49. Paris: Paris es Universitaires de France, 1958.

Chisholm, Robert B. Jr. "Does God 'Change His Mind'?" *Bibliotheca Sacra* 152.4 (1995) 387–89.

———. "When Prophecy Appears to Fail, Check Your Hermeneutic." *Journal of the Evangelical Theological Society* 53.3 (2010) 561–77.

Clark, David J., and Howard Hatton. *A Handbook on Malachi.* Ubs Handbook Series. New York: United Bible Society, 2002.

Clines, David J. A. *Word Biblical Commentary: Job 1–20*. Word Biblical Commentary 17. Dallas, TX: Word, 2002.
Cohen, A. *The Psalms*. London: Soncino, 1958.
Cole, Robert Luther. "An Integrated Reading of Psalms 1 and 2." *Journal for the Study of the Old Testament* 26.4 (2002) 75–88.
Collins, Adela Yarbro, and Harold W. Attridge. *Mark: A Commentary on the Gospel of Mark*. Minneapolis: Fortress, 2007.
Collins, Adela Yarbro, and John J. Collins. *King and Messiah as the Son of God*. Grand Rapids: Eerdmans, 2008.
Collins, John J. *The Bible after Babel: Historical Criticism in a Postmodern Age*. Grand Rapids: Eerdmans, 2005.
———. *The Scepter and the Star*. Grand Rapids: Eerdmans, 2010.
Conzelmann, Hans. *Acts of the Apostles: A Commentary on the Acts of the Apostles*. Edited by Eldon Jay Epp and Christopher R. Matthews. Translated by James Limburg, et al. Hermeneia—A Critical and Historical Commentary on the Bible. Philadelphia: Fortress, 1987.
Copan, Paul. *"True for You but Not for Me."* Minneapolis: Bethany House, 2009.
Coppes, Leonard J. "1652 עָנָה." In *Theological Workbook of the Old Testament*, edited by Robert Laird Harris, et al. Chicago: Moody, 1999.
Corley, Bruce, et al. *Biblical Hermeneutics: A Comprehensive Introduction to Interpreting Scripture*. 2nd ed. Nashville: Broadman & Holman, 2002.
Craig, William Lane. *Reasonable Faith: Christian Truth and Apologetics*. Rev. ed. Wheaton, IL: Crossway, 1994.
Craig, William Lane, et al. *Jesus' Resurrection: Fact or Figment? A Debate between William Lane Craig & Gerd LüDemann*. Downers Grove, IL: InterVarsity, 2000.
Craigie, Peter C. *Word Biblical Commentary: Psalms 1–50*. Word Biblical Commentary 19. Dallas, TX: Word, 2002.
Creach, Jerome F. D. "Like a Tree Planted by the Temple Stream: The Portrait of the Righteous in Psalm 1:3." *The Catholic Biblical Quarterly* 61.1 (1999) 34–46.
Cullmann, Oscar. *The Christology of the New Testament*. Translated by Shirley C. Guthrie and Charles A. M. Hall. Rev. ed. Philadelphia: Westminster, 1963.
Cyprian. "Three Books of Testimonies against the Jews." In *Fathers of the Third Century: Hippolytus, Cyprian, Novatian, Appendix*. Vol. 5 of *The Ante-Nicene Fathers*, edited by Alexander Roberts, et al. Buffalo, NY: Christian Literature Company, 1886.
Cyril of Jerusalem. *The Catechetical Lectures of S. Cyril, Archbishop of Jerusalem*. Translated by R. W. Church and Edwin Hamilton Gifford. Vol. 7 of *A Select Library of the Nicene and Post-Nicene Fathers of the Christian Church*, edited by Philip Schaff and Henry Wace. New York, NY: Christian Literature Company, 1894.
Dagg, John L. *The Evidences of Christianity*. Macon, GA: J. W. Burke, 1869.
Dahl, Nils Alstrup. *Studies in Paul*. Eugene, OR: Wipf and Stock, 2002.
Dahood, Mitchell Joseph. *Psalms 1–50: Introduction, Translation, and Notes*. Anchor Yale Bible 16. New Haven, CT: Yale University Press, 2008.
———. "Root 'zb Ii in Job." *Journal of Biblical Literature* 78.4 (1959) 303–9.
David, Martin. *Die Adoption Im Altbabylonischen Recht*. Leipziger Rechtswissen-Schaftliche Studien. Leipzig, Germany: T. Weicher, 1927.
Davies, W. C., and Dale C. Allison, Jr. *A Critial and Exegetical Commentary on the Gospel According to Saint Matthew*. Vol. 1. Edinburgh: T&T Clark, 1988.
Day, John. *Psalms*. London: T&T Clark, 1999.

Day, John, ed. *King and Messiah in Israel and the Ancient near East*. New York, NY: Bloomsbury, 2013.

Deissmann, Adolf, and Lionel Richard Mortimer Strachan. *Light from the Ancient East: The New Testament Illustrated by Recently Discovered Texts of the Graeco-Roman World*. London: Hodder & Stoughton, 1910.

Delitzsch, Franz. *Messianic Prophecies in Historical Succession*. Translated by Samuel Ives Curtiss. Edinburgh: T&T Clark, 1891.

Dines, Jennifer M., and Michael A. Knibb. *The Septuagint*. London: T&T Clark, 2004.

Driver, Samuel R. *A Critical and Exegetical Commentary on Deuteronomy*. 3rd ed. International and Critical Commentary. Edinburgh: T&T Clark, 1902.

Driver, Samuel R., and Walter F. Adeney, eds. *The Minor Prophets: Nahum, Habakkuk, Zephaniah, Haggai, Zechariah, and Malachi*. New York: Henry Frowde; T. C. & E. C. Jack, 1906.

Duling, Dennis C. "Promises to David and Their Entrance into Christianity: Nailing Down a Likely Hypothesis." *New Testament Studies* 20.1 (1973) 55–77.

———. "The Therapeutic Son of David: An Element in Matthew's Christological Apologetic." *New Testament Studies* 24.3 (1978) 394–410.

Dunn, James D. G. *Beginning from Jerusalem: Christianity in the Making*. Grand Rapids: Eerdmans, 2009.

———. *Did the First Christians Worship Jesus?: The New Testament Evidence*. London: Westminster John Knox, 2010.

Dupont, Jacques. *The Salvation of the Gentiles*. Translated by John R. Keating. New York: Paulist, 1979.

Eaton, J. H. *Kingship and the Psalms*. Studies in Biblical Theology. Naperville, IL: Allec R. Allenson, 1975.

Edersheim, Alfred. *The Life and Times of Jesus the Messiah*. Vol. 2. Bellingham, WA: Logos Research Systems, 1896.

———. *The Temple: Its Ministry and Services as They Were at the Time of Jesus Christ*. London: James Clarke & Co., 1959.

Edghill, Ernest Arthur, and Herbert E. Ryle. *An Inquiry into the Evidential Value of Prophecy*. Kessinger Legacy Reprints, 2010.

Ehrman, Bart D. *Did Jesus Exist:The Historical Argument for Jesus of Nazareth*. New York: Harper Collins, 2012.

———. *Jesus Apocalyptic Prophet of the New Millennium*. New York: Oxford University Press, 1999.

———. *Jesus Interrupted: Revealing the Hidden Contradictions in the Bible (and Why We Don't Know About Them)*. New York: Harper One, 2009.

Eichrodt, Walther. *Theology of the Old Testament*. Translated by J. A. Baker. The Old Testament Library 2. Philadelphia: Westminster, 1967.

"Epistle of Barnabas." In *The Apostolic Fathers with Justin Martyr and Irenaeus*. Vol. 1 of *The Ante-Nicene Fathers*, edited by Alexander Roberts, et al., 133–50. Buffalo, NY: Christian Literature Company, 1885.

Eusebius. "Ecclesiastical History, Books 1–5." Edited and translated by Roy Joseph Deferrari. The Fathers of the Church 19. Washington DC: Catholic University of America Press, 1953.

Evans, Craig A. "The Aramaic Psalmer and the New Testament: Praising the Lord in History and Prophecy." In *From Prophecy to Testament*, edited by Craig A. Evan, 44–91. Peabody, MA: Hendrickson, 2004.

Eve, Eric. *The Jewish Context of Jesus' Miracles*. Journal for the Study of the New Testament Supplement Series 231. London: Sheffield Academic, 2002.

Fairbairn, Patrick. *The Typology of Scripture*. Kindle edition: Titus, 2013.

Fales, Evan. "Successful Defense?: A Review of in Defense of Miracles." *Philosophia Christi* 3.1 (2001) 7–35.

Falls, Thomas B., and Justin Martyr. *The First Apology, the Second Apology, Dialogue with Trypho, Exhortation to the Greeks, Discourse to the Greeks, the Monarchy or the Rule of God*. Vol. 6. Washington DC: Catholic University of America Press, 1948.

Feinberg, Charles Lee. "The Dating of the Psalms." *Bibliotheca Sacra* 104 (1947) 426–40.

Ferguson, Paul. *Ezra, Theology Of*. Evangelical Dictionary of Biblical Theology. Edited by Walter A. Elwell. Grand Rapids: Baker 1996.

Fitzmyer, Joseph A. "David, 'Being Therefore a Prophet' (Acts 2:30)." *The Catholic Biblical Quarterly* 34.3 (1972) 332–39.

———. *The One Who Is to Come*. Grand Rapids: Eerdmans, 2007.

Flavius, Josephus, and William Whiston. "Antiquities of the Jews." In *The Works of Josephus: Complete and Unabridged*. Peabody, MA: Hendrickson, 1987.

Flint, Peter W. "Dead Sea Scrolls Psalms." In *The Lexham Bible Dictionary*, edited by John D. Barry, et al. Bellingham, WA: Lexham, 2015.

Foreman, Benjamin A. "Matthew's Birth Narrative." In *Lexham Geographic Commentary on the Gospels*, edited by Barry J. Beitzel and Kristopher A. Lyle. Electronic edition. Bellingham, WA: Lexham, 2016.

France, R. T. *The Gospel of Mark: A Commentary on the Greek Text*. Grand Rapids: Eerdmans, 2002.

———. *The Gospel of Matthew*. The New International Commentary on the New Testament. Grand Rapids: Eerdmans, 2007.

———. "The Infancy Narratives of Mathew." In vol. 2 of *Gospel Perspectives: Studies in History and Traditon in the Four Gospels*, edited by R. T. France and David Wenham, 239-66. Eugene, OR: Wipf and Stock, 1981.

Fruchtenbaum, Arnold G. *Messianic Christology: A Study of Old Testament Prophecy Concerning the First Coming of the Messiah*. Tustin, CA: Ariel Ministries, 1998.

Funk, Robert W., and Roy W. Hoover. *The Five Gospels: The Search for the Authentic Words of Jesus*. New York: Harper Collins, 1997.

Garcia Martinez, Florentino, and Eibert J. C. Tigchelaar. *The Dead Sea Scrolls: Study Edition (Transcriptions)*. Leiden: Brill, 1997.

———. *The Dead Sea Scrolls Study Edition (Translations)*. Leiden: Brill, 1997.

Gauch, Hugh G. Jr. "Best Practices for Prophecy Arguments." *Philosophia Christi* 16.2 (2014) 255–82.

Gauch, Hugh G. Jr., et al. "Public Theology and Scientific Method: Formulating Reasons That Count across Worldviews." *Philosophia Christi* 4.1 (2002) 45–88.

Geisler, Norman L. *Christian Apologetics*. Grand Rapids: Baker Book House, 1976.

Geisler, Norman L., and Paul D. Feinberg. *Introduction to Philosophy: A Christian Perspective*. Grand Rapids: Baker, 1980.

Geisler, Norman L., and Thomas A. Howe. *When Critics Ask: A Popular Handbook on Bible Difficulties*. Wheaton, IL: Victor, 1992.

Gillingham, Sue E. "The Messiah in the Psalms." In *King and Messiah in Israel and the Ancient near East Proceedings of the Oxford Old Testament Seminar*, edited by John Day, 209–37. Sheffield, UK: Sheffield Academic, 1998.

Gillman, Neil. "Death and the Afterlife, Judaic Doctrines of." In *Encyclopedia of Judaism*, edited by Jacob Neusner, et al., vol. 1., 196–212. Leiden: Brill, 2000.

Ginzberg, Louis, et al. *Legends of the Jews*. 2nd ed. Philadelphia: Jewish Publication Society, 2003.

Goldingay, John. *Psalms 1–41*. Baker Commentary on the Old Testament, edited by Tremper Longman III. Grand Rapids: Baker Academic, 2006.

Gordis, Robert. "'Begotten' Messiah in the Qumran Scrolls." *Vetus Testamentum* 7.2 (1957) 191–94.

"Gospel of the Nativity of Mary." In *Fathers of the Third and Fourth Centuries: The Twelve Patriarchs, Excerpts and Epistles, the Clementina, Apocrypha, Decretals, Memoirs of Edessa and Syriac Documents, Remains of the First Ages*. Vol. 8 of *Ante-Nicene Fathers*, edited by Alexander Roberts, et al. Buffalo, NY: Christian Literature Company, 1886.

Got Questions Ministries. *Got Questions? Bible Questions Answered*. Bellingham, WA: Logos Research Systems, 2010.

Green, Joel B. *The Theology of the Gospel of Luke*. Cambridge: Cambridge University Press, 1995.

Gundry, Robert H. *The Use of the Old Testament in St. Matthew's Gospel with Special Reference to the Messianic Hope*. Leiden: Brill, 1975.

Gunkel, Hermann. *Genesis*. Translated by Mark E. Biddle. Macon, GA: Mercer University Press, 1997.

———. *Introduction to the Psalms: The Genres of Religious Lyric of Israel*. Translated by James D. Nogalski. Macon, GA: Mercer University Press, 1998.

Gunn, George A. "Psalm 2 and the Reign of the Messiah." *Bibliotheca Sacra* 169.676 (2012) 427–42.

Habermas, Gary R. "Evidentialist Apologetics." In *Five Views on Apologetics*, edited by Steven B. Cowan, 91–121. Grand Rapids: Zondervan, 2000.

———. *The Historical Jesus: Ancient Evidence for the Life of Christ*. Joplin, MO: College, 2009.

———. "The Minimal Facts Approach to the Resurrection of Jesus: The Role of Methodology as a Crucial Component in Establishing Historicity." *Southeastern Theological Review* 3.1 (2012) 15–26.

———. *The Risen Jesus and Future Hope*. New York: Rowman and Littlefield, 2003.

Hanson, Paul D. *The Dawn of Apocalyptic: The Historical and Sociological Roots of Jewish Apocalyptic Eschatology*. Philadelphia: Fortress, 1979.

Harris, Robert Laird. "2343 שָׁוָה." In *Theological Wordbook of the Old Testament*, edited by Robert Laird Harris, et al. Chicago: Moody, 1999.

Harrison, Peter. "Prophecy, Early Modern Apologetics, and Hume's Argument against Miracles." *Journal of the History of Ideas* 60.2 (1999) 241–56.

Hays, J. Daniel. *The Message of the Prophets*. Edited by Tremper Longman III. Grand Rapids: Zondervan, 2010.

Heinemann, Mark H. "An Exposition of Psalm 22." *Bibliotheca Sacra* 147.587 (1990) 286–308.

Heirs, Richard H. "Purification of the Temple: Preparation for the Kingdom of God." *Journal of Biblical Literature* 90.1 (1971) 82–90.

Heiser, Michael S., and Vincent M. Setterholm. *Glossary of Morpho-Syntactic Database Terminology*. Bellingham, WA: Lexham, 2013.

Hemer, Colin J. *The Book of Acts in the Hellenistic History*. Edited by Conrad H. Gemph. Winona Lake, IN: Eisenbrauns, 1990.

———. "Luke the Historian." *Bulletin of the John Rylands University Library of Manchester* 60.1 (1977) 28–51.

Hengel, Martin. *The Zealots: Investigations into the Jewish Freedom Movement in the Period from Herod I until A.D. 70*. Edinburgh: T&T Clark, 1989.

Hengstenberg, E. W. *Christology of the Old Testament and a Commentary on the Messianic Predicitons*. Vol. 1. Translated by Theodore Meyer. Kindle edition: Public Domain, 2010.

———. *Commentary on the Psalms*. Vol. 1. Edinburgh: T&T Clark, 1869.

Henry, Matthew. *Matthew Henry's Commentary on the Whole Bible: Complete and Unabridged in One Volume*. Peabody, MA: Hendrickson, 1994.

Henten, Jan Willhem Van. "The Hasmonean Period." In *Redemption and Resistence: The Messianic Hopes of Jews and Christians in Antiquity*, edited by Markus Bockmuehl and James Carleton Paget. New York: T&T Clark, 2007.

Hill, Andrew E. *Malachi: A New Translation with Introduction and Commentary*. Vol. 25. The Anchor Yale Bible. New Haven, CT: Yale University Press, 2008.

Hillers, Delbert R. *Micah: A Commentary on the Book of the Prophet Micah*. Edited by Paul D. Hanson and Loren R. Fisher. Philadelphia: Fortress, 1984.

Hinckley, Mitchell G., John Merlin Powis, and Julius A. Brewer. "A Critical and Exegetical Commentary on Haggai, Zechariah, Malachi, and Jonah." In *International Critical and Exegetical Commentary on the Holy Scriptures of the Old and New Testament*, edited by Samuel Driver Rolles, et al., 1–88. New York: Scribner and Sons, 1912.

———. "A Critical and Exegetical Commentary on Micah, Zephaniah, Nahum, Habakkuk, Obadiah and Joel." In *International Critical and Exegetical Commentary on the Holy Scriptures of the Old and New Testament*, edited by Samuel Driver Rollses, et al., 5–156. New York: Scribner and Sons, 1912.

Hindson, Ed. "Messianic Prophecy." In *The Popular Encyclopedia of Bible Prophecy*, edited by Tim LaHaye and Ed Hindson, 217-23. Eugene, OR: Harvest House, 2004.

Hirch, Emil G. "Shemoneh Esreh." In *The Jewish Encyclopedia: A Descriptive Record of the History, Religion, Literature, and Customs of the Jewish People from the Earliest Times to the Present Day*. Vol. 11, edited by Isidore Singer, 270–82. New York: Funk & Wagnalls, 1901.

"History of Joseph the Carpenter or Death of Joseph." In *The Apocryphal New Testament: Being the Apocryphal Gospels, Acts, Epistles, and Apocalypses*, edited by Montague Rhodes James, 84–86. Oxford: Clarendon, 1924.

Hitchcock, Roswell D. and Francis Brown, eds. *The Teaching of the Twelve Apostles: Greek*. Translated by Roswell D Hitchcock and Francis Brown. London: John C. Nimmo, 1885.

Holladay, William Lee. *Jeremiah 1: A Commentary on the Book of the Prophet Jeremiah, Chapters 1-25*. Hermeneia—A Critical and Historical Commentary on the Bible, edited by Paul D. Hanson. Philadelphia: Fortress, 1986.

Holmes, Michael William. *The Apostolic Fathers: Greek Texts and English Translations*. Updated ed. Grand Rapids: Baker, 1999.

Horbury, William. *Messianism among Jews and Christians: Twelve Biblical and Historical Studies*. London: T&T Clark, 2003.

Hossfeld, Frank-Lothar, and Erich Zenger. *Psalms 3: A Commentary on Psalms 101–150*. Translated by Linda M. Maloney. Hermeneia—A Critical and Historical Commentary on the Bible, edited by Klaus Baltzer. Minneapolis: Fortress, 2011.

Huckel, Tom. *The Rabbinic Messiah*. Philadelphia: Hananeel House, 1998.

Huey, F. B. "An Exposition of Malachi." *Southwestern Journal of Theology* 30.1 (1987) 12–21.

Hume, David. *An Enquiry Concerning Human Understanding and Selections from a Treatise of Human Nature*. Chicago: Open Court, 1921.

Hurtado, Larry W. *How on Earth Did Jesus Become God?* Grand Rapids: Eerdmans, 2005.

Irenaeus of Lyons. "Irenæus against Heresies." In *The Apostolic Fathers with Justin Martyr and Irenaeus*. Vol. 1 of *Ante-Nicene Fathers*, edited by Alexander Roberts, et al., 315–67. Buffalo, NY: Christian Literature Company, 1885.

James, Montague Rhodes, ed. *Apocryphal New Testament: Being the Apocryphal Gospels, Acts, Epistles, and Apocalypses*. Oxford: Clarendon, 1924.

———. "Protevangelium of James." In *Apocryphal New Testament: Being the Apocryphal Gospels, Acts, Epistles, and Apocalypses*, 38–49. Oxford: Clarendon, 1924

Jamieson, Robert, et al. *Commentary Critical and Explanatory on the Whole Bible*. Oak Harbor, WA: Logos Research Systems, 1997.

Jenson, Philip P. "Models of Prophetic Prediction and Matthew's Quotation of Micah 5:2." In *The Lord's Anointed Interpretation of Old Testament Messianic Texts*, edited by Philip E. Satterthwaite, et al. Grand Rapids: Baker, 1995.

Jeremias, J. "Μωυσῆς." In *Theological Dictionary of the New Testament*. Vol. 4, edited by Gerhard Kittel, et al., 622–25. Grand Rapids: Eerdmans, 1964.

Johnson, Marshall D. *The Purpose of the Biblical Genealogies with Special Reference to the Genealogies of Jesus*. 2nd ed. Eugene, OR: Wipf and Stock, 1969.

Johnston, Gordon H. "Messianic Trajectories in Amos, Hosea, and Micah." In *Jesus the Messiah: Tracing the Promises, Expectations, and Coming of Israel's King*, edited by Herbert W. Bateman IV, et al., 107–32. Grand Rapids: Kregel Academic, 2012.

———. "Messianic Trajectories in Genesis and Numbers." In *Jesus the Messiah: Tracing the Promises, Expectations, and Coming of Israel's King*, edited by Herbert W. Bateman IV, et al., 37–58. Grand Rapids: Kregel Academic, 2012.

———. "Messianic Trajectories in God's Covenant Promise to David." In *Jesus the Messiah: Tracing the Promises, Expectations, and Coming of Israel's King*, edited by Herbert W. Bateman IV, et al., 59–74. Grand Rapids: Kregel Academic, 2012.

———. "Messianic Trajectories in Psalm 2." In *Jesus the Messiah: Tracing the Promises, Expectations, and Coming of Israel's King*, edited by Herbert W. Bateman IV, et al., 74–83. Grand Rapids: Kregel Academic, 2012.

Johnston, Philip S. "Left in Hell? Psalm 16, Sheol, and the Holy One." In *The Lord's Anointed Interpretation of Old Testament Messianic Texts*, edited by Philip E. Satterthwaite, et al. Grand Rapids: Baker, 1995.

Josephus, Flavius, and William Whiston. "Antiquities of the Jews." In *The Works of Josephus: Complete and Unabridged*. Peabody, MA: Hendrickson, 1987.

Kaiser, Walter C. Jr. "Psalm 72: An Historical and Messianic Current Example Antiochen Hermeneutical *Theoria*." *Journal of the Evangelical Theological Society* 52.2 (2009) 257–70.

Kaiser, Walter C. Jr. *The Messiah in the Old Testament*. Grand Rapids: Zondervan, 1995.

Kaiser, Walter C. Jr., et al. *Three Views on the New Testament Use of the Old Testament.* Zondervan Counterpoints Collection. Grand Rapids: Zondervan, 2008.

Kaiser, Walter C., Jr. and Moises Silva, eds. *Introduction to Biblical Hermeneutics: The Search for Meaning.* Grand Rapids: Zondervan, 2007.

Kaufmann, Yeḥezkel. "The Messianic Idea: The Real and the Hidden Son-of-David." *Jewish Bible Quarterly* 22.3 (1994) 141–50.

Kee, H. C. "The Testament of the Twelve Patriarchs." In *The Old Testament Pseudepigrapha.* Vol. 1, edited by James H. Charlesworth, 775–828. New York: Yale University Press, 1983.

Keener, Craig S. *Introduction and 1:1–2:47.* Vol. 1 of *Acts: An Exegetical Commentary.* Grand Rapids: Baker, 2012.

———. *Miracles: The Credibility of the New Testament Accounts.* Vol. 1. Grand Rapids: Baker Academic, 2011.

Keil, Carl Friedrich, and Franz Delitzsch. *Commentary on the Old Testament.* Peabody, MA: Hendrickson, 1996.

Keith, Alexander. *Evidence of the Truth of the Christian Religion Derived from the Literal Fulfillment of Prophecy; Particularly as Illustrated by the History of the Jews, and by the Discoveries of Recent Travellers.* Classic Reprint Series. New York: Forgotton, 2012.

Kenyon, F. G. "The Berlin Papyri." *Classical Review* 7.3 (1893) 108–111.

Kepple, Robert J. "Hope of Israel, the Resurrection of the Dead, and Jesus: A Study of Their Relationship in Acts." *Journal of the Evangelical Theological Society* 20.3 (1977) 231–41.

Kingsbury, Jack Dean. *The Christology of Mark's Gospel.* Philadelphia: Fortress, 1983.

Klayman, Elliot, ed. *What the Rabbis Know About Messiah.* Columbus, OH: Messianic Publishing Company, 2002.

Klein, William W., et al. *Introduction to Biblical Interpretation.* Nashville: Thomas Nelson, 2004.

Kligerman, Aaron Judah. *Messianic Prophecy in the Old Testament.* Grand Rapids: Zondervan, 1957.

Klippenstein, Rachel Stark. *The Lexham Bible Dictionary.* Bellingham, WA: Lexham, 2015.

Koehler, Ludwig, et al. *The Hebrew and Aramaic Lexicon of the Old Testament.* Leiden: Brill, 1999.

Kohler, Kaufmann. "Saul of Tarsus." In *The Jewish Encyclopedia: A Descriptive Record of the History, Religion, Literature, and Customs of the Jewish People from the Earliest Times to the Present Day.* Vol. 11, edited by Isidore Singer, 79–87. New York: Funk & Wagnalls, 1906.

Kokkinos, N. "The Titulus Tiburtinus, Symes's Piso, Sentius Saturninus and the Provice of Syria." *Scripta Judaica Cracoviensia* 10 (2012) 37–69.

Köstenberger, Andreas J. *John.* Baker Exegetical Commentary on the New Testament. Grand Rapids: Baker Academic, 2004.

Kraus, Hans-Joachim. *Psalms 1–59.* A Continental Commentary. Minneapolis: Fortress, 1993.

———. *Psalms 60–150.* A Continental Commentary. Minneapolis: Fortress, 1993.

Krentz, Edgar. *The Historical-Critical Method.* Philadelphia: Fortress, 1975.

Kuenen, Abraham. *The Prophets and Prophecy in Israel: A Historical Critical Inquiry.* Kindle edition: Amazon Digital Services, 2014.

La Sor, William Sanford, et al. *Old Testament Survey: The Message, Form, and Background of the Old Testament*. 2nd ed. Grand Rapids: Eerdmans, 1996.
Ladd, George E. *A Theology of the New Testament*. Grand Rapids: Eerdmans, 1993.
LaHaye, Tim, and Ed Hindson, eds. *The Popular Bible Prophecy Commentary*. Eugene, OR: Harvest House, 2006.
Lane, William L. *The Gospel of Mark*. The New International Commentary on the New Testament. Grand Rapids: Eerdmans, 1974.
Lange, Harvey D. "The Relationship of Psalm 22 and the Passion Narratives." *Concordia Theological Monthly* 43.9 (1972) 610–21.
Lange, John Peter, et al. *Psalms*. A Commentary on the Holy Scriptures. Bellingham, WA: Logos Research Systems, 2008.
Lanier, Gregory R. "The Rejected Stone in the Parable of the Wicked Tenants: Defending the Authenticity of Jesus' Quotation of Ps 118:22." *Journal of the Evangelical Theological Society* 56.4 (2013) 733–51.
Levin, Yigal. "Jesus, 'Son of God' and 'Son of David': The 'Adoption' of Jesus into the Davidic Line." *Journal for the Study of the New Testament* 28.4 (2006) 415–42.
Licona, Michael R. *The Resurrection of Jesus: A New Historiographical Approach*. Downers Grove, IL: InterVarsity, 2010.
Lim, Timothy H., et al. *The Dead Sea Scrolls in Their Historical Context*. London: T&T Clark, 2004.
Lipson, Irene. *Blessing the King of the Universe: Transforming Your Life through the Practice of Biblical Praise*. Baltimore, MD: Messianic Jewish Publishers, 2004.
Locke, John. *The Reasonableness of Christianity, as Delivered in the Scriptures*. London: Stirling and Slade, 1824.
Lövestam, Evald. *Son and Saviour: A Study of Acts 13, 32–37. With Appendix: 'Son of God' in the Synoptic Gospels*. Translated by Michael J. Petry. Copenhagen: G. W. K. Gleerup, 1961.
Lowery, David K. "Review of Jesus, 'Son of God' and 'Son of David': The 'Adoption' of Jesus into the Davidic Line by Yigal Levin." *Bibliotheca Sacra* 164 (2007) 101–2.
Lunde, Jonathan. "An Introduction to Central Questions in the New Testament Use of the Old Testament." In *Three Views on the New Testament Use of the Old Testament*, 10–35. Zondervan Counterpoints Series. Grand Rapids: Zondervan, 2008.
Lust, Johan, et al. *A Greek-English Lexicon of the Septuagint*. Rev. ed. Stuttgart, Germany: Deutsche Bibelgesellschaft, 2003.
Luz, Ulrich. *Matthew 1–7: A Commentary on Matthew 1–7*. Hermeneia—A Critical and Historical Commentary on the Bible. Minneapolis: Fortress, 2007.
———. *Matthew 21–28: A Commentary on Matthew 21–28*. Hermeneia—A Critical and Historical Commentary on the Bible. Minneapolis: Fortress, 2005.
MacArthur, J., and R. Mayhue. *Biblical Doctrine: A Systematic Summary of Bible Truth*. Crossway, 2017.
Mach, R. *Der Zaddik in the Talmud Und Midrasch*. Leiden: Brill, 1957.
Maier, Paul L. "The Infant Massacre—History or Myth?" *Bible and Spade* 6.4 (1977) 97–104.
Maimonides, Moses. *Maimonides Commentary on the Mishnah Tractate Sanhedrin*. Translated by Fred Rosner. New York: Sepher-Hermon, 1981.
Malone, Andrew S. "Is the Messiah Announced in Malachi 3:1?" *Tyndale Bulletin* 57.2 (2006) 215–28.

Marshall, I. Howard. *Luke: Historian and Theologian*. Milton Keynes, UK: Paternoster, 1970.
Martyr, Justin. "Dialogue of Justin with Trypho, a Jew." In *The Apostolic Fathers with Justin Martyr and Irenaeus*. Vol. 1 of *The Ante-Nicene Fathers*, edited by Alexander Roberts, et al., 194–270. Buffalo, NY: Christian Literature Company, 1885.
———. "The First Apology of Justin." In *The Apostolic Fathers with Justin Martyr and Irenaeus*, Vol. 1 of *The Ante-Nicene Fathers*, edited by Alexander Roberts, et al., 163–86. Buffalo, NY: Christian Literature Company, 1885.
Mayhew, Eugene J. "Current Trends in Messianology." *Michigan Theological Journal* 1.1 (1990) 35.
Mazar, Amihai. *Archaeology of the Land of the Bible 10,000–586 B.C.E.* New Haven, CT: Yale University Press, 1990.
McConville, Gordon J. "Micah." In *Dictionary of Old Testament Prophets*, edited by Mark J. Boda and Gordon J. McConville, 544–54. Downers Grove, IL: Intervarsity, 2012.
McCown, Chester Charlton. *The Promise of His Coming: A Historical Interpretation and Revaluation of the Idea of the Second Advent*. New York: The Macmillan Company, 1921.
McCullagh, C. Behan. *Justifying Historical Descriptions*. Cambridge, UK: Cambridge University Press, 1984.
Meier, John P. *A Marginal Jew: Rethinking the Historical Jesus: The Roots of the Problem and the Person*. Vol. 1. New York: Doubleday, 1991.
Meldau, Fred John. *The Prophets Still Speak: Messiah in Both Testaments*. Bellmawr, NJ: Friends of Israel Gospel Ministry, 1988.
Merrill, Eugene H. "שָׁחַת (Šaḥat)." In *New International Dictionary of Old Testament Theology & Exegesis*. Vol. 4, edited by William VanGemeren, 93–94. Grand Rapids: Zondervan, 1997.
Meyers, Caroll L. and Eric M. Meyers. *Haggia, Zechariah 1–8*. The Anchor Yale Bible 25. New Haven, CT: Yale University Press, 2010.
Mitchell, David C. *Message of the Psalter: An Eschatological Programme in the Book of Psalms*. Journal for the Study of the Old Testament. Sheffield, UK: Sheffield Academic, 1997.
Moehring, Horst, R. "The Census in Luke as an Apologetic Device." In *Studies in the New Testament and Early Christian Literature: Essays in Honor of Allen P. Wikgren*, edited by David Edward Aune, 144–60. Novum Testamentum Supplements 33. Leiden: Brill, 1972.
Moreland, J. P., and William Lane Craig. *Philosophical Foundations for a Christian Worldview*. Downers Grove, IL: InterVarsity, 2003.
Morey, Robert A. *Death and the Afterlife*. Minneapolis: Bethany House, 1984.
Morris, Leon. *The Gospel According to John*. The New International Commentary on the New Testament. Grand Rapids: Eerdmans, 1995.
Mowinckel, Sigmund. *He That Cometh: The Messiah Concept in the Old Testament and Later Judaism*. Translated by G. W. Anderson. Grand Rapids: Eerdmans, 2005.
———. *The Psalms in Israel's Worship*. Vol. 2. Biblical Resource Series. Grand Rapids: Eerdmans, 2004.
Murphy, Roland E. "ŠAḥat in the Qumran Literature." *Biblica* 39.1 (1958) 61–66.
Myers, Allen C. *The Eerdmans Bible Dictionary*. Grand Rapids: Eerdmans, 1987.

Neusner, Jacob, ed. *The Babylonian Talmud: A Translation and Commentary*. 22 vols. Peabody, MA: Hendrickson, 2011.

———, ed. *Parashiyyot 34 through 67 on Genesis 8:15–28:9.* Genesis Rabbah: The Judaic Commentary to the Book of Genesis. Atlanta, GA: Scholars, 1985.

———, ed. *Parashiyyot 68 through 100 on Genesis 28:10–50:26.* Genesis Rabbah: The Judaic Commentary to the Book of Genesis. Atlanta, GA: Scholars, 1985.

———, ed. *The Jerusalem Talmud: A Translation and Commentary*. Peabody, MA: Hendrickson, 2008.

Neusner, Jacob, et al., eds. *Judaism and Their Messiahs at the Turn of the Christian Era*. New York: Cambridge University Press, 1987.

———. "Messiah in Rabbinic Judaism." In *Encyclopedia of Judaism*, 550–883. Leiden: Brill, 2000.

Newman, Robert C. "Fulfilled Prophecy as Miracle." In *In Defense of Miracles a Comprehensive Case for God's Action in History*, edited by Douglas Geivett and Gary R. Habermas, 214–25. Downers Grove, IL: InterVarsity, 1997.

———. *Jesus: The Testimony of Prophecy and History*. Kindle edition. Biblical Seminary Hatfield, PA: Interdiciplinary Biblical Research Institute Research Report 39, 1990.

———. "On Fulfilled Prophecy as Miracle." *Philosophia Christi* 3 (2001) 63–67.

———. *Prophecies About the Coming Messiah*. Vol. 42. Kindle edition. Biblical Seminary Hatfield, PA: Interdiciplinary Biblical Research Institute Research, 2014.

Nickelsburg, George W. E., and James C. VanderKam. *1 Enoch 2: A Commentary on the Book of 1 Enoch, Chapters 37–82*. Hermeneia—A Critical and Historical Commentary on the Bible. Minneapolis, MN: Fortress, 2012.

Noland, B. M. *The Royal Son of God: The Christology of Matthew 1–2 in the Setting of the Gospel*. Göttingen: Vandenhoeck & Ruprecht, 1979.

Noth, Martin. *Numbers: A Commentary*. Translated by James D. Martin. Philadelphia: Westminster, 1968.

Origen. "Commentary on the Gospel of John." In *The Gospel of Peter, the Diatessaron of Tatian, the Apocalypse of Peter, the Visio Pauli, the Apocalypses of the Virgil and Sedrach, the Testament of Abraham, the Acts of Xanthippe and Polyxena, the Narrative of Zosimus, the Apology of Aristides, the Epistles of Clement (Complete Text), Origen's Commentary on John, Books I–X, and Commentary on Matthew, Books I, II, and X–XIV*. Vol. 9 of *The Ante-Nicene Fathers*, edited and translated by Allan Menzies, 297–345. New York: Christian Literature Company, 1897.

———. "Origen against Celsus." In *Fathers of the Third Century: Tertullian, Part Fourth; Minucius Felix; Commodian; Origen, Parts First and Second*. Vol. 4 of *The Ante-Nicene Fathers*, edited by Alexander Roberts, et al., 395–669. Buffalo, NY: Christian Literature Company, 1885.

Osborne, Grant R. *Revelation*. Baker Exegetical Commentary on the New Testament. Grand Rapids: Baker Academic, 2002.

Oswalt, John N. *The Book of Isaiah, Chapters 40–66*. The New International Commentary on the Old Testament. Grand Rapids: Eerdmans, 1998.

Oxtoby, Gurdon C. *Prediction and Fulfillment in the Bible*. Philadelphia: Westminster, 1964.

Paffenroth, Kim. "The Story of Jesus According to L." PhD diss., University of Notre Dame, 1995.

Patterson, Richard D. "Psalm 22: From Trial to Triumph." *Journal of the Evangelical Theological Society* 47.2 (2004) 213–33.

Payne, J. Barton. *Encyclopedia of Biblical Prophecy*. Grand Rapids: Baker Book House, 1989.
Pervo, Richard I. *Acts: A Commentary on the Book of Acts*. Minneapolis: Fortress, 2009.
Pocock, E. "Doctrinal and Ethical." In *A Commentary on the Holy Scriptures: Malachi*, edited by John Peter Lange, et al. Bellingham, WA: Logos Research Systems, 2008.
Pohlig, James. *An Exegetical Summary of Malachi*. Dallas, TX: Summer Institute of Linguistics, 1998.
Poirier, John C. "Psalm 16:10 and the Resurrection of Jesus 'on the Third Day' (1 Corinthians 15:4)." *Journal for the Study of Paul and His Letters* 4.2 (2014) 149–67.
Ramm, Bernard. *Protestant Christian Evidences*. Chicago: Moody, 1953.
Ramsay, William Mitchell. *The Bearing of Recent Discoveries on the Trustworthiness of the New Testament*. 2nd ed. London: Hodder and Stoughton, 1915.
———. *Was Christ Born at Bethlehem: A Study on the Credibility of St. Luke*. Primedia eLaunch, 2011.
Rashi. *Rashi's Commentary*: Chabad.org. http://www.chabad.org/library/bible_cdo/aid/16223#showrashi=true&lt=both.
Richard, Earl. *Jesus: One and Many—The Christological Concept of New Testament Authors*. Wilmigton, DE: Michael Glazier, 1988.
Riehm, Eduard Karl August. *Messianic Prophecy: Its Origin, Historical Character, and Relation to New Testament Fulfillment*. Edinburgh: T&T Clark, 2012.
Roberts, J. J. M. *The Bible and the Ancient near East: Collected Essays*. Winona Lake, IN: Eisenbrauns, 2002.
———. "The Old Testament's Contribution to Messianic Expectations." In *The Messiah: Developments in Earliest Judaism and Christianity*, edited by James H. Charlesworth. Minneapolis: Fortress, 1992.
Robertson, A. T. *Luke the Historian in the Light of Research*. New York: Scribner's Sons, 1930.
Robinson, James McConkey, et al., eds. *Critical Edition of Q: Synopsis Including the Gospels of Matthew and Luke, Mark and Thomas with English, German, and French Translations of Q and Thomas*. Minneapolis: Fortress, 2000.
Ross, Allen P. "Psalms." In *The Bible Knowledge Commentary: An Exposition of the Scriptures*. Vol. 1, edited by J. F. Walvoord and R. B. Zuck, 778–899. Wheaton, IL: Victor, 1985.
Rowell, Earle A. *Prophecy Speaks: Dissolving Doubts*. Washington DC: Review and Herald, 1933.
Rydlelnik, Michael. *The Messianic Hope: Is the Hebrew Bible Really Messianic?* Kindle edition. Nac Studies in Bible and Theology. Nashville: B & H, 2010.
Sailer, William J., et al., eds. *Religious and Theological Abstracts*. Myerstown, PA: Religious and Theological Abstracts, 2012.
Sanders, E. P. *The Historical Figure of Jesus*. New York: Penguin, 1993.
Satterthwaite, Philip E., et al., eds. *The Lord's Anointed Interpretation of Old Testament Messianic Texts*. Grand Rapids: Baker, 1995.
Saucy, Mark. "The Kingdom-of-God Sayings in Matthew." *Bibliotheca Sacra* 151 (1994) 175–97.
Schaeffer, Francis A. *The Complete Works of Francis A. Schaeffer: A Christian Worldview*. Vol. 2. Westchester, IL: Crossway, 1982.
Schnackenburg, Rudolf. *Jesus in the Gospels: A Biblical Christology*. Translated by O. C. Dean Jr. Louisville, KY: Westminster John Knox, 1995.

Schaper, Joachim. "The Persian Period." In *Redemption and Resistance*, edited by Markus Bockmuehl and James Carleton Paget, 3–14. New York: T&T Clark, 2009.

Schiffman, L. H. "Messianic Figures and Ideas in the Qumran Scrolls." In *The Messiah: Developments in Earliest Judaism and Christianity*, edited by James H. Charlesworth, 116–29. Minneapolis: Fortress, 1992.

Schley, Donald G. "The Traditions and History of Biblical Shiloh." In *Shiloh: A Biblical City in Tradition and History*, 185–201. Sheffield, UK: JSOT, 1989.

Scott, R. B. Y. "The Relation of Isaiah, Chapter 35, to Deutero-Isaiah." *The American Journal of Semitic Languages and Literatures* 52.3 (1936) 178–91.

Seligsohn, Max. "Stephen." In *The Jewish Encyclopedia: A Descriptive Record of the History, Religion, Literature, and Customs of the Jewish People from the Earliest Times to the Present Day*. Vol. 11, edited by Singer Isidor, 548. New York: Funk & Wagnalls, 1906.

Selman, Martin. *2 Chronicles: An Introduction and Commentary*. Tyndale Old Testament Commentaries. Downers Grove, IL: InterVarsity Press, 1994.

Septuginta: With Morphology. Stuttgart, Germany: Deutsche Bibelgesellschaft, 1996.

Shenton, Tim. *Haggai: An Expositional Commentary*. Exploring the Bible Commentary. Leominster, UK: Day One, 2007.

Skinner, John. *A Critical and Exegetical Commentary on Genesis*. International Critical Commentary. New York: Scribner, 1910.

Smith, Gary V. *The Prophets as Preachers: An Introduction to the Hebrew Prophets*. Nashville: Broadman & Holman, 1994.

Smith, George Adam. "The Book of Isaiah." In *Psalms to Isaiah*. Vol. 3 of *The Expositor's Bible*, edited by Robertson W. Nicoll, 611–846. Hartford, CT: S. S. Scranton Co, 1903.

Smith, James E. *The Wisdom Literature and Psalms*. Joplin, MO: College, 1996.

Smith, Ralph L. "The Shape of Theology in the Book of Malachi." *Southwestern Journal of Theology* 30.1 (1987) 22–27.

Smith, William. *Dictionary of Greek and Roman Antiquities*. 2nd ed. Boston: Little, Brown, and Company, 1865.

Son, Kiwoong. *Zion Symbolism in Hebrews: Hebrews 12:18–24 as a Hermeneutical Key to the Epistle*. Milton Keynes, UK: Paternoster, 2005.

Stern, David H. *Jewish New Testament Commentary: A Companion Volume to the Jewish New Testament*. Clarksville, MD: Jewish New Testament Publications, 1996.

Strack, Hermann L. and Paul Billerbeck. *Kommentar Zum Neuen Testament Aus Talmud Und Midrasch*. 3 Vols. München: C. H. Beck'sche Verlagsbuchhandlung Oskar Beck, 1922–1926.

Strauss, David Friedrich. *The Life of Jesus: Critically Examined*. 4th ed. London: Swan Sonnenschein & Co., 1902.

Strauss, Mark L. "David." In *New Dictionary of Biblical Theology*, edited by T. Desmond Alexander and Brian S. Rosner, 435–43. Downers Grove, IL: InterVarsity, 2000.

Strauss, Mark L. *The Davidic Messiah in Luke–Acts: The Promise and Its Fulfillment in Lukan Christology*. Journal for the Study of the New Testament Supplement Series 413. Sheffield, UK: Sheffield Academic, 1995.

Strawn, Brent A. "Psalm 22:17b: More Guessing." *Journal of Biblical Literature* 119 (2000) 439–51.

Stronstad, Rodger. *The Charismatic Theology of St. Luke*. Peabody, MA: Hendrickson, 1984.

Sutcliffe, Edmund F. "The Replies of the Biblical Commission: Translated with Introductory Note." In *A Catholic Commentary on Holy Scripture*, edited by Bernard Orchard and Edmund F. Sutcliffe, 67–75. Toronto, Canada: Thomas Nelson, 1953.

Swanson, James. *Dictionary of Biblical Languages with Semantic Domains: Hebrew (Old Testament)*. Oak Harbor, WA: Logos Research Systems, 1997.

Swenson, Kristin M. "Psalm 22:17: Circling around the Problem Again." *Journal of Biblical Literature* 123 (2004) 637–48.

Swinburne, Richard. "Violation of a Law of Nature." In *Miracles*, edited by Richard Swinburne, 75–84. New York: Macmillan, 1989.

Tacitus, Cornelius. *Historiae (Latin)*. Edited by Charles Dennis Fisher. Medford, MA: Perseus Digital Library, 1911.

Taylor, Richard A., and E. Ray Clendenen. *Haggai, Malachi*. The New American Commentary 21. Nashville: Broadman & Holman, 2004.

Terry, Milton S. *Biblical Apocalyptics*. Eugene, OR: Wipf and Stock, 2001.

———. *Biblical Hermeneutics: a Treatise on the Interpretation of the Old and New Testaments*. Rev. ed. New York: Eaton & Mains; Curts & Jennings, 1890.

Thomson, Thomas L. *The Historicity of the Patriarchal Narratives*. New York: de Gruyter, 1974.

Tigay, Jeffrey H. *Deuteronomy*. The JPS Torah Commentary. Philadelphia: Jewish Publication Society, 1996.

Tigay, Jeffrey H., et al. "Adoption." In *Encyclopaedia Judaica*. Vol. 1, edited by Michael Berenbaum and Fred Skolnik, 415–20. Detroit, MI: Macmillan Reference USA, 2007.

Tostengard, Sheldon. "Psalm 22." *Interpretation* 46.2 (1992) 167–70.

Tranquillus, C. Suetonius. *Suetonius: The Lives of the Twelve Caesars; an English Translation, Augmented with the Biographies of Contemporary Statesmen, Orators, Poets, and Other Associates*. Edited by Alexander Thomson. Medford, MA: Gebbie & Co., 1889.

Troeltsch, Ernst. "Historiography." In *Encyclopedia of Religion and Ethics*, edited by James Hastings, et al., vol. 6, 718. New York, NY: T&T Clark, 1908–26.

Trull, Gregory V. "An Exegesis of Psalm 16:10a." *Bibliotheca Sacra* 161 (2004) 304–21.

———. "Views on Peter's Use of Psalm 16:8–11 in Acts 2:25–32." *Bibliotheca Sacra* 161 (2004) 194–214.

Turtullian. "Apology." In *Latin Christianity: Its Founder, Tertullian*. Vol. 3 of *The Ante-Nicene Fathers*, edited by Alexander Roberts, et al., 17–55. Buffalo, NY: Christian Literature Company, 1885.

———. "The Prescription against Heretics." In *Latin Christianity: Its Founder, Tertullian*. Vol. 3 of *The Ante-Nicene Fathers*, edited by Alexander Roberts, et al., 243–65. Buffalo, NY: Christian Literature Company, 1885.

Twelftree, Graham H. *Jesus the Miracle Worker: A Historical and Theological Study*. Downers Grove, IL: InterVarsity, 1999.

———. "Miracles and Miracle Stories." In *Dictionary of Jesus and the Gospels*, edited by Joel B. Green, et al., 594–604. Downers Grove, IL: Intervarsity, 2013.

Ulrich, Dean. "Dissonant Prophecy in Ezekiel 26 and 29." *Bulletin for Biblical Research* 10 (2000) 130–31.

Utley, Robert James. *Luke the Historian: The Book of Acts*. Vol. 3B. Study Guide Commentary Series. Marshall, TX: Bible Lessons International, 2003.

VanGemeren, William A. *Expositors Bible Commentary*. Edited by Frank E. Gaebelein and J. D. Douglas. Grand Rapids: Zondervan, 1992.

Vermes, Geza. *The Dead Sea Scrolls in English*. Rev. and extended 4th ed. Sheffield, UK: Sheffield Academic, 1995.

———. *Jesus the Jew: A Historian's Reading of the Gospels*. Philadelphia: Fortress, 1973.

Viereck, P. "Die Aegyptische Steuereinschätzungs-Commission in Römischer Zeit." *Philologus: Zeitscrift für das classische Alterthum* 52 (1894) 219–47.

Waetjen, Herman C. "Genealogy as the Key to the Gospel According to Matthew." *Journal of Biblical Literature* 95.2 (1976) 205–30.

Waltke, Bruce K. "A Canonical Process Approach to the Psalms." In *Tradition and Testament: Essays in Honor of Charles Lee Feinberg*, edited by John S. Feinberg and Paul D. Feinberg, 3–18. Chicago, IL: Moody, 1981.

———. "Psalms." In *New International Dictionary of Old Testament Theology & Exegesis*. Vol. 4, edited by William VanGemeren, 1100–116. Grand Rapids: Zondervan, 1997.

Waltke, Bruce K., et al. *The Psalms as Christian Worship: A Historical Commentary*. Grand Rapids: Eerdmans, 2010.

Waltke, Bruce K. and Michael Patrick O'Connor. *An Introduction to Biblical Hebrew Syntax*. Winona Lake, IN: Eisenbrauns, 1990.

Walvoord, John F. *Every Prophecy of the Bible*. Colorado Springs, CO: Cook Communications Ministries, 1999.

Watts, John D. W. *Isaiah 1–33*. Word Biblical Commentary 24. Dallas, TX: Word, 1998.

Weil, Gérard E., et al. *Biblia Hebraica Stuttgartensia*. 5. Aufl., rev. ed. Stuttgart: Deutsche Bibelgesellschaft, 1997.

Weir, Jack. "Analogous Fulfillment: The Use of the Old Testament in the New Testament." *Perspectives in Religious Studies* 9.1 (1982) 65–76.

Westermann, Claus. *A Continental Commentary: Genesis 37–50*. Minneapolis, MN: Fortress, 2002.

Whiting, Mark J. "Psalms 1 and 2 as a Hermeneutical Lens for Reading the Psalter." *The Evangelical Quarterly* 85.3 (2013) 246–62.

Whitsett, Christopher G. "Son of God, Seed of David: Paul's Messianic Exegesis in Romans 1:3–4." *Journal of Biblical Literature* 119.4 (2000) 661–81.

Wilcken, Ulrich. "Ἀπογραφαι." *Hermes* 28.1 (1893) 230–51.

Wildberger, Hans. *A Continental Commentary: Isaiah 1–12*. Minneapolis: Fortress, 1991.

———. *A Continental Commentary: Isaiah 28–39*. Minneapolis: Fortress, 2002.

Williams, A. Lukyn. *A Manual of Christian Evidences from the Jewish People*. Vol. 2. New York: Society for Promoting Christian Knowledge, 1919.

Williamson, H. G. M. "The Messianic Text of Isaiah 1–39." In *King and Messiah in Israel and the Ancient near East Proceedings of the Oxford Old Testament Seminar*, edited by John Day, 238–70. Sheffield, UK: Sheffield Academic, 1998.

Willis, John T. "A Cry of Defiance—Psalm 2." *Journal for the Study of the Old Testament* 47 (1990) 33–50.

Wilson, Gerald Henry. "The Use of Royal Psalms at the 'Seams' of the Hebrew Psalter." *Journal for the Study of the Old Testament* 11.35 (1986) 85–94.

Wiseman, Donald J. *1 and 2 Kings: An Introduction and Commentary*. Tyndale Old Testament Commentaries 9. Downers Grove, IL: InterVarsity, 1993.

Witherington, Ben III. *The Acts of the Apostles: A Socio-Rhetorical Commentary*. Grand Rapids: Eerdmans, 1998.

———. *Jesus, Paul and the End of the World*. Downers Grove, IL: InterVarsity, 1992.

———. *The Jesus Quest: The Third Search for the Jew of Nazareth*. 2nd ed. Downers Grove, IL: InterVarsity, 1997.

———. "The Nativity According to Luke." *Bible Review* 20.6 (2004) 46–47.

Witthoff, David, et al. "Psalm 2." In *Psalms Form and Structure*, edited by Eli Evans, s.v. Psalm 2. Bellingham, WA: Faithlife, 2014.

———. "Psalm 16." In *Psalms Form and Structure*, edited by Eli Evans, s.v. Psalm 16. Bellingham, WA: Faithlife, 2014.

Wolff, Hans Walter. *A Continental Commentary: Micah*. Minneapolis: Augsburg Fortress, 1990.

———. *Hosea: A Commentary on the Book of the Prophet Hosea*. Hermeneia—A Critical and Historical Commentary on the Bible. Philadelphia: Fortress, 1974.

Wood, Bryant G, ed. *Bible and Spade* 7 (1978).

Wright, N. T. *Jesus and the Victory of God*. Christian Origins and the Question of God 2. London: Society for Promoting Christian Knowledge, 1996.

———. *The New Testament and the People of God*. Christian Origins and the Question of God 1. Minneapolis: Society for Promoting Christian Knowledge, 1992.

———. *The Resurrection of the Son of God*. Christian Origins and the Question of God 3. Minneapolis: Society for Promoting Christian Knowledge, 2003.

Young, Edward J. *An Introduction to the Old Testament*. Grand Rapids: Eerdmans, 1977.

Zimmerli, Walther. *Ezekiel: A Commentary on the Book of the Prophet Ezekiel*. Philadelphia: Fortress, 1979.

Zodhiates, Spiros. *The Complete Word Study Dictionary: New Testament*. electronic ed. Chattanooga, TN: AMG, 2000.

Zuck, Roy B. *A Biblical Theology of the New Testament*. Chicago: Moody, 1994.

Subject Index

Abijah, king of Judah, 105–6
"accidental truths of history," 8
Achtemeier, Paul J., 158
Acta Senatus, of Rome, 147n5
Acts 2, 197–200, 217
Acts 2:34-35, quotation of Psalm 110:1 in, 199n146
Acts 4:25-26, relation to Psalm 2, 180
Acts 13, relation to Psalm 16, 200–201
Acts 13:34, relation to Psalm 16:10, 180n64
Acts of Pontius Pilate (Justin), 146
adoption, 118, 168, 173n37
Against Celsus (Origen), 5, 128, 141
agent of the judgment, reappearing in Psalm 2:6, 170
Akkadian verb *walādu*, 168
Allen, Leslie C., 76, 181
Allison, David, 196
analogy, principle of, 38, 42, 55, 143n71
ancient texts, strategy for analyzing, 16
angels, attending the body of Abraham until the third day, 196
Ankerberg, John, 23
Anointed One, 3, 171, 175
Apocalypse of Peter, 196n134
Apocalypse of Zephaniah, 196
apocalyptic prediction, 156
Apocrypha, 128n20, 206, 209
apologetic device, prophecy as, 30
apologetic value, of prophecy, 31
apostolic testimony, 52
apostolic witness, 53

Aramaic Psalter, on the stone that the builders reject, 76
Archaeology of the Land of the Bible (Mazar), 65n15
archeological evidence, analyzing, 16
Arndt, William, 161
Attridge, Harold W., 181
Augustine, 103n145, 110
Augustus, registration ordered by, 138–41
author, presuppositions of, 18
authorial intent, establishing facts about, 59
authorship
  of any canonical or other works, 16n38
  of Psalm 16, 189
autonomy, of the historian, 42
'āzōb, in Psalm 16:10, 190–91

Babylonian Talmud, 74, 160, 193n119
baby-slaughter-and-rescue story, in Matthew, 143n71
Balaam oracles, basis of, 67, 67n25
baptism in water, offered by John the Baptist, 98
Bar Kochba (Simeon ben Kosibah), as a messianic figure, 116n46
Barfield, Kenny, 30–33, 66
Bartimaeus, 73, 115–16
Barton, John, 156
2 Baruch 32:1-4, 86
4 Baruch, 196n133

249

Bateman, Herbert W., IV, 40–41
Bauckham, Richard J., 114n34, 196
Bauer, Walter, 161
Beale, Gregory K., 182
Beegle, Dewey M., 48–49
begetting, in Psalm 2:7 and John 1:14, 178–79
"begotten"
   cannot be truncated to mean adopted, 185, 223
   Hebrew term found in no other narrative and never applied to a known Israelite king, 186
   Hebrew term translated found in no other near-eastern enthronement narrative and never applied to a known historical Israelite king, 226
   in Psalm 2:7, 167, 168
"Behold I send," Malachi's use of, 91–93
beliefs, hypothesis disconfirmed by fewer accepted, 14
Bethlehem of Judea
   association with the eschatological ruler of Israel, 226
   as the birthplace of Jesus, 135
   confused with "Bethlehem" located in Galilee (*Beit Lahm*), 133
   as the home of Joseph and Mary before the birth of Jesus, 137n49
   as the home of Joseph's relatives, 131–32
   Jesus' family in, 221
   Messiah having genealogical roots in, 125
   as the place from which Israel's predicted ruler emerges, 220
   textual and historical evidence for, 134–35
Bible
   accepting the claims of, 15
   percentage containing prophetic material, 23
The Bible after Babel: Historical Criticism in a Postmodern Age (Collins), 41–42
biblical *autographa*, as inerrant in content, 37
biblical data, evaluative framework for, 15–16
biblical figures, eliminating non-predictive, 38
biblical inerrancy, 37, 49
biblical narratives, accuracy of, 42
biblical prophecy, volumes devoted to, 23
biblical texts
   criteria for selecting, 12
   first group of, 11, 215–18
   second group of, 11, 105–24, 218–20
   third group of, 11, 125–44, 220–21
   fourth group of, 11, 145–65, 221–22
   fifth group of, 12, 166–211, 223–24
biblical thought, streams of, 43
Billerbeck, Paul, 151, 159, 177
birth narratives, 134, 141n66, 220
birth/begotten nomenclature, used in Psalm 2:7, 184
birthplace, evidence against a contrived, 136–38
blind, giving sight to, 162
Bock, Darrell L., 21, 40–41, 200
Brannan, Rick, 204
Bratcher, Robert G., 187
Briggs, Charles Augustus, 68, 188, 194
Briggs, Emilie Grace, 188
"brothers of the Lord," 114
Brown, Michael L.
   on the expectation of a miracle-working Messiah, 148
   on Mary descending from the Davidic line, 119
   on the Messiah's descent, 118
   on the Second Temple, 91
   on signs associated with Isaiah 35:5-6, 160
   on the title "Son of David" meaning "Messiah," 163
Brown, Raymond E.
   on the integrity of the infancy narratives, 134
   on Jesus being from Davidic stock, 116
   on Jesus denying his or the Messiah's Davidic status, 121

SUBJECT INDEX

on a parallel expectation of a hidden messiah, 136
Bruce, F. F., 140
Bultmann, Rudolf Karl, 121–22
Burger, Christoph, 131

High Priest Caiaphas, 3, 15–16, 99
Campbell, Keith, 203, 203n156
canon, 25, 40
"canonical process approach," of Waltke, 185n87
canonical reading, 25, 57
Carroll, Robert P., 7n16
caves, for the protection of livestock, 128
Celsus, 5, 7, 147. *See also Against Celsus* (Origen)
Charles, Robert Henry, 70n36, 136, 157
Charlesworth, James H., 197n136
Chevallier, Max-Alain, 176
chiastic structure, of Malachi 3:1, 93–95
chief priests and the Pharisees, John using the terminology of, 100n136
Chilton, Bruce, 106, 133
Christ. *See also* Jesus; messiah
prophecy preparing the way for, 43–44
Christian literature, on Psalm 22, 210
Christian messianic titles, 50
Christian motifs, examples of stylized, 123
Christian religion, explaining origins of, 53
Christology of the Old Testament (Hengstenberg), 28n15–29n15
The City of God (Augustine), on Psalm 89, 110
1 Clement, 179, 206–7
Clines, David J. A., 193
Clopas, a brother of Joseph, 136
Cohen, A., 184
Cole, Robert Luther, 170–71
Collins, Adela Yarbro, 157, 174
Collins, John J.
on 1QSa, 174

on the accuracy of biblical narratives, 41–42
on the "begets" reading of 1QSa, 174
identifying the title "Son of Man" with "Messiah," 157
on the kingly identity of the individual in the Psalm 118, 73–74
stressing the futuristic intent of 4Q174, 174
coming of the Lord, 93
coming of the Messiah, 215–16
Commentarii principis, 147n5
"concrete data," need for, 30
"conflation," of *Yahweh* and the king in Psalm 110, 171
Constantine, 129
continuity, in the birth narratives, 220
conversion experience, of Saul of Tarsus, 4
Conzelmann, Hans, 88n97, 199, 201
Coppes, Leonard J., 161
cornerstone image, from Isaiah 28:16, 75
correspondence, fulfillment as, 47
correspondence theory of truth, 18
corruption
of the body, 195
death and resurrection before, 199
Jesus never to see, 200
Lazarus exhibiting obvious signs of, 197
physical, 192
preservation from, 194, 203, 227
šāḥat associated with, 195
covenant promise, in the text of 2 Samuel 7:13, 16, 172
Craig, William Lane, 54
Craigie, Peter C., 167, 179–80
Creach, Jerome F. D., 170
creedal statements, within the four gospels, 21n48
criteria-verifying conditions, 5
criticism, principle of, 42
crucifixion
aspects also present in Psalm 22, 208, 210
attributing Psalm 22 to, 224

Cullmann, Oscar, 121
cultural-historical characteristics, affecting prophecy, 31–32
Cyprian, 110
Cyril of Jerusalem, 102–3

Dagg, John L., 63n8
Dahl, Nils Alstrup, 71n40
Dahood, Mitchell Joseph, 190–91
Damascus Documenta, 195
Daniel (book of), 25, 32
Daniel 9:24-27, conundrum of, 25
Danker, Fredrick, 161
David
    anointing of versus coronation, 184
    argument against a literal descendant of, 45
    as the author of Psalm 2, 180
    considered to have prophetic gifts, 199n143
    enthroned in 2 Samuel 7 with sons, 173
    Jesus a descendant of, 220, 221
    Joseph's ancestor as, 144
    making great the name of, 105
    Messiah springing from the linage of, 11
    perpetuity of the line of, 105, 171, 226
    Philistines rebelled against, 183
    physical descendant of, ruling Israel and the nations, 113
    portrayed with some second-Moses themes, 151
    promised son of as the physical offspring of David, 106
    prophetic insight into the future appearance of the Messiah, 198–99
David, Martin, 168
Davidic and divine sonship, of Jesus, 114
Davidic authorship, of Psalm 16, 189
Davidic Covenant
    celebrating the institution of, 173
    discussion of, 45
    elements in, 201
    embedded in the Jewish messianic consciousness, 123–24, 220
    everlasting nature of, 200
    integral in the theology of the OT, 105
    involved a messianic hope, 198
    predicted David's death and the rise of his offspring, 190n109
    reference to, 168
    requiring offspring to be established forever, 218
Davidic descent of Jesus, as a given in the early church, 113
Davidic dynasty, perpetuity of, 105, 171, 226
Davidic heritage, of Jesus, 114, 115–17
Davidic king
    hope for during the pre-exilic period, 107
    Jewish people's anticipation of, 219
    overseeing the temple cult and serving as a priest, 172
    postponing the realization of, 108
    prophetic eschatological expectation of, 72, 216
Davidic kingship, Yahweh's rejection of, 172
Davidic leader, 69, 107
Davidic line, clear break with in Ezekiel, 69
Davidic messiah, 108, 174
Davidic monarchy, *vaticinia ex eventu* affirmation of, 67
Davidic ruler, 108, 126
Davidic sonship, as the prevailing view of the Messiah, 115n41
Davidic status, of Jesus, 124, 226
Davidic thinking, as a form of Jewish messianism, 110–12
day of Pentecost, 88, 89, 90
Day of *Yahweh*, expectation of Israel regarding, 152
Dead Sea Scrolls
    approach to Genesis 49:10, 64, 70
    depicting miracles in relation to the Messiah or the messianic age, 165
    eschatological idea prominent in, 86

SUBJECT INDEX

linking miraculous deeds with the messianic era, 158-59
on Psalm 22, 205
deaf, enabled to hear the words of the writing, 153
Delitzsch, Franz, 28
demons, Jesus' actions against, 163
desert, blossoming of, 155
Deutero-Isaiah, basic thoughts of, 155
Deuteronomist (D) source, dated seventh century BC, 65n14
Deuteronomy 18:15, expectation of an eschatological prophet, 86
Deuteronomy 18:15-18, Moses/Messiah typology, 148-52
Deuteronomy 18:15-22, non-messianic referent for, 221-22
Deuteronomy 33, containing a list of blessings, 65n17
Dialogue with Trypho (Justin), on Bethlehem as the place of Jesus' birth, 128
Didache, on the family of Jesus rooted in the Davidic line, 114
disciples, citing Psalm 118 in reference to the Triumphal Entry, 77n60
divination, associated with pagan prophets, 47
divine inspiration, 41, 57
documents, earliest interpreting Psalm 2 from an eschatological messianic perspective, 185, 186
"drapery," of the OT forms, 27
dreams, interpretation of establishing historical facts, 33
Driver, Samuel R., 149
Duling, Dennis C., 113, 115
Dunn, James D. G., 199n146, 220n146

Eagle vision, of 4 Ezra as a reference to the Davidic Messiah, 70n39
early church
on Jesus was the ultimate descendant of David, 112
on Psalm 22 as both prophetic and messianic, 206-7
understanding Jesus' relationship to the house of David, 119, 124
early extra-biblical sources, attesting Jesus' Davidic status, 226
early Jewish interpretation, of Deuteronomy 18:15-18, 151
economic relationship, of Jesus to God the Father, 179
Edersheim, Alfred, 207n174
Edghill, Ernest Arthur, 43-46
Edom, 154, 154n33
Ehrman, Bart D., 131, 162-63
Elijah, 98n127, 151, 218
Elohist (E) source, dated ninth century BC, 65n14
Encyclopedia of Biblical Prophecy (Payne), 37-39
Enlightenment, rationalist arguments of, 6
1 Enoch, theology of a general resurrection, 197
1 Enoch 37-71 (the Parables or Similitudes), 175
1 Enoch 52, 175
An Enquiry Concerning Human Understanding (Hume), 24, 52-57
epistemological certainty, not possible with historical investigations, 58
Epistle of Barnabas, 115n41, 146, 207
eschatological connotations, of both Psalms 1 and 2 together, 169
eschatological dimension, of Psalm 1 and 2, 170
eschatological king, rejection of, 184
eschatological Melkisedek, bearing significant messianic resemblance, 158n48
eschatological messianic interpretation of Psalm 2, objections to, 182-84
eschatological prophet, 86, 150
eschatological role, of the Messiah, 152
eschatological vision, individual and cosmic elements, 152
eschatology, equated with miracle-working, 158n48

Essenes, messianic expectation of two messiahs, 108
Eusebius, 136, 146
evaluative framework, for biblical data, 15–16
evangelical "prophetic criticism" method, 49
Eve, Eric, 147
evidence, 16, 43
Evidence of the Truth of the Christian Religion (Keith), 25–26
evidential approaches to OT messianic prophecy, 7n13
evidential verification, 42
excluded middle, law of, 18n44
exegetical and hermeneutical approaches, replicating to the Old Testament from the New Testament, 20
exile, return from, 85
exorcism, 162, 163
expected prophet like Moses pattern, Jesus as the image of, 164
explanatory power/scope, of the hypothesis, 14, 227n5
extra-biblical data, on miracles and the Messiah, 157–64
extra-biblical evidence
  on Malachi 3:1, 102–3
  on messianic understanding of Psalm 2 as no late entry, 178
  on Micah 5:2, 128–30
  on Psalm 16, 196–97
extra-biblical literature, on the messianic interpretation of Psalm 22, 210
extra-biblical primary sources, needed for study of the OT, 229
extra-biblical texts, regarding 2 Samuel 7:13, 108–10
Ezekiel, temple vision of, 90n103
Ezekiel 21, exilic oracle of, 69
Ezekiel 21:27b, marking the end of formal Judahite rule in Israel, 69
Ezekiel 34:23-24, relation to 2 Samuel 7:13, 107, 219–20
Ezra, 151, 151n20

Fairbairn, Patrick, 39
Fales, Evan, 123n70
false birthplace, as indiscriminate and arbitrary, 137
family members, of Jesus having ministries, 122
Ferguson, Paul, 151n20
"fill this house with glory," 85, 90
first-century thought, miracles and the Messiah in, 158–60
Fitzmyer, Joseph A.
  on characteristics of the messianic figure, 110
  on David widely held to be a prophet, 199n143
  on Jesus fulfilling Malachi 3:1, 96
  on messianic prophecy, 49–51
  not finding a connection between Psalm 2 and Psalms of Solomon 17, 176n51
  on the NT use of the Psalm 22, 203
  on Psalm 2, 173–74, 185
  on reading 4Q521, 159
The Five Gospels, 21
Flint, Peter W., 205
foreign nations, treasures of being brought to God's temple, 85
Foreman, Benjamin A., 125
forerunner, existence of a plausible, 97–98
foretelling, 30
France, R. T., 96–97, 132
Fruchtenbaum, Arnold G., 106
Fulfilled Prophecy as Miracle (Newman), 20, 34–35
fulfillment
  as "correspondence," 47
  defined, 16–17
  determining of particular prophecies, 39
  in an impartial manner, 31
  semantic range of the expression, 46–47
future tone, of Psalm 16:10, 189
futurum instans participle, 91

Gamaliel, 100
"gate liturgies," 74
Genesis, personal names in West Semitic form, 65n15
Genesis 49:1-27, as a poem, 65
Genesis 49:10
  on the ascendancy and rulership of the tribe of Judah, 72
  interpretation of in exilic and post-exilic Judaism, 68–72
  investigation of, 61–72
  literary and textual analysis, 61–68
  on the Messiah being from the tribe of Judah, 71
  prophesies, inconsistency of maintaining an unbroken line of Davidic kings, 63
  reading in its traditional patriarchal context, 67
  when first interpreted as a reference to the Messiah, 71
  yielded no evidence to validate an affirmative minimal-facts statement, 216
Genesis Rabbah, on healing, 160
Genesis Rabbah 44:8, traces of messianic interpretation, 178n57
Genesis Rabbah 100.7. Section X, on the three day connection of soul to body, 196
geographical location, associated with the birth and early life of the Messiah, 11
Gilat, Yisrael, 168
glory, 84, 87, 88–89
God
  of the Bible, 24
  coming to save, 155
  covenant-keeping righteousness, 113
  decreed beforehand events according to His plan, 181n67
Gordis, Robert, 174–75
gospel writers, believed Jesus was the particular prophet and Messiah, 165, 222
gospels, all four confirming Jesus' presence in the temple, 97
grammatical-historical method, 15
grave/pit, early Jewish understanding of, 187n94
Green, Joel B., 158
Gundry, Robert H., 117
Gunkel, Hermann
  affirming ten Royal Psalms, 172
  on dating the finished Psalter, 190n109–91n109
  on the enthronement and dominionist poetry employed by Israel, 183
  on Genesis 49:1-27 as a poem, 65
  grounding Psalm 2 in the historical Israelite monarchy, 185
Gunn, George A., 184
Gurion family, wealth of, 100n136

Habermas, Gary R.
  on the inability of science to postulate absolutes, 54–55
  on minimal facts, 5n10–6n10, 17
  pointing out eyewitnesses to miracles, 146
  on sources for studying the historical Jesus, 21, 21n48
Haggada-question, 121n62
Haggai 2:1-9, 82–90, 217
Haggai 2:9, 83
Hanina Ben Dosa, 160
Hanson, Paul D., 156
Harris, Robert Laird, 192
Harrison, Peter, 56
Hasmoneans, 108
healing
  Christians reporting multitudes of, 53
  in Isaiah 29:18-19 as physical or spiritual, 153
  physical aspect of versus spiritual aspect, 222
  of the physically afflicted, 155
Hebrew Psalter, division into units, 172
Hebrews (book of), affirming the OT exegesis of Paul, 181
Hegesippus, 115
Heinemann, Mark H., 204, 208

Heirs, Richard H., 92
Hengel, Martin, 140
Hengstenberg, E. W., 28n15–29n15
Henten, Jan Willem Van, 175
hermeneutic, use of a three-fold, 40
hermeneutical approaches, of modern scholarship, 15n34
hermeneutical methodology, in the study of messianic prophecy, 229
Herod the Great, 85, 111, 127, 131n31, 137
high priest, presenting Jesus as, 116n46
high priests, obedient to the faith, 100
Hindson, Ed, 29
historians, bias and dispositions of, 13
historical bedrock, 21, 22
historical data, 15, 16
historical descriptions
 applying criteria for justifying, 227–29, 227n5
 based on probabilities, 5
 conclusions drawn, 9
 as less than certain, 228
historical events, 7, 59
historical evidence
 on early Jewish understanding of Haggai, 86
 refuting that Jesus directly fulfilled a prophecy, 215
 supporting Jesus' presence in Egypt, 143n71
 weighed against plausible competing hypotheses, 10
historical facts, as different from minimal facts, 72n42
historical fulfillment
 denying the possibility of, 42
 for Malachi 3:1 after AD 70, 228
 positive evidence for a, 184
historical investigation, principle of analogy applied to, 55
historical Jesus, sources studying, 21
"historical life of Christ," prophecy preparing the way for, 44
historical naturalism, failing as a scientific methodology, 55
historical sense, of prophecy, 26

historical sources, claiming prophecy was fulfilled by Jesus, 18
historical-critical methodology, 41, 42
historical-critical methods, applying to ancient oracles, 5
historical-evidential basis, for the NT claims of Jesus' origin, 179
historical-evidential conclusions
 related to Genesis 49:10, 72
 related to Haggai 2:1-9, 90
 related to Malachi 3:1, 104
 related to Micah 5:2 and the birth narratives, 144
 related to Psalm 2:1-12, 186
 related to Psalm 16:9-10, 202
 related to Psalm 22:1-31, 210
 related to Psalm 118, 81
 related to the OT and NT Davidic claim, 124
 from the study of the miracles in relation to Jewish messianism, 164
historical-evidential facts
 related to Genesis 49:10, 72
 related to Haggai 2:1-9, 90
 related to Malachi 3:1, 104
 related to Micah 5:2 and the birth narratives, 144
 related to miracles in relation to Jewish messianism, 164–65
 related to Psalm 2, 186
 related to Psalm 16:9-10, 203
 related to Psalm 22:1-31, 210–11
 related to Psalm 118, 82
 related to the OT and NT Davidic claim, 124
historical-evidential minimal facts
 in textual group one, 225
 in textual group two, 226
 in textual group three, 226
 in textual group four, 226
 in textual group five, 226–27
historical-evidential reasons, for believing that Jesus is the direct fulfillment of OT messianic texts, 6
historicity
 denying for persons and events, 42

SUBJECT INDEX

establishing, 54, 54n79
of Peter's speech in Acts 2, 198n140
historiographical method, 13, 13n30
historiography, 10, 42
history
    consisting of factual data, 16n39
    defined, 16
    realist view of, 18
Hodayot, elements present in but absent from Psalm 22, 205–6
Holy Spirit, 52, 89n98
Honi the Circle Drawer, 160
Horbury, William, 110–11
horizons, disclosing authorial, 13, 13n30
"horn of salvation," common to Luke 1:69 and 2 Samuel 22:3, 109
"Hosanna," recorded by all evangelists except Luke, 79
Hosea 3:4-5, relation to 2 Samuel 7:13, 107–8, 219–20
Hossfeld, H. L., 169
house for *Yahweh*'s name, David's offspring building, 105
Houston, James M., 169–70
human disunity, reversal of, 89
human testimony, Hume's unwillingness to accept for miracle claims, 53
Hume, David, 9n23, 24, 52–57
humiliation and exaltation, of Christ, 73
hypothesis
    exceeding other incompatible hypotheses, 227n5
    formulating, 15
    implying observable data, 14

ideal Davidic scion, prophecies foreseeing, 126
ideal leader, enjoying total victory, 170
identity, law of, 18n44
Ignatius, Bishop of Antioch, 114, 128–29
imaginary thought forms, analogy containing, 55
Immanuel, in Isaiah and Matthew, 48
"in the days to come," prophetic and eschatological meaning of, 68

incarnation, prophetic images leading to, 44
incompatible hypotheses, exceeding, 14
individual supplicant, text of Psalm 22 recording the pleas of, 224
infancy narratives, 130, 134
An Inquiry into the Evidential Value of Prophecy (Edghill and Ryle), 43–46
interpretive perfection, within the reader's grasp, 24–25
interpretive principle, considering for a specific prophecy, 49n62
intertestamental and extra-biblical literature, related to Psalm 118, 78
intertestamental evidence
    related to 2 Samuel 7:13, 108–10
    related to Genesis 49:10, 70
    related to Haggai 2:1-9, 85–88
    related to Micah 5:2, 127
    related to Psalm 16 as scarce, 195
    related to Psalm 22, 205–6
    related to the interpretation of Psalm 2, 173–78
Irenaeus, on John the Baptist, 103
iron rod, in Psalm 2:9, 176
Isaiah, 45, 74, 101
Isaiah 6, 157
Isaiah 11:1, 106, 219–20
Isaiah 28:16-17, 74
Isaiah 29, 152, 154, 222
Isaiah 35, 155, 164
Isaiah 35:1-5, 154–57, 222
Isaiah 45:23, 99
Israel
    expecting some form of second Exodus, 152, 164
    inability to hear and see the truth, 153
    never enjoyed universal dominion, 183
    spiritual blindness and deafness of, 157
    as a vassal state to a non-Israelite king, 63

Israelite leaders, as an unbroken line from the tribe of Judah until the birth of Jesus, 63

Jacob, 65n15, 67
James, 136
Janneus, Alexander, battle against, 108n8
Jeremiah 23:5-6, relation to 2 Samuel 7:13, 107, 219–20
Jeremias, J., 150, 151
Jeroboam II, 107
Jerome, translation of Haggai, 83
Jerusalem Talmud, Bethlehem stated as the birthplace of the Messiah-king, 127
Jesse, ideal ruler stemming from the house of, 106
Jesus. *See also* Christ; messiah; Savior
acted out the fulfillments associated with Zechariah 9:9, 80
as the anointed king/son in Psalm 2, 178
as the anointed one, 223
apostolic ministry of his brothers, 114
believed he was the Messiah and Son of David, 163
believed he was the particular prophet and Messiah, 165, 222
as the best identifiable candidate for the LORD and the messenger of the covenant in Malachi 3:1, 225
birth in Bethlehem, 125, 125n1, 226
commanding the healed leper to show himself to the priests for a proof to them, 161
connection with Moses, 149
considered himself to be the stone and directly related to the vineyard owner (*Yahweh*), 80
on the cross, citing Psalm 22:1, 208
declared as the son of God in Romans 1:4, 181
declared himself as the Messiah and King of Israel, 88
declared his role of judge in Mark 14:62, 101
as a descendant of King David, 11, 45–46, 105, 116, 119–20, 124, 220
as direct fulfillment of the OT messianic texts, 6, 13
elusive answer regarding his descent, 120
encounter with Bartimaeus not displaying any disapproval of the title Son of David, 116
entering Jerusalem, 73
entering the second temple during his life, 97, 101–2
as equal with *Yahweh*, 98–101, 104
family fleeing Herod and living in Egypt, 143n71
flesh not seeing corruption, 195
fulfilled OT predictions, 24
fulfilled OT prophecies, 117, 164
fulfilling Malachi 3:1, 103
gave the disciples power to work miracles, 162
genealogical and family data of, 113–24
holding both a special economic and metaphysical relationship to God, 179
as identical with *Yahweh*, 99n134
identification with Malachi 3:1, 96–97
identified with the supplicant in Psalm 22, 210
identifying with Psalm 22, 206
as an illegitimate child, 137–38, 141
invoked the processional images related to Psalm 118, 81, 216
as the Jewish Messiah and judge of Israel, 104, 218
linking the stone metaphor to the new eschatological temple, 80
as the messenger of the covenant, 103, 104
as Messiah, 3
ministry summarized, 162
as a miracle worker, 145–48, 221
mother of, 118–19

nascent church declared the divinity
of, 199n146
neither affirmed nor denied Peter's
statement, 120
as the new Moses, 162
not denying his Davidic status, 121
NT documents attesting the divinity
of, 200n148
OT prophesying regarding life and
ministry of, 228
as the particular son of David, 202
Paul's affirmation of as a son of
David, 122
performed miracles with reference
to the implications of the OT,
222
personal identification with Psalm
22, 210
placing within the Davidic house,
124
as the probable fulfillment of
Malachi 3:1, 96
receiving the kingdom described in
Daniel 7:13-14, 4n5
recognized as an exorcist by his
contemporaries, 162–63
rejected Peter's attempt to intrude
into his agenda, 120
relationship with God, 178
relatives of, 114, 124, 136
reply to the high priest, 99
self-identifying as the prophet
predicted by Moses, 149
self-perception of, 120
sojourn in Egypt, 143n71
as Son of God by position and by
nature, 179
as son of "Pandera" or "Pantera," 138
view of his task, 120
work involving more than the
individual miracles, 164
as *Yahweh's* son, 180
Jesus Seminar
as hypercritical in approaching the
historical Jesus, 21
on Jesus acting against the temple,
101
on Jesus cleansing the temple, 80

rejecting that Jesus asked Peter the
question regarding his identity,
122–23
*Jesus the Messiah: Tracing the Promises,
Expectations, and Coming of
Israel's King* (Bateman, Bock,
and Johnston), 19, 40–41
*Jesus: The Testimony of Prophecy and
History* (Newman), 33–34
Jewish belief, on corruption of the body,
195
Jewish conceptual overlap, between
corruption in Sheol/the pit and
the grave, 195
Jewish documents (LXX), on Psalm
16:10, 203, 227
Jewish leaders, not denying that Jesus
was born in Bethlehem, 137, 142
Jewish literature, depicting miracles in
relation to the Messiah, 165
Jewish liturgical material, that the
throne of David would be
reestablished, 109
Jewish messianic thought, 19, 157
Jewish messianism, Davidic thinking as
a form of, 110–12
Jewish polemical literature, on Jesus,
110n16
Jewish rabbis
on Psalm 2:7, 178n57
on Psalm 118, 78
Jewish Talmud, considering Ezra as the
second Moses, 151n20
Jewish teachers, withheld information
about the birthplace of Jesus,
142
Jews
associated feats of power with the
coming of the messianic age, 162
believed that the Messiah would
have roots in Bethlehem of
Judea, 142
believed the soul remained near a
dead body for approximately
three days, 202
disposition toward messianic
expectation, 32

Jews *(continued)*
  expectation and desire that *Yahweh* would return to Zion, 86
  expecting a messiah born in Bethlehem of Judea, 136
  expecting a miracle-working Messiah, 148–65
  expecting a specific eschatological prophet, 149
  on Genesis 49:10 including the whole series of Jewish kings, 111
  hope for a restored kingdom ruled by the scion of David, 111
  theology of resurrection, 189n100
Job, 196
John (apostle), 98, 101
John 5:22-29, 101
John the Baptist (JTB)
  affirming Jesus as the fulfillment of OT prophetic messianic predictions, 3
  as the best identifiable candidate for the forerunner, 97, 103, 104, 218
  dressed in the same clothing as Elijah, 97
  fulfilling Malachi 3:1, 103
  as a historical person, 98
  identified as Elijah in the Synoptic Gospels, 218
  knew the truth about the birthplace of Jesus, 136
  messengers from, questioning Jesus concerning his messiahship, 160
  ministry decreased while Jesus' ministry increased, 98
  self-designation as a prophet in the OT tradition, 97
  as a separate and distinct witness to a connection of Jesus with Malachi, 96
  as a witness to the light, 98
Johnson, Marshall D., 116
Johnston, Gordon H., 40–41, 184–85
Johnston, Philip S., 191
Jordan River, stoppage of, 150
Joseph (husband of Mary), 118, 119, 132
Joseph and Mary, geographical locations of, 131–33

Josephus
  affirming the approximate time of the Messiah's appearance, 26
  attributing the destruction of the temple and Jerusalem to ancient prophecy, 101n141–2n141
  on the battle against Alexander Janneus, 108n8
  confirming the conceptual connection between the promised prophet and the Messiah, 152
  on Herod the Great's expenditures and embellishment of the temple, 85
  making mention of Jesus in the context of a virtuous life, 147n7
  silent on deaths in Bethlehem, 133
Joshua, 63, 150
JTB. *See* John the Baptist (JTB)
Jubilees (book of), 158
Judah, 63, 68, 72
Judaism, 44, 168
judge, role of Jesus as, 101
judgment, at an unexpected moment, 93
judgment and replacement motif, projecting, 66
Julius Africanus, 115
Justin Martyr (Justin), 5, 131n31, 146

Kaiser, Walter C., Jr., 172
Kaufman, Yeḥezkel, 115
Keener, Craig S., 54, 89n98, 148
Keith, Alexander, 25–26
Kepple, Robert J., 198
king
  hope for Israel's ideal, 112
  ruling from Zion, 171
"King of Israel," John calls Jesus the, 78
king of Israel, ordained to Saul from the tribe of Benjamin, 63
kingdom
  of David's offspring, 105
  that shall stand forever, 33
Kingsbury, Jack Dean, 163, 163n68
Koester, Helmut, 181
Kohler, Kaufmann, 100

SUBJECT INDEX

Kokkinos, Nikos, 140
Kuenen, Abraham, 46n54

"L" group of material, 134
Ladd, George E., 200n146
Lange, Harvey D., 204, 205–6
Lanier, Gregory R., 74–75
law
    compared to something universally true (inviolable), 55
    perfect adherence to guaranteeing success, 170
laws
    of logic, 18n44
    of nature, 55, 56
Lazarus, 197
leader, ideal, 170
Lebanon, as a symbol of magnificence, 155
less ad hoc, hypothesis as, 14
Lessing, G. E., 6–7
Letter to Aristides (Julius Africanus), 115
Levin, Yigal, 116, 118n51
levirate marriage, thesis of, 118–19
lexical evidence, regarding Psalm 16, 202
Licona, Michael R., 208–9, 208n177
light-to-the-Gentiles prophecy, of Isaiah 42 and 49, 36
literature, summary of important, 18–21
Literature Review
    overview of, 23–24
    section 1, 23, 24–25, 25–41
    section 2, 23–24, 41
    section 3, 24, 51
Locke, John, 125
logic, laws of, 18, 18n44
Loken, Israel, 204
long-range predictions, Oxtoby rejecting, 47
"the LORD," in Joel as *Yahweh*, 99
Lord YHWH of Hosts, ripping off the branches at one wrench, 108
Lövestam, Evald, 200–201
Lowery, David K., 119n55

Luke
    arguing for death and subsequent resurrection before corruption, 199
    on Bethlehem of Judea as the birthplace of Jesus, 126, 130, 134
    describing theophanic phenomena associated with the day of Pentecost, 90
    excluding Herod's order to kill the children of Bethlehem, 132
    identifying John the Baptist using language from Malachi, 97–98
    indicating the unique relationship of Jesus to God, 179
    pointing out the mistake of readers who may be thinking in terms of Matthew's genealogy, 118n52
    sources for birth narratives, 144, 220
    writing history to help Theophilus gain certainty, 129
    writing in historiographical style, 130
    writing to a Gentile audience, 133
LXX, agreeing with other Hebrew manuscripts on Psalm 22:16, 204

MacArthur, J., 179
Mach, R., 195
Maier, Paul, 143n71
Maimonides, 177n57, 178n57
mal' ak, meaning messenger, 95
Malachi
    as not primarily concerned with the eschatological future, 92
    temple envisioned by, 225
    use of the terms "Behold I Send" and "Suddenly," 91–93
Malachi 3, context of, 93
Malachi 3:1
    chiastic structure of, 93–95
    depicting *Yahweh* coming into his temple for judgment, 217, 225
    direct historic fulfillment of a prophecy by Jesus, 225

Malachi 3:1 *(continued)*
    directed to the second temple, 102
    distinguishing between three distinct individuals, 218
    interpretation of, 91–104
    possibility of a *terminus ad quem* for the advent of the Messiah, 217
Malone, Andrew S., 94
mankind, constantly seeking a messiah, 32
Mark
    appropriation of Psalm 2, 180
    citing Isaiah 40:3, 97
Mark 1:2b, 96
Mark 1:11, 180
Martha, despair exhibited by, 197
Mary
    authors of the birth narratives risking stigmatizing, 137
    described by Luke as treasuring up things and events, 129
    placing in the Davidic line, 118
    as the source of Jesus' Davidic status, 119
    as the source of Luke's infancy narrative, 130
Mary (sister of Martha), despair exhibited by, 197
Matthew
    birth narrative, 134
    mentioning knowledge of the chief priests and scribes in reference to Jesus' birth in Bethlehem, 125
    placing Jesus in the judge's seat, 101
    sources for birth narratives, 144, 220
    stating that Jesus was born in "Bethlehem of Judea," 126, 130
    as telling some of the story and Luke telling the rest of it, 131
    theological agenda of, 143n71
    tying the Herodian order to kill the children to OT prophecy, 133
    on the unique relationship of Jesus to God, 179
Mayhue, R., 179
Mazar, Amihai, 65n15
McCullagh, C. Behan, 14–15
Meier, John P. A., 129–30

Melchizedek, perpetual priesthood according to the order of, 172
Melkisedek, bearing significant messianic resemblance, 158n48
memorabile, depicting a historical event in one central point, 107
messenger
    as human, angelic, or divine, 95
    not identical with the forerunner "my messenger," 94
    preceding the messenger of the covenant, 102n143
messenger of the covenant, 93, 94, 95
Messiah
    to be born into a house of lowliness, 106
    bearing the power of the miracle-working Holy Spirit, 157
    entering the second or rebuilt temple, 25–26, 73, 76
    establishing the time of, 32
    furnished with a council to assist him, 127n16
    God begetting, 174–75
    as greater than any earthly king, 121
    Jesus' redemptive works identifying him as, 115
    mentioned on several occasions in the Pseudepigrapha, 157–58
    as the prophet like Moses, 164
    raising the dead in 1 Enoch, 157
    relationship to David, 45
    roots in Bethlehem of Judea, 220
    as a son of Mariamne and Herod, 137
    as springing from the linage of King David, 105
    terminus ad quem for the coming of, 61
messianic age
    affirmation of the presence of, 160
    diseases and other calamities finding no place in, 156
    Jewish expectation for the working of miracles, 148
    marked by miracles according to the Qumran sect, 159

as the period described in Isaiah 35
and 40, 155
messianic commentary, on the Balaam
oracle, 67
messianic expectation, 116n46, 124
messianic figure, 110, 127
messianic hope, existence of, 111
messianic ideal, 45
messianic implication, of Isaiah 29, 154
messianic interpretation
of Genesis 49:10, 32, 67, 216
of Psalm 16, 224
of Psalm 22, 204–5, 210
related to messiah ben David, 177
messianic pretenders, miracle-working
power of, 160
*Messianic Prophecies in Historical
Succession* (Delitzsch), 28
messianic prophecy. *See also* prophecy
analyzing, 21
developed along a continuum, 27
opening up new research
possibilities for, 9
progressive development of, 50
review of the traditional argument
from, 25–41
revitalization of the study of, 5
summary of the literature related
to, 18
works specifically treating, 23
*Messianic Prophecy: Its Origin, Historical
Character, and Relation to New
Testament Fulfillment* (Riehm),
26–28
"messianic psalter," 169
messianic significance, of 4Q174, 174
messianism
influence felt during the life of Jesus,
19
of the OT and pseudepigraphal
works, 110–11
as a universal phenomenon, 32
metaphysical relationship, of Jesus as
God incarnate, 179
methodological naturalism, 55
methodology, steps of, 215
Meyers, Carol L. and Eric M., 86
Micah 5:2

claims about Bethlehem, 220
declaring that a ruler will come
from Bethlehem Ephrathah, 125
literary and textual analysis, 126–31
as a prophecy naming Bethlehem of
Judea, 226
prophesying the birth of a future
ideal ruler, 126
Midrash, birth narratives as, 116
Midrash Rabbah, 70n39, 127
minimal facts
Bethlehem of Judea as the birthplace
of Jesus, 221
compared to historical facts, 72n42
criteria, 20, 215
as criteria-verifying, 5
defined, 17
evidence rising to a level of, 10
fifteen historical-evidential emerged,
225
italicized because of methodological
significance, 6n10
items specifically labeled as, 59
meeting the criteria for justifying
historical descriptions, 228
posing, 13
reducing data to, 8
reporting only the historical
evidence, 228
minimal-fact statements
related to the statement of the
problem, 225–27
supported by the present observable
data, 228
miracles
accompanied by preaching of the
good news, 162
alone not enough to confirm a true
prophet, 56n88
attended with multiple independent
witnesses, 54
expected in association with the
advent of the Messiah, 221
giving a moral certainty of the truth
of Christianity to the believer, 56
human testimony regarding as
untrustworthy, 53
Hume on the rejection of, 9n23

miracles *(continued)*
   implying that the messianic age had arrived, 161
   impossibility of, 7
   of Jesus, 221
   performed by Jesus in accordance with the OT, 226
   possibility of, 51–57
   rationale for not rejecting *a priori*, 24
   rejecting the possibility of, 9, 51
   as a violation of the laws of nature, 9n23
miracle-working activity, required for a prophet like Moses, 149
miracle-working strand, of Jewish messianism, 162
miraculous acts, attributed to Jesus in a variety of ancient books, 145
Mitchell, David C., 171
Moab and Edom, subjugation of by David, 66–67
Moehring, Horst R., 141n66
Moore, Erika, 169–70
Moreland, J. P., 54
Morey, Robert A., 193
Moses, 63, 148–49, 150
Moses/Christ typology, 149, 150
mother of Jesus, 118–19. *See also* Mary
Mowinckel, Sigmund
   on dating the final form of the psalms, 169
   on eschatological sayings of prophetic books, 152
   on Ezekiel contributing to the overall idea of the Messiah, 70
   on the king, as *Yahweh*'s anointed son, having a rightful claim to dominion over the whole world, 183
   on Psalm 16, 188n98
   on Psalm 22, 203
   on Psalm 118:25ff, 79
   rejecting Psalm 2 as a direct reference to the eschatological Messiah, 185

MT's (Masoretic Text), consistently different spelling for the place Shiloh, 62
Murphy, Roland E., 195

narrative smoothing, Matthew and Luke not showing evidence of, 144
"nations," perishing in a universal judgment, 170
naturalistic assumptions, *a priori* rejection of miracles based on, 54–55
naturalistic means, explaining the phenomenon of predictive prophecy, 35
nature, of an individual inherited from his progenitors, 179
Nazareth of Galilee, 144, 221
near-eastern royal-adoption formulas, not containing "begotten" language, 173
Nebuchadnezzar, 69
New Testament (NT)
   affirming Jesus as performing various miracles, 145–46
   apocryphal works in agreement with the historicity of Jesus' birth in a cave near Bethlehem, 128n20
   applying Psalm 2 to Jesus as the Messiah, 182
   applying the image of Psalm 22 to the death of Jesus, 36
   attesting Jesus' Davidic status, 226
   attributing prophetic fulfillments to Jesus, 19
   attributing Psalm 16 to David and verse 10 as a direct prophecy of the resurrection of Jesus, 202
   citing Psalm 22 on no less than fourteen occasions, 208, 208n176
   consistent messianic exegesis of Psalm 2 by, 180
   correlating Jesus' suffering with the supplicant of Psalm 22, 211
   declaring the divinity of Jesus, 219n2

declaring the unique metaphysical relationship of Jesus to the Father, 223
depicting the expectation of a particular prophet, 222
on the expectation of a particular prophet, 165
on Genesis 49:10, 71
on Haggai 2:1-9, 88–89
identifying the suffering in Psalm 22 with Jesus, 224
insight into how the Hebrew Scriptures were traditionally understood, 182
on Jesus as the fulfillment of Psalm 22, 210
on Jesus representing the coming of *Yahweh*, 94
on John the Baptist as the forerunner of Jesus, 96
as a legitimate source, 182
on Malachi 3:1, 96
on Micah 5:2, 130–31
on the miracle-working Messiah, 160–63, 165
on prophecy fulfilled, 18
on Psalm 2, 178–84
on Psalm 16, 197–201
on Psalm 16:10, 203, 227
on Psalm 22, 208–9, 210
on Psalm 118, 78–80
reading into OT prophecies things they did not contain, 46n54
recording that Jesus performed miracles in accordance with the OT, 165, 226
on 2 Samuel 7:13, 112–24
writers explaining the New Testament use of the Old Testament, 20
Newman, Robert C.
on messianic prophecy, 33–34, 36
placing the location of Israelite kings in the land of Judah, 63–64
on predictive prophecy, 34–35
works by, 20
Nickelsburg, George W. E., 175
Nicodemus, 99–100, 100n136, 115

non-biblical sources
earliest for studying messianic thought, 19
predating the historical Jesus, 20
non-canonical Jewish writers, verifying the expectation of a miracle-working messianic figure, 53
non-canonical texts, interpreting prophecy as messianic, 17
noncontradiction, law of, 18n44
Numbers 24:14, 66
Numbers 24:17, 67, 71

"office of Christ and his Church," prophecy preparing the way for, 43
Old Testament (OT)
containing implicit, ambiguous messianic concepts, 40
deficiencies of contemporary treatments of prophecy, 8
envisioning the sort of event alleged to be its NT fulfillment, 12
evidential approaches to messianic prophecy, 7n13
examining specific prophecies and their NT counterparts, 13
fulfillment of messianic prophecies, 229
fulfillment of predictions, 39
Genesis 49:10, 68–70
Haggai 2:1-9, 82–85
on Jesus as the fulfillment of prophecies, 29
on a Jewish expectation of a miracle-working Messiah, 148–57
limited sense of canon, 40
messianic prophecies rarely limiting perspective, 19
Micah 5:2, 126–27
original understanding of messianic texts, 50
passages connecting Moses and messianic redemption with a second Moses motif, 150, 151
pertaining to "Messiah as a light to the Gentiles," 33

Old Testament *(continued)*
  portraying several prophets with some second-Moses themes, 151
  on the possibility of a canonical reading of, 40
  proper method for interpreting prophecy in, 229
  prophecies, directly associated with Jesus' messianic status, 160
  prophecies, fulfilled by Jesus, 146
  prophecies, not invented or staged by the NT church, 36
  prophecies, on aspects of Jesus' life and ministry, 228
  prophecies, predicting events that did not come to pass, 47
  Psalm 2, 166–73
  Psalm 16, 187–94
  Psalm 22, 203–5
  relationship of prophecies with NT fulfillments, 10
  2 Samuel 7:13, 105–8
  texts pertaining to the Messiah, 33–34
  types of prophecy, 35
  witnessing the prophets and nation of Israel, 53
omniscience, as supernatural, 51
"One who is to come," derived from Malachi 3:1, 96
The One Who Is to Come (Fitzmyer), 49
oracle of salvation, depicted in Isaiah 35, 156
oral traditions of the Jews, incomplete transmission of, 182
Origen
  accusation of a sexual relationship between Mary and a Roman soldier (Panthera), 141
  employing OT prophecy to defend the Messiah, 5
  on the Gospel of John identifying John the Baptist as the forerunner of Jesus, 103
  on historical events, 59, 59n90
  on Jewish teachers withholding information from the public about the birthplace of Jesus, 127
  on the place where Jesus was born, 137
  understanding and evidence that Jesus was born in Bethlehem, 128
Oswalt, John N., 161
Oxtoby, Gurdon C., 46–48

Paffenroff, Kim, 134
Palestinian Judaism, messianic beliefs of, 176–77
Panthera, refering to any Roman soldier, 142
Parable of the Tenants, 80
parthenos (virgin), term originally applied to Mary, 138
path of life, leading into the presence of *Yahweh*, 188
"pattern and prophecy," dynamic nature of, 40
Patterson, Richard D., 206, 206n165
Paul (Saul of Tarsus)
  advocating Jesus as the Messiah through the words of the OT prophets, 4
  affirming the suffering of the Messiah, 4n6
  alignment of Jesus and *Yahweh*, 99
  as another source of information concerning the testimony of Jesus, 100
  believed Jesus to be the uniquely begotten Son never to see corruption, 200
  citing OT prophecy, 5n7
  claimed Jesus was a physical descendant of King David, 124
  closely aligning Jesus with *Yahweh*, 99
  consenting to the stoning of Stephen, 100
  on Genesis 49:10, 71n40
  on Jesus as the fulfillment of prophecies, 4n7

on Jesus being raised after three days "according to the Scriptures," 195
on "the Lord" as clearly Jesus, 99
persecutions of the new Jewish sect (Christians), 4
placing John the Baptist in the role of forerunner, 98
on Psalm 2:7 in Romans 1:4, 180
repeated references to the OT prophets, 4
on the resurrection of Jesus as fulfillment of the Davidic Covenant, 200
on 2 Samuel 7:13, 112–13
on the sonship concept in Acts and Romans, 180
spreading knowledge of Jesus as the son of David, 122
Payne, J. Barton
  on biblical prophecy, 37–39
  on dating of Isaiah 29, 153
  on Psalm 16, 188n98
  on Psalm 22, 203
Pentecost. *See* day of Pentecost
Peter
  argument in Acts 2:24-31 for the resurrection of Jesus, 198
  identifying Jesus as the particular descendant of David, 198
  on Jesus as the fulfillment of OT promises, 4
  on Jesus was a miracle-worker, 146
  on Psalm 16:10 as applied to the resurrection of Jesus, 199
  transferring the messianic Davidic throne from Jerusalem to God's right hand in heaven, 200n146
Pharisees, John using the terminology of, 100n136
Philo, 26
physical corruption, 192
pierced-one prophecy, of Psalm 22, 36, 204, 224
Pilate, Pontius, 4, 146
pit, 192, 201
Plumber, Rolles, 194
Pohlig, James, 92–93

Poirier, John C., 195
the "poor," 161
The Popular Encyclopedia of Bible Prophecy, article on messianic prophecy, 29
post-apostolic sources, believing prophecy was fulfilled, 18
post-exilic era, changes in the way the Jewish people viewed death and Sheol, 193
post-exilic redaction and arrangement, evidence from regarding Psalm 2, 169–71
pre-Christian Jewish texts, associated with Psalm 2, 176
pre-Christian Judaism or other pre-Christian Jewish writings, messianic titles used in a messianic sense, 50
pre-Christian verification, on Psalm 2, 175
predicative prophecy, assessing the claims of, 31
prediction, 31
Prediction and Fulfillment in the Bible (Oxtoby), 46
predictive elements, Payne's criteria for determining legitimate, 37–38
predictive prophecy. *See also* prophecy
  altering or eliminating the traditional approach to, 41–51
  criteria or techniques employed to disallow the existence of genuine, 35
  as dynamic and accurate, 31
  Hume's arguments and, 55–57
  as miraculous in nature, 34–35
  scholars avoiding as subject matter, 9
  as a sub-species of miracle, 10
pre-Matthean sources, material attributed to, 135
preservation, in Psalm 16, 192–93, 227
presuppositions
  about supernatural activity, 28
  of the author, 18
  of an inspired text and canonical readings, 41

presuppositions *(continued)*
  regarding prophecy, 24
  role in the traditional argument from OT messianic prophecy to the conclusion that Jesus is the Messiah, 29
Priestly source (P), dated sixth century BC, 65n14
primary sources, demonstrating familiarity with, 18
principle of analogy. *See* analogy
probabilities, determining by the methodology explicated by C. Behan McCullagh, 13–15
probability, of historical events, 54, 59
progression, from the metaphorical (Isa 6:10) to the literal (Isa 35:5-6), 155
Prophecies about the Coming Messiah (Newman), 20, 36
prophecy. *See also* messianic prophecy; predictive prophecy
  actualized in human experience, 30
  apologetic value of, 30, 31
  aspects of Matthew's appropriation of, 48
  classic or traditional argument from, 23
  considered messianic within Judaism, 17
  criteria for identifying in Payne's work, 39
  criteria to evaluate miraculous, 35
  determining fulfillment of, 39
  evaluated unfilled, 89n102
  implication of unfulfilled, 17–18
  as incapable of staged fulfillments, 12
  including predictive elements, 29–30
  as a legitimate apologetic tool, 5
  made prior to its alleged fulfillment, 12
  as a multi-strand work of preparation, 27
  not necessarily bound to second-hand testimony, 56
  outcomes for, 6, 57n89, 215, 225
  predicting literal events, 15
  reducing to an ideal, 42
  responses on failed, 47n58
  spoken before the alleged fulfillment, 17
  as a subspecies of miracle, 20
  traditional argument from, 24
  treating as a whole, 43
  true evidence of, 46
  as verifiable historically, 56
Prophecy and Prediction (Beegle), 48–49
The Prophet Motive (Barfield), 30–33
prophetic fulfillment in Christ, 27
prophetic language, 15
prophetic protagonist
  escaping decay, 223
  existence in the realm of the dead as not permanent, 201
  as a future "holy one" experiencing preservation, 194
  identity of, 191, 194n125
  not permanently left in Sheol, 201
  as the referent of Psalm 16, 189n105
  whole being preserved by Yahweh, 194, 201–2
prophets
  calling Israel to holiness, 37
  distinguishing true, 30
Protestant Christian Evidences (Ramm), 29–30
Psalm 1 and 2, as the introduction to the Hebrew Psalter, 166–67, 171
Psalm 2
  celebrating the institution of the Davidic covenant, 173
  as eschatological, 185, 223, 227
  facts evident in relation to, 185
  Fitzmyer's treatment of, 51n67
  interpretations of, 166, 174, 177n56
  no certain historical king or occasion assigned to, 185, 226
  not a private acknowledgment, 180
  originally written as prophecy, 185, 186
  parallelisms in, 183
  prefixed to the finished collection, 169, 172
  quoted or alluded to in the NT, 178

restricting to metaphorical
adoption, 173
timing of acquiring a messianic
eschatological interpretation,
176
universal scope of requiring a
messianic referent, 182–83
Psalm 2:1-12, emphasizing verse 7,
166–86, 223
Psalm 2:7, applied to Jesus, 181
Psalm 2:7-8, containing adoptive
language, 173n37
Psalm 8 and 110, accepted as
compositions of David, 121n64
Psalm 16, 187–203, 223–24
authorship and referent of, 202, 224
classified as a psalm of "confidence,"
187
grammatical difficulties in verses
9-10, 189
indicative of the resurrection of
Jesus, 166
no consensus on the overall
interpretation of, 188
on preservation from corruption,
203, 227
as a prophecy of Jesus' resurrection,
187
Psalm 16:10, "corruption" translation
versus "pit," 223
Psalm 22
as controversial, 203
depicting a suffering person, 20, 204
evidence against a directly messianic
intent for the original work, 209
interpretive history of prior to the
Christian era, 204
literary and textual analysis, 203–11
as messianic, 166
Newman's reasons for viewing as
a depiction of the suffering of
Jesus, 36
partially preserved in three of the
Dead Sea Scrolls, 205
personal application of by a psalmist
in Qumran, 206, 209, 224
study results, 224
Psalm 22:16, 210

Psalm 110, 121n64, 168
Psalm 116, parallels with 118, 76n60–
77n60
Psalm 118
containing eschatological motifs
from its origin, 76
historical period of the composition
of, 77
incidental nature of the temple to
the meaning of, 216–17
interpretation of, 72–82
literary and textual analysis, 72–77
message of eschatological
deliverance, 77
originally included eschatological
elements, 81
used by NT writers, 72–73
Psalms, final form of, 169
Psalms of Solomon, 108, 176
Pseudepigrapha
containing messianic components,
127
depicting miracles in relation to the
Messiah or the messianic age,
157, 165
not giving attention to Psalm 22,
206
overview of miracles and the
Messiah in, 157–60
paucity of clearly identifiable
references attributable to Psalm
22, 209
Puech, Pace, 176

Q, 97, 100, 101
Q 3:16b-17, 98
Quadratus, 146
Quirinius, 139
Qumran
associated *šāhat* with corruption,
195
evidence from concerning Psalm 16
as inconclusive, 202
expected miracles to accompany the
age of the Messiah, 159
Isaiah 28:16 referenced in relation
to, 75n53

Qumran *(continued)*
  overview of miracles and the Messiah in, 158–59
  portions of Psalm 15 in the scrolls of, 194
  referencing Messiah as a branch or scion of David, 173–75

rabbinic literature, attributing miraculous power to Jesus through sorcery, 147
Ramm, Bernard, 29–30
Ramsay, William Mitchell, 129, 138–39
Rashi, 177
rebuilt temple. *See* temple
the redeemed, joyful return of, 155
registration, of Luke 2, 139, 141
rejected stone, reset as the Messiah/cornerstone, 81
relatives of Jesus, in the first-century church, 114
repentance, linked with the coming of the messiah, 115n42
research, recommendations for future, 229
restoration, in Isaiah 34–35, 156
resurrection
  associated with Jesus' appointment as judge, 181n67
  of the dead, 193
  earliest mentions of in the OT, 188n98
  guaranteeing fulfillment of the mercies of David, 201
  implication of in Psalm 16, 194
  pointing directly to Psalm 2, 180
  as a universal declaration of Jesus' divine sonship for Luke and Paul, 180n64
  witnesses to, 54
Revelation, references to Psalm 2, 181–82
Revelation 11, two unknown witnesses dead for three and a half days, 196n134
Reyburn, William David, 187
Riehm, Eduard Karl August, 26–28

righteous and the unrighteous, separate fates for, 193
righteous branch, of David, 107, 219
Roberts, J. J. M., 126–27, 168
Robertson, A. T., 139–40
"rod of iron," ruling the nations with, 182
Roman Catholic Church, official interpretation of Psalm 16, 188
Roman historians, verifying messianic expectation, 32
Roman world, Herod dealt harshly with sedition, 133
Ross, Alan P., 168
Royal Psalms
  affirming the Davidic Covenant and its promises, 171
  Gunkel affirming ten, 172
  poetic language and devices of, 183
  Psalm 2 classified as, 166
ruler of Israel, from the tribe of Judah, 64
"ruler's staff" (xx), meaning of, 62
Rydelnik, Michael, 151
Ryle, Herbert E., 43–46

Sadducees, 112
šāhat, translating as "corruption" or pit, 191–92
Samaritan woman, knowledge of the coming one expressed by, 96
2 Samuel 7:1-17, 105–6
2 Samuel 7:13, 105–24, 218–19
2 Samuel 7:13, 16, 226
Sanders, E. P.
  arguing that the Jewish people were not expecting a miracle-working messianic figure, 148
  on the historicity of Jesus' entry into Jerusalem, 79
  on the historicity of the movements of Jesus' family, 131
  on Luke having the family returning directly to Galilee after the scene at the temple, 132
Sanhedrin, 99, 120
Saucy, Mark, 157, 162

Saul, from the tribe of Benjamin, 63
Saul of Tarsus. *See* Paul (Saul of Tarsus)
Savior. *See also* Jesus
    time of the coming of, 25
scepter, as an emblem of royal authority, 63
"scepter" (xx), meaning of, 62
Schaper, Joachim, 169, 172
Schereschewsky, Ben-Zion, 168
Schiffman, L. H., 174
scholarly opinions, regarding Psalm 16, 187–88
scholars
    consensus that Jesus was a miracle-worker, 147
    defined, 18
scholarship, providing interaction with the assertions of critical, 34
science, inability to "postulate absolutes," 55
scientific method, changing and evolving as knowledge increases, 54
Scott, R. B. Y., 154–55
second song of the Servant of YHWH, Isaiah 49:1-9 as, 177
second temple. *See* temple
second temple period, establishing the *terminus ad quem* associated with Malachi 3:1, 92
secondary meanings, transcending the understanding of the original oracle, author, and recipients, 16
second-Moses concept, 151, 222
seed of David, as a physical descendant, 110
sensus plenior, explaining the New Testament use of the Old Testament, 19
Septuagint
    analysis of allegedly messianic OT texts presented in, 50
    as a commentary on the *Tanakh*, 50
    Hebrew text used by for Psalm 22:16, 205
    translation of Psalm 15 (English 16) as undoubtedly pre-Christian, 194

seventy-weeks prophecy, of Daniel 9, 36
Shemoneh Esreh, 73, 109, 197
Sheol, 188, 193
shepherds, annunciation to paralleled by the magi story, 135
Shiloh, 61–62, 68n31
signs, the Messiah will give, 160–61
Similitudes (Parables), 175
"sinister reinterpretation," of Ezekiel, 69
Smith, George Adam, 154
Smith, James E., 183
Solomon, as the "Son of David" and the only king to be called "God's son," 163
Solomon's temple, former glory of "this house" as a reference to, 82
son
    meaning of in Psalm 2:7, 167
    as a term applied at the point of exaltation, 181
Son, Kiwoong, 176
Son of David
    as a Christological messianic title, 163
    Edghill and Ryle on, 44–45, 46
    Matthew identifies Jesus as, 78
    not adequate to depict the office of Jesus, 121
son of God
    in a controversial Aramaic fragment from Qumran as the Davidic messiah, 64
    Edghill and Ryle on, 46
    future Davidic scion as, 174
    in Israelite settings as a title of official sonship, 44
    by position and nature, 179
    as preparation for a Son of God, 44
son of man
    centered in the frailty of man but also a messianic designation, 44
    Edghill and Ryle on, 46
    exalted functions, 157
    Jesus evoking the image of, 4
sons of God, designating beings of a higher metaphysical order, 44
sonship, 180, 181
sorrow and pain, banishment of, 155

soul of the dead, remained near for approximately seventy-two hours after death, 202
spiritual blindness and deafness, making the nation poor and weak, 154
spoken prophecy, minimal fact referring to, 17
statement of the problem, minimal-fact statements related to, 225–27
Stephen, mentioning the coming of the Righteous One, 4
Stern, David H., 118n52, 160
stone
  interpreting in Psalm 118 as the nation of Israel, 75
  that the builders rejected, 74
stone metaphor
  in exilic and post-exilic literature, 75
  no historical-evidential way to demonstrate directly identifying with the Messiah, 81
  other significant uses of, 75n53
  as a reference to Israel in Psalm 118, 75n56
  used by Jesus, 80
Strack, Hermann L., 177
Strack and Billerbeck, Paul, 151, 159
Strauss, David Friedrich, 116
Strauss, Mark L., 109, 171–72
study, results of, 215–29
stylization, proving that the early church understood Jesus to be the Davidic Messiah, 219
"suddenly," Malachi's use of, 91–93
Suetonius, 26, 32
sufferer in Qumran, language of Psalm 22 appropriate to his own suffering, 205
suffering supplicant, in Psalm 22, 208
suffering-servant prophecy, of Isaiah 53, 36
superhuman characteristics, messianic figures with, 112, 112n26
supernatural activity, 18, 28
supernatural inspiration, 24
supernaturalism, 49
Swinburne, Richard, 55
Symeon, son of Clopas, 136

Tacitus, Cornelius, 26, 32, 32n24
Talmud
  overview of miracles and the Messiah in, 159–60
  reference to the Messiah in association with the "day of the Lord," 103
Tanakh, translation of as a composite work, 50
Targum, on Psalms 2 as eschatologically and messianically oriented, 177
Targum Jonathan to the Prophets, 127
Targum Onkelos, 70
"teaching of Christ," prophecy preparing the world for, 43
temple
  as a central feature in the book of Malachi, 217
  cleansing of, 73, 79, 101
  during the composition of Psalm 118 as probably the rebuilt temple, 81
  dissatisfaction with the first-century, 111
  as the one Jesus entered, 82, 97
  possessed great material splendor, 90
  things missing from, 87n94
  torn down by the Romans, 95
"tent peg" image, from Isaiah 22:20–23, 75
terminology, definitions of key, 16–18
terminus ad quem, for the advent of the Messiah, 11, 61, 72, 82, 90
Terry, Milton S., 15
Tertullian, 133n36, 146
Testament of Benjamin, 86
Testament of Jacob, 71, 216
Testament of Judah, 70
textual and historical evaluation, accepted standards for, 3n3
thanksgiving song
  in Isaiah 12:1-6, 76
  Psalm 118 as, 73
theologoumenon theory, 116, 116n46, 136
Theophilus, 129, 130
Theudas, 152

SUBJECT INDEX

"this house"
    as ambiguous terminology, 90
    in Haggai 2:1-9, 82–83
    Malachi not employing the ambiguous language related to, 92
Thompson, Marianne Meye, 158
Three Views on the New Testament Use of the Old Testament (Kaiser Jr.), 19
Tigay, Jeffrey Howard, 149, 168
titular nomens
    of Jesus, 145
    Jesus' self-described, 221
Titulus Tiburtinus, 140
Titulus Venetus, 140
"to fill with glory," referring to the manifest presence of God, 87
Tostengard, Sheldon, 209
treasures (xx), textual-historical ground for understanding, 83–84
tree of life, as a symbol for the Israelite monarchy, 106
tree-related terminology
    in Jeremiah 23:5, 107
    recounting the Davidic promise, 219
tribes of Israel, in the Testament of Jacob, 65–66
Triumphal Entry
    all four evangelists narrating a version of, 78
    historicity of the basic story line of, 79
    of Jesus into the temple, 216
    NT attestations of, 82
    Psalm 118 in the narrative of, 73
    royal manifestation of, 73
Troeltsch, Ernst, 55
A True Discourse (Celsus), 147
Trull, Gregory V.
    dividing the range of opinions concerning the meaning of Psalm 16 into categories, 188n99
    hermeneutical approaches of modern scholarship, 15n34
    on Peter's argument in Psalm16:10, 198–99, 199n143
    on resurrection intended by David in Psalm 16:10, 197

truth, 18, 52
Trypho the Jew, on Christ as a man of solely human birth, 98n127
Twelftree, Graham H., 147, 162
types, 38–39
typology, 20, 38

unclean, excluded, 155
underworld, placement in, 190
unfulfilled prophecy, cannot be evaluated evidentially, 89n102
"unit ideas," of Deutero-Isaiah, 155
unrighteous rulers, response to the scoffing of, 171
"until he comes," Ezekiel's appropriation of the expression, 69
unwed mother, in first-century Jewish culture could mean death, 137

VanderKam, James C., 175
VanGemeren, William A., 187, 192
vaticinia ex eventu, Genesis 49:1-27 as, 65
vaticinium ex eventu prophecy (late dating), claiming, 42
vengeance and recompense, of God, 155
verification
    Barfield's principles for, 31
    evidential, 42
    pre-Christian on Psalm 2, 175
    of prophecy as inspired, 37
Vermes, Geza, 175
Vespasian, 32
virgin conception, 138

Waltke, Bruce K., 169–70, 185n87
Watts, John D. W., 153
weak and fearful, encouraging, 155
Weldon, John, 23
"well-attested grounds," Habermas giving priority to, 6n10
Westermann, Claus, 65
Whiting, Mark J., 170
Whitsett, Christopher G., 180–81
wicked, as chaff, 170
wild beasts, no longer present, 155
Wildberger, Hans, 106, 153, 156

wilderness, rejoicing of, 155
Williams, A. Lukyn, 178n57
Williamson, H. G. M., 155
Willis, John T., 167, 182, 184
Wilson, Gerald Henry, 169, 172
Witherington, Ben III, 112
Wolff, Hans Walter, 107
Wright, N. T., 111, 197, 197n137

Yahweh
    begetting in relation to, 168
    coming into his temple for judgment, 104, 225
    coming of, 93, 94
    continued rejection of, 157
    covenant with King David and his descendants, 105
    glory of manifest, 155
    Jesus as, 98
    perpetual judgment on Edom, 154
    promising to be with Joshua "as" with Moses, 150
    relationship with the "begotten" son, 170
    rescue by, 76
    seeing the psalmist through the imminent crisis, 191
    stone originally meaning, 75
    supplied Israel with a succession of prophets, 149
    visual phenomena associated with the presence of, 84
Yahwist source (J), dated tenth century BC, 65n14
Yalkut Shimeoni, 207n174–8n174, 209

Zadokites, 136–37
Zealots, 136
Zedekiah, 69
Zenger, E., 169
Zerubbabel, 49, 112, 115
Zion, 183
Zodhiates, Spiros, 179
Zoroastrianism, 195n131
Zuck, Roy B., 161–62

Ancient Document Index

Old Testament

Genesis 197

6:2	44
12:7	71n40
14:18-20	33
21:17	95
35:19-21	135
49:1	66
49:1-26	68n31
49:1-27	65, 65n17, 66, 67
49:1b	65, 66, 72
49:8-10	66
49:10	11, 19, 25, 32, 33, 61–72, 70n38, 70n39, 71n40, 111, 216, 217
97	70n39
98:8-9	70n39
99	70n39

Exodus

4:11	162
7-12	162
14:19	95
15	76
15:2	76
40	85
40:34	87

Leviticus, 9 85

Numbers

24	86
24:7, 17 LXX	177n54
24:9, 17	113n30
24:14	66, 66n21
24:17	66n23, 67, 71

Deuteronomy

1:15, 18	150
4:30	66
15:18-22	222
18	30, 151
18:15	86
18:15, 18	150
18:15-18	11, 145, 148–52
18:15-22	30, 221
31:29	66
32:4, 37	74
33	65, 65n17
34:9-12	150

Joshua

1:5	150
1:7	170
3:7	150
6:20	150
10:13	150
19:15	133n37

Judges, 5:14-18 65, 65n17

1 Samuel

9:16	63
9:20	83
16:1	184
16:13	184
21:11	183

2 Samuel

5:17	177
7	80, 173
7:1-17	105–6, 218
7:8-16	200
7:9b	105
7:11-14	174
7:11c	64
7:12	64, 71n40, 105, 106, 191
7:12-14	108, 113
7:12-16	67
7:13	11, 64, 105–8, 218–20
7:13, 16	172, 200, 226, 228
7:13-16	201
7:13a	105
7:13b	105
7:14	64, 168, 179
7:16	105, 218
7:22-23	189
22:3	109
22:15	105
22:51	199n143
23:1	199n143
23:5	201

1 Kings

2:45	105
8	85

2 Samuel, 2:1-4 184

2 Kings, 1:8 97

1 Chronicles

5:2	68
14	183
22:6-10	107

2 Chronicles

5:14	87
7:1-4	87
13:5	106
21:20	84
32:27	83
36:10	83

Job

1:6	44
14:22	196
17:13-16	193
17:14	192

Psalms

1	170, 172
1 and 2	166, 169, 170, 170n21, 171, 173
1:1	170
1:1a	169
1:2	169
1:3	170
1:5	170
1:6	170
2	12, 51n67, 166, 167, 168, 169, 170, 171, 172, 173, 174, 175, 176, 176n51, 177, 178, 178n57, 179, 180, 181, 182, 183, 184, 185, 186, 223, 226, 227

ANCIENT DOCUMENT INDEX 277

2:1	169, 177	18:50	105, 171
2:1-9	172	18:51	199n143
2:1-12	12, 166–86, 223	20:1-9	172
2:2	175, 176n51	21:1-13	172
2:2, 7-8, 10	182	22	12, 20, 33, 36, 166, 184, 203–11, 224
2:4	170, 171		
2:4-6	172		
2:4a	170, 171	22:1	208, 208n176, 208n177, 210
2:6	170, 171		
2:7	12, 166–86, 178n57, 200, 223, 228	22:1-31	12, 166, 203–11
		22:5	208n176
		22:7	206n165, 208n176
2:7-8	173n37	22:7-8	208n177
2:8	172, 178n57	22:8	208n176
2:8-12	170	22:15	208n177
2:9	176, 182	22:15 (16 in Hebrew)	208n174
2:12	170, 183	22:16	12, 166, 203–11, 208n177, 209n177, 224
2:12b	169		
2-89	169, 172		
3-41	169, 172	22:16 (LXX 21:17)	207n170, 207n171
4:23	194n125		
4:25	194n125	22:17	209n177
8	44, 121n64	22:18	208n176, 208n177
8:6	121	22:18 (LXX 21:19)	207n172
8:23	194n125	22:20	205
13:10	194n125	22:20 (LXX 21:21)	207n168
14:3, 10	194n125	22:21a	205
14:6	194n125	22:21b	205
15	74, 194	22:22	208n176
15 (English 16)	194	22:22 (LXX 21:23)	207n173
15:10ff	188	22:23	208n176
16	12, 166, 187–203, 198n142, 223–24, 227	22:31	208n176
		42:2 (LXX 41:3)	207n173
		42-89	169, 172
16:7	199n143	45:5	172
16:8-11	198	45:6, 16-17	171
16:9	118n98	45:7	172
16:9-10	12, 166, 187–203, 223–24	49:16	190
		56-60	189
16:10	118n98, 180n64, 188, 198, 199n146, 223, 224, 227, 228	72	172
		72:1-4, 7	172
		72:8-11	172
		72:9-11	172
16:11	194	72:16	172
17:21 LXX	108n7	73:24	190
17:23	113n30	79:25	113n30
18	74	82:6-7	44
18:31-42	172	89	110, 172

Psalms *(continued)*

89:4, 29	171
89:27-30	176
89:30	201
106:24	84
110	33, 115n41, 121, 121n64, 168, 171, 173, 179, 185, 198, 199n143, 199n146, 223
110:1	171, 172, 199n146, 200n146
110:1-2, 5-6	172
110:2	172
110:3	168, 171, 176
110:4	118n98, 171
110:4 nrsv	172
110:5	171
116	77n60, 78
116:3	77n60
116:3-4, 7-9, 15	77n60
116:4, 13, 17	77n60
116:4, 16	77n60
116:6, 13	77n60
116:17	77n60
118	11, 72–82, 216–17
118 (LXX 117)	207n171
118:1, 19, 21, 28, 29	77n60
118:5	77n60
118:10-12, 26	77n60
118:14, 15, 21, 25	77n60
118:17-18	77n60
118:20	78
118:21	76
118:22	78, 81
118:22-23	80
118:25	77n60
118:25, 26	73
118:25ff	79
118:26	61, 74
118:27	78
118:27, 28	78
118:28	78
119 (LXX 118)	207n170
120 (LXX text form only)	207n170
132:10-12, 17	171
132:11	198, 199n143
132:12	171
132:17	113n30
146:8	162
149	170n21

Proverbs, 19:21 70n39

Isaiah

1-12	76
1-39	156
2:2	66n21
2:16	83
4:23N	160
6	85, 155, 157
6:1ff	101
6:10	153, 155
7:14	45, 48
8:22	153
9:7	112
9:10	113n30
10:33	45
10:33-34	108
11	106, 108, 153, 154, 155, 176, 177
11:1	45, 106, 112, 219
11:1-2	11, 105, 160, 218
11:1-5	108
11:1-10	176
11:10-16	149
11:11	151
12	76
12:1-2	76
12:1-6	76
12:2b	76
17:13	170
22:20-23	75
26:19	118n98, 194, 199
28:16	74, 75, 75n53
28:16-17	74
29	152, 153, 154, 164, 221, 222
29:9-11	153
29:18	11, 145, 152–54, 155, 160, 162, 221, 222
31:9	75n52
32:1-5	155

34	154
34:10	154
34-35	156
35	154, 155, 156, 164, 221
35:1	155
35:1-2	154, 155
35:1-5	154–57, 222
35:2	155
35:3-4	155
35:3-4, 10	154
35:4	155
35:5	160, 162
35:5-6	11, 145, 153, 155, 160, 221, 222
35:6	153, 160
35:6-7	155
35:6a	156
35:7, 9	155
35:8	155
35:9-10	155
35:10	155, 156
40:1-2	155
40:1-5	155
40:3	97, 155
40:3-5	102n143
40:5	155
40:10	155
40:16	155
40:29	155
40-56	35
41	30
41:10, 13-14	155
41:15	170
41:18	155
41:19	155
41:22-23	30
42	36
42:6-7	33
42:7	153, 162
42:7, 16	155, 222
42:11	155
42:16	153
43:1, 5	155
43:8	153
43:19	155
43:19-20	155
43:20	155
44:2	155
44:3	155
45:17	155
45:23	99
46:13	155
48:20	155
48:21	151
49	36
49:1-9	177
49:5-6	33
49:10	155
49:11	155
49:25	155
49:25-26	155
51:1	75n52
51:3	155
51:7	155
51:11	156
51:22	155
52:1, 11	155
52:8-9	155
52:9	155
52:13-53:12	33
53	36
54:4, 14	155
54:14	155
55:3	200, 201
56-66	156
57:1-2	194
61	153, 221
61:1	160, 161, 162
61:1-2	11, 31, 145, 153n32, 160, 221

Jeremiah

3:19	84
12:10	84
18:7-10	49n62
22:30	45
23:5	107, 112, 113n30
23:5-6	11, 105, 107, 218, 219
25:34	83
28:9	30
30:9	113n30
33:14-15	113n30

Jeremiah (continued)

33:15-17	112
48:47	66n21
49:39	66n21

Lamentations

1:16	127
1:16, 51	70n39

Ezekiel

21	69
21:27	69
21:27b	69
26:7-13	49
26:12	83
33:33	30
34:23-24	11, 105, 107, 112, 218, 219
37:25	112
40-48	90n103
43:5	87
44:4	87
47:12	170

Daniel

	44
2	32, 80
2:34	75n53
2:44	33
3:25	44
7:13-14	4, 4n5, 33
9	32, 36
9:24-27	25, 26, 34, 35, 35n30, 102
9:26	102n141
11:8	83
11:37	83
12:2	118n98, 199

Hosea

1:1	112
2:16	151
3:1-5	107, 219
3:4-5	11, 105, 107-8, 218, 219
3:5	112
11	151
11:1	143n71, 146
12:10	151
13:3	170
13:15	83

Joel

2:28-32	199n146
2:32	99, 199n146

Amos

5:18	152
9:11	108, 112

Micah

3:12	49
4:1	66n21
4-5	135
5	127
5:2	11, 33, 125, 126-44, 219n2, 220, 226, 228
5:4	127
7:15	151

Nahum, 2:6   83

Zephaniah   111

2:2	170

Haggai   111

1:13	95
2:1-9	82-90, 120n59, 217
2:3	82, 83, 84
2:3, 7, 9	84, 92
2:3-9	33
2:6-7	83
2:7	82, 84, 85, 86

2:7, 9	11, 61, 216	48:3, 6	112n26
2:7a	83	48:4-7	112n26
2:9	26, 83, 85, 87, 87n94, 89n100	48:8a	175
		48:10	157, 173, 175
2:21b-23	83	49:1-4	177n54
2.9	86	49:2	112n26
3:7	83	51:1	157, 197
		52	175
		52:4	157, 175
		52:8	175

Zechariah 111

1:11	95	52:10	175
3:8	107, 113n30, 219	61:5	157, 197
3:9	75n53	92-105	197n136
4:7	75n53	104:13	197n136
6:12	113n30		
6:12-13	49		
7:14	84		

2 Baruch

9:9	33, 73, 80	29:3	158
12:3	75n53	32:1-4	86
12:10	33	51:7	157
14:21	101		

2 Enoch, 71:34-35   158n48

Malachi 111

4 Ezra 127

1:10-11	103n145	7:29	158
2:5-7	103n145	12:31-34	109
3	93	12:32	158
3:1	11, 25, 61, 91–104, 216, 217–18, 225, 228		

2 Esdras 70n39

3:1, 3	101	3-14	111n21
3:2	103	13:3	112n26
4	98n127	13:9-13	112n26
4:5	218	13:26	112n26
4:5-6	98		

1 Maccabees, 2:57   201

Apocrypha

2 Maccabees, 14   197

1 Enoch 111n21, 127

2 Baruch

17-19	199n145	29:3	112n26
22-27	196–97	29:3-5	112n26
37-71	127	39:7-40:3	112n26
46:3-6	177n54		
48:2-5	177n54		

the Syriac Apocalypse
of Baruch   111n21

Ecclesiasticus   206n165

Sirach
47:11   177n54, 201
51:12   109

Pseudepigrapha

4 Baruch, 9:12-14   196n133

Apocalypse of Zephaniah
4:7   196

Fifth Sibylline book   111n21

Jubilees, 23:29-30   158

Psalms of Solomon   108,
                         111n21
17   173, 176,
                         176n51, 177
17, 4   201
17-18   127
17:23-45   177n54
17:36   157
18:6, 8   158
18:6-10   176
23:4   78

Sibylline Oracles
4.115-114.118   228n6
5:14-28   112n26
5:414   112n26

Testament of Benjamin   86
822   86n89
829   86n89

Testament of Dan, v.10
                         113n30

Testament of Job, 5-7   196

Testament of Judah
1:6   70
22:3   70
24:1, 5b   113n30

Testament of Simeon, 1bF
                         113n30

Third Sibylline book
                         111n21

Dead Sea Scrolls

1Q28b, Col. v:, 20-28   108

1QH
3:18   195
3:19   195
8:28-29   195

1QH I, 31-34   206

1QH II, 13-15   206

1QH IV
20-22   206
27, 29-30, 33-35   206
27-28   206

1QH IX, 23-28   206

1QH V
15-18   206
23-25   206

1QH VI, 29-33	206	4Q175	152
1QH XI, 8-14	206	CD 7:19-20	66n23
1QH XII, 18-20	206	4Q252	64n12
1QH XIII, 13-17	206	Col. v	70

1QH XVIII

6-12	206	4Q521	158–59, 197
18-30	206	4QDa, 3 iii 20-21	66n23
		4Qflor	113n30
1QM	127	4QPs^f	205
11:6-7	66n23	4QPs^w	205
		4QTestimonia, I 5-8	86

1QS

9:16	195	5/6HevPs	205
9:17	195	11QPsa, 27:2-11	199n143
9:22	195		
10:19	195	Nahal Hever,	
10:20	195	Psalms Col. 11	
11:13	195	(Frgs. 8 + 9)	205
Col. ix:11	152		
IX 10-11	86	Nahal Hever Psalms:	
		Col. 7 (Frg. 4),	
1QSa	173, 174, 175, 176, 223	Psalms Col. 7 (Frg. 4)	194n124
II 11-12	86	Q173a	

4Q85, Psalms c: Frg. 1		1	78
	194n124	3	78
4Q161		Scroll of Isaiah,	
Frags. 8-10:11-25	108	Asc Isa 11:2	114n34
Frags. 168-110:111	108		

4Q174	173, 174, 176
Frags. 1 i, 21, 2:10-13	108
Frags. 1 i, 21, 2	64

Ancient Jewish Writers

Damascus Documenta

CD 6:15	195
CD 13:14	195
CD 15:7-8	195

Josephus

Antiquities of the Jews	85n85
4.388	102n141
6:166	199n143
8.45	163n65
13.379	108n8
18:3	140n61
18:4	140n61
20, 97	152
20, 169	152
20:11	100n136
20.5.1	158n49
20.8.6	158n49
29.166	228n6
386.109	102n141

Testimonium Flavianum	147n7

War of the Jews	
2.13.5	158n49
6.304	209n177

Rabbinic Writings

b. Sabb, 104b	143n71

b. Sanh

6:1h, II.1	147n7
107b	143n71

b. Sukk, 52A	177n55

Tosephta, *Hullin*,

II 22-23	143n71

Babylonian Talmud

Aboda Zara, 40d	143n71
b. Bat. 1:1, III.5.C-6.C. y. Meg. 1:12, I.11.R	85n85
b. Erub., 2:1, I.19.D	193n119
b. Shabb. 16:12, II.17.B.	103n148
b. Yoma 39B	228n6
Sabbath, 14d	143n71
Sukkah, 52a	160
y. Ber. 8:8, I.2.G	74n49

Jerusalem Talmud

y. Ber., 2:4, II.3.N	127n17
y. Meg. 1:1, II.3.F-G	133n37
y. Meg. 2:1, I.2.J	78n64

Talmud

y. Ber. 2:4, II.1.I-K	78n63
y. Meg 2:1, 1.2.H, I, J	78

Targum

Isaiah 9:1	113n30
Psalm 2	177

Targum Jonathan to the Prophets	127

Targum Onkelos	70

Targum Pseudo Jonathan	70

Genesis Rabbah

44:8	178n57
95:1	160
100.7.Section X	196
XCVII:II.7	68n31
XCVIII:VIII.1	68n31

Leviticus. Rabbah.

18.1	196n133

Midrash Rabbah	127

Yalkut Shimeoni,
on Psalms 22:7   207n173

Maimonides

Commentary

148	177n57
148n273	178n57

Rashi

b. Ber 7B	177
Rashi's Commentary, Psalm 2	177n55

Shemoneh Esreh

Benedictions 2 and 3	197
Eighteen Benedictions, 14 and 15	109

New Testament

Matthew

1:1	179
1:1, 20	163
1:1-17	11, 105, 218
1:6, 17, 20	114n34
1-10	162
1:18	179
1:20-21, 24-25	135
1:21-23	48
1:23	200n148, 219n2
2	135
2:1	134
2:1-12	11, 126, 135, 220
2:5-6	130
2:6	125, 142
2:11	132
2:13-15	133
2:13-15a	135
2:15	143n71, 146
2:19-21	135
3:17	179
4:23	162
5-7	162
8-9	160, 162
9:27	11, 145, 163, 221
9:27-31	116
9:35	11, 145, 162, 221
11:3	96
11:3-6	160
11:4-6	11, 145, 221
11:4b-5	160
11:5	156
11:10	97, 102n143
11:14	218
11:56	149, 152n27
12:22-32	163
12:23	11, 145, 163, 221
12:24	163
12:28	163
15:22	11, 145, 163, 221
16:16	163n68
17:5	179
17:10-13	218
20:30-31	163
21:1-11	81n76
21:1-17	78, 216
21:9	11, 73, 145, 221
21:9, 15	163
21:12	97
21:12-14	85
21:12-17	81n76
21:13	102
21:33-43	81n76
21:33-43pp	80
25:31-46	101
26:25	120
26:63	163n68
26:64	119, 120
27:1	120
27:11, 37	112
27:35	208n176, 208n177
27:38	209n177
27:39	208n176
27:39-43	208n177
27:43	208n176
27:46	36, 208n176, 208n177
27:47-48	208n177
28:19	200n148, 219n2

Mark

1:1	163
1:1-2	97
1:2	97, 102n143
1:2-8	96
1:2b	96
1:6	97
1:10	3
1:11	180, 181
1:11pp	178, 180
1:44	161
8:27-30	119
8:29	120
8:32	120
8:33	120
9:7	181
9:11-13	218
10:46-52	116
10:47	11, 145, 221
10:47-48	113, 114n34
11:1-11	78, 216
11:9	73
11:9-10	79
11:10	79
11:15-18	102
12:35	45, 97, 120, 121, 163
12:35-37	113, 115n41, 119, 121, 121n64, 121n65
12:36	199n146, 200n146
13:22	158
13:26	112n26
14:49	97
14:61	119, 163
14:61-62	11, 145, 221
14:61-65	119
14:62	4n5, 11, 99, 101, 112n26, 120, 145, 199n146, 200n146, 200n148, 219n2, 221
14:62b	3
15:2	120
15:2, 26	112
15:2-5	119
15:2b	4
15:24	208n176, 208n177
15:27	209n177
15:29	208n176
15:29-32, 35-36	208n177
15:32	163
15:34	36, 208n176, 208n177, 210
15:36-37	208n177

Luke

1:16-17	97
1:17	218
1:17, 76	97
1:27, 32	114n34
1:32	118, 180n64
1:32-33	198, 201
1:35	179, 200n148, 219n2
1:39-45, 54	137
1:69	109
1:79	89n100
2	141
2:1-7	11, 126, 220
2:2	140n61
2:4	11, 105, 218
2:4-6	130
2:6-20	135
2:7	132
2:11	200n148, 219n2
2:11, 15	134
2:14	89n100
2:19, 51	129
2:22	130
2:22ff, 46	97
3:4-6	97
3:22	180n64
3:23	105, 118n52
3:23-28	11
3:23f	218
3:31	114n34
4:17-19	11, 145, 221
4:18	153n32, 161
4:18-19	149, 152n27
4:21	31
7:18-23	160

7:19	96	7:26, 48	100n136
7:22-23	11, 145, 221	7:27	136
7:27	97, 102n143	7:31	158
10:34	132	7:32, 45	100n136
19:28-48	78, 216	7:41-42	125n1
19:38	73	7:42	125, 142, 220
19:42	89n100	7:50-52	100
19:45-47	102	8:14	182
19:47	97	8:23, 58	112n26
22:11	132	8:41	110n16, 138
23:3, 38	112	8:58	200n148, 219n2
23:32-34	209n177	9:39	101
23:34	208n176	10:23	97
23:35	208n176	10:30	101
23:35-39	208n177	11:17	197
23:36	208n177	11:47, 57	100n136
24:13-27	114	11:49c-50	16
		12:12-15	78, 216
		12:13	73

John

		12:40-41	200n148, 219n2
1:1	112n26	12:41	101
1:1-2, 18	200n148, 219n2	12:42	100n136
1:7-8	98	12:52	100
1:14	178	13:3	182, 200n148, 219n2
1:14, 18	178		
1:15	98	13:22	198
1:18	101	14:16	200n148, 219n2
1:21	149, 152n27	16:5, 28	182
1:22-23	218	16:28	200n148, 219n2
1:32	3	17:5, 24	200n148, 219n2
1:33	98	18:3	100n136
1:35-45	122n67	18:33-34	112
2:13-17	101	19:18	209n177
2:13-22	102	19:19-22	112
3:1	100n136	19:23-24	208n177
3:2	115	19:24	208n176
3:13	182	19:28	208n177
3:13, 31	200n148, 219n2	19:30	208n176
3:16	178	19:39	100n136
3:30	98	20:28	101
5:17-18	200n148, 219n2		
5:22-29	101	## Acts	
6:4-42, 62	200n148, 219n2		
6:14	149, 152n27	2	88, 197–200, 199n146
6:14b	149		
6:15	158, 164	2:2	89, 90
6:66-69	122n67	2:17-21	199n146
7:14	97		

Acts (continued)

2:22	146
2:24-31	198
2:24-33	188
2:25-32	198
2:30	114n34
2:31	195
2:34-35	199n146, 200
3:18-25	4
4	180
4:11	78n64
4:25-26	180
4:25-28	181n67, 185, 223
4:25ff	178
4:28	181
5:37	139, 140n61
6:7	100
7:37	86
7:52	4
9:20	122
10:36	89n100
10:42	181n67
10:42-43	4
13	200–201
13:5, 14	122
13:23	98, 114n34, 198
13:26-36	200
13:27	4
13:33	178, 179, 180, 180n64
13:34	180n64, 201
13:35	195
13:35-37	188
14:1	122
15	136
15:16	114n34
17:1	122
17:1, 10	122
17:13	178
17:31	180, 181n67
18:4	122
19:4	98
22:3	100
26:22ff	4
26:27	4n7
28:23	4
28:26-27	5n7

Romans

1:1-6	180
1:2-3	4
1:3	11, 113, 114n34, 122, 179, 218
1:3-4	113, 182, 200n148, 219n2
1:4	178, 180, 181
3:5	208n176
3:21	4
5:5	89n98
7	114n38
8:3	179
8:34	200n146
9:5	200n148
9:5, 33	219n2
9:33	200n148
10:9, 13	200n148, 219n2
10:13	99, 199n146
11:36	200n148, 219n2
15:12	113

1 Corinthians

2:7	181
2:7-8	181
8:6	99n134, 200n148, 219n2
9:5	114
15:3	4n6
15:3-4	4
15:4	195
15:8	4
15:25	199n146, 200n146

2 Corinthians

4:5	200n148, 219n2
8:6	112n26

Galatians 98–99

1:11-17	4
3:19b, NA27	71n40
4:4	179

Ephesians

1:13-14	200n148, 219n2
1:20	200n146
2:18, 22	200n148, 219n2
2:20-21	78n64
3:14-17	200n148, 219n2
4:4-6, 8	200n148, 219n2
18, 20	114n38

Philippians

2:5-11	99
2:6, 9-11	200n148, 219n2
2:7, 8	179

Colossians

1:16-17	112n26
1:22	179
2:9	99n134
3:1	200n146

1 Thessalonians

4:17	112n26
5:3	112n26

2 Thessalonians, 1:5-9   112n26

1 Timothy, 3:16   179, 182

2 Timothy

2:8	114n34
2:8-9	113–14, 114n31

Titus, 3:5-6   89n98

Hebrews

1:3	200n146
1:5	178, 179, 181
1:8	200n148, 219n2
2:12	208n176
2:14	179
5:5	178, 181
7:14	114n34
13:6	78n64

1 Peter

1:10-12	4
2:4-8	78n64

2 Peter, 3:7   112n26

1 John, 4:2   179

2 John, 7   179

Revelation

1:7	112n26
2:26-27	178, 182
3:7	114
5:5	114, 114n34
11	196n134
12:5	178, 181
17:14	112
19:5	208n176
19:11-21	112n26
19:15	178, 181, 182
19:16	112
21:24	87
22:16	114, 114n32, 114n34

Apocrypha (New Testament)

1 Clement

6-8	206–7
36:4	179

Acts of Pontius Pilate   146

Apocalypse of Peter, Syriac (Clementine) version   196n134

Didache

9:2	114
10:6	114n34, 114n37

Epistle of Barnabas

4	228n6
5:8	146
5:13	207
6:6	207
6:16	207
145	115n41

Gospel of James

22.21	143n71

Gospel of Thomas

13:1-8	122n67

History of Joseph the Carpenter or Death of Joseph, VIII

143n71

Odes of Solomon

28, 31:9	209n180

Q Document

Q

3:16b-17	98
3:21	100
3:21-22	3
7:18-19, 20-21, 22-23	96
11:31-32	101
13:35	97

Early Christian Writings

Africanus, Julius

Letter to Aristides	115
125-27	115n40

Ambrose of Milan, *De fide*, 4:7

206n166

Augustine

The City of God	110
2:381	103n145
349-51	110n14
De civ. Dei, 17:1, 17:17	206n166
Expositions on the Book of Psalms, 22:17	206n166
Letters of St. Augustine	
76:1	206n166
140:16	206n166
199:50	206n166

Batei Midrashot 2

24:11	87n94

Celsus, *A True Discourse*

147

Constitutions of the Holy Apostles

5:14	206n166

Cyprian, "Three Books"

515	110n15

Cyril, *Catechetical Lectures of S. Cyril*

74	102n144

Eusebius

Ecclesiastical History, Books 1-5	
1.7	119n53
3.11	115n39, 136n44
3.32.6	115n39
4.22.4	115n39
210	146n2

Theophania, Bk 4,35   152

Ignatius of Antioch

Letter to the Ephesians
18:2	114n34
20:2	114n34

Letter to the Smyrnaeans
1	114n38
1:1	114n34

Irenaeus of Lyons, "Irenæus Against Heresies"

Adv haer 3.11.14   103n147

Justin Martyr

Dialogue with Trypho	98n127, 128, 128n19
250	131n31
First Apology	5n8
35, 48	143n71
178–79	146n4

Novation, *Trinity*

28:12   206n166

Origen

"Commentary on the Gospel of John," 367	103n146
"Origen against Celsus"	128, 141–42
1:38	110n16
1.28	142n67
1.35	5n9
1.38	138n50, 147n6
1.42	59
1.51	127n18, 128n21
1.57	152
2.28	7n14, 7n15

Tacitus, Cornelius, *Historiae (Latin)*

5.13   32n24

Tertullian

Answer to the Jews, 8, 10	206n166
Apology	
21	146n5
21.24	143n71
Against Marcion, 3:19	206n166

Greco-Roman Literature

Acta Senatus	147n5
Commentarii pincipis	147n5
Homer, *Odyssey*	199n145
Plato, *Republic*	199n145

Unknown

Jes
11, 11	151?? German
48, 21	151?? German

As Mos, 11:16   149??

Tractates on the Gospel of John

86:1-2   206n166

www.ingramcontent.com/pod-product-compliance
Lightning Source LLC
Chambersburg PA
CBHW071235230426
43668CB00011B/1441